Approaches to Studying World-Situated Language Use

Learning, Development, and Conceptual Change

Lila Gleitman, Susan Carey, Elissa Newport, and Elizabeth Spelke, editors

Approaches to Studying World-Situated Language Use

Bridging the Language-as-Product and Language-as-Action Traditions

edited by John C. Trueswell and Michael K. Tanenhaus

A Bradford Book
The MIT Press
Cambridge, Massachusetts
London, England

MIT Press books may be purchased at special quantity discounts for business or sales promotional use. For information, please e-mail special_sales@mitpress.mit.edu or write to Special Sales Department, The MIT Press, 5 Cambridge Center, Cambridge, MA 02142.

This book was set in Stone serif and Stone sans on 3B2 by Asco Typesetters, Hong Kong.
Printed and bound in the United States of America.

Library of Congress Cataloging-in-Publication Data

Approaches to studying world-situated language use : bridging the language-as-product and language-as-action traditions / edited by John C. Trueswell and Michael K. Tanenhaus.
    p.   cm. — (Learning, development, and conceptual change)
  Includes bibliographical references and index.
  ISBN 0-262-20149-6 (alk. paper) — ISBN 0-262-70104-9 (pbk. : alk. paper)
  1. Psycholinguistics. I. Trueswell, John C. II. Tanenhaus, Michael K. III. Series.
P37.A754   2004
401'.9—dc22   2004040257

10 9 8 7 6 5 4 3 2 1

Contents

17   Evaluating Explanations for Referential Context Effects: Evidence for Gricean Mechanisms in Online Language Interpretation   345
Julie C. Sedivy

Series Foreword

This series in learning, development, and conceptual change includes state-of-the-art reference works, seminal book-length monographs, and texts on the development of concepts and mental structures. It spans learning in all domains of knowledge, from syntax to geometry to the social world, and is concerned with all phases of development, from infancy through adulthood.

The series intends to engage such fundamental questions as

The nature and limits of learning and maturation: the influence of the environment, of initial structures, and of maturational changes in the nervous system on human development; learnability theory; the problem of induction; domain-specific constraints on development.

The nature of conceptual change: conceptual organization and conceptual change in child development, in the acquisition of expertise, and in the history of science.

Lila Gleitman
Susan Carey
Elissa Newport
Elizabeth Spelke

Preface

What are the central questions we should pose about humans' use of language for communication? And which methods should we use to investigate these issues?

In his book *Arenas of Language Use*, Clark (1992) noted that although there have been many different approaches to answering these questions, two distinct traditions have emerged within psycholinguistics, which he called the "language-as-product" and "language-as-action" traditions.

The product tradition, which has dominated psycholinguistics, has its roots in George Miller's (1962) synthesis of the then-emerging information-processing approach to cognition with Chomsky's (1957, 1959) revolutionary approach to linguistic knowledge as a cognitive system of rules and representations. Clark labeled this the language-as-product tradition because it focuses on the cognitive processes by which listeners recover, and speakers create, linguistic representations—the "product" of comprehension.

The second tradition sketched by Clark, the language-as-action tradition, has its roots in work by the Oxford philosophers of language use (e.g., Austin 1962, Grice 1957, and Searle 1969), and work on conversational analysis (e.g., Schegloff and Sachs 1973). The action tradition in language processing has been extended by psycholinguists focusing primarily on pragmatics and by computational linguists working in dialogue. This approach focuses on how people use language to perform acts in conversation, arguably the most basic form of language use. Psycholinguistic research within the action tradition focuses primarily on investigations of interactive conversation using natural tasks, typically in settings with real-world referents and well-defined behavioral goals.

This edited volume represents what we hope is the early stages of a movement to merge these traditions. Before we turn to a review of the contents of the book, we briefly describe the product and action traditions in more detail and lay out some of the reasons we believe that combining these traditions is both desirable and tractable.

Differences between the Product and Action Approaches

Although a broad range of perspectives can be found in the product tradition, most researchers in this tradition share a common set of methodological and theoretical assumptions. For instance, language comprehension and production are treated almost entirely as cognitive processes. As a result, experimental investigations focus on how individual "comprehenders"—that is, readers or listeners—assemble the (primarily syntactic) linguistic representations necessary for interpretation and how individual "speakers" translate thoughts into linguistically structured utterances. The emphasis on syntactic representations can be traced to the influence that generative linguistics has had on the study of language comprehension. Linguistics has focused on syntactic phenomena in large part because of key recursive functions that are believed to underlie the productive aspects of language, especially at the level of sentence descriptions.

Because the product tradition is also heavily influenced by information-processing approaches to cognition, many of the important theoretical issues are also rooted in questions about how information from different subsystems is processed and how information is integrated during different stages in information processing (e.g., Fodor 1983; Garfield 1987). One consequence is that most researchers in the product tradition consider "online" measures to be the methodological gold standard. For example, in sentence processing, researchers focus on the moment-by-moment syntactic choices made by readers and listeners (e.g., see Clifton, Frazier, and Rayner 1994) in order to evaluate linguistically motivated theories of sentence syntactic processing (e.g., Frazier 1989; Tanenhaus and Trueswell 1995; MacDonald, Pearlmutter, and Seidenberg 1994). Several decades of research in this area has established that processing decisions at these levels are closely time-locked to the input. With only a few notable exceptions (e.g., Altmann and Steedman 1988; Crain and Steedman 1985), theories of these processes have emphasized "noncontextual" linguistic contributions to language understanding. Context is viewed as a correlated constraint that can inform decisions at points of temporary ambiguity or is used to instantiate interpretations that build on context-independent linguistic representations (for discussion see Tanenhaus, Chambers, and Hanna, forthcoming).

In the action tradition, dialogue, including the form of utterances, is viewed as emerging from joint actions created by collaboration between interlocutors in a conversation (Clark 1996). From this theoretical perspective the processing of an utterance is inextricably intertwined with the place, time, and situation of its use. Participants in conversations are believed to establish and update their common ground, which forms the backdrop against which utterances are generated and interpreted. As a result, psycholinguistic research in the action tradition has focused on conversational issues, including the assessment of interlocutors' intentions and the coordination processes necessary to establish reference to familiar and novel objects in the world (cf. Clark 1992, 1996). Unlike the product tradition, in which experimental approaches typically examine a single person in the act of reading or speaking, psycholinguistic studies in the action tradition have focused on the behavior of multiple participants engaged simultaneously in both speaking and listening. Moreover, because real-time measures of comprehension have not been well suited to the study of situated language use, most research in this tradition has relied on offline measures, with theoretical accounts focusing on the more global properties of dialogue and reference.

The methodological differences in the approaches can be illustrated by comparing two well-known experimental methods from the product and action traditions. Figure P.1 illustrates a schematic of a prototypical product-based task, cross-modal lexical priming (Swinney et al. 1978). Cross-modal priming builds on the classic finding that response times to a target word are faster when the target is preceded by a semantically related prime word (Meyer and Schvanaveldt 1970). The subject, who is wearing headphones, listens to sentences prerecorded by the experimenter. A sentence or short sequence of sentences is presented on each trial. At some point in the sentence a target letter string appears on a computer monitor, allowing for experimenter control over the timing of the probe with respect to the input. The subject's task is to make a forced-choice lexical decision indicating whether the letter string is a word or not. The pattern of lexical-decision times is used to assess comprehension processes. For example, when

Figure P.1
Schematic of prototypical product experiment: Cross-modal lexical priming with lexical decision.

the target word follows *testified*, a verb whose object, *doctor*, has been fronted in a relative clause, lexical decisions on words that are associatively related to the fronted object are faster than lexical decisions on unrelated target words. Comprehension questions or a memory test are presented to ensure that the subject attends to the sentence.

A prototypical example of an action-based task is the referential communication task originally introduced by Krauss and Weinheimer (1966). A schematic of a well-studied variant of this task introduced by Clark and his colleagues (e.g., Clark and Wilkes-Gibbs 1986) is illustrated in figure P.2. Two naive participants, a matcher and a director, are separated by a barrier. Each has the same set of shapes arranged in different positions on a numbered grid. These objects are not very "codable" in the sense that a single word does not typically come to mind for all participants when describing such objects. Their goal is for the matcher to rearrange the shapes on his grid to match the arrangement on the director's grid. The resulting conversation can then be analyzed to provide insights into the principles that guide interactive conversation.

Figure P.2
Schematic of prototypical action task: Referential communication task with Tangrams.

Given the theoretical concerns and methodological tools used by the action and product traditions, it is not surprising that each has viewed the other with a certain amount of skepticism. For instance, researchers in the action tradition have criticized the product tradition for running "phone-booth" psycholinguistic studies (Clark 1992) in which willing-but-confused human participants are seated in a dark room and bombarded with written or spoken material that is devoid of much relevant context, or any possibility for assessing the speakers' goals. Thus, one may question whether experiments conducted within traditional paradigms using relatively "decontextualized" materials will generalize to more normal modes of language use. Likewise, the product tradition has criticized the action researchers for taking what might be called a "let-all-flowers-bloom" approach to psycholinguistics, in which research problems are left open ended, theoretical accounts are rarely mechanistic, and fewer links to linguistic or computational formalisms are made.

These biases aside, it is clear that detailed complex linguistic knowledge is a central component of human-language comprehension and production. Moreover, language is comprehended and generated in real time using basic information-processing mechanisms. However, it is *also* clear that much of this process is necessarily intertwined with the ongoings of the ambient world, as well as the intention of language users to communicate perspectives on that world. It therefore seems that attention to both sides of the language coin, the cognitive and social, will be important for understanding how language is processed in natural settings.

A Bridging of Traditions

A confluence of methodological and theoretical developments in psycholinguistics, linguistics, and computational linguistics, all related to the goal of providing mechanistic accounts of language use within rich referential environments, suggest that the time is ripe to bridge the product and action traditions.

Within psycholinguistics, the opportunity of such a merger has arisen with the advent of world-situated eye-tracking techniques (e.g., see Cooper 1974; Tanenhaus et al. 1995). In this technique, a listener's eye gaze is followed as he or she responds to spoken instructions to move objects about in the world (e.g., Tanenhaus et al. 1995), generates utterances (e.g., Eberhard 1998; Griffin and Bock 2000), or listens to spoken descriptions of visually copresent scenes (e.g., Altmann and Kamide 1999). This technique has allowed researchers to conduct studies that, from the subject's perspective, are like the contextually rich conversation studies devised in the action tradition, but from the experimenters' perspective, are studies that (behind the scenes) generate linguistically time-locked behavioral data relevant to the product tradition. This Wizard-of-Oz approach, in which the product tradition's experimental gadgets and gizmos are hiding behind a curtain, permits the study of the inner workings of the comprehension and production machinery while manipulating factors central to the action tradition. This work has already revealed examples of amazingly rapid coordination of the listener's linguistic knowledge with his or her knowledge about the relevant visual-referent world (e.g., Tanenhaus et al. 1995; Spivey et al. 2002; Sedivy et al. 1999; Altmann and Kamide 1999), the listener's assessment of the speaker's perspective on that same world (Keysar, Barr, Balin, and Paek 1998; Keysar, Barr, and Horton 1998; but see also Hanna, Tanenhaus, and Trueswell 2003), discourse organization (Arnold et al. 2000), and even the development of these interactive and integrative mechanisms in young children (Trueswell et al. 1999).

However, research using these techniques has barely scratched the surface in terms of addressing issues that arise in studying language generated in natural conversational interactions. It has also been largely uninformed by new theoretical developments within computational linguistics and formal semantics. Until recently, most implemented computer models of conversation operated in only very restricted domains, typically processing a handful of scripted dialogues. These systems did not make contact with psycholinguistic phenomena at a useful grain. However, the dramatic increase in the speed and power of computers, along with improvements in real-time speech recognition and visual-pattern recognition, has made it possible to explore a new generation of conversational agents that engage in interactive conversation with people in practical dialogue (e.g., task-oriented dialogue). For example, Allen and his colleagues at Rochester have developed a system that engages in cooperative problem solving using unrestricted spoken language to coordinate and plan the most efficient train routes in a model world, given existing constraints of that world (e.g., Allen et al. 1995, 1996; Heeman and Allen 1999). Cassell and colleagues at MIT, in collaboration with Stone and his colleagues at Rutgers, have been exploring embodied conversational agents that coordinate gestures, utterances, and postural signals in generating and understanding interactive conversation (e.g., Cassell, Stone, and Yan 2000). These working systems incorporate theoretical proposals about real-time cross-modality integration and generation that cry out for experimental evaluation. As computer systems become more realistic, they are likely to serve as useful hypothesis-testing domains for evaluating how interactional variables influence human-language comprehension and production. Indeed, Brennan and colleagues have pioneered such an approach, examining computer-dialogue performance in an experimental setting (Brennan and Hulteen 1995; Brennan 1998).

Steps toward Formalizing Situated Language Use

The writing of the chapters in this book arose out of a special session of the 2001 CUNY Human Sentence Processing conference, held at the University of Pennsylvania with the generous support of the National Science Foundation (BCS-0096377) and the Institute for Research in Cognitive Science. Indeed, the signature conference for the product tradition has been the CUNY conference originally founded by Janet Fodor in 1987. More than 200 linguists, cognitive psychologists, and computational linguists now gather annually at this conference to address issues in sentence processing.

The goals of the special session were to bring together key researchers from the product and action traditions who shared the interest of further connecting cognitive and social approaches to language processing within dynamic models of language use. Chapters based on both the invited and submitted presentations of this session appear in this book.

Part I of the book, titled "Reviews and Theoretical Perspectives," features a set of four review/position papers. In chapter 1, Tanenhaus and Trueswell argue for the importance of conducting real-time studies that investigate action-type variables. They outline methodological desiderata for such approaches and argue that eye tracking meets the central criteria for a product-based measure, while generalizing to action-based paradigms. They conclude with a review of how this technique can be used to study a wide range of issues that bridge the product and action traditions.

Next, in chapter 2, Stone lays out a representational and computational framework for utterance interpretation in human dialogue, specifically within a Gricean view of language use as an intentional activity. We believe this chapter makes significant theoretical advances for how best to connect Gricean observations to formal language-processing systems. Stone begins the chapter by considering a set of task-oriented dialogues, which he uses to motivate the need for detailed pragmatic representations that interface with linguistic representations. These dialogues highlight the complexity of the problem facing interlocutors in almost every exchange, but Stone provides some rather elegant solutions to these problems via a set of representations pertaining to pragmatic interpretations. He then cashes in on the advantages of such a representational system when he explores how utterance understanding and utterance production can be viewed as operations on these pragmatic representations. Stone discusses how this formalism might operate within a constraint-satisfaction system, and even considers connections to experimental work presented in other sections of this book.

In chapter 3, Keysar and Barr review a more specific attempt at bridging the product and action traditions within a theory of coordinated reference among interlocutors. The authors address directly the important issue of how to reconcile context-independent linguistic representation and processes (the mainstay of the product tradition) and context-dependent mechanisms (emphasized in the action tradition). Based on a range of eye-gaze and other online data, they propose a staged model of reference resolution by both speakers and listeners in which initial reference computation is determined using relatively little conversational knowledge regarding a fellow interlocutor's perspective. This early egocentric stage generates representations that may only later be evaluated against broader conversational knowledge, in particular the referential common ground established between interlocutors. This line of research has generated a lively debate about the time course with which common-ground information is used during definite and pronominal reference, with other researchers arguing against staged approaches in favor of the simultaneous application of multiple constraints (see in particular Hanna and Tanenhaus, chapter 5, this book).

In chapter 4, Brennan details her view of reference coordination, which has been heavily influenced by the action tradition. Brennan reviews the Clark and Wilkes-Gibbs (1986) reference-contribution model, which defines reference as a coordination process between interlocutors. Brennan expands on this account by providing more detailed predictions about the dynamics of reference coordination during conversation. And, in an interesting twist, she reviews a previously unpublished study from the 1980s where she collected real-time comprehension measures of interlocutors engaged in a referential communication task. This work foreshadowed much current research activity and sheds light on some present controversies in the field.

The remaining sections of this book consist of shorter reports of experimental findings in the literature. Taken together, these chapters offer a snapshot of current work that begins to bridge the product and action approaches. We have organized these chapters into four groups.

The first group, comprising Part II "Speakers and Listeners as Participants in Conversations," examines language-processing issues as they occur in natural and seminatural conversational settings. Multiple research methods are represented here. Hanna and Tanenhaus (chapter 5) and Brown-Schmidt, Campana, and Tanenhaus (chapter 6) both examine reference using eye-gaze measures; Bard and Aylett (chapter 7) provide spoken-corpus data; and the contributions from McLean, Pickering, and Branigan (chapter 8) and from Schafer and Speer (chapter 9) examine linguistic and behavioral measures in dialogue settings. These chapters have a common thread in that all explore conversational phenomena that have competing explanations from product and action approaches to language use.

Part III, "Language-Scene Interactions," examines how nonlinguistic information, gleaned from visual scenes, can be used by listeners to constrain and predict linguistic hypotheses. In chapter 10, Kamide, Altmann, and Haywood examine predictive linguistic processing in both English and Japanese listeners. This work shows that verbs and other lexical items, when interpreted with respect to visual scenes, allow for rapid predictions of upcoming, yet-to-be-heard, constituents. In chapter 11, Gennari, Meroni, and Crain examine how prosodic and visual-scene information interact to constrain the interpretation of quantifiers. In chapter 12, Arnold, Brown-Schmidt, Trueswell, and Fagnano examine referential issues from a developmental perspective, asking how linguistic and nonlinguistic cues contribute to the development of online pronoun interpretation.

The contributions in Part IV, "Product Approaches to Action Variables," use measures from the product tradition to explore issues traditionally discussed in the action tradition. In chapter 13, Almor describes a computational model of reference that emphasizes how assumptions regarding information-processing load interact with pragmatic considerations. In chapter 14, Bailey and Ferreira examine disfluencies, and how they influence syntactic-ambiguity resolution. In chapter 15, Fitneva and Spivey examine how perceived speaker authorship constrains lexical-ambiguity resolution.

Part V, "Gricean Phenomena," discusses how phenomena typically construed as examples of Grice's cooperative principle are instantiated in language use, focusing specifically on reference. In chapter 16, Barr presents a set of artificial-language simulations that explore how referential systems can emerge from formal-language users whose behavior is egocentric. Sedivy (in chapter 17), on the other hand, uses Gricean considerations to explain key online referential findings on the generation and interpretation of different classes of prenominal adjectives.

Clearly the body of work presented in this book represents only the first hesitant steps toward bridging the action and product traditions. We hope that the work presented here will motivate more researchers in the computational, psycholinguistic, and linguistic communities to pursue research that builds on and transcends these initial efforts.

References

Allen, J. F., Schubert, L. K., Ferguson, G., Heeman, P., Hwang, C. H., Kato, T., Light, M., Nathaniel, G., Martin, N. G., Miller, B. W., Poesio, M., and Traum, D. R. 1995. The TRAINS Project: A case study in building a conversational planning agent. *Journal of Experimental and Theoretical AI*, 7.

Allen, J. F., Miller, B. W., Ringger, E. K., and Sikorski, T. 1996. A Robust System for Natural Spoken Dialogue. In *Proceedings of the 1996 Annual Meeting of the Association for Computational Linguistics*, 62–70.

Altmann, G., and Kamide, Y. 1999. Incremental interpretation of verbs: Restricting the domain of subsequent reference. *Cognition*, *73*, 247–264.

Altmann, G., and Steedman, M. 1988. Interaction with context during human sentence processing. *Cognition*, *30*, 191–238.

Arnold, J. E., Eisenband, J. G., Brown-Schmidt, S., and Trueswell, J. C. 2000. The rapid use of gender information: Evidence of the time course of pronoun resolution from eyetracking. *Cognition*, *76*, b13–b26.

Austin, J. L. 1962. *How to Do Things with Words*. Cambridge, MA: Harvard University Press.

Brennan, S. E. 1998. The grounding problem in conversations with and through computers. In S. Fussell and R. J. Kreuz, eds., *Social and cognitive psychological approaches to interpersonal communication*, 201–225. Mahweh, NJ: Erlbaum.

Brennan, S. E., and Hulteen, E. 1995. Interaction and feedback in a spoken language system: A theoretical framework. *Knowledge-Based Systems*, *8*, 143–151.

Cassell, J., Stone, M., and Yan, H. 2000. Coordination and context-dependence in the generation of embodied conversation. *INLG 2000*, 171–178.

Chomsky, N. 1957. *Syntactic Structures*. Gravenhage, Holland: Mouton.

Chomsky, N. 1959. *Review of Skinner's Verbal Behavior. Language*, *35*, 26–58.

Clark, H. H. 1992. *Arenas of Language Use*. Chicago: University of Chicago Press.

Clark, H. H. 1996. *Using Language*. New York: Cambridge University Press.

Clark, H. H., and Wilkes-Gibbs, D. 1986. Referring as a collaborative process. *Cognition*, *22*, 1–39.

Clifton, C., Frazier, L., and Rayner, K., eds. 1994. *Perspectives on Sentence Processing*. Hillsdale, NJ: Erlbaum.

Cooper, R. M. 1974. The control of eye fixation by the meaning of spoken language. A new methodology for the real-time investigation of speech perception, memory, and language processing. *Cognitive Psychology*, *6*, 84–107.

Crain, S., and Steedman, M. J. 1985. On not being led up the garden path: The use of context by the psychological parser. In D. Dowty, L. Karttunen, and A. Zwicky, eds., *Natural Language Parsing: Psychological, Computational, and Theoretical Perspectives*. Cambridge, UK: Cambridge University Press.

Eberhard, K. M. 1998. Watching speakers speak: Using eye movements to study language production. Invited paper presented at the Seventieth Annual Meeting of the Midwestern Psychological Association, Chicago.

Fodor, J. A. 1983. *The Modularity of Mind*. Cambridge, MA: MIT Press.

Frazier, L. 1989. Against lexical generation of syntax. In W. D. Marslen-Wilson, ed., *Lexical Representation and Process*. Cambridge, MA: MIT Press.

Garfield, J. L., ed. 1987. *Modularity in Knowledge Representation and Natural-Language Understanding*. Cambridge, MA: MIT Press.

Grice, P. 1957. Meaning. *Philosophical Review, 66*, 377–388.

Griffin, Z. M., and Bock, K. 2000. What the eyes say about speaking. *Psychological Science, 11(4)*, 274–279.

Hanna, J. E., Tanenhaus, M. K., and Trueswell, J. C. 2003. The effects of common ground and perspective on domains of referential interpretation. *Journal of Memory and Language, 49*, 43–61.

Heeman, P., and Allen, J. 1999. Speech repairs, intonational phrases, and discourse markers: Modeling speakers' utterances in spoken dialog. *Computational Linguistics, 25(4)*, 527–571.

Keysar, B., Barr, D. J., Balin, J. A., and Paek, T. S. 1998. Definite reference and mutual knowledge: Process models of common ground in comprehension. *Journal of Memory and Language, 39*, 1–20.

Keysar, B., Barr, D. J., and Horton, W. S. 1998. The egocentric basis of language use: Insights from a processing approach. *Current Directions in Psychological Sciences, 7*, 46–50.

Krauss, R. M., and Weinheimer, S. 1966. Concurrent feedback, confirmation, and the encoding of referents in verbal communication. *Journal of Personality and Social Psychology, 4*, 343–346.

MacDonald, M. C., Pearlmutter, N. J., and Seidenberg, M. S. 1994. The lexical nature of syntactic ambiguity resolution. *Psychological Review, 101*, 676–703.

Meyer, D. E., and Schvanveldt, R. W. 1971. Facilitation in recognizing words: Evidence of dependence upon retrieval operations. *Journal of Experimental Psychology, 90*, 277–234.

Miller, G. 1962. Some psychological studies of grammar. *American Psychologist, 17*, 748–762.

Schegloff, E. A., and Sacks, H. 1973. Opening up closing. *Semiotica, 8*, 289–327.

Searle, J. 1969. *Speech Acts: An Essay in the Philosophy of Language*. Cambridge, UK: Cambridge University Press.

Sedivy, J. C., Tanenhaus, M. K., Chambers, C. G., and Carlson, G. N. 1999. Achieving incremental semantic interpretation through contextual representation. *Cognition, 71*, 109–147.

Spivey, M. J., Tanenhaus, M. K., Eberhard, K. M., and Sedivy, J. C. 2002. Eye movements and spoken language comprehension: Effects of visual context on syntactic ambiguity resolution. *Cognitive Psychology, 45*, 447–481.

Swinney, D. A., Onifer, W., Prather, P., and Hirshkowitz, M. 1978. Semantic facilitation across sensory modalities in the processing of individual words and sentences. *Memory and Cognition, 7*, 159–165.

Tanenhaus, M. K., Chambers, C. G., and Hanna, J. E. Forthcoming. Referential domains in spoken language comprehension: Using eye movements to bridge the product and action traditions. In J. M. Henderson and F. Ferreira, eds., *The Interface of Language, Vision, and Action: Eye Movements and the Visual World*. New York: Psychology Press.

Tanenhaus, M. K., Spivey-Knowlton, M. J., Eberhard, K. M., and Sedivy, J. C. 1995. Integration of visual and linguistic information in spoken language comprehension. *Science, 268*, 1632–1634.

Tanenhaus, M. K., Spivey-Knowlton, M. J., Eberhard, K. M., and Sedivy, J. C. 1996. Using eye-movements to study spoken language comprehension: Evidence for visually-mediated incremental interpretation. In T. Inui and J. McClelland, eds., *Attention and Performance XVI: Integration in Perception and Communication*, 457–478. Cambridge, MA: MIT Press.

Tanenhaus, M. K., and Trueswell, J. C. 1995. Sentence comprehension. In J. L. Eimas and P. D. Miller, eds., *Handbook in Perception and Cognition, Volume 11: Speech, Language, and Communication*, 217–262. New York: Academic Press.

Trueswell, J. C., Sekerina, I., Hill, N. M., and Logrip, M. L. 1999. The kindergarten-path effect: Studying on-line sentence processing in young children. *Cognition, 73(2)*, 89–134.

I Reviews and Theoretical Perspectives

1 Eye Movements as a Tool for Bridging the Language-as-Product and Language-as-Action Traditions

Michael K. Tanenhaus and John C. Trueswell

Introduction: The Product and Action Approaches

The language-as-action and language-as-product traditions, as sketched in the preface to this book, have each had their own characteristic theoretical concerns and preferred experimental methods. For the most part, the product tradition has sought to understand the individual cognitive processes by which listeners recover linguistic representations, whereas the action tradition has sought to understand how people use language to perform joint acts in interactive conversation.

Psycholinguistic research within the product tradition has typically examined moment-by-moment processes in language processing, using fine-grained reaction-time measures designed to tap processes that occur during the perception of a word or of a sentence (Tanenhaus and Trueswell 1995). The rationale for using real-time measures comes largely from the sequential nature of language comprehension. For instance, when comprehending text, readers are known to make successive fixations on individual words rather than taking in entire phrases, with attention focused on the word that is being fixated and the next word to be fixated (Rayner 1998). Fixation patterns from these studies are consistent with the hypothesis that readers assign provisional interpretations to the input essentially on a word-by-word basis (e.g., Rayner 1998; Tanenhaus and Trueswell 1995). Comprehension of spoken language necessarily involves sequential input because speech unfolds as a sequence of rapidly changing acoustic events. As in reading, experimental studies that probe the listeners' developing representations show that they make provisional commitments as soon as the input arrives (Marlsen-Wilson 1973, 1975). In both reading and listening, then, language processing is closely time-locked to the input, which is processed more or less sequentially.

The combination of sequential input and time-locked processing means that the processing system is continuously faced with temporary ambiguity. For example, the initial portion of the spoken word *beaker* is temporarily consistent with many potential lexical candidates, including *beaker, beetle, beeper, beagle,* and so on. An understanding of spoken-word recognition within the product tradition requires a mechanistic account of how these potential lexical candidates are activated and evaluated with respect to the unfolding input. Similarly, as the utterance *Put the apple on the towel into the box* unfolds, the phrase *on the towel* is temporarily consistent with several syntactic analyses. In one analysis, *on the towel* introduces a Goal argument for the verb *put* (the location where the apple is to be put). In another analysis, it modifies the Theme argument, *the apple,* specifying the location of the Theme (on the towel). Again, a mechanistic account of how people understand utterances requires specifying the nature of the linguistic representations that are accessed and constructed and how these representations are integrated as the utterance unfolds over time. Similar arguments for the importance of time-locked response measures can be made for studies of language production where the speaker must rapidly map thoughts onto linguistic forms that are produced sequentially (Levelt, Roelof, and Meyer 1999). Note, however, that the focus on real-time measures and mechanisms has led most researchers to study comprehension and production separately, often within limited but highly controlled contexts.

In contrast, psycholinguistic research within the action tradition has typically focused on interactive conversation involving two or more subjects engaged in a task that typically has real-world referents and well-defined goals. One reason is that many aspects of utterances in a conversation can only be understood with respect to the context of the language use, which includes the time, place, and participants' conversational goals, as well as the collaborative processes intrinsic to conversation. For example, Clark (1992) points out that in the utterance *Look at the stallion,* the expression *the stallion* could refer to a horse in a field, a painting of a horse, or even a test tube containing a blood sample taken from a stallion, depending on the context of the utterance. Moreover, many of the characteristic features of conversation emerge only when interlocutors have joint goals and when they participate in the dialogue as both a speaker and an addressee.

We can illustrate some of these characteristics by examining a fragment of a conversation from a study by Brown-Schmidt, Campana, and Tanenhaus (chapter 6, this volume). Brown-Schmidt and colleagues used a modified version of a referential communication task, originally introduced by Krauss and Weinheimer (1966). Pairs of participants, separated by a curtain, worked together to arrange blocks in matching configurations and to confirm those configurations. The excerpt includes many well-documented aspects of task-oriented dialogue, including fragments that can only be understood as combinations of utterances between two speakers, false starts, over-lapping speech (marked by asterisks), and negotiated referential terms (e.g., *vertically* meaning up and down).

Speaker	Utterance
1	*ok, ok I got it* ele ... ok
2	alright, *hold on*, I got another easy piece
1	*I got a* well wait I got a green piece right above that
2	above this piece?
1	well not exactly right above it
2	it can't be above it
1	it's to the ... it doesn't wanna fit in with the cardboard
2	it's to the right, right?
1	yup
2	w- how? *where*
1	*it's* kinda line up with the two holes
2	line 'em right next to each other?
1	yeah, vertically
2	vertically, meaning?
1	up and down
2	up and down

Analyses of participants' linguistic behavior and actions in these tasks has provided important insights into how interlocutors track information to achieve successful communication (Clark 1992, 1996). Moreover, the findings from these studies illustrate that the establishment of a referent is not simply an individual cognitive process. Rather it is arrived at as the result of coordinated actions among two or more individuals across multiple linguistic exchanges (Clark and Wilkes-Gibbs 1986).

Why Bridge?

It is tempting to view research in the action and product traditions as complementary. Research in the product tradition examines the early perceptual and cognitive processes that create linguistic representations, whereas research in the action tradition focuses on subsequent cognitive and social-cognitive processes that build on and use these representations. Although there is some truth to this perspective, it can also be misleading. First, as we have seen, the language used in interactive conversation is dramatically different from the scripted, carefully controlled language studied in the product tradition. The characteristics of natural language illustrated in the excerpt from Brown-Schmidt and colleagues (chapter 6, this volume) are ubiquitous, yet they are rarely studied outside of the action tradition. On the one hand, they raise important challenges for models of real-time language processing within the product tradition, which are primarily crafted to handle fluent, fully grammatical well-formed language. On the other hand, it will be difficult to evaluate models of how and why these conversational phenomena arise without explicit mechanistic models that can be evaluated using real-time methods.

Second, and perhaps most importantly, the theoretical constructs developed within each tradition offer competing explanations for phenomena that have been the primary concern of the other tradition. For example, the product-based construct of *priming* provides an alternative mechanistic explanation for phenomena such as lexical and syntactic entrainment (the tendency for interlocutors to use the same words and/ or the same syntactic structures). A priming account does not require appeal to the action-based claim that such processes reflect active construction of common ground between interlocutors (cf. Pickering and Garrod, forthcoming). Likewise, the tendency of speakers to articulate lower-frequency words more slowly and more carefully, which has been used to argue for speaker adaptation to the needs of the listener, has a plausible mechanistic explanation in terms of the attentional resources required to sequence and output lower-frequency forms.

Conversely, the interactive nature of conversation may provide an explanation for why comprehension is so relentlessly continuous. Most work on comprehension within the product tradition takes as axiomatic the observation that language processing is continuous. If any explanation for *why* processing is incremental is offered, it is typically that incremental processing is necessitated by the demands of limited working memory: the system would be overloaded if it buffered a sequence of words rather then interpreting them immediately. However, working-memory explanations of this type are not particularly compelling. One could alternatively argue that delaying interpretation might reduce demands on working memory, by allowing comprehenders to avoid computing multiple analyses and having to revise premature commitments that could be avoided by taking into account immediately upcoming information. In fact, the first-generation models of language comprehension—models that were explicitly motivated by considerations of working-memory limitations—assumed that comprehension was a form of sophisticated catch-up in which the input was buffered long enough to accumulate enough input to reduce ambiguity (e.g., Fodor,

Bever, and Garrett 1974; Marcus 1980). However, there is a clear need for incremental comprehension in interactive conversation. Participants, who are simultaneously playing the roles of speaker and addressee, need to plan and modify utterances in midstream in response to input from an interlocutor. This type of give-and-take requires incremental comprehension.

Finally, the action and product traditions often have different perspectives on constructs that are viewed as central within each tradition. Consider, for example, the notion of *context*. Within the product tradition, context is typically viewed either as information that enhances or instantiates a context-independent core representation or as a *correlated constraint* in which information from higher-level representations can, in principle, inform linguistic processing at lower levels of representation. Specific debates about the role of context include whether, when, and how (1) lexical context affects sublexical processing, (2) syntactic and semantic context affect lexical processing, and (3) discourse and conversational context affect syntactic processing. Each of these questions involves debates about the architecture of the processing system and the flow of information between different types of representations—classic information-processing questions. In contrast, we have already noted that within the action tradition context includes the time, place, and participants' conversational goals, as well as the collaborative processes intrinsic to conversation. A central tenet is that utterances can only be understood relative to these factors. Although these notions can be conceptualized as a form of correlated constraint, they are much more intrinsic to the comprehension process than that characterization would suggest.

Given these factors, we believe that combining and integrating the product and action approaches is likely to prove fruitful by allowing researchers from each tradition to investigate phenomena that would otherwise prove intractable. Moreover, research that combines the two traditions is likely to deepen our understanding of language processing by opening up each tradition to empirical and theoretical challenges from the other tradition.

The Methodological Challenge

With the exception of an occasional shot fired across the bow (e.g., Clark and Carlson 1981; Clark 1997), the action and product traditions have not fully engaged one another. We believe that one reason is methodological. The traditional techniques in the psycholinguist's toolkit for studying real-time language processing have required using either text or prerecorded audio stimuli in contextually limited environments that cannot be used with more naturalistic tasks.

Table 1.1
Desiderata for a response measure bridging the action and product traditions

Action-based requirements:
1. Measure can be used with *conversational language.*
2. Measure can be used to monitor *language production and language comprehension*
3. Measure should not *interrupt* or *interfere* with the primary task of engaging in conversation

Product-based requirements:
4. Measure must be *sensitive* to rapid, unconscious processes underlying production and comprehension.
5. Measure should be closely *time-locked* to the input (for comprehension) and output (for production).
6. Measure should have a well-defined *linking hypothesis.*

Requirement for understanding development and deficits:
7. Measure can be used with young *children* and *special populations.*

Table 1.1 lists seven desiderata for a methodology that bridges the action and product traditions of psycholinguistic research. The first three desiderata are essential if the paradigm is to be useful in studies of interactive conversation. First, the method must be usable with *conversational language* in relatively natural behavioral contexts. Second, because both speaking and understanding are integral components of inter-active conversation, the response measure should provide insights into both *language production and language comprehension.* Third, the response measure should not *interrupt* or *interfere* with the primary task of the participants—engaging in a conversation.

The next three desiderata are essential for investigating the time course of language processing with a fine-enough grain to meet the criteria of a successful product method. Specifically, the fourth desideratum states that the response measure must be *sensitive* to the rapid, typically unconscious processes that underlie comprehension and production. Fifth, the response measure must be closely *time-locked* to the input in order to provide insights into the rapidly occurring processes that underlie compre-hension and production. Sixth, the response measure should have a well-defined *link-ing hypothesis.* By this we mean a theory, ideally one that can be formalized, that maps hypothesized underlying processes onto behavioral patterns. Without clear linking hypotheses, it is difficult to relate behavioral data patterns to theoretical constructs (Tanenhaus, Spivey-Knowlton, and Hanna 2000). Finally, if we are to understand the development of the relevant processes, the method should allow us to investigate comprehension and production processes in *children* and *special populations.*

In the remainder of this chapter we argue that monitoring saccadic eye movements as people engage in spoken-language processing in natural tasks satisfies all seven of these methodological criteria. In the next section, we briefly review the properties of saccades in natural-scene perception and investigate how they reflect momentary states of attention. We then illustrate how lightweight visor systems could be applied to common dialogue tasks in the action tradition, thus satisfying the three desiderata for an appropriate action-based response measure. In the following section, which forms the core of the chapter, we demonstrate that the eye-gaze paradigm meets the central criteria for product methods, namely, sensitivity, time locking, and availability of a linking hypothesis. We also use this section to introduce the reader to the methods employed to collect and analyze data, and provide some illustrative examples, focusing on word recognition and syntactic processing, in adults and in children. We conclude that section by discussing a potential limitation of the visual-world paradigm—the constraints imposed by a restricted task-relevant visual world—and summarize work addressing these *closed-set* concerns. We conclude the chapter with a discussion of present and future uses of eye gaze in studies of conversational language, highlighting issues that we believe will increasingly take center stage in psycholinguistic research.

Fixation as a Measure of Attention in Natural Tasks

During everyday tasks involving vision, such as reading a newspaper, looking for the car keys, making a cup of coffee, and conversing about objects in the immediate environment, people rapidly shift their gaze to bring task-relevant regions of the visual field into the central area of the fovea (e.g., for reviews see Hayhoe 2000; Kowler 1995). Eye movements are necessary because visual sensitivity differs across the retina. Acuity is greatest in the central portion of the fovea, then markedly declines. The organization of the retina can be viewed as a compromise between the need to maintain sensitivity to visual stimuli across a broad range of the visual field, while also allowing detailed spatial resolution for task-relevant aspects of the visual field. In addition, this division of labor helps restrict most processing to a relevant subset of the visual field, reducing the amount of information being made available from the visual environment. However, it also requires an eye-movement system to quickly bring new regions of the field into the fovea, where visual acuity is greatest. These gaze shifts are accomplished by saccadic eye movements (Hayhoe 2000; Kowler 1995, 1999; Liversedge and Findlay 2001).

Saccades are rapid ballistic eye movements. During a saccade, the eye is in motion for 20 to 60 ms, with the duration of the saccade related to the distance that the eye travels. At peak velocity, the eye can be moving between 500 and 1,000 degrees per second. During a saccade, sensitivity to visual information is dramatically reduced. Suppression of visual information occurs in part because of masking, and in part because of central inhibition (see the following sources and references therein: Kowler 1995; Liversedge and Findlay 2001; Rayner 1998).

A saccade is followed by a fixation that typically lasts for 200 ms or more depending on the task. The minimal latency for planning and executing a saccade is approximately 150 ms when there is no uncertainty about target location. In reading, visual search, and other tasks in which there are multiple target locations, saccade latencies are somewhat slower, typically about 200 to 300 ms. The pattern and timing of saccades, and the resulting fixations, are among the most widely used response measures in the cognitive sciences, providing important insights into the mechanisms underlying attention, visual perception, reading, and memory (Rayner 1998). Overviews of eye movements in scene perception are provided by Henderson and Hollingsworth (2003) and Henderson and Ferreira (forthcoming).

Eye Gaze in Interactive Conversation

The development of accurate, relatively inexpensive head-mounted and remote eye-tracking systems has made it possible to monitor eye movements as people perform natural tasks.[1] Eye movements naturally occur rapidly in response to even low-threshold signals, and because they are ballistic, there is little uncertainty about when a saccade has been initiated and what part of the visual field is being fixated. Crucially, they are closely linked to attention. Although attention *can* be directed to regions of space not currently being fixated, or about to be fixated, a growing body of behavioral and neurophysiological research supports a close link between fixation and spatial attention (Findlay, forthcoming; Kowler 1999; Liversedge and Findlay 2001). Thus, to the extent that attention and shifts in attention are closely time-locked to the processes that underlie comprehension and production, eye movements should be informative about real-time language processing.

Monitoring eye movements as people understand and produce language related to ongoing tasks in a circumscribed visual world would seem to meet the important criteria for an action-based measure. For example, monitoring eye movements in a referential communication task would not modify the basic task. This is illustrated in figure 1.1, which presents a schematic of a well-studied variant of a referential communication task introduced by Clark and his colleagues (e.g., Clark and Wilkes-Gibbs 1986).

Two naive participants, a matcher and a director, are separated by a barrier. Each has the same set of shapes arranged in different positions on a numbered grid. The participants' goal is for the matcher to rearrange the shapes on his grid to match the arrangement on the director's grid. In the schematic both the director and the matcher

Figure 1.1
Schematic of using eye tracking in a referential communication task with Tangrams.

are wearing visor-mounted eye trackers. With a screen-based variant of the task, one could monitor eye movements using a remote eye tracker without placing anything on the head of the participants. The crucial question, then, is whether eye movements in natural tasks in a circumscribed visual world are sensitive to comprehension and production processes. Also, we would like to know if the eye movements meet the necessary criteria for a product-based measure, namely, sensitivity, time locking, and the presence of a well-defined linking hypothesis.

The use of eye movements as a real-time measure of spoken-language processing was pioneered by Cooper (1974), who demonstrated that the timing of participants' eye movements to pictures was closely time-locked to relevant information in a spoken story. More recently, Tanenhaus et al. (1995) showed that when participants follow spoken instructions to manipulate objects in a task-relevant "visual world," fixations to task-relevant objects are closely time-locked to the unfolding utterance. Since then, a body of research has demonstrated that eye movements can be used to trace the time course of language comprehension and, more recently, language production (see Henderson and Ferreira, forthcoming).

The Visual-World Paradigm Applied to Issues in the Product Tradition

We now review three applications of the visual-world paradigm to address classic language-as-product questions. We begin with a review of a study by Allopenna, Magnuson, and Tanenhaus (1998) that traces the time course of lexical access in continuous speech. We use the Allopenna et al. study to illustrate how eye-movement data are analyzed. We also use this study to illustrate *sensitivity*, *time locking*, and a formalized *linking hypothesis* between underlying processes and fixations. We then review work by Spivey, Tanenhaus, and colleagues that illustrates how the paradigm can be extended to syntactic processing, suggesting that such a method taps processes at multiple levels of representation. We conclude with work by Fernald, Swingley, Trueswell, and colleagues that illustrates how the paradigm can be extended to investigations of language processing in children (desideratum 7).

Tracking Lexical Access in Continuous Speech

Allopenna, Magnuson, and Tanenhaus (1998) evaluated the time course of activation for lexical competitors that shared initial phonemes with the target word (e.g., *beaker* and *beetle*) or that rhymed with the target word (e.g., *beaker* and *speaker*). In the studies by Allopenna and colleagues, participants were instructed to fixate a central cross and then followed a spoken instruction to move one of four objects displayed on a computer screen with the computer mouse (e.g., *Look at the cross. Pick up the beaker. Now put it above the square*).

A schematic of a sample display of pictures is presented in figure 1.2, panel (a). The pictures include the target (the beaker), the cohort (the beetle), a picture with a name that rhymes with the target (*speaker*), and the unrelated picture (the carriage). For purposes of illustrating how eye-movement data are analyzed, we will restrict our attention to the target, cohort, and unrelated pictures. The particular pictures displayed are used to exemplify types of conditions and are not repeated across trials. Panel (b) shows five hypothetical trials. The 0 ms point indicates the onset of the spoken word *beaker*. The dotted line begins at about 200 ms—the earliest point where we would expect to see signal-driven fixations. On trial 1, the hypothetical participant initiated a fixation on the target about 200 ms after the onset of the word, and continued to fixate on it (typically until the hand brings the mouse onto the target). On trial 2, the fixation on the target begins a bit later. On trial 3, the first fixation is on the cohort, followed by a fixation on the target. On trial 4, the first fixation is on the unrelated picture. Trial 5 shows another trial where the initial fixation is on the cohort. Panel (c)

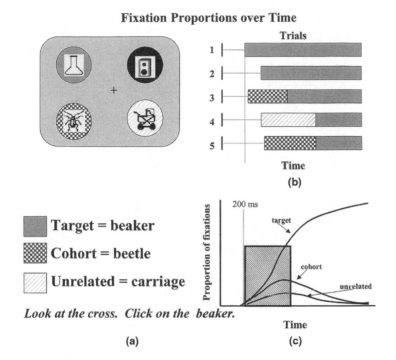

Figure 1.2
Schematic showing how proportions of fixations are calculated and plotted over time.

illustrates the proportion of fixations over time for the target, cohort, and unrelated pictures, averaged across trials and participants. These fixation proportions are obtained by determining the proportion of looks to the alternative pictures at a given time slice, and they show how the pattern of fixations changes as the utterance unfolds. The fixations do not sum to 1.0 as the word is initially unfolding because participants are often still looking at the fixation cross.

Researchers often define a window of interest, illustrated by the rectangle in panel (c). For example, one might want to focus on the fixations on the target and cohort in the region from 200 ms after the onset of the spoken word to the point in the speech stream where disambiguating phonetic information arrives. The proportion of fixations on pictures or objects, the time spent fixating on the alternative pictures (essentially the area under the curve, which is a simple transformation of proportion of fixations), and the number and/or proportion of saccades generated to pictures in this region can then be analyzed. These measures are all highly correlated.

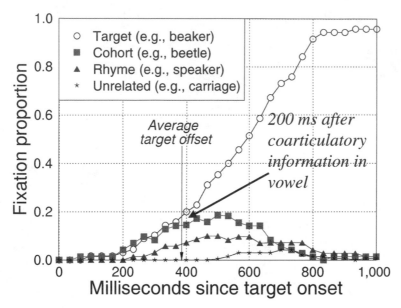

Figure 1.3
Results of Allopenna, Magnuson, and Tanenhaus 1998.

Figure 1.3 shows the actual data from the experiment by Allopenna and colleagues (1998). The figure plots the proportion of fixations on the target, cohort, rhyme, and unrelated picture. Until 200 ms, nearly all of the fixations are on the fixation cross. These fixations are not shown. The first fixations on pictures begin at about 200 ms after the onset of the target word. These fixations are equally distributed between the target and the cohort. These fixations are remarkably time-locked to the utterance: input-driven fixations occurring 200 to 250 ms after the onset of the word are most likely programmed in response to information from the first 50 to 75 ms of the speech signal. At about 400 ms after the onset of the spoken word, the proportion of fixations on the target began to diverge from the proportion of fixations on the cohort. Subsequent research has established that cohorts and targets diverge approximately 200 ms after the first phonetic input, including coarticulatory information in vowels, that provides probabilistic evidence favoring the target (Dahan et al. 2001; Dahan and Tanenhaus, forthcoming).

Shortly after fixations on the target and cohort begin to rise, fixations on rhymes start to increase relative to the proportion of fixations on the unrelated picture. This result discriminates between predictions made by the cohort model of spoken-word recognition and its descendants (e.g., Marslen-Wilson 1987, 1990, 1993), which assume that any featural mismatch at the onset of a word is sufficient to strongly inhibit a lexical candidate, and continuous mapping models, such as TRACE (McClelland and Elman 1986), which predict competition from similar words that mismatch at onset (e.g., rhymes). The results strongly confirmed the predictions of continuous mapping models.

We can now illustrate a simple linking hypothesis between an underlying theoretical model and fixations. The assumption providing the link between word recognition and eye movements is that the activation of the name of a picture determines the probability that a subject will shift attention to that picture and thus make a saccadic eye movement to fixate it.[2]

Allopenna and associates formalized this linking hypothesis by converting activations into response strength, following the procedures outlined in Luce 1959. The Luce choice rule is then used to convert the response strengths into response probabilities. Panel (a) in figure 1.4 shows the activation values for *beaker*, *beetle*, *carriage*, and *speaker*, generated by a TRACE simulation. Panel (b) shows the equations used in the linking hypothesis.

The Luce choice rule assumes that each response is equally probable when there is no information. Thus when the initial instruction is *look at the cross* or *look at picture X*, we scale the response probabilities to be proportional to the amount of activation at each time step using the following equations, where max_t is the maximum activation at a particular time step, m is a constant equal to the maximum expected activation (e.g., 1.0), i is a particular item, and d_t is the scaling factor for time step t. Thus the predicted fixation probability is determined both by the amount of evidence for an alternative and the amount of evidence for that alternative compared to the other possible alternatives. Finally, we introduce a 200 ms delay because programming an eye movement takes approximately 200 ms (Matin, Shao, and Boff 1993). In experiments without explicit instructions to fixate on a particular picture, initial fixations are randomly distributed among the pictures. Under these conditions, the simple form of the choice rule can be used (see Dahan et al. 2001). When the linking hypothesis is applied to TRACE simulations of activations for the stimuli used by Allopenna and colleagues, it generates the predicted fixations over time shown in figure 1.4, panel (c). Note that the linking hypothesis transforms the shape of the functions because it introduces a nonlinear transformation. This highlights the importance of developing and using explicit linking hypotheses. The actual data are repeated figure 1.4, panel (d). The fixations over time on the target, the cohort competitor, and a rhyme competitor closely matched the predictions generated by the hypothesis linking activation levels in TRACE to fixation probabilities over time.

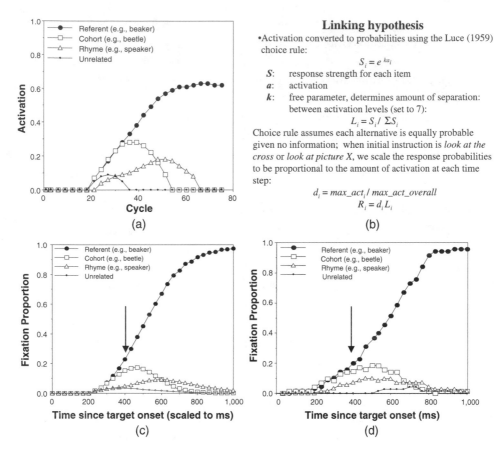

The portion at the right of the figure reads:

Linking hypothesis

•Activation converted to probabilities using the Luce (1959) choice rule:

$$S_i = e^{ka_i}$$

S: response strength for each item

a: activation

k: free parameter, determines amount of separation: between activation levels (set to 7):

$$L_i = S_i / \Sigma S_i$$

Choice rule assumes each alternative is equally probable given no information; when initial instruction is *look at the cross* or *look at picture X*, we scale the response probabilities to be proportional to the amount of activation at each time step:

$$d_i = max\_act_i / max\_act\_overall$$
$$R_i = d_i L_i$$

Figure 1.4
Results compared to model. Adapted from Allopenna, Magnuson, and Tanenhaus 1998.

Syntactic-Ambiguity Resolution in Sentence Processing

Temporary "attachment" ambiguities like those we illustrated with the example *Put the apple on the towel* ... have long served as a primary empirical test bed for evaluating models of syntactic processing (Tanenhaus and Trueswell 1995). Crain and Steedman (1985) (also Altmann and Steedman 1988) called attention to the fact that many classic structural ambiguities involve a choice between a syntactic structure in which the ambiguous phrase modifies a definite noun phrase and one in which it is a syntactic complement (argument) of a verb phrase. Under these conditions, the argument analysis is typically preferred. For instance, in *Put the apple on the towel in the box*, readers and listeners will initially misinterpret the prepositional phrase *on the towel* as in-

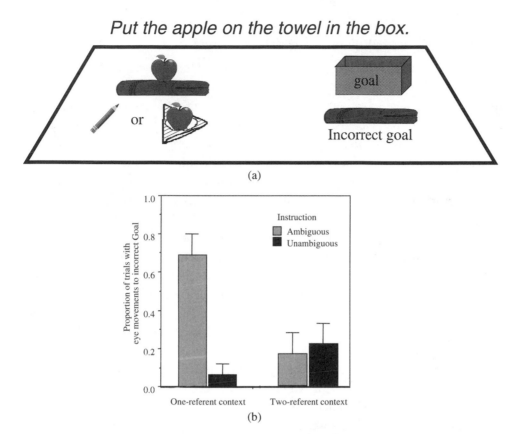

Figure 1.5
Proportion of fixations on Incorrect Goal. Adapted from Spivey et al. 2002.

troducing the Goal argument of *put*, resulting in temporary confusion if later-arriving information required treating the prepositional phrase as an adjunct modifying the Theme argument, *the apple*.

Tanenhaus et al. (1995) and Spivey et al. (2002) presented participants with temporarily ambiguous sentences such as (1) and unambiguous control sentences such as (1b), in contexts like the one illustrated in panel (a) of figure 1.5, which is adapted from Spivey et al. 2002. The objects illustrated in the figure were placed on a table in front of the participant. Participants' eye movements were monitored as they performed the action in the spoken instruction. The objects of interest are the referent of the Theme (the apple on the towel), the garden-path Goal (the empty towel), and the true Goal (the box).

(1)   a.   Put the apple on the towel in the box.
      b.   Put the apple that's on the towel in the box.

The figure presents the proportion of looks to each of these objects as the instruction unfolded. The fixations are again remarkably time-locked to the utterance. Toward the end of the word *apple*, fixations on the apple begin to rise sharply. During the middle of the word *towel*, participants begin to fixate on the empty towel, indicating that it is being considered as the Goal. The left-hand side of the graph in figure 1.5, panel (b), presents the proportion of trials with fixations on the garden-path Goal for the temporarily ambiguous (1a) and unambiguous (1b) instructions. Crucially, there were far more fixations on the garden-path Goal with the ambiguous instruction.

Crain and Steedman (1985) also noted that one use of modification is to differentiate an intended referent from other alternatives. For example, it would be odd for (1a) to be uttered in a context in which there was only one perceptually salient apple, such as the scene. However, the instruction in (1a) would be natural in a context with more than one apple—for instance, a display with two apples, one on a towel and one on a napkin. In this context, the modifying phrase *on the towel* provides information about which of the apples is the intended Theme. Crain and Steedman proposed that listeners might initially prefer the modification analysis to the argument analysis in situations that provided the appropriate referential context. Moreover, they suggested that referential fit to the context, rather than syntactic complexity, was the primary factor controlling syntactic preferences (also see Altmann and Steedman 1988).

The apple-on-the-towel experiment also included a condition with two potential referents—for example, an apple on a towel and an apple on a napkin. In the two-referent context, looks to the garden-path Goal were dramatically reduced in the two-referent context (right-hand side of the graph, panel (b) of figure 1.5). Crucially, there was not even a suggestion of a difference between the proportion of looks to the false goal with the ambiguous and the unambiguous instructions. Moreover, the timing of the fixations provided clear evidence that the prepositional phrase was being immediately interpreted as modifying the noun phrase. Participants typically looked at one of the potential referents as they heard the beginning of the instruction—for instance, *put the apple*. On trials in which participants looked first at the incorrect Theme (e.g., the apple on the napkin), they immediately shifted to the correct Theme (the apple on the towel) as they heard *towel*. Moreover, the timing was identical for the ambiguous and unambiguous instructions. Signs of garden pathing in the one-referent ambiguous instruction appeared almost immediately on hearing the potentially ambiguous *on the towel* (figure 1.6).

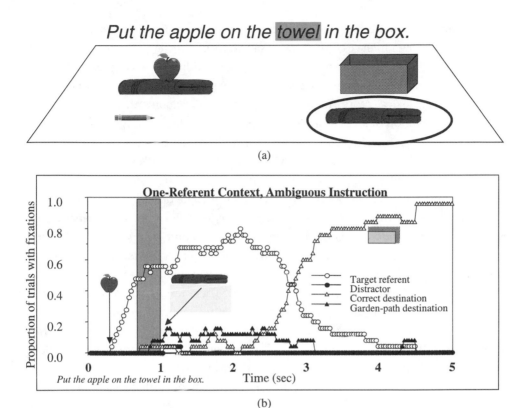

(a)

(b)

Figure 1.6
Proportion of fixations on Incorrect Goal over time. Adapted from Spivey et al. 2002.

Development of Language Use

Researchers have also begun to use eye gaze during listening with infants, toddlers, and young children to address developmental issues in language processing (e.g., Swingley, Pinto, and Fernald 1998, 1999; Swingley and Aslin 2002; Trueswell et al. 1999). The time course of children's eye movements is established either by inspecting a videotape of the child's face frame by frame (Swingley, Pinto, and Fernald 1999), or by analyzing the output of a lightweight eye-tracking visor worn by the child (Trueswell et al. 1999). These eye-movement techniques have the potential to revolutionize how we examine the child's emerging understanding of language because they provide a natural measure of how linguistic knowledge is accessed and used in real-time interpretation. Initial studies demonstrate that, like adults, children rapidly access and use their linguistic knowledge in real-time processing, so long as they know the relevant words and structures.

For example, Fernald, Swingley, and colleagues have shown that reference to an object with a known name (e.g., *ball*) results in shifts in direction of gaze to that object within 600–700 ms of the name's onset, even in children as young as 24 months (Fernald et al. 1998). More recent research has explored the extent to which there is continuity in lexical processing over the course of development. For instance, the parallel consideration of lexical candidates appears to be a fundamental property of the spoken-language comprehension system even at its earliest stages of development. Swingley, Pinto, and Fernald (1999) provided 24-month-olds with spoken instructions to look at a particular object (e.g., *Look at the tree*) in the presence of either lexical-cohort competitor (pictures of a tree and a truck) or some other object (pictures of a tree and a dog). Like Allopenna and colleagues' (1998) adult subjects, toddlers showed temporary consideration of both the target and the cohort competitor early in the perception of the word, which resolved toward the target soon after the word's offset (also see Swingley and Aslin 2002). Consideration of the alternative object did not occur when the object was not a cohort member. These results demonstrate that the developing word-recognition system makes use of fine-grained phonemic contrasts, and from the start is designed to interface this linguistic knowledge (how the word sounds, what the word means) with knowledge about how the word might plausibly behave referentially when making contact with the ambient world.

Other work has begun to examine the development of sentence-parsing abilities using eye-gaze measures. This research began with studies conducted with 5-year-olds and 8-year-olds, first reported in Trueswell et al. 1999. The experiments were modeled after the adult apple-on-the-towel study described earlier (Tanenhaus et al. 1995; Spivey et al. 2002). Here children's eye movements were recorded using a lightweight visor system as they acted on spoken instructions that contained temporary ambiguities such as *Put the frog on the napkin in the box* (see figure 1.7). Like the apple example, the phrase *on the napkin* is briefly ambiguous between a Goal argument of the verb *put* and a Modifier of the noun phrase *the frog*, specifying a property of a particular frog. The phrase is disambiguated in favor of the Modifier interpretation by the presence of a second Goal phrase (*in the box*).

The striking finding was that 5-year-olds showed a strong preference for interpreting *on the napkin* as the Goal of *put*, even when the referential scene supported a Modifier interpretation (e.g., two frogs, one on a napkin; figure 1.7). On hearing *on the napkin*, 5-year-olds typically looked over to a potential Goal in the scene, the empty napkin, regardless of whether there were two frogs present (supporting a Modifier interpretation) or one frog present (supporting a Goal interpretation). The timing of these eye movements was similar to what was observed in the one-referent condition of adults—

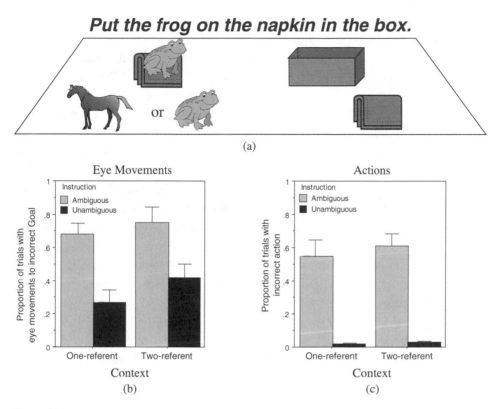

(a)

(b)   (c)

Figure 1.7
Child Parsing Data. Proportion of fixations on Incorrect Goal. Adapted from Trueswell et al. 1999.

that is, approximately 600 ms after the onset of the word *napkin*—but for children this pattern of Goal looks also arose in two-referent contexts. In fact, 5-year-olds' preference for the Goal interpretation was so strong that they showed little sign of revising it; on hearing *napkin*, children looked to the empty napkin as a potential goal and then frequently moved a frog to that location. In two-referent cases, children were equally likely to move the frog that was on the napkin and the frog that was not on the napkin, suggesting they never considered a Modifier interpretation.

Importantly, this child parsing behavior was localized to the ambiguity and not to the complexity of the sentence. Five-year-olds' eye movements and actions became adultlike when the temporary ambiguity was removed, as in the unambiguous modifier form, *Put the frog that's on the napkin in the box*. The nearly perfect performance with unambiguous sentences rules out a potentially mundane explanation of the results, namely, that long "complicated" sentences confuse young children. Here an even longer sentence with the same intended structure does not cause difficulty, precisely because the sentence lacks the temporary ambiguity.

In contrast to the responses of 5-year-olds, 8-year-olds' and adults' responses to the temporarily ambiguous stimuli were found to depend on the referential scene provided. In particular, the mere presence of a two-referent scene eliminated measurable signs of syntactic misanalysis of the ambiguous phrase: there were few looks to the potential Goal and few incorrect actions as compared to one-referent scenes. This finding is consistent with the earlier apple-on-the-napkin studies described above (Tanenhaus et al. 1995; Spivey et al. 2002).

Both of these findings (from Swingley, Pinto, and Fernald 1999 and Trueswell et al. 1999) suggest that there is considerable continuity in the language-processing system throughout development: lexical and sentential interpretation proceed incrementally and are designed to coordinate multiple information sources (e.g., linking what is heard to what is seen within milliseconds). However, the differences between 5- and 8-year-old children reported by Trueswell et al. (1999) suggest that significant developmental differences exist. These differences likely pertain to how children learn about sources of evidence relevant to linguistic and correlated nonlinguistic constraints. Highly reliable cues to structure, such as the argument-taking preferences of verbs, are learned earlier than other sources of evidence that may be less reliable or more difficult to discover.

Closed-Set Issues

We have established that the eye-movement paradigm meets the three essential criteria for a measure of real-time spoken language processing: the response measure is sensitive, it is time-locked, and it has a clear linking hypothesis. There is, however, an aspect of the methodology that is potentially problematic. The use of a visual world with a limited set of pictured referents and a limited set of potential actions creates a more restricted environment than language processing in many, if not most, contexts. Certainly, these characteristics impose more restrictions than most psycholinguistic tasks. We will refer to this as the *closed-set* problem.

Two aspects of the closed-set problem could, in principle, limit the usefulness of the visual-world paradigm. The first is that the closed set might create task-specific strategies that result in language processing that does not generalize beyond the specific situations created within the experiment. The second is that the paradigm might not be sensitive to characteristics of linguistic knowledge and experience lying outside of the closed set that has been established on a given trial. We will illustrate these two potential problems using the experiment by Allopenna, Magnuson, and Tanenhaus (1998).

We know that as a spoken word unfolds over time, recognition takes place against a backdrop of partially activated alternatives that compete for recognition. As a consequence the recognition of a spoken word is influenced by the similarity structure created by those lexical candidates that most closely match the input. The number of competitors, their frequency of occurrence in the language, and the frequency of occurrence of the target word itself all affect recognition (e.g., Luce and Pisoni 1998; Marslen-Wilson 1987, 1990).

We can use the linking hypothesis discussed earlier to help clarify the distinction between the task-specific strategy and the sensitivity issues. Recall that the linking hypothesis assumes that the equation that determines the response strength for each lexical candidate at a moment in time is computed using the activation of its lexical representation. The activation of a lexical candidate will be affected by the entire lexicon—that is, it will be determined in part by its neighbors. However, only the items in the response set enter into calculations for response selection. The task-specific strategy concern is that processing of the input might bypass the activation process. The sensitivity concern is that the effects of response selection, or alternatively, the effects of presenting the response set, are so strong that they mask any effects of lexical neighborhoods.

Strategies   In the experiment by Allopenna and colleagues, the potential response set on each trial was limited to four pictured items. If participants adopted a task-specific strategy, such as implicitly naming the pictures, then the unfolding input might be evaluated against these activated names, effectively bypassing the usual activation process. A related argument could be made for the parsing studies. Here the argument would be that listeners process the language shallowly, extracting only the information necessary to inform the action.

Along with our colleagues, we have tried to articulate the task-specific strategy concerns and to address them empirically (see Dahan and Tanenhaus, forthcoming). For example, the patterns of results observed in the Allopenna et al. studies are observed even when the preview time for the pictures is limited. In addition, we find robust effects of frequency for targets and cohort competitors (Dahan, Magnuson, and Tanenhaus 2001). These are unexpected with a closed-set strategy because the a priori probability of each of the pictured names is equated, which should eliminate or strongly reduce frequency effects. Crucially, the prenaming strategy is inconsistent with the fact that we observe input-driven looks to pictures whose names are not related to the target but are visually similar to its referent—for example, a picture of a turtle for the target *igloo* (Dahan and Tanenhaus 2003). This result is unexpected if participants are implicitly naming the pictures. However, it is predicted by the hypothesis that the link to the pictured referents is made via perceptual/conceptual representations that are accessed as the target word is being processed.

A crucial empirical test of the task-specific strategies argument in sentence processing comes from work by Craig Chambers and colleagues (Chambers et al. 2002; Chambers 2001). In Chambers et al. 2002, experiment 2, participants were presented with six objects in a workspace. On critical trials, the objects included a large and a small container—for example, a large can and a small can. The critical variable manipulated in the workspace was whether a to-be-mentioned (Theme) object, like a cube, could fit into both of the containers, as was the case for a small cube, or could only fit into the larger container, as was the case for a large cube. Thus the size of the Theme object determined whether one or two potential Goal objects were compatible referents. The instructions—for instance, *Pick up the cube. Put it inside a/the can*—manipulated whether the Goal was introduced with the definite article *the*, which presupposes a unique referent, or the indefinite article *a*, which implies that the addressee can choose from among more than one Goal.

As expected, when the definite article, which assumes a uniquely identifiable referent, was used in the instruction with the small cube, participants were confused compared to when an indefinite article was used in the instruction. Eye-movement latencies to fixate the Goal object chosen by the participant were slower in the definite condition than in the indefinite condition. However, for the large cube, confusion with the definite article (relative to a baseline with only a single large container) was eliminated. This result by itself is consistent with two explanations, both of which assume that listeners dynamically update referential domains to include only objects that afford the required action—that is, containers that the object in hand would fit into. The first explanation is that participants simply adopt a task-specific strategy. After picking up the cube and hearing *put it inside*, they focus their attention on the only Goal object compatible with the action, therefore bypassing more detailed linguistic processing. This hypothesis predicts that participants will not be confused when the indefinite article *a* is used because there is still only one possible action. The second explanation is that the participants fully process the instruction, using the information provided by each word. This explanation predicts that the indefinite article should be infelicitous when there is only one compatible Goal object because it implies that there is more than one possible Goal. The results were clearly inconsistent with the task-specific strategy explanation: latencies in the indefinite condition increased in the one-compatible-Goal condition compared to the two-compatible-Goal condition, despite the fact that the one-Goal condition afforded only one possible action.

Sensitivity   Evaluating sensitivity outside of the closed set is relatively straightforward in the case of spoken-word recognition. We need to determine whether the visual-world paradigm shows effects of the nondisplayed, nonmentioned lexical neighbors. A body of such results now exists. For example, Dahan et al. (2001) introduced misleading coarticulatory information about upcoming place of articulation by creating cross-spliced tokens such as *neck* in which the onset and vowel were taken from either a word (e.g., *net*) or a nonword (e.g., *nep*). The effects of the cross-splicing was stronger when the initial portion of the target was consistent with a word compared to a nonword, even though that word was never mentioned and its referent was never displayed. This result demonstrates strong effects of a nondisplayed, nonmentioned lexical competitor.

Perhaps the most compelling evidence for sensitivity comes from a series of studies by Magnuson and colleagues (Magnuson 2001; Magnuson, Tanenhaus, and Aslin 2003). Magnuson and colleagues used a variant of the Allopenna et al. paradigm to examine the effects of lexical neighbors on recognition of spoken words. Target words matched in frequency were chosen that varied in whether they came from high- or low-density neighborhoods, where density was defined as either the number of words that differed by only a single phoneme (neighborhood density) or whether they had few or many cohorts (cohort density). The displays presented a picture of a target along with three pictures with unrelated names. Cohorts and noncohort neighbors were never pictured or mentioned throughout the course of the experiment. Nonetheless, clear effects of both cohort and neighborhood density were found, including theoretically significant time-course differences that had not been previously observed with other paradigms (also see Magnuson et al. 2003 for similar results with artificial lexicons). Despite the closed set, then, the paradigm is sensitive to effects coming from the full lexicon. Interestingly, similar conclusions have been made about the eye-gaze patterns of 24-month-olds. Swingley and Fernald (2002) looked at the speed of response to known and unknown words and found that on this task, children sought out a ball on hearing *ball* even when no ball was present. All of these results confirm the most basic claim of the Allopenna et al. linking hypothesis, namely, that the activation of the lexical candidates is determined by the entire lexicon, with the visual world operating as a response selection set.

There is also an emerging literature that addresses sensitivity concerns in sentence processing. In the adult PP-attachment studies we reviewed earlier, the two-referent contexts completely eliminated any hint of a garden path for the temporarily ambiguous instructions. This result is somewhat surprising, because the verb *put* obligatorily occurs with a goal argument. In the parallel literature in reading there is clear evidence that referential factors are partially modulated by the availability of syntactic alternatives, especially those tied to verb-based frequencies (see MacDonald, Pearlmutter, and Seidenberg 1994; Snedeker, Thorpe, and Trueswell 2001; Snedeker and Trueswell 2004; Trueswell and Tanenhaus 1994). Consider, for example, a well-known study by Britt (1994).

Britt manipulated referential context and verb bias in a study using self-paced reading. The discourse context introduced one or two potential referents (e.g., a book about the Civil War and another book). The target sentence contained a temporarily ambiguous PP-phrase (e.g., *Susan dropped the book <u>on the Civil War</u> onto the table*) that was preceded by a verb that optionally takes a Goal argument (e.g., *Susan dropped the book ...*) or a verb that obligatorily takes a Goal argument (e.g., *Susan put the book ...*). Britt found that two-referent contexts eliminated garden paths due to the Goal-argument bias for the optional-Goal verbs, but not for the obligatory-Goal verbs.

Why then were the context effects so strong in the visual-world, *put-the-apple-on-the-towel* studies? Certainly, referential-context effects might be stronger in visual-world situations because the context is copresent with the linguistic input rather than held in memory, as in reading studies. Nonetheless, the fact that a constraint as strong as verb bias was completely overridden raises concerns about sensitivity and/or strategies because of the highly constraining visual context and limited set of potential actions that could be performed with the objects in the workspace.

However, several visual-world studies have demonstrated clear effects of verb-based constraints. For example, using the anticipatory-looks paradigm introduced by Altmann and Kamide (1999), Boland (2002) found that as they heard a verb, participants were more likely to make anticipatory looks to referents of likely recipient arguments than to referents of plausible adjuncts. Moreover, Snedeker, Thorpe, and Trueswell (2001) have demonstrated an interaction between referential context and verb-bias in syntactic-ambiguity resolution. These studies used instructions such as *Tickle/Feel/Choose the frog with the feather*. The verb had a strong instrument bias (e.g., *tickle*) or was equibiased between taking an instrument or a modifier (*feel*) or had a strong modifier bias (*choose*). The contexts contained an instrument (e.g., a large feather), and either a single frog with a small feather (one-referent context) or two frogs, one of which was holding a small feather and one of which was holding another object (two-referent context). As expected, one-referent scenes did induce more instru-ment actions than two-referent scenes (i.e., two-referent scenes supported a restrictive modifier reading of *with the feather* and hence reduced the instrument interpretation). However, the extent to which the two-referent contexts reduced instrument responses was modulated by verb bias. For equibias and modifier-bias verbs, two-referent scenes resulted in very few instrument actions (i.e., picking up the feather to do the action occurred on only about 5 percent of the trials for both verb types). A substantial num-ber of instrument responses were observed, though, in two-referent scenes when the verb was instrument biased (65 percent instrument responses). Snedeker and Trueswell (2004) suggest this pattern arises because lexical biases in this condition so strongly support an instrument reading that the competing NP-modifier interpretation is often inaccessible to the listener. Thus, like the results of Magnuson et al. 2003, these data suggest that eye-gaze responses are guided in part by the availability of linguistic alter-natives; here verb-specific frequency information modulates the influence of the refer-ential scene.

Why then would referential context have such strong effects in the *put-the-apple/frog* studies even though *put* obligatorily requires a Goal argument and thus is more strongly biased than a verb such as *tickle*, for which an instrument in not obligatory? More research is needed to provide a definitive answer but the outline of a plausible explanation is beginning to emerge (Snedeker and Trueswell 2004). First, in an in-struction such as *Put the apple on the towel* . . . , the preposition introducing the PP, *on*, specifies a location, regardless of whether the PP modifies the noun phrase or the verb. In contrast, in the Britt 1994 study, the sense of *on* in the prepositional phrase differed when it introduced a Goal argument and when it modified the noun. The location sense of *on*, which corresponds to the Goal argument, is the more frequent sense, es-pecially when *on* follows a noun phrase after a verb. The sense of the preposition *with* also differs for the modifier and the instrument attachment in *tickle the frog with the feather*, with the instrument sense more frequent when *with* follows a verb. Thus in the Britt 1994 and Snedeker and Trueswell 2004 studies, the referential constraints from the two-referent context are pitted against two opposing constraints for strongly biased Goal or Instrument verbs. One bias comes from the preposition, the other from the verb. The preposition bias is especially strong in Goal constructions like those used by Britt.

A second possible factor is specific to the noun modification/instrument ambiguity. In natural tasks, people typically fixate on an object before reaching for it (cf. Ballard et al. 1997). Instrument actions, such as tickling a frog with a feather, require the par-ticipant to first grasp the instrument (the feather) before using it to perform the action on the Theme (the frog). Thus attention for action needs to be directed to potential instruments. As a result, on hearing a Theme-instrument verb such as *tickle*, the participant's attention for action is already biased toward an instrument, even before encountering the definite noun phrase. In contrast, for Theme-Goal verbs such as *put*, attention for action will be directed toward the Theme. Thus the combination of the verb bias, preposition bias, and attention-for-action bias may conspire against the referential constraint in the *tickle-the-frog* studies. In sum, then, the strength of the referential-context effects in the *put-the-apple* and the *tickle-the-frog* studies interacts with other constraints, including lexically based verb preferences and frequency-based sense biases for prepositions. Further, visual-world parsing studies, including those involving actions, are sensitive to the lexical preferences that have been documented with other paradigms. Crucially, the differences between the Britt (1994) results and those of Tanenhaus et al. (1995), Spivey et al. (2002), and Trueswell et al. (1999) cannot be due to exaggerated context effects in visual-world tasks, in which sensitivity to well-established linguistic variables was somehow masked: Snedeker, Thorpe, and Trueswell (2001) showed sensitivity to these variables in such a task. Rather, the different findings arise precisely because both measures (reading fixations and visual-world fixations) are sensitive to subtle linguistic properties, pertaining to lexical information and lexical biases, that differed across these studies.

Bridging the Action and Product Traditions

We conclude by first briefly reviewing some ongoing work that we and our colleagues have been pursuing that uses eye gaze to bridge the product and action traditions and then outlining some future challenges.

The availability of eye gaze as a real-time response measure that can be used with nonlinguistic contexts and natural tasks makes it possible to more strongly integrate action-based constructs into product-based experimental designs. One example is the line of research initiated by Chambers and colleagues on when and how actions, intentions, and affordances affect the context with respect to which an utterance is processed. Consider, for example, a variant of the *put-the-apple* study with a two-referent context in which only one of the two potential referents is compatible with the action. In a context that includes a liquid egg in a bowl and a hard-boiled egg in a cup, the instruction *Pour the egg in the bowl over the flour* contains a temporarily ambiguous prepositional phrase (*in the bowl*) with two potential referents (two eggs) that are consistent with a context-independent sense of *the bowl*. In these circumstances, listeners are temporarily garden-pathed, mistakenly interpreting the prepositional phrase as introducing the Goal argument, just as they would in a one-referent context. This result, along with related findings, demonstrates that syntactic ambiguity is resolved with respect to a dynamically updated referential domain that takes into account plausible actions and intention-relevant affordances of objects (Chambers 2001; Chambers, Tanenhaus, and Magnuson, forthcoming). A second example is research by Arnold and colleagues on disfluency and reference resolution. There is growing interest in how characteristics of natural utterances, such as disfluent productions, affect real-time language processing (Brennan and Schober 2001; Bailey and Ferreira, chapter 14, this volume). Using the paradigm of Allopenna and colleagues (1998), Dahan, Tanenhaus, and Chambers (2002) showed that an accented definite noun phrase is preferentially interpreted as referring to a discourse-old entity that is not in focus, rather than to a new entity. Arnold noted that a disfluent production is more likely to occur when a speaker is introducing a new discourse entity than when a speaker is mentioning a given entity. Using the paradigm of Allopenna and associates (1998) to examine looks to cohort competitors, Arnold and colleagues showed that a disfluent noun phrase modulates, and sometimes reverses, the given bias for accented noun phrases (e.g., Arnold, Fagnano, and Tanenhaus 2003). An important unresolved question is whether the real-time effects of disfluency reflect learned contingencies based on statistical correlations among types of forms or whether the listener's attributions of plausible sources of the disfluency also modulate the effects. For instance, would the new bias created by a disfluency disappear if difficulty in lexical retrieval was no longer a plausible source of the disfluency, if, for example, the speaker was distracted by an external noise?

The question of how a listener's attributions about the speaker might affect the processing of a disfluent utterance raises perhaps the most hotly contested issue in current work that bridges the product and action traditions: to what extent do speakers and listeners compute common ground? Most work in the action tradition assumes that participants in a conversation monitor each other's intentions, including making distinctions between speaker and hearer knowledge. It is also frequently assumed that the speaker crafts his or her message with the listener in mind, including sending fine-grained signals about upcoming difficulty in production and choosing forms to limit ambiguity. However, an emerging literature suggests that speakers do not avoid constructions that are ambiguous or otherwise difficult for listeners (Arnold et al. 2004; Brown and Dell 1986; Ferreira and Dell 2000), though under some circumstances speakers use prosody to disambiguate an otherwise ambiguous utterance (Snedeker and Trueswell 2004).

More controversially, Keysar and colleagues (e.g., Keysar et al. 2000; Keysar and Barr, chapter 3, this volume) have presented evidence that listeners initially ignore salient aspects of common ground, such as visual copresence—an important heuristic for common ground, identified by Clark and Marshall (1981). The strongest form of the Keysar proposal was that listeners' initial interpretations are computed egocentrically, with speaker knowledge consulted only in a second stage if a misunderstanding arises (Keysar, Barr, and Horton 1998).

More recent work has qualified that conclusion. While common ground does not completely circumscribe the listeners' referential domain, it does affect even the earliest moments of reference resolution (Arnold, Trueswell, and Lawentmann 1999; Hanna and Tanenhaus, chapter 5, this volume; Hanna, Tanenhaus, and Trueswell 2003; Keysar and Barr, chapter 3, this volume). Moreover, even young children engaged in this task show a similar time course of consideration of common ground (Nadig and Sedivy 2002). Use of eye gaze has been crucial for evaluating when information about common ground is used, and we believe it will be increasingly important in linking the literature on use of common ground with the parallel literature in theory of mind, and its development (see Nadig and Sedivy 2002; Sabbagh and Baldwin 2001).

Thus far work on common ground in real-time processing has used tasks in which one of the participants is a confederate, following a script. Although this class of studies has contributed and will continue to contribute important insights, use of confederates eliminates one of the crucial ingredients of spontaneous interactive conversation: interlocutors cooperating to create a relevant discourse, in a task with joint goals. In our opinion, the question of how speakers and addressees coordinate with one another cannot be satisfactorily answered until we can monitor real-time comprehension in nonscripted interactive conversation. Doing so raises a difficult methodological challenge because traditional psycholinguistic experiments use carefully controlled stimuli. However, Brown-Schmidt and her colleagues (e.g., Brown-Schmidt, Campana, and Tanenhaus, chapter 6, this volume) have demonstrated that it is possible to use eye gaze to monitor real-time comprehension in natural interactive conversation. The initial studies replicate some effects observed in more controlled experiments, but also shed light on how common goal structures can result in closely aligned referential domains. We anticipate that extension of this line of research to more complex goal structures as well as to face-to-face interactive conversation is likely to shed light on when and how interlocutors achieve coordination. This work also parallels the environments in which children are first exposed to words, and we expect that developmental parallels will shed light on long-standing issues in language acquisition (Snedeker and Trueswell 2004; Trueswell and Gleitman, forthcoming).

As real-time work on interactive conversation develops, we are hopeful that psycho-linguistic work can complement, and be complementary to, work on intelligent com-municative systems that make use of spoken language (Allen et al. 2001). Dialogue systems are beginning to tackle the problem of incremental or continuous generation and understanding in domains that involve interactive conversation with a human user. Because these systems must integrate knowledge of a domain with language processing, they offer the potential for providing a theoretical test bed for explicit computational models of dialogue. We believe that such models will be necessary if psycholinguistic research on dialogue is to seriously explore interactive conversation within an explicit theoretical framework. We also anticipate that eye movements will play an important methodological role in this research.

We close by noting that eye-movement measures need not and should not be the only measures used by researchers to map the time course of processes in conversation. We expect that other methods will emerge that meet many or all of the desiderata sketched earlier in this chapter. We strongly suspect, though, that the most ground-breaking work will come from those using increasingly rich (and complex) data arrays to understand the dynamics of comprehension and production in conversa-tion. For instance, other body movements pertaining to gestures and actions are likely to be highly informative when connected to the timing of speech and eye-gaze events. This movement toward connecting language and action in rich goal-directed tasks is likely to influence theoretical developments in natural language, just as it has begun to enrich theories of perception and cognition (Ballard et al. 1997; Barsalou 1999).

Notes

This research was partially supported by NIH grants HD-27206 and DC-05071 to MKT and NIH grant HD-37507 to JCT.

1. Studies with action-based tasks increasingly use video-based trackers that monitor the pupil and the cornea, with independent tracking of the head or compensation for head movement, when stimuli are presented on a screen. Measuring head movement can be bypassed by super-imposing fixations on a head-based videorecord, though this limits analysis to videorates (60 Hz).

2. By using the word *attention*, we do not intend to suggest that participants are consciously shifting attention. In fact, people are typically unaware of making eye movements and even of exactly where they are fixating. One possibility is that the attentional shifts take place at the level of unconscious visual routines that support accessing information from a visual scene (Hayhoe 2000).

References

Allen, J. F., Byron, D. K., Dzikovska, M., Ferguson, G., Galescu, L., and Stent, A. 2001. Towards conversational human-computer interaction. *AI Magazine, 22,* 27–35.

Allopenna, P. D., Magnuson, J. S., and Tanenhaus, M. K. 1998. Tracking the time course of spoken word recognition: Evidence for continuous mapping models. *Journal of Memory and Language, 38,* 419–439.

Altmann, G. T. M., and Kamide, Y. 1999. Incremental interpretation of verbs: Restricting the domain of subsequent reference. *Cognition, 73,* 247–264.

Altmann, G. T. M., and Steedman, M. J. 1988. Interaction with context during human sentence processing. *Cognition, 30,* 191–238.

Arnold, J., Fagnano, M., and Tanenhaus, M. K. 2003. Disfluencies signal theee, um, new information. *Journal of Psycholinguistic Research, 32,* 25–36.

Arnold, J., Trueswell, J. C., and Lawentmann, S. M. 1999, November. Using common ground to resolve referential ambiguity. Paper presented at the Fortieth Annual Meeting of the Psychonomic Society, Los Angeles.

Arnold, J., Wasow, T., Asudeh, A., and Alrenga, P. Avoiding attachment ambiguities: The role of constituent ordering. Unpublished manuscript.

Austin, J. L. 1962. *How to Do Things with Words.* Oxford: Oxford University Press.

Ballard, D. H., Hayhoe, M. M., Pook, P. K., and Rao, R. P. N. 1997. Deictic codes for the embodiment of cognition. *Behavioral and Brain Sciences, 20(4),* 723–767.

Barsalou, L. W. 1999. Perceptual symbol systems. *Behavioral and Brain Sciences, 22(4),* 577–660.

Boland, J. E. 2002. Listeners use verb argument structure to focus visual attention on potential arguments. Paper presented at the 15th annual meeting of the CUNY Sentence Processing Conference, New York, March 2002.

Brennan, S. E., and Schober, M. F. 2001. How listeners compensate for disfluencies in spontaneous speech. *Journal of Memory and Language, 44,* 274–296.

Britt, M. A. 1994. The interaction of referential ambiguity and argument structure in the parsing of prepositional phrases. *Journal of Memory and Language, 33,* 251–283.

Brown, P. M., and Dell, G. S. 1986. Adapting production to comprehension: The explicit mention of instruments. *Cognitive Psychology, 19,* 441–472.

Chambers, C. G. 2001. The Dynamic Construction of Referential Domains. Unpublished doctoral dissertation, University of Rochester.

Chambers, C. G., Tanenhaus, M. K., Eberhard, K. M., Carlson, G. N., and Filip, H. 2002. Circumscribing referential domains during real-time language comprehension. *Journal of Memory and Language, 47,* 30–49.

Chambers, C. G., Tanenhaus, M. K., and Magnuson, J. S. Forthcoming. Action-based affordances and syntactic ambiguity resolution. *Journal of Experimental Psychology: Learning, Memory, and Cognition.*

Clark, H. H. 1992. *Arenas of Language Use.* Chicago: University of Chicago Press.

Clark, H. H. 1996. *Using Language.* Cambridge, UK: Cambridge University Press.

Clark, H. H. 1997. Dogmas of understanding. *Discourse Processes, 23,* 567–598.

Clark, H. H., and Brennan, S. E. 1989. Grounding in communication. In L. Resnick, J. Levine, and S. Teasley, eds., *Perspectives on Socially Shared Cognition,* 127–149. Washington, DC: American Psychological Association.

Clark, H. H., and Carlson, T. 1981. Context for comprehension. In J. Long and A. Baddeley, eds., *Attention and Performance IX,* 313–330. Hillsdale, NJ: Erlbaum.

Clark, H. H., and Marshall, C. R. 1981. Definite reference and mutual knowledge. In A. H. Joshi, B. Webber, and I. A. Sag, eds., *Elements of Discourse Understanding,* 10–63. Cambridge, UK: Cambridge University Press.

Clark, H. H., and Wilkes-Gibbs, D. 1986. Referring as a collaborative process. *Cognition, 22,* 1–39.

Colby, C. L., and Goldberg, M. E. 1999. Space and attention in parietal cortex. *Annual Review of Neuroscience, 22,* 97–136.

Cooper, R. M. 1974. The control of eye fixation by the meaning of spoken language: A new methodology for the real-time investigation of speech perception, memory, and language processing. *Cognitive Psychology, 6,* 84–107.

Crain, S., and Steedman, M. 1985. On not being led up the garden path: The use of context by the psychological parser. In D. Dowty, L. Karttunen, and A. Zwicky, eds., *Natural Language Parsing: Psychological, Computational, and Theoretical Perspectives,* 320–358. Cambridge, UK: Cambridge University Press.

Dahan, D., Magnuson, J. S., and Tanenhaus, M. K. 2001. Time course of frequency effects in spoken word recognition: Evidence from eye movements. *Cognitive Psychology, 42,* 317–367.

Dahan, D., Magnuson, J. S., Tanenhaus, M. K., and Hogan, E. M. 2001. Subcategorical mismatches and the time course of lexical access: Evidence for lexical competition. *Language and Cognitive Processes, 16,* 507–534.

Dahan, D., and Tanenhaus, M. K. 2003. Activation of visually based conceptual representations during spoken-word recognition. Unpublished manuscript.

Dahan, D., and Tanenhaus, M. K. Forthcoming. Continuous mapping from sound to meaning in spoken-language comprehension: Evidence from immediate effects of verb-based constraints. *Journal of Experimental Psychology: Learning, Memory, and Cognition.*

Dahan, D., Tanenhaus, M. K., and Chambers, C. G. 2002. Accent and reference resolution in spoken language comprehension. *Journal of Memory and Language, 47,* 292–314.

Eberhard, K. M., Spivey-Knowlton, M. J., Sedivy, J. C., and Tanenhaus, M. K. 1995. Eye-movements as a window into spoken language comprehension in natural contexts. *Journal of Psycholinguistic Research, 24*, 409–436.

Fernald, A., Pinto, J. P., Swingley, D., Weinberg, A., and McRoberts, G. 1998. Rapid gains in speed of verbal processing by infants in the second year. *Psychological Science, 9*, 228–231. Reprinted in M. Tomasello and E. Bates, eds., *Language Development: The Essential Readings*. Oxford: Blackwell, 2001.

Ferreira, V., and Dell, G. 2000. Effects of ambiguity and lexical availability on syntactic and lexical production. *Cognitive Psychology, 40*, 296–340.

Findlay, J. M. Forthcoming. Eye scanning and visual search. In J. M. Henderson and F. Ferreira, eds., *The Interface of Language, Vision, and Action: Eye Movements and the Visual World*. New York: Psychology Press.

Fodor, J. A., Bever, T. G., and Garrett, M. F. 1974. *The Psychology of Language: An Introduction to Psycholinguistics and Generative Grammar*, 313–372. New York: McGraw-Hill.

Grice, H. P. 1957. Meaning. *Philosophical Review, 66*, 377–388.

Hanna, J. E., Tanenhaus, M. K., and Trueswell, J. C. 2003. The effects of common ground and perspective on domains of referential interpretation. *Journal of Memory and Language, 49*, 43–61.

Hayhoe, M. 2000. Vision using routines: A functional account of vision. *Visual Cognition, 7*, 43–64.

Henderson, J. M., and Ferreira, F. 2003. *The Interface of Language, Vision, and Action: Eye Movements and the Visual World*. New York: Psychology Press.

Henderson, J. M., and Hollingworth, A. 2003. Eye movements, visual memory, and scene representation. In M. A. Peterson and G. Rhodes, eds., *Analytic and Holistic Processes in the Perception of Faces, Objects, and Scenes*, 356–383. New York: Oxford University Press.

Horton, W. S., and Keysar, B. 1995. When do speakers take into account common ground? *Cognition, 59*, 91–117.

Keysar, B., Barr, D. J., Balin, J. A., and Brauner, J. S. 2000. Taking perspective in conversation: The role of mutual knowledge in comprehension. *Psychological Science, 11*, 32–37.

Keysar, B., Barr, D. J., and Horton, W. S. 1998. The egocentric basis of language use: Insights from a processing approach. *Current Directions in Psychological Science, 7*, 46–50.

Kowler, E. 1995. Eye movements. In S. M. Kosslyn and D. N. Osherson, eds., *An Invitation to Cognitive Science, Volume 2: Visual Cognition*, 2nd ed., 215–265. Cambridge, MA: MIT Press.

Kowler, E. 1999. Eye movements and visual attention. In R. A. Wilson and F. C. Keil, eds., *The MIT Encyclopedia of the Cognitive Sciences*, 306–309. Cambridge, MA: MIT Press.

Krauss, R. M., and Weinheimer, S. 1966. Concurrent feedback, confirmation, and the encoding of referents in verbal communication. *Journal of Personality and Social Psychology, 4*, 343–346.

Levelt, W. J. M., Roelof, A., and Meyer, A. S. 1999. A theory of lexical access in speech production. *Behavioral and Brain Sciences*, *22*, 1–75.

Levinson, S. C. 2000. *Presumptive Meanings*. Cambridge, MA: MIT Press.

Liversedge, S., and Findlay, J. 2001. Saccadic eye movements and cognition. *Trends in Cognitive Sciences*, *4*, 6–14.

Luce, R. D. 1959. *Individual Choice Behavior*. New York: Wiley.

Luce, P., and Pisoni, D. 1998. Recognizing spoken words: The Neighborhood Activation Model. *Ear and Hearing*, *19*, 1–38.

MacDonald, M. C. 1994. Probabilistic constraints and syntactic ambiguity resolution. *Language and Cognitive Processes*, *9*, 157–201.

MacDonald, M. C., Pearlmutter, N. J., and Seidenberg, M. S. 1994. The lexical nature of syntactic ambiguity resolution. *Psychological Review*, *101*, 676–703.

Magnuson, J. S. 2001. The Microstructure of Spoken Word Recognition. Unpublished doctoral dissertation, University of Rochester.

Magnuson, J. S., Tanenhaus, M. K., and Aslin, R. 2003. Time course of spoken word recognition: effects of frequency, cohort density and lexical neighbors. Unpublished manuscript.

Magnuson, J. S., Tanenhaus, M. K., Aslin, R. N., and Dahan, D. 2003. The time course of spoken word learning and recognition: Studies with artificial lexicons. *Journal of Experimental Psychology: General*, *132*, 202–227.

Marcus, M. P. 1980. *A Theory of Syntactic Recognition for Natural Language*. Cambridge, MA: MIT Press.

Marslen-Wilson, W. D. 1973. Linguistic structure and speech shadowing at very short latencies. *Nature*, *244*, 522–523.

Marslen-Wilson, W. D. 1975. Sentence perception as an interactive parallel process. *Science*, *189*, 226–228.

Marslen-Wilson, W. D. 1987. Functional parallelism in spoken word-recognition. *Cognition*, *25*, 71–102.

Marslen-Wilson, W. D. 1990. Activation, competition, and frequency in lexical access. In G. Altmann, ed., *Cognitive Models of Speech Processing: Psycholinguistic and Computational Perspectives*. Cambridge, MA: MIT Press.

Marslen-Wilson, W. D. 1993. Issues of process and representation in lexical access. In G. Altmann and R. Shillcock, eds., *Cognitive Models of Language Processes: The Second Sperlonga Meeting*. Hove, England: Erlbaum.

Matin, E., Shao, K. C., and Boff, K. R. 1993. *Information-processing time with and without saccades*. *Perception and Psychophysics*, *53(4)*, 372–380.

McClelland, J. L., and Elman, J. L. 1986. Interactive processes in speech perception: The TRACE Model. In D. E. Rumelhart and J. L. McClelland, eds., *Parallel Distributed Processing*, vol. 2. Cambridge, MA: MIT Press.

McMurray, B., Tanenhaus, M. K., and Aslin, R. N. 2002. Gradient effects of within-category phonetic variation on lexical access. *Cognition, 86*, B33–B42.

Miller, G. A., and Chomsky, N. 1963. Finitary models of language users. In R. D. Luce, R. R. Bush, and E. Galanter, eds., *Handbook of Mathematical Psychology*. New York: Wiley.

Nadig, A. S., and Sedivy, J. C. 2002. Evidence of perspective-taking constraints in children's on-line reference resolution. *Psychological Science, 13*, 329–336.

Pickering, M., and Garrod, S. A. Forthcoming. Towards a mechanistic psycholinguistics of dialogue. *Brain and Behavioral Sciences*.

Rayner, K. 1998. Eye movement in reading and information processing: 20 years of research. *Psychological Bulletin, 124(3)*, 372–422.

Sabbagh, M. A., and Baldwin, D. A. 2001. Learning words from knowledgeable versus ignorant speakers: Links between preschoolers' theory of mind and semantic development. *Child Development, 72*, 1054–1070.

Schegloff, E. A., and Sacks, H. 1973. Opening up closings. *Semiotica, 8*, 289–327.

Searle, J. R. 1969. *Speech Acts: An Essay in the Philosophy of Language*. Cambridge, UK: Cambridge University Press.

Sedivy, J. C., Tanenhaus, M. K., Chambers, C. G., and Carlson, G. N. 1999. Achieving incremental processing through contextual representation: Evidence from the processing of adjectives. *Cognition, 71*, 109–147.

Snedeker, J., Thorpe, K., and Trueswell, J. 2001. On choosing the parse with the scene: The role of visual context and verb bias in ambiguity resolution. *Proceedings of the Twenty-Third Annual Conference of the Cognitive Science Society*, 964–969. Hillsdale, NJ: Erlbaum.

Snedeker, J., and Trueswell, J. C. 2003. Using prosody to avoid ambiguity: Effects of speaker awareness and referential context. *Journal of Memory and Language, 48(1)*, 103–130.

Snedeker, J., and Trueswell, J. C. 2004. The developing constraints on parsing decisions: The role of lexical-biases and referential scenes in children's sentence processing. *Cognitive Psychology*. Forthcoming.

Spivey, M. J., Tanenhaus, M. K., Eberhard, K. M., and Sedivy, J. C. 2002. Eye movements and spoken language comprehension: Effects of visual context on syntactic ambiguity resolution. *Cognitive Psychology, 45*, 447–481.

Swingley, D., and Aslin, R. N. 2002. Lexical neighborhoods and the word-form representations of 14-month-olds. *Psychological Science, 13*, 480–484.

Swingley, D., and Fernald, A. 2002. Recognition of words referring to present and absent objects by 24-month-olds. *Journal of Memory and Language, 46*, 39–56.

Swingley, D., Pinto, J. P., and Fernald, A. 1998. Assessing the speed and accuracy of word recognition in infants. *Advances in Infancy Research, 12*, 257–277.

Swingley, D., Pinto, J. P., and Fernald, A. 1999. Continuous processing in word recognition at 24 months. *Cognition, 71*, 73–108.

Tanenhaus, M. K., Spivey-Knowlton, M. J., Eberhard, K. M., and Sedivy, J. C. 1995. Integration of visual and linguistic information during spoken language comprehension. *Science, 268*, 1632–1634.

Tanenhaus, M. K., Spivey-Knowlton, M. J., and Hanna, J. E. 2000. Modeling thematic and discourse context effects on syntactic ambiguity resolution within a multiple constraints framework: Implications for the architecture of the language processing system. In M. Pickering, C. Clifton, and M. Crocker, eds., *Architecture and Mechanisms of the Language Processing System*, 90–118. Cambridge, UK: Cambridge University Press.

Tanenhaus, M. K., and Trueswell, J. C. 1995. Sentence comprehension. In J. Miller and P. Eimas, eds., *Speech, Language, and Communication*, 217–262. San Diego, CA: Academic Press.

Trueswell, J. C., and Gleitman, L. Forthcoming. Children's eye movements during listening: Developmental evidence for a constraint-based theory of sentence processing. In J. M. Henderson and F. Ferreira, eds., *The Interface of Language, Vision, and Action: Eye Movements and the Visual World*. New York: Psychology Press.

Trueswell, J. C., Sekerina, I., Hill, N., and Logrip, M. 1999. The kindergarten-path effect: Studying on-line sentence processing in young children. *Cognition, 73*, 89–134.

Trueswell, J. C., and Tanenhaus, M. K. 1994. Toward a lexicalist framework for constraint-based syntactic ambiguity resolution. In C. Clifton, K. Rayner, and L. Frazier, eds., *Perspectives on Sentence Processing*. Hillsdale, NJ: Erlbaum.

2 Communicative Intentions and Conversational Processes in Human-Human and Human-Computer Dialogue

Matthew Stone

Introduction

The topic of this chapter is *pragmatic interpretation*—that is, our understanding of an utterance as an action chosen by its speaker to contribute to a conversation. In (1a), for example, we understand that *A* utters *hello* in order to greet *B* and get the conversation started. This is our pragmatic interpretation of (1a).

(1) a. *A:* Hello.
    b. *B:* Hello.

(2) a. *A:* Where are the measuring cups?
    b. *B:* In the middle drawer on the far right.

(3) a. *A:* Pass the cake mix.
    b. *B:* Here you go [handing over the package].

Examples (2) and (3) are parallel, though more involved. In (2a), when *A* utters *Where are the measuring cups?*, we understand that *A*'s strategy is for *B* to reply by identifying a place where the cups *A* has in mind can be found, so that *A* will have this information. In (3a), when *A* utters *Pass the cake mix*, we understand that *A*'s strategy is for *B* to perform the intended action, so that *A* will then obtain the mix *A* has in mind. Each of these attributed plans counts as an interpretation; it gives a rationale that explains why *A* used the utterance *A* did. Our ability to signal and recognize these interpretations holds our conversations together. In (1b), (2b), and (3b), for example, *B* simply recognizes the strategy behind *A*'s utterance, adopts that strategy, and follows through on it.

This chapter offers a formal, computational perspective on the role of representations of pragmatic interpretation in explaining our competence in contributing to conversation. In considering conversational competence, I will adopt the perspective of the knowledge level (Newell 1982) or the level of computational theory (Marr 1982) in cognitive science, and attempt to characterize our general ability, idealizing away from incidental errors and failings, to successfully formulate, use, and understand utterances in conversation, as in (1), (2), and (3).[1] By formalizing representations of pragmatic interpretation, I hope to show in a precise way how these representations might serve as a bridge between the *language-as-product* tradition in the cognitive science of language use, which characterizes language processing in terms of the construction of symbolic grammatical representations, and the *language-as-action* tradition, which characterizes language processing in terms of the actions and interactions of collaborating interlocutors.

In particular, I will show how results from computational logic allow us to formalize a pragmatic representation as an abstract but systematic explanation of what a speaker is trying to do with an utterance. The formalization captures important insights from both traditions because its representations of interpretation enjoy these three properties simultaneously:

- They are recursive, symbolic structures. Thus, they are characteristically linguistic in being constituted by formal rules; they do not attempt, as our more general world knowledge might, to encode empirical regularities in a general way.

- They are sufficiently detailed to encompass all steps of disambiguating a linguistic structure. Thus, in important respects, we can characterize linguistic processes in terms of these representations; understanding is the process by which the hearer infers the representation behind a speaker's utterance, while production is the process by which the speaker infers a new representation with the potential to mediate a desired contribution to a conversation.

- They represent utterances as actions, and are in fact structured as reasons to act. Thus, deliberation in conversation can also be characterized in terms of these representations; doing so connects with a broader literature on intentions in communication and collaboration.

To achieve this, the formalism itself draws closely and evenly from both traditions. For example, to model linguistic problems such as disambiguation in terms of pragmatic representations, we must connect the rules that structure pragmatic representations directly with our knowledge of language—indeed, more specifically, with the derivations licensed by the mental grammar (Larson and Segal 1995). At the same time, to connect such symbolic structures to choices in an uncertain and open-ended world, we must understand them as records of agents' commitments in linguistic action (Pollack 1992), and recognize how keeping track of these commitments supports the diverse deliberative and collaborative processes we need for conversation

(Clark 1996). This balanced synthesis offers a number of advantages. This proposal is readily implemented (see Stone 2001; Stone et al. 2003). It is simpler than formalizations of speech act theory in the tradition of Cohen and Perrault 1979 and Allen and Perrault 1980, and more perspicuous than previous formal attempts to use action theory to link grammatical knowledge to participation in conversation (Appelt 1985; Heeman and Hirst 1995). In addition, this proposal strengthens and extends the genuine points of overlap between the language-as-action tradition and dynamic formalisms for meaning in dialogue (such as Kamp and Reyle 1993; Stokhof and Groenendijk 1999; Ginzburg and Cooper 2001; Asher and Lascarides 2003), which already represent change—and by extension, action—as fundamental to interpretation.

In this chapter, I hope to suggest how an account of such representations can help to explain our impressive abilities in language use, and how it may provide working hypotheses for the qualitative and quantitative characterization of those abilities. At the same time, I hope to provide an introduction to research on intentions in cooperative dialogue from artificial intelligence (AI) and computational linguistics. Despite its engineering focus, this research increasingly holds peoples' utterances and meanings in conversation up to empirical scrutiny, and so increasingly converges with psycholinguistics both in its methods and in its results.

The structure of this chapter is as follows. I first describe task-oriented dialogue, a prototypical setting in which pragmatic competence reveals itself. This description helps to motivate representations of speakers' intentions as essential for language users. Then I review philosophical and formal accounts of intentions in deliberation and agency, and suggest an understanding of intentions as complex mental representations structured to support decision making and collaboration. This understanding, together with some assumptions about the syntactic structure and semantic representations of utterances, suffices to flesh out communicative intentions in particular (though of course many challenges remain). The payoff comes in later sections, where we look at understanding and production as operations on pragmatic representations. We can sketch how to implement understanding as a constraint-satisfaction process in which a language user reconstructs the interpretation of an utterance. When we take these interpretations to describe speakers' intentions systematically and abstractly, we help explain how language users infer consistent interpretations that are faithful to the grammar, faithful to the context and goals of the conversation, and also faithful to a wide range of probabilistic regularities in language use. Conversely, we can sketch how to implement production as a process of deliberation, in which a speaker formulates a suitable communicative intention. In production, the account helps explain how a speaker might exploit that same grammar, the same understanding of context, and perhaps even the same statistical regularities, to plan concise, grammatical, and easily understood contributions to a conversation.

Motivating Pragmatic Representations

One important source of evidence about the processes behind ordinary language use comes from conversation known as task-oriented dialogue, in which interlocutors aim to accomplish some practical real-world purpose, and language use serves this collaboration. The real-world focus of task-oriented dialogue offers analysts independent evidence from the world about the uses people make of language in cooperative interaction. Moreover, task-oriented dialogue represents a constrained form of language use; it offers analysts an idealized setting to investigate cooperative conversation that abstracts away from important elements of conversation, such as politeness, humor, or small talk, which reflect other functions of dialogue, such as supporting interlocutors' social relationships.[2] In this respect, task-oriented dialogue attracts enduring interest as the form of linguistic interaction that might most usefully be recreated in machines.[3]

Task-oriented dialogue exhibits a rich and detailed functional organization, which we can use to characterize the specific goals of individual utterances. This organization is best described by example; (4) offers a fragment (constructed to illustrate a range of typical phenomena in a short space), of a hypothetical dialogue in which interlocutors *A* and *B* prepare dinner together.

(4) a. *A:* So are we all set?
     b. *B:* The vegetables [pointing] are still too crunchy.
     c. *A:* The zucchini there?
     d. *B:* Yeah, the zucchini …
     e. *A:* OK, I'll take care of it.

The dialogue suggests the effort that people make when they collaborate to maintain a detailed shared understanding of the status and direction of their joint activity. This effort goes well beyond simply keeping track of the real-world tasks that have been accomplished and the real-world tasks that remain (though such research as Power 1977 shows what a substantial endeavor this alone can be). This additional effort involves interlocutors' *attention* in dialogue and their *intentions* for dialogue.

As an activity progresses, new objects, actions, and relationships in the world may come into play. Collaborators must redirect their attention accordingly. Interlocutors can draw on this coordinated attention to talk about their task more concisely and more coherently (Grosz and Sidner 1986). More generally, in using utterances that describe particular objects, actions, and relationships, interlocutors can also set up strong expectations about where to center attention for subsequent utterances (Grosz, Joshi, and Weinstein 1995).

Example (4) illustrates both aspects of coordinated attention. A and B are able to use *the vegetables* and *the zucchini* to refer specifically to the zucchini that they have planned to cook for dinner, because their attention to the task distinguishes this zucchini from other things they might have cause to talk about more generally—tomorrow's zucchini, still in the fridge, perhaps. Subsequent utterances about the zucchini reflect this attention and cement it linguistically. More spectacularly, with *I'll take care of it*, A is able to identify a specific task and commit to doing it—putting the zucchini back in the microwave and heating them some more, let us suppose—without this task having being described explicitly in the recent conversation. A and B can be presumed to be attending to the task A identifies because of its relevance to their ongoing discussion and collaboration.

Meanwhile, as an activity progresses, further problem solving and negotiation may be required to address outstanding goals. Collaborators' intentions in dialogue must address these metalevel tasks in addition to real-world tasks. Characteristic problem-solving activities include identifying goals that need to be achieved, identifying subtasks to perform and selecting suitable parameters for them, allocating them to individual agents, and jointly assessing the results once agents have acted. Modeling this problem solving means recognizing the indirect role utterances play in achieving real-world goals (Litman and Allen 1990; Lambert and Carberry 1991; Carberry and Lambert 1999) and the explicitly collaborative stake participants have in problem-solving discourse as well as real-world action (Grosz and Sidner 1990; Lochbaum 1998; Blaylock, Allen, and Ferguson 2003).

Example (4) gets its coherence in part from the collaborative problem-solving strategy A and B exhibit. For example, B takes A's opening question (4a) as advancing a specific problem-solving activity: identifying any further task that remains to be done for dinner. B's response in (4b) furthers this same problem solving. B offers an indirect answer to A's literal question; the two are not all set. But B also proposes, again indirectly, that finishing the zucchini is an outstanding subtask of preparing dinner that A and B should pursue next.

By characterizing the functional organization of task-oriented dialogue along these different dimensions, we are able to identify specific functional roles for individual utterances in collaboration. Consider (4a). By (4a), A makes the specific proposal in (5):

(5)   The dialogue should continue with an answer as to whether *A* and *B* are finished
      cooking as of the current moment.

In so doing, *A* draws on the joint attention *A* and *B* maintain to the overall task they
are engaged in, and suggests a way of identifying further subtasks to be done and
thereby contributing to their collaboration.

Spelling out these functions explicitly, as in (5), enables a more precise characterization of interlocutors' collaboration in conversation. Clearly, people do not have to
agree with one another completely to have a cooperative conversation. Our actions
reflect our personal preferences, even in task-oriented dialogue. In (4b), for example,
perhaps *B* proceeds this way in part because *B* does not really like zucchini, and pri-
vately hopes that *A* might now overcook tonight's batch into an inedible mush. Even
if *B* has this nefarious ulterior motive, *B*'s response is still collaborative in that *B* uses
it to acknowledge the evident meaning in what *A* has said, and to build on *A*'s contribution to develop the conversation further. In other words, what makes this a collaborative conversation is not that *A* and *B* have all the same goals, but simply that *A* and
B are jointly attempting to integrate one another's utterances into a conversational
record that gives a shared interpretation to what they are doing together (Thomason
1990). This kind of collaboration seems indispensable; after all, as (4c) (*The zucchini
there?*) and (4d) (*Yeah, the zucchini . . .*) show, achieving such a shared interpretation can
be problematic. Imagine if *B* were to answer uncooperatively with *I'm not telling* instead
of (4d). It would not be nefarious: it would end the conversation. Accordingly, it makes
sense to circumscribe the analysis of the collaborative intentions and deliberation behind utterances and to consider only functions like (5) that address the agreed content
and direction of the conversation.

Even when we consider these circumscribed functions, interlocutors' conversational
abilities are remarkable. Particularly astounding is the generality of the linguistic
knowledge that interlocutors rely on to signal and recognize these functions. The
grammar associates an utterance such as (4a) with a complex and abstract syntactic
structure, and an equally complex and abstract meaning. For (4a), the syntax
represented in (6a) and the semantics represented in (6b)—both undoubtedly
oversimplified—are indicative of the gap that language users must bridge to apply their
linguistic knowledge in collaboration.

(6) a.

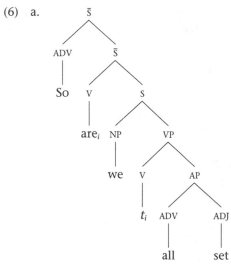

b.   At the current moment does the group containing the speaker have the property they require to be ready for the upcoming event?

It is difficult to characterize the relationship between representations like (6) and the specific function of utterances in collaboration like (5), even theoretically. We know that inference is required from philosophical models of discourse interpretation, such as implicature (Grice 1975) and relevance (Sperber and Wilson 1986), and in more explicitly computational frameworks for discourse interpretation, such as abductive interpretation (Hobbs et al. 1993) and commonsense entailment (Lascarides and Asher 1991; Asher and Lascarides 2003). But in conversation, inference must look beyond discourse, to embrace the collaborative setting and collaborative functions of language. This inference must lay out the resolution of ambiguity in linguistic terms while simultaneously describing utterances as actions that contribute to joint projects. This is a tall order—requiring representations of interpretation, for example, that respect both language-as-product and language-as-action traditions!

Despite the apparent gap between function and grammar apparent in (5) and (6), language users make connections to their ongoing collaboration quickly and easily in their word-by-word understanding of one anothers' utterances. Hanna and Tanenhaus (chapter 5, this volume) offer one clear demonstration. In their experiments, subjects were able to use knowledge of the goals and requirements of an ongoing collaboration to disambiguate referring expressions in instructions such as (7).

(7)   Now pass me the cake mix.

Instruction (7) was uttered by a confederate cook in a situation with two packages of cake mix. At stages of the collaboration where the cook needed help to reach only distant objects, subjects took *the cake mix* in (7) to refer to the distant package. At other stages of collaboration, when the cook needed help with all objects, subjects regarded *the cake mix* in (7) as ambiguous. Amazingly, subjects' eye movements showed that by the time they recognized the word *pass*, they had already arrived at strong expectations for the real-world location where the referent of the object noun phrase could be found.

Such inferences seem just as essential for interlocutors' spontaneous language use. Brown-Schmidt, Campana, and Tanenhaus (chapter 6, this volume) collected task-oriented dialogue from naive pairs of subjects, and found that speakers systematically produce abbreviated referring expressions, as in (7), to exploit pragmatic constraints on reference. The analysis of hearers' eye-tracking data in these dialogues attests that the abbreviated references pose no difficulty for hearers either.

Such experiments provide strong evidence that peoples' representation and reasoning for interpretation can assess different ways of resolving linguistic ambiguities in light of the consequences for ongoing collaborations. This chapter draws on formal and computational research in pragmatics to explore one scheme by which this might be realized. I have implemented this scheme in a basic dialogue agent, so the agent can achieve the pragmatic disambiguation human subjects exhibit in (7). A preliminary description of this implementation from a computational perspective appears as Stone 2001; Stone et al. 2003 fully describes a more substantial but less general implementation of a related framework.

The starting point for this exploration is Grice's proposal that interpretation is a species of intention (Grice 1957, 1969). For Grice, a pragmatic interpretation simply represents what the speaker was trying to do with an utterance; to understand an utterance, language users must simply construct an appropriate such representation.

This idea might be taken as an almost tautological restatement of our problem—to understand an utterance, language users must recognize what the speaker intended. Indeed, when we speak of the intended analysis of an ambiguous expression, or the intended referent of a pronoun, or other intended aspects of utterance interpretation, we rarely stop to consider our implicit appeal to Grice's theory. However, I will show here how Grice's proposal places strong constraints on pragmatic formalization. Grice's proposal suggests that we must develop an account of interpretation by drawing on independent accounts of intention. This means that we must use the same kind of formal structures to record what a speaker was trying to do with an utterance as we use to record agents' commitments in taking other actions in support of collaboration.

Likewise, Grice's proposal suggests that we must frame an account of processes in conversation in terms of independent accounts of deliberation and collaboration. This means that we must explain the work interlocutors do to understand one another with the same constructs we use to account for other interactions among people working together in dynamic and unpredictable environments. Grice's proposal is thus a deep and provocative one, whose consequences are yet to be fully worked out.

Intention, Collaboration, and Communication

Our first step in describing pragmatic representations is to develop a more precise account of intention. Such an account must involve at least two ingredients: an account of individual intentions and rational deliberation, and an account of joint intentions and collaboration. In this section, I review one formal approach to these problems, and apply it to the case of communication. The approach is based on an understanding of intentions not simply as goals, propositions, or commitments to specific actions, but rather as rich, complex, and symbolic representations of reasons to act.

Individual Intentions and Deliberation

Let us first understand a plan as a mental representation with a complex structure, as in AI (Pollack 1990, 1992). An agent's plan must set out, specifically or abstractly, what the agent is to do, when and in what circumstances the agent is to act, and what outcome the agent will thereby achieve. For the purposes of this chapter, I understand an intention as a plan that an agent is committed to.

The simplest case involves plans and intentions that concern physical action in the world. Imagine that agent A plans to turn on a light, for example. The corresponding plan representation might set out that the agent is to flip the switch, in a situation where the light is off (but functional), and thereby yield the result that the light is on.

Laying out the content of a real-world plan this way recalls formal reasoning about action from AI, a tradition that begins with work on the situation calculus (McCarthy and Hayes 1969; Green 1969) and continues with work on more sophisticated models and ontologies today (including Shanahan 1997; Thielscher 1999). Indeed, one specific representation for the content of a plan is an argument or inference in a formal theory of actions and their effects. A planning inference sets out an array of hypotheses—that the world starts out in a specified condition, that the agent performs a selected action, and that the world obeys specified causal principles. The inference then links these assumptions together to characterize the events that must ensue if these assumptions hold. For example, to record A's plan to turn on the light, we might use the inference in (8). (Here ∧ represents logical conjunction, ⊃ represents logical implication, and [N]p represents change over time; [N]p means that p holds in the agent's *next* cycle of deliberation, after one step of action.)

(8) a. *off*   Hypothesized situation
     b. *flip*   Hypothesized action
     c. *off* ∧ *flip* ⊃ [N]*on*   Cause and effect
     d. [N]*on*   Modus ponens, (8a)–(8c)

Representation (8a) specifies the condition of the world by hypothesizing that the light is *off*; (8b) specifies A's action, that A is going to *flip* the switch. Representation (8c) makes a general hypothesis about the domain, that if you flip the switch and light is off, it then goes on. Representation (8d) is the consequence that follows under these hypotheses: A is going to turn on the light.

Such inferences encapsulate the information intentions must make explicit if they are to guide agents' deliberation. These representations thereby connect with the systematic accounts of rational deliberation proposed by researchers such as Bratman (1987). Inferences such as (8) map out actions for the agent to take (8b), they draw attention to circumstances (8a) and causal connections in the world (8c) that the agent must rely on to take that action, and they record the effects for which the agent might select the action (8d). In committing to this plan, an agent must take all these considerations into account. The agent must believe that the circumstances laid out in the plan will obtain (8a); the agent must expect to decide on the actions in the plan and carry them out in those circumstances (8b); the agent must believe that the outcome spelled out by the plan will occur ((8c)–(8d)), and must on the whole regard that outcome as favorable. If the agent reconsiders any of these conditions, the agent has reason to abandon the intention as unworkable or undesirable. But as long as the agent persists in its commitment to the plan, the agent can refer to the plan to determine how to act. In this way, the intention can play a causal role in the agent's pursuit and realization of its desires.

Further evidence for this understanding of intentions comes from the criteria people use to attribute intentions to one another. (See Malle and Knobe 1997, or in AI, Pollack 1990.) Suppose we have observed an agent A flip a light switch, and consider what we must implicitly accept about A to attribute to A the intention of turning on the light. At some point, A must have been committed to flipping the switch. A must have understood that the light was then off but would go on once the switch was flipped. At that time A must, on the whole, have desired that outcome.

In contrast, if any of these conditions fails, we are more reluctant to attribute this intention to A. If A set out to bump the switch but not flip it, A had a different intention and failed to carry it off. Likewise if A thought the light was already on, or thought that flipping the switch would do something else instead, A had a different intention and failed to carry it off. It is more problematic if A was causally motivated to act by the plan to flip the switch and turn on the light, but without in any sense thinking that this course of action had anything to recommend it (even subconsciously). In this implausible situation, perhaps we must give up our idealization that A is engaged in rational deliberation at all.

Thus, to attribute an intention to an agent through a representation such as (8) is to say that the agent was guided in acting by that inference, and therefore to take on assumptions about the agent's beliefs about the current circumstances, the agent's causal knowledge, and the agent's desires for the future. This understanding may seem to diverge from ordinary ascriptions of intention. We normally say agents intend to do something, or to bring about some result, as though the content of the intention was simply an action or a goal. In fact, the theory assigns intentions a more complex structure, linking actions to effects in context, in order to interpret intentions as mental representations that guide agents' deliberation and action. We should not regard our ordinary language as an objection to the theory. Any English report of mental state describes both the content of an individual's attitude and the cognitive representations behind it. However, it is impossible to describe the objective meaning of an individual's mental state, as natural languages appear to do, while still reporting individuals' representations exactly; representations with equivalent objective content can have important differences, for example in the form in which they are represented. Because of this, semantic accounts of mental-state sentences require substantial flexibility in linking content and representations. (See for example Crimmins 1992.) Our theory of intention, which links action content to inference representations, is therefore no exception. Nevertheless, it will be important to remember that when I describe an intention, I refer not just to an action or goal, but to the complete ensemble of considerations that guide an agent's choice.

The planning inference in (8) describes the results of specific actions that the agent can already identify and commit to. Of course, intentions must also allow for agents to postpone planning and decision making until subsequent steps of deliberation. For example, the agent may anticipate that future information will affect its upcoming decisions.

The simplest way to accommodate future decisions is to model individual intentions as inferences not about what an agent *will do*, as in (8), but about what an agent *would be able to do*. This suggestion can be cashed out formally using theories of knowledge and action (Moore 1985; Davis 1994). To carry out a program of action, an agent must meet two conditions at each step where action is required. First, the agent will have to know what to do next: the agent must anticipate that there will be a specific suitable real-world action to do. Second, the agent will have to be able to construct a further intention that it can carry successfully through the remaining cycles of deliberation and action. The intention representations we arrive at are symbolic, recursive structures that appeal to logical accounts of knowledge and time to characterize actions and their effects in context. (Fuller technical details are available in Stone 1998, 2001.)

Proofs such as (8) may look like they express knowledge about the world, but it is better to think of them as *programs* that are annotated with assumptions that say when they can be executed safely in an uncertain world. Seeing plans and intentions simultaneously as proofs and as programs is a central idea in computation (Green 1969; Howard 1980). This idea is independent of the more contentious view that our knowledge of the world has the content of logical axioms. The difficulty with logic is that our empirical claims about the world are usually approximate or statistical in character. Our best-guess predictions about the future, for example, will inevitably involve uncertainty among different outcomes with different probabilities. A corresponding statement of our knowledge of the world will be either incomplete or false if expressed in first-order logic. However, intentions make explicit an agent's *commitments* for the future, not an agent's predictions or guarantees about what will happen. The uncertainty of our predictions has no bearing on whether logical structures can record these commitments accurately and precisely. In fact, the commitments agents make in executing specific actions in their current circumstances certainly can have the definite content of logical statements.

Although this understanding of the role of logic is intrinsic to representations of programs as proofs, it is rarely noted explicitly in the literature. Nonetheless, in what follows, I will draw repeatedly on it to motivate simplified representations of action while sidestepping well-known difficulties. In (8), (8c) exemplifies this strategy. The axiom, repeated as (9) below, cannot be read as expressing what we know about lights.

(9) *off* ∧ *flip* ⊃ [N]*on*

As such, (9) would be quite a poor description of the world. Actually, we know that flipping the switch turns the light on only when the bulb is operational, the power is flowing to the switch, the switch is capable of making a connection, the circuit to the bulb is functioning, and so on. To describe the world in a general way, we would have to supply an indefinite number of further conditions to (9). The impossibility of specifying these conditions completely is known as the *qualification problem*. Meanwhile, we also know that flipping the switch has many other effects, both direct and indirect, that (9) omits. In these circumstances, flipping the switch might contribute to the wear on the bulb, it might heat the room slightly, it might leave a smudge of dirt on the wall or the switchplate, and so on. The impossibility of specifying these effects completely is known as the *ramification problem*.[4]

All the same, when agent *A* decides to flip the switch and turn on the light—that is, when agent *A* adopts the intention in (8)—agent *A* really is committed to the truth of (9) in this instance. The qualification problem is important for understanding what *A*'s commitment means; AI researchers now understand that in making commitments such as (9), *A* must be understood as reasoning in a certain *context*, which depends in an indefinite way on unspecified further assumptions (McCarthy and Buvač 1994). But the qualification problem does not stand in the way of representing *A*'s commitment logically.

Conversely, when agent *A* adopts the intention in (8), *A* is not committed to all the ramifications of flipping the switch. For example, if the ramifications do not take place, *A* will not have failed to carry off this intention. And if *A* discovers an obstacle to this intention, *A* will not reason and act to make sure these ramifications take place anyway. Again, the ramification problem may be important for understanding what *A*'s commitment means. Rationally (and ethically), *A* must strive to identify and defuse potential negative consequences of intended actions. But the ramification problem does not stand in the way of representing *A*'s commitment logically.

We can make similar observations about the idealizations involved in reporting inferences about knowledge in logic. I will use [c] to describe the information that interlocutors presuppose in conversation: their mutual knowledge (Stalnaker 1973) or common ground (Clark and Marshall 1981); [c]p means that p is shared. I describe [c] (like [N]) using the logical machinery of *modal logic*, so that the common ground is assumed to give a consistent but incomplete picture of the world. (For an introduction to modal logic, see Fitting and Mendelsohn 1998.) The inference from (10a) and (10b) to (10c) is a consequence of this assumption.

(10) a. [c]p
     b. [c]$(p \supset q)$
     c. [c]q

If we make unrestricted use of these inferences in assessing our real mental states, we find a problem of *logical omniscience*. We predict that we know all the consequences of what we know, all the theorems of mathematics for example. It is a rather poor description of what our knowledge actually is, and as such could certainly be improved (Konolige 1985).

But again, this is no obstacle to the use of logic to formalize our epistemic commitments in deliberation. Any one plan is a finite structure that involves only a fixed number of inferences about knowledge. Each such inference requires an agent to perform a specified cognitive operation in the course of carrying out the plan. The agent may have to remember some fact, or link two facts together in a predetermined way. When an agent commits to an intention involving inferences about knowledge, then, the agent commits to these operations, and nothing more. And commit the agent must: if the agent fails to remember, or fails to draw an inference, the agent will lose track of the plan's upcoming choices, or of the rationale behind them.

By the foregoing considerations, I hope to underscore that representations of intentions as inferences such as (8) are circumscribed and economical. They offer parsimonious specifications of an agent's commitment to act in a certain way, because they presuppose sophisticated deliberative processes that manage these commitments. For example, the agent's planning processes must use inference about action to identify commitments that the agent can make consistently. The agent's updating processes for plans must use reason maintenance to assess the continued appropriateness of the agent's commitments in a dynamic and unpredictable environment. And the agent's execution mechanisms must ensure that the agent keeps track of the right information, makes the right choices, and completes the right actions while pursuing its plans.

Thus far, of course, we have considered these deliberative processes themselves only in the most general way. So it should be clear that intention representations are compatible with quite different characterizations of these processes, and quite different characterizations of the information and representations that these processes may require in addition to intentions. For instance, since decision theory provides a normative characterization of rational action, we might envision processes that commit to specific intentions based on calculations of probabilities and utilities derived from empirical regularities. (See Pollack and Horty 1999 for AI research along these lines.) For example, an agent's decision to commit to $off \wedge flip \supset [\text{N}]on$ might reflect the agent's judgment of the probability that the light will go on in circumstances where the light is off and the agent flips the switch. That conditional probability might in turn be estimated from empirical observations. Nevertheless, we need not expect any representations of these empirical generalizations to figure explicitly in intentions; indeed, we need not even expect them to be represented in the same kind of way as intentions.[5]

Joint Intentions and Collaboration

When groups of agents collaborate to achieve goals they share—and conversation must be considered such a case—groups of agents must sometimes commit to plans that lay out programs of coordinated action for the group. I will understand these collaborative plans by analogy to individual plans, as complex mental representations. Collaborative plans set out, specifically or abstractly, what each agent is to do, when and in what circumstances each agent is to act, and what outcome the group will thereby achieve. These plans can again be represented as formal inferences, in a logic of knowledge and time, which describe what members of the group would be able to do together.

As a simple example of collaboration on a real-world task, let's consider taking a posed picture, as you and a companion might do on vacation in front of a famous landmark. In this case we have two agents A and B, and a situation in which agent B has a ready camera. A first poses, adopting some distinctive expression and attitude toward B; this gets A set to be photographed. Then B snaps the shutter, with the result that A's pose is recorded for posterity. The inference in (11) records the content of this plan in a simple inferential form that parallels (8).

(11) a. *ready*   Hypothesized situation
      b. *pose*   Hypothesized action
      c. *pose* ⊃ [N]*set*   Cause and effect
      d. *ready* ∧ *pose* ⊃ [N]*ready*   Persistence
      e. [N]*set*   Modus ponens, (11b), (11c)
      f. [N]*ready*   Modus ponens, (11a), (11b), (11d)
      g. [N]*snap*   Hypothesized action
      h. [N](*ready* ∧ *set* ∧ *snap* ⊃ [N]*pic*)   Cause and effect
      i. [N][N]*pic*   Modus ponens, (11f), (11e), (11g), (11h),
                                                            and temporal logic

Here (11a) specifies the condition of the world by hypothesizing that the camera is *ready*; (11b) specifies A's action, that A will *pose*. Later, (11g) specifies B's action, to *snap*. Causal assumptions include axioms (11c) and (11h) about change, and the axiom of persistence (11d). The result that follows, by a chain of intermediate reasoning from these hypotheses, is that A and B will record the picture after the two steps of action, [N][N]*pic* in (11i).

In view of the formal structure of such plans, and the function that commitment to them plays in the deliberation of members of the group, it is reasonable to understand them as joint intentions. As before, these inferences encapsulate the considerations that agents must take into account in committing to and pursuing a course of action. For example, in committing to their collaboration, A and B must jointly believe that the circumstances described in the plan will fit the situation in which they must act. They must agree that each will decide on their own actions and carry them out as specified in the plan. They must expect that the outcome spelled out by the plan will occur, and agree that this outcome is favorable. (These attitudes are described more precisely in Cohen and Levesque 1991; Grosz and Kraus 1996.) On this understanding, a joint intention simply reflects the coordination of agents' individual commitments and deliberation (rather than an irreducibly joint mental state as in Searle 1990).

The actions that agents may have to take to carry out a joint project are significantly more involved than a single agent's commitment with an individual intention, however. These additions serve to ensure that agents achieve the most successful possible conclusion, in a coordinated way, even in the face of potential obstacles.

Thus, an agent must not only carry out the actions it commits to do as part of a collaboration, but it must do so in a way that allows its collaborators to recognize the contribution it is making to the joint activity. Otherwise collaborators might suspect that something has gone wrong. In our photography example, A must not only adopt a pose; A must allow B to recognize that A has done so. Of course, A has a variety of devices for this, from stylized flourishes of movement to simple verbal announcement: "Here I go" (beforehand) or "OK" (afterward).

Conversely, each agent must work to recognize the actions of the other agents in the context of the ongoing collaboration. Otherwise one agent may remain unaware of another's failures. Before B takes the picture, if B is serious about having the picture come out, B must attend to A, recognize whether A has attempted to achieve the right look, and judge whether A has succeeded. In addition, when an agent detects that the intention has failed, the agent must communicate this to the group as a whole. Likewise, when an agent achieves success, the agent must make sure that the group as a whole is aware of this.

Joint intentions as represented in (11) thus presuppose sophisticated processes of coordination, just as individual intentions as represented in (8) presuppose sophisticated processes of deliberation. In computational agents, such processes have proved essential in allowing groups of agents to work together on tasks from robotic soccer to search and rescue (Tambe et al. 1999) and in allowing individual agents to be understood by their human partners (Sengers 1999). Of course, we also find such processes of coordination in psychological accounts of language use (Clark 1996) and computational models of dialogue (Cassell et al. 2000). Again, representations of intentions provide only a partial framework for characterizing these processes; these processes must have access to many other kinds of information, and this information may involve very different form and content from intentions, especially when it is derived from experience in a general way. However, our systematic appeal to these processes of coordination makes it possible for us to understand simple logical structures such as (11) as principled representations. Intention representations formalize commitments, independent of the effort required to manage and pursue those commitments.

Cooperative Conversation

Earlier, I argued that to account for peoples' language use in task-oriented dialogue, we must view interpretations as pragmatic representations that link different ways of resolving linguistic ambiguities to their consequences for an ongoing collaboration. Grice (1957, 1969) theorized that speakers' intentions are what establish such links. He argued that in making a meaningful contribution to conversation with an utterance, a speaker must intend to make this contribution, in a recognizable way, through the ordinary process of linguistic communication. Ordinary linguistic communication depends on the fact that speakers manifest their intentions in utterances and hearers recognize them in this way. This is just what we would expect from analyzing conversation as a deliberative and collaborative process, as characterized in previous sections.

Accordingly, we can now draw on Grice's theory to specify the content and representation of utterance interpretations in dialogue more precisely. Interpretations record the speaker's commitments in using an utterance to advance a cooperative conversation. Specifically, they hypothesize an event of utterance, and perhaps further actions as well. They specify the assumed context in which the utterance is to be made, and they draw on an assumed idealization of the way utterances and other actions bring about context change. They link these assumptions together into an argument that shows how the speaker's use of the utterance in context can advance the status of a joint project. When formalized, such arguments serve as the *representations of pragmatic interpretation* introduced and motivated in earlier sections—abstract but systematic explanations of what a speaker is trying to do with an utterance.

Let us proceed by formalizing a simple example, and examining the result from the perspective of the language-as-product and language-as-action traditions. Consider (12b).

(12) a. *A:* Did the man stay?
      b. *B:* The man left.

What are the speaker *B*'s commitments in offering this answer? *B* proposes to utter *The man left*, in a context that provides a discourse referent *m* under discussion. *B* assumes that, in virtue of its meaning, this utterance will contribute the information that m left. B further presumes that if m left, he did not stay. In this way B has answered A's question and resolved an outstanding shared goal of the conversation.

Representation (13) lays out these commitments as an inference. In tracing the argument, note that premises (13c) and (13e) contain a free variable M, which is instantiated to (that is, replaced with) m when drawing conclusions from it.

(13) a. $[\text{c}]man(m)$ Hypothesized contextual situation

     b. $utter(\text{“The man left”})$ Hypothesized action

     c. $([\text{c}]man(M)) \wedge utter(\text{“The man left”})$ Cause and effect (grammar)
$$\supset [\text{n}][\text{c}]left(M)$$

     d. $[\text{n}][\text{c}]left(m)$ Modus ponens and instantiation, (13a)–(13c)

     e. $[\text{n}][\text{c}](left(M) \supset \neg stayed(M))$ Hypothesized contextual situation, persistence

     f. $[\text{n}][\text{c}]\neg stayed(m)$ Modus ponens and instantiation, (13d), (13e), and logic of knowledge and time

By inspecting (13), you can check that it exhibits the characteristics advertised for such representations in the introductory section of this chapter.

• (13) is a recursive, symbolic structure, constructed according to formal rules—the rules of logical deduction. As we have seen, (13) formalizes a commitment rather than expressing knowledge and so abstracts away from the additional processes of coordination that may be required to follow up (12b), and the corresponding uncertainty in whether (12b) will achieve its intended effect.

• (13) details the precise contribution of the grammar in determining interpretation. Premise (13c) is the crucial one. It says that, provided the common ground saliently provides a man M, then the action of uttering *The man left* will contribute the fact that M left to the common ground. This statement is a record of the commitments of the language faculty to a theorem about the analysis of a sentence of English, in the spirit of the knowledge of meaning investigated in Larson and Segal 1995. In particular, we can easily imagine (and readily implement) a process of inference that would derive this statement from a suitable compositional syntax and semantics.

• (13) describes B's utterance as an action, and is structured as a reason to act. In particular, premise (13c) characterizes the potential that the utterance has to draw on the evolving context of collaboration and to update it. Descriptions of context change are also familiar in linguistics from discourse representation theory and dynamic semantics (Kamp and Reyle 1993; Stokhof and Groenendijk 1999). What makes this different is that premise (13c) is a hypothesis about cause and effect that the speaker represents and commits to, as part of a communicative intention. The behavior of (13c) in language use follows from its status as a represented commitment. For example, the antecedent condition [c]*man*(*M*) functions as an anaphoric presupposition (Kripke 1991; van der Sandt 1992) in the sense that the speaker *B* intends the common ground to supply a specific resolution for this condition, and in particular to supply the salient value *m* for its free variable *M*. The hearer *A* must recognize this link to understand (12b) as (13).

In generalizing from this small example, the formalism allows us to include two further kinds of inferences that link meaning to context. First, where (13) includes premises that specify contextual parameters like *m* for *M* directly, such parameters may also be derived by inference. For example, in the bridging anaphora first described by Clark (1975), context supplies an entity that is new to the discourse but that is related to one evoked previously.

(14) Chris peeled the cucumber and removed the seeds.

In the case of (14), *the seeds* are understood to be the seeds of the cucumber Chris has just peeled. Such relationships can be recorded in pragmatic representations as inferences that establish the antecedents of rules such as (13c) by appeal to premises describing salient objects and general world knowledge. This provides a general interface to link utterance interpretation to attentional state in dialogue. (See also Hobbs et al. 1993; Piwek 1998; Webber et al. 2003.)

A second set of inferences may spell out the contribution the utterance makes to the ongoing task. Representation (13) includes the simplest case of such inference; (13e) and (13f) describe why *B*'s utterance answers *A*'s question. More generally, as in (11), these inferences may also proceed by hypothesizing further actions that participants will take as part of their collaboration. This provides a general interface to link utterance interpretations to the intentional structure of dialogue.

The utterances in (4) or (7) depend for their analysis on all three kinds of inferences—grammatical inferences, attentional inferences, and intentional inferences. To describe these utterances, I will emphasize the content that we can now assign to speakers' intentions, and leave the formalism for future presentations. (But for provisional attempts with related examples consult Stone 2000, 2001; Stone et al. 2003.)

Consider the interpretation of (7), *Now pass me the cake mix*. In the circumstances of Hanna and Tanenhaus's experiments, the argument behind the speaker's utterance must proceed along the following lines. The speaker assumes that the context provides a package of cake mix p, and hypothesizes uttering (7) in this situation. Drawing on a representation of the syntactic structure of (7) and its dynamic meaning, the speaker is thereby committed that the utterance will impose an obligation on the hearer to pass p. Now as a further development, the speaker hypothesizes that the hearer does pass p. The result of this action, inferred by a logical representation of the speaker's commitments in action, is that the speaker will have p, and can therefore use p for further steps in the unfolding recipe. This chain of inference, as needed, links the reference resolution required to interpret *the cake mix* with goals and expectations that the speaker has for the collaboration.

And consider (4a), *So are we all set?* We can reconstruct the speaker A's intention with this utterance as the following argument. A begins with a suite of assumptions about the context: that participants A and B form a group containing the speaker; that there is a specific current moment, say 6:30 p.m.; that *dinner* is an upcoming event; and that being *finished cooking* is a property that A and B must have to be ready for dinner. A hypothesizes uttering *So are we all set?*, as analyzed in (6a), under these circumstances. The meaning of this utterance—in contexts where G is a group containing the speaker, N is the current moment, E is an upcoming event, and P is a property that G must have to be ready for E—is to ask the hearer to provide an answer as to whether G does have property P at time N. With this semantics we specify (6b) in terms of an anaphoric presupposition and a dynamic contribution to the conversation, by analogy to (13c). By inference in this case, then, A commits to asking whether A and B are *finished cooking* as of 6:30. To account for the function of this question in the collaboration, the interpretation may map out the further course of A and B's collaborative conversation. Suppose B responds with an answer, *yes* or *no*: in either case, we can envisage A and B proceeding to conclude the collaboration thereafter. After a *yes*, A and B achieve common ground that the goal is achieved. After a *no*, A and B proceed to work out how to achieve the specific further tasks that they can then identify.

In our Gricean framework, intentions such as these are the objects of interlocutors' deliberation and coordination in conversation. For example, in offering an utterance in conversation as part of a specific plan or intention, the speaker is committed that the circumstances and conditions laid out in the plan obtain, and that the outcome envisaged in the plan is advantageous. These commitments are a standard feature of formal analyses in the speech act tradition (Searle 1969; Cohen and Perrault 1979; Allen and Perrault 1980). Yet even though these commitments can be derived from the role of intentions in deliberation (Cohen and Levesque 1990), prior analyses have not offered representations of intentions that abstract away from these commitments in a general way.

Meanwhile, since the conversation is a collaboration, the speaker must also ensure that the intention behind the utterance will be recognizable to the other interlocutors. At the same time, collaboration allows the speaker to presume that interlocutors maintain coordinated attention and intentions toward the ongoing task, and it allows the speaker to presume that interlocutors will recognize the plan and pursue it, by carrying its actions through and by grounding its success or failure. Again, previous formalizations in the speech act tradition recognize speakers' anticipation of such collaborative effort in understanding and grounding (Appelt 1985; Traum 1994; Heeman and Hirst 1995). But this general reasoning has been formalized explicitly as part of the content of speakers' intentions, offering no interpretation of language as action that abstracts away from it. The formalism sketched here is therefore substantially simpler than what has previously been available—simple enough, in fact, to enable a straight-forward, efficient first-principles implementation.

Understanding as Intention Recognition

The rich but parsimonious pragmatic representations introduced earlier can help us, in certain circumscribed ways, to characterize conversational processes. For example, I have used these pragmatic representations to implement processing modules for computational agents whose language use exhibits interesting commonalities with our own.

I start with the problem of interpretation. From this perspective, interpretation is what AI researchers call a plan-recognition problem (Thomason 1990; Carberry 2001). The hearer perceives some actions (an utterance), and must determine what the speaker was trying to do by reconstructing a representation of the speaker's intention. When the hearer perceives utterance (7), for example, the plan-recognition problem is to reconstruct the argument for it sketched in the previous section.

Reconstructing such an argument involves reconciling constraints from grammar and logic with constraints from attention and intention in dialogue. Consider (7) in the unambiguous context where the cook needs help getting objects near the subject (and we find that subjects do go on to pass the mix near them). The grammar of English analyzes (7) so as to assign it the intended semantic form, presupposing some cake mix and introducing an obligation that the hearer pass it. But the grammar doubtless offers other analyses; one and only one must figure in the recognized

interpretation. This is one constraint—one that might be modulated further by probabilistic knowledge about the frequency with which such constructions are used in
English.

The attentional state of the conversation is another constraint. The speaker's presuppositions must be resolved by supplying salient individuals and facts from the
environment; indeed, perhaps the matches must be as salient as possible. For (7) there
is the intended package of cake mix p near the hearer; perhaps there are others elsewhere in the environment. Again, exactly one match must figure in the recognized
interpretation.

From the intentional state, we get constraints on the overall goals that the utterance
can be meant to achieve. For (7), we know the speaker would initiate a joint project to
get some objects, including p, but not others. Of course, the collaboration might have
other outstanding goals, and the hearer must identify which of them figures in the
recognized interpretation (if any).

Finally, of course, these different components of interpretation must be fit together
compatibly into a single inference about what speaker and hearer would be able to do
together. In the case of (7) as represented here, the intended argument is the only one
that fits these constraints. That is, only by taking (7) as an instruction to pass p can we
reconcile grammatical options with the salient objects, including p, that the speaker
might refer to, and the outstanding goals, including potentially obtaining p, that the
collaboration provides.

We can implement this constraint-satisfaction analysis directly in computational
logic (Stone 2001). This is sufficient to create a system that resolves references by linking evoked discourse referents to speakers' high-level goals via linguistic descriptions,
as in (7). Indeed, by representing grammatical knowledge in a suitable form and
applying all constraints incrementally in utterance interpretation, as in Haddock 1989
or Schuler 2001, such an implementation would even be able to replicate the online
resolution of ambiguity that Hanna and Tanenhaus describe.

Methodologically, such implementations bear on what Newell (1982) calls the
knowledge level and Marr (1982) calls the level of computational theory: they give
evidence about the represented regularities in the world that that make it possible
for computational devices (ourselves included) to perform a real-world task. Such
implementations have rather less to say about what algorithms might be involved in
human-language understanding. The case of the grammar is a familiar microcosm.
Reconstructing an intended grammatical analysis might be a case of strategic exploration of logical possibilities set out by our knowledge of language, as with the different

algorithms explored in Altmann 1988 and Frazier and Clifton 1996. Alternatively, grammatical reasoning might be informed by probabilistic generalizations on language use over and above whatever knowledge of grammaticality we may have (as in Tanenhaus and Trueswell 1995; Seidenberg and MacDonald 1999).

To consider the additional constituents of pragmatic interpretation is to introduce such possibilities anew. Attentional state may have a purely logical implementation or it may take into account many kinds of probabilistic influence; either case leaves open wide ranges of processing strategy. The same goes for the outstanding goals of a collaboration. We might consider this a negative, were it not for a suspicion that all such cases, and many others, are governed by common cognitive constraints and common principles of biological computation. (And were it not for our appreciation for the complexity and significance of the problem of language understanding itself!)

Production as Intention Generation

In production, the speaker starts with a contribution that might usefully be made to an ongoing collaboration. What the speaker needs is a specific utterance that will make this contribution. The utterance can achieve this effect only if the speaker's intention in using it is recognizable. So the speaker's production problem is to formulate a suitable pragmatic representation for a potential utterance. The speaker must judge that the hearer can use shared information, the utterance, the grammar, and the attentional and intentional state of the discourse, to reconstruct this interpretation. Thus, pragmatic representations are the *outputs* of both understanding and production! This fact nicely emphasizes the algorithmic flexibility we have observed.

This is the formulation of the language-production problem that I and my colleagues arrived at in the generation system SPUD (for *sentence planning using description*) (Stone and Doran 1997; Stone and Webber 1998; Stone et al. 2003). SPUD can generate concise, contextually appropriate utterances, including both speech and concurrent nonverbal behavior, by applying a simple, uniform, and efficient decision-making strategy. This strategy gradually constructs an interpretation by refining the generator's existing commitments and considering new actions compatible with those commitments. In this sense, this strategy can be regarded as a special case of more general processes of deliberating with intentions.

Specifically, SPUD's strategy exploits the lexicalized tree-adjoining grammar (LTAG) formalism in which SPUD's grammar is represented (Joshi, Levy, and Takahashi 1975; Schabes 1990). LTAG grammars derive sentences by incorporating meaningful elements one by one into a provisional syntactic structure. SPUD makes these choices headfirst and incrementally, in the order its grammar provides. (Compare also Ferreira 2000; Frank and Badecker 2001.)

At each stage of derivation, SPUD determines both the intended interpretation for a provisional utterance and the interpretation that the hearer would recognize from it. SPUD again implements this interpretation process directly in computational logic. (SPUD's interpretations do not hypothesize actions that follow the utterance, so SPUD does not account for the role of conversational goals in disambiguation; in all other respects SPUD implements the formal account sketched earlier.)

These pragmatic representations guide SPUD's choices of what elements to add to an incomplete sentence. The structure of the utterance suggests ways the sentence may be elaborated with further meaningful elements. The intended pragmatic interpretation of each elaboration makes explicit the specific information that the utterance could contribute, and the specific links with the context that the utterance establishes. Meanwhile the recognized interpretation records SPUD's progress toward unambiguous formulation of referring expressions. These representations allow SPUD to assess by simple heuristics which choice might best suit the ongoing conversation, and to commit to that choice.

Conclusion

Let us return to (4), to take stock of the principles of the account, and the many further problems that remain.

(15) a. *A:* So are we all set?
      b. *B:* The vegetables [pointing] are still too crunchy.
      c. *A:* The zucchini there?
      d. *B:* Yeah, the zucchini . . .
      e. *A:* OK, I'll take care of it.

To account for such collaborative conversations, I have suggested a broadly Gricean formalization of language use as intentional activity. Each utterance in a dialogue such as (15) manifests its speaker's intention: a complex, symbolic mental representation that characterizes the speaker's utterance in grammatical terms, links the utterance to the context, and describes the contribution to the collaboration that the speaker commits to making with the utterance. The dialogue itself proceeds through interlocutors' reasoning about these intentions: the speaker produces each utterance by formulating suitable intentions, while the hearer understands each utterance by recognizing the intention behind it. When this coordination is successful, interlocutors succeed in considering the same representations of utterance meaning as the dialogue proceeds.

Of course, representations of pragmatic interpretation, like all intention representations, should provide a resource for action and cooperation beyond just acting and understanding. A recognized interpretation may help shape questions and elaborations, as in (15b) and (15c). In response to B's answer, A proposes a possible refinement of B's interpretation. A specializes B's vocabulary but preserves much of the structure of B's utterance, its links to context, and its function for the ongoing task. (See Clark and Wilkes-Gibbs 1986; Heeman and Hirst 1995.) Coordination at the level of pragmatic interpretation may also help to signal satisfactory understanding, as in (15d). Here B repeats not only A's words themselves, but also their interpretation, in order to mark this interpretation as recognized and its contribution as shared (Brennan 1990; Brennan and Clark 1996).

More generally, of course, a cognitive science of language use is responsible not only for explaining adult conversation, but also for elucidating its relationship to other cognitive abilities in ourselves and other species, and for accounting in particular for infants' ability to learn language. I am intrigued by the synergy with related work that a computational theory of pragmatics along Gricean lines might afford. For example, in characterizing language use in terms of representations of intentions, it plays into a tradition beginning with Aristotle and continuing with such work as Sperber 2000 in linking human language to a representational understanding of one's own and others' mental states that is uniquely human. Meanwhile, intention-based pragmatic representations seem necessary to flesh out the rich bootstrapping view of language acquisition that theorists increasingly adopt (see Gillette et al. 1999; Seidenberg and MacDonald 1999; Bloom 2000; Arnold and colleagues, chapter 12, this volume). In this approach, the acquisition of language depends on integrating multiple sources of evidence, including not only observed utterances and innate constraints of grammar but also learners' understanding of and interaction with the people whose language they learn.

Notes

This chapter has benefited from feedback from audiences at the CUNY conference in Philadelphia, at the Rutgers Cognitive Science Center, at Rutgers Semantics Workshops, and at Johns Hopkins, Harvard, UCLA, USC, MIT, and King's College London. Thanks to John Trueswell, Doug DeCarlo, and Louis ten Bosch for detailed comments on the written version. The work described here was supported in part by NSF research instrumentation 9818322, by a sabbatical leave from Rutgers, and of course by the organizers of CUNY 2001.

1. As observed from quite different perspectives by Geis (1995) and Seidenberg and MacDonald (1999), pragmatics seems to invite this broadening of the traditional understanding of competence. Barry Schein, John Hale, and Robert Frank independently observed the relevance of this issue to my research.

2. Of course this idealization should not obscure the potential importance of such social language not only for cognitive science (Brown and Levinson 1987) but even for human-computer dialogue (Cassell and Bickmore 2002).

3. Computational researchers' interest in task-oriented dialogue has persisted from early work on domain-specific question-answering systems (Green et al. 1961; Woods 1968; Winograd 1973) to such current efforts in spoken dialogue agents as Allen et al. 1995, Ferguson and Allen 1998, and Wahlster 2000.

4. In formal psychology, these problems are regarded as part of a common *frame problem*. However, in the AI literature, the frame problem refers to a technical problem of axiomatizing temporal change compactly, for which numerous solutions are now available. So I stick to the more specific terms here. For the AI terminology, see particularly Shoham 1988.

5. In this connection, it is instructive to regard intentions as metarepresentations that duplicate or re-represent information available to one cognitive system so as to expose that information to other kinds of processing. See the papers in Sperber 2000.

References

Allen, J. F., and Perrault, C. R. 1980. Analyzing intention in utterances. *Artificial Intelligence*, *15*, 143–178.

Allen, J. F., Schubert, L. K., Ferguson, G., Heeman, P., Hwang, C. H., Kato, T., Light, M., Martin, N. G., Miller, B. W., Poesio, M., and Traum, D. R. 1995. The TRAINS project: A case study in building a conversational planning agent. *Journal of Experimental and Theoretical AI*, *7*, 7–48.

Altmann, G. 1988. Ambiguity, parsing strategies and computational models. *Language and Cognitive Processes*, *3*, 73–98.

Appelt, D. 1985. *Planning English Sentences*. Cambridge, UK: Cambridge University Press.

Asher, N., and Lascarides, A. 2003. *Logics of Conversation*. Cambridge, UK: Cambridge University Press.

Blaylock, N., Allen, J., and Ferguson, G. 2003. Managing communicative intentions with collaborative problem solving. In J. van Kuppevelt and R. Smith, eds., *Current and New Directions in Discourse and Dialogue*. Dordrecht: Kluwer.

Bloom, P. 2000. *How Children Learn the Meanings of Words*. Cambridge, MA: MIT Press.

Bratman, M. E. 1987. *Intention, Plans, and Practical Reason*. Cambridge, MA: Harvard University Press.

Brennan, S. E. 1990. Seeking and providing evidence for mutual understanding. Unpublished doctoral dissertation, Stanford University.

Brennan, S. E., and Clark, H. H. 1996. Conceptual pacts and lexical choice in conversation. *Journal of Experimental Psychology: Learning, Memory and Cognition, 22(6)*, 1482–1493.

Brown, P., and Levinson, S. C. 1987. *Politeness: Some Universals in Language Use.* Cambridge, UK: Cambridge University Press.

Brown-Schmidt, S., Campana, E., and Tanenhaus, M. K. 2002. Reference resolution in the wild: On-line circumscription of referential domains in a natural interactive problem-solving task. In *Proceedings of the Twenty-fourth Annual Conference of the Cognitive Science Society*, 148–153.

Carberry, S. 2001. Techniques for plan recognition. *User Modeling and User-Adapted Interaction, 11(1)*, 31–48.

Carberry, S., and Lambert, L. 1999. A process model for recognizing communicative acts and modeling negotiation subdialogues. *Computational Linguistics, 25*, 1–53.

Cassell, J., and Bickmore, T. 2002. Negotiated collusion: Modeling social language and its relationship effects in intelligent agents. *User Modeling and Adaptive Interfaces, 12(1)*, 1–44.

Cassell, J., Bickmore, T., Campbell, L., Vilhjalmsson, H., and Yan, H. 2000. Human conversation as a system framework. In J. Cassell, J. Sullivan, S. Prevost, and E. Churchill, eds., *Embodied Conversational Agents*, 29–63. Cambridge, MA: MIT Press.

Clark, H. H. 1975. Bridging. In R. Schank and B. Nash-Webber, eds., *Theoretical Issues in Natural Language Processing*, 169–174. Cambridge, MA: MIT Press.

Clark, H. H. 1996. *Using Language.* Cambridge, UK: Cambridge University Press.

Clark, H. H., and Marshall, C. R. 1981. Definite reference and mutual knowledge. In A. K. Joshi, B. L. Webber, and I. Sag, eds., *Elements of Discourse Understanding*, 10–63. Cambridge, UK: Cambridge University Press.

Clark, H. H., and Wilkes-Gibbs, D. 1986. Referring as a collaborative process. *Cognition, 22*, 1–39.

Cohen, P. R., and Levesque, H. J. 1990. Rational interaction as the basis for communication. In P. R. Cohen, J. Morgan, and M. E. Pollack, eds., *Intentions in Communication*, 221–256. Cambridge, MA: MIT Press.

Cohen, P. R., and Levesque, H. J. 1991. Teamwork. *Nous, 24(4)*, 487–512.

Cohen, P. R., and Perrault, C. R. 1979. Elements of a plan-based theory of speech acts. *Cognitive Science, 3(3)*, 177–212.

Crimmins, M. 1992. *Talk about Beliefs.* Cambridge, MA: MIT Press.

Davis, E. 1994. Knowledge preconditions for plans. *Journal of Logic and Computation, 4(5)*, 721–766.

Ferguson, G., and Allen, J. F. 1998. TRIPS: An intelligent integrated problem-solving assistant. In *Proceedings of AAAI*, 567–573. Menlo Park CA: AAAI Press.

Ferreira, F. 2000. Syntax in language production: An approach using tree-adjoining grammars. In L. Wheeldon, ed., *Aspects of Language Production*, 291–330. New York: Psychology Press.

Fitting, M., and Mendelsohn, R. L. 1998. *First-Order Modal Logic*. Dordrecht: Kluwer.

Frank, R., and Badecker, W. 2001. Modeling syntactic encoding with incremental tree-adjoining grammar: How grammar constrains production and how production constrains grammar: Abstract. In *CUNY Conference on Human Sentence Processing*, 19. Philadelphia: IRCS, University of Pennsylvania.

Frazier, L., and Clifton, C. 1996. *Construal*. Cambridge, MA: MIT Press.

Geis, M. 1995. *Speech Acts and Conversational Interaction*. Cambridge, UK: Cambridge University Press.

Gillette, J., Gleitman, H., Gleitman, L., and Lederer, A. 1999. Human simulations of lexical acquisition. *Cognition*, *73*, 135–176.

Ginzburg, J., and Cooper, R. 2001. Clarification, ellipsis and the nature of contextual updates in dialogue. Unpublished manuscript, King's College London and Gőteborg University.

Green, B., Wolf, A., Chomsky, C., and Laugherty, K. 1961. BASEBALL: an automatic question answerer. In *Proceedings of the Western Joint Computer Conference*, 219–224. Reprinted in B. Grosz, K. Sparck Jones, and B. Webber, eds., *Readings in Natural Language Processing*. Los Altos, CA: Morgan Kaufmann, 1986.

Green, C. 1969. Theorem-proving by resolution as a basis for question-answering systems. In B. Meltzer and D. Michie, eds., *Machine Intelligence*, vol. 4, 183–205. Edinburgh: Edinburgh University Press.

Grice, H. P. 1957. Meaning. *Philosophical Review*, *66(3)*, 377–388.

Grice, H. P. 1969. Utterer's meaning and intention. *Philosophical Review*, *78(2)*, 147–177.

Grice, H. P. 1975. Logic and conversation. In P. Cole and J. Morgan, eds., *Syntax and Semantics III: Speech Acts*, 41–58. New York: Academic Press.

Grosz, B., Joshi, A. K., and Weinstein, S. 1995. Centering: A framework for modeling the local coherence of discourse. *Computational Linguistics*, *21(2)*, 203–225.

Grosz, B., and Kraus, S. 1996. Collaborative plans for complex group action. *Artificial Intelligence*, *86(2)*, 269–357.

Grosz, B., and Sidner, C. 1986. Attention, intentions, and the structure of discourse. *Computational Linguistics*, *12*, 175–204.

Grosz, B., and Sidner, C. 1990. Plans for discourse. In P. Cohen, J. Morgan, and M. Pollack, eds., *Intentions in Communication*, 417–444. Cambridge, MA: MIT Press.

Haddock, N. 1989. Incremental semantics and interactive syntactic processing. Unpublished doctoral dissertation, Edinburgh University.

Heeman, P., and Hirst, G. 1995. Collaborating on referring expressions. *Computational Linguistics, 21(3)*, 351–382.

Hobbs, J., Stickel, M., Appelt, D., and Martin, P. 1993. Interpretation as abduction. *Artificial Intelligence, 63*, 69–142.

Howard, W. A. 1980. The formulae-as-types notion of construction. In *To H. B. Curry: Essays on Combinatory Logic, Lambda Calculus, and Formalism*, 479–490. New York: Academic Press.

Joshi, A. K., Levy, L., and Takahashi, M. 1975. Tree adjunct grammars. *Journal of the Computer and System Sciences, 10*, 136–163.

Kamp, H., and Reyle, U. 1993. *From Discourse to Logic: Introduction to Modeltheoretic Semantics of Natural Language, Formal Logic and Discourse Representation Theory*. Dordrecht: Kluwer.

Konolige, K. 1985. A computational theory of belief introspection. In *Proceedings of IJCAI*, 502–508. Los Altos, CA: Morgan Kaufmann.

Kripke, S. 1991. Presupposition and anaphora: Remarks on the formulation of the projection problem. Transcript of a lecture given at Princeton University.

Lambert, L., and Carberry, S. 1991. A tripartite plan-based model of dialogue. In *Proceedings of ACL*, 47–54. East Stroudsburg, PA: Association for Computational Linguistics.

Larson, R., and Segal, G. 1995. *Knowledge of Meaning: An Introduction to Semantic Theory*. Cambridge, MA: MIT Press.

Lascarides, A., and Asher, N. 1991. Discourse relations and defeasible knowledge. In *Proceedings of ACL*, 55–62. East Stroudsburg, PA: Association for Computational Linguistics.

Litman, D. J., and Allen, J. F. 1990. Discourse processing and commonsense plans. In P. R. Cohen, J. Morgan, and M. E. Pollack, eds., *Intentions in Communication*, 365–388. Cambridge, MA: MIT Press.

Lochbaum, K. E. 1998. A collaborative planning model of intentional structure. *Computational Linguistics, 24(4)*, 525–572.

Malle, B. F., and Knobe, J. 1997. The folk concept of intentionality. *Journal of Personality and Social Psychology, 33*, 101–121.

Marr, D. 1982. *Vision: A Computational Investigation into the Human Representation and Processing of Visual Information*. San Francisco: W. H. Freeman.

McCarthy, J., and Buvač, S. 1994. Formalizing context (expanded notes). Technical Report STAN-CS-TN-94-13, Stanford University.

McCarthy, J., and Hayes, P. 1969. Some philosophical problems from the standpoint of artificial intelligence. In B. Meltzer and D. Michie, eds., *Machine Intelligence*, vol. 4, 473–502. Edinburgh: Edinburgh University Press.

Moore, R. C. 1985. A formal theory of knowledge and action. In J. R. Hobbs and R. C. Moore, eds., *Formal Theories of the Commonsense World*, 319–358. Norwood, NJ: Ablex.

Newell, A. 1982. The knowledge level. *Artificial Intelligence, 18*, 87–127.

Piwek, P. 1998. Logic, information and conversation. Unpublished doctoral dissertation, Eindhoven University of Technology.

Pollack, M. E. 1990. Plans as complex mental attitudes. In P. Cohen, J. Morgan, and M. Pollack, eds., *Intentions in Communication*, 77–103. Cambridge, MA: MIT Press.

Pollack, M. E. 1992. The uses of plans. *Artificial Intelligence, 57*, 43–68.

Pollack, M. E., and Horty, J. F. 1999. There's more to life than making plans: Plan management in dynamic, multi-agent environments. *AI Magazine, 20(4)*, 71–84.

Power, R. 1977. The organisation of purposeful dialogues. *Linguistics, 17*, 107–152.

Schabes, Y. 1990. Mathematical and computational aspects of lexicalized grammars. Unpublished doctoral dissertation, University of Pennsylvania.

Schuler, W. 2001. Computational properties of environment-based disambiguation. In *Proceedings of ACL*, 466–473. East Stroudsburg, PA: Association for Computational Linguistics.

Searle, J. R. 1969. *Speech Acts: An Essay in the Philosophy of Language*. Cambridge, UK: Cambridge University Press.

Searle, J. R. 1990. Collective intentions and actions. In P. R. Cohen, J. Morgan, and M. E. Pollack, eds., *Intentions in Communication*, 401–416. Cambridge, MA: MIT Press.

Seidenberg, M. S., and MacDonald, M. C. 1999. A probabilistic constraints approach to language acquisition and processing. *Cognitive Science, 23(4)*, 569–588.

Sengers, P. 1999. Designing comprehensible agents. In *Proceedings of IJCAI*, 1227–1232. Los Altos, CA: Morgan Kaufmann.

Shanahan, M. 1997. *Solving the Frame Problem*. Cambridge, MA: MIT Press.

Shoham, Y. 1988. *Reasoning about Change*. Cambridge, MA: MIT Press.

Sperber, D., ed. 2000. *Metarepresentations: An Interdisciplinary Perspective*. Oxford: Oxford University Press.

Sperber, D., and Wilson, D. 1986. *Relevance: Communication and Congition*. Cambridge, MA: Harvard University Press.

Stalnaker, R. 1973. Presuppositions. *Journal of Philosophical Logic, 2(4)*, 447–457.

Stokhof, M., and Groenendijk, J. 1999. Dynamic semantics. In R. Wilson and F. Keil, eds., *MIT Encyclopedia of Cognitive Science*. Cambridge, MA: MIT Press.

Stone, M. 1998. Abductive planning with sensing. In *Proceedings of AAAI*, 631–636. Menlo Park, CA: AAAI Press.

Stone, M. 2000. Towards a computational account of knowledge, action and inference in instructions. *Journal of Language and Computation, 1*, 231–246.

Stone, M. 2001. Representing communicative intentions in collaborative conversational agents. In B. Bell and E. Santos, eds., *Intent Inference for Collaborative Tasks*, 58–65. Technical report FS-01-05. Menlo Park, CA: AAAI Press.

Stone, M., and Doran, C. 1997. Sentence planning as description using tree-adjoining grammar. In *Proceedings of ACL*, 198–205. East Stroudsburg, PA: Association for Computational Linguistics.

Stone, M., Doran, C., Webber, B., Bleam, T., and Palmer, M. 2003. Microplanning with communicative intentions: The SPUD system. *Computational Intelligence, 19(4)*, 311–381.

Stone, M., and Webber, B. 1998. Textual economy through close coupling of syntax and semantics. In *Proceedings of the International Natural Language Generation Workshop*, 178–187. East Stroudsburg, PA: Association for Computational Linguistics.

Tambe, M., Adibi, J., Al-Onaizan, Y., Erdem, A., Kaminka, G. A., Marsella, S. C., and Muslea, I. 1999. Building agent teams using an explicit teamwork model and learning. *Artificial Intelligence, 110*, 215–240.

Tanenhaus, M., and Trueswell, J. 1995. Sentence processing. In P. Eimas and J. L. Miller, eds., *Handbook in Perception and Cognition: Speech Language and Communication*, 217–262. New York: Academic Press.

Thielscher, M. 1999. From situation calculus to fluent calculus: State update axioms as a solution to the inferential frame problem. *Artificial Intelligence, 111(1–2)*, 277–299.

Thomason, R. H. 1990. Accommodation, meaning and implicature. In P. R. Cohen, J. Morgan, and M. E. Pollack, eds., *Intentions in Communication*, 325–363. Cambridge, MA: MIT Press.

Traum, D. R. 1994. A computational theory of grounding in natural language conversation. Unpublished doctoral dissertation, University of Rochester.

van der Sandt, R. 1992. Presupposition projection as anaphora resolution. *Journal of Semantics, 9(2)*, 333–377.

Wahlster, W., ed. 2000. *Verbmobil: Foundations of Speech-to-Speech Translation*. Heidelberg: Springer.

Webber, B., Stone, M., Joshi, A., and Knott, A. 2003. Anaphora and discourse semantics. *Computational Linguistics, 29(4)*, 545–587.

Winograd, T. 1973. A procedural model of language understanding. In R. Schank and K. Colby, eds., *Computer Models of Thought and Language*, 152–186. San Francisco: W. H. Freeman. Reprinted in B. Grosz, K. Sparck Jones, and B. Webber, eds., *Readings in Natural Language Processing*. Los Altos, CA: Morgan Kaufmann, 1986.

Woods, W. 1968. Procedural semantics for a question-answering machine. In *Proceedings of the Joint Computer Conference*, 457–471. New York, NY: American Federation of Information Processing Societies.

3 Coordination of Action and Belief in Communication

Boaz Keysar and Dale J. Barr

Conversation is a stunning human achievement; it is as easy to do as it is difficult to study. In attempting to explain such a complex activity there is a tendency to appeal to complex mechanisms. We suggest that interlocutors resort to relatively simple action routines that converge on the complex activity of a conversation.

The Problem

Fundamental to understanding how conversation works is understanding what actions participants perform when they converse (Austin 1962). When I say "you know the fellows' names" I might be asking if you know the names, suggesting you do, requesting that you tell me the names, or asking you to leave me alone because you already know the names. Such speech acts are at the heart of the classic American comedy sketch where Costello asks Abbott about the players on a baseball team:

Costello: You know the fellows' names?

Abbott: Yes.

Costello: Well, then who's playing first.

Abbott: Yes.

Costello: I mean the fellow's name on first base.

Abbott: Who.

Costello: The guy on first base.

Abbott: Who is on first base.

"Who is on first base" is a true statement because the player named "Who" is indeed playing on first, but it is also an excellent question if you do not know who is on first. In the face of such ambiguity, identifying the action a speaker is performing is a fundamental problem for conversationalists. Even when speakers explicitly label their speech act, it does not necessarily solve the problem:

Abbott: Who is on first base.

Costello: What are you asking me for?

Abbott: I'm not asking you—I'm telling you. WHO IS ON FIRST.

Costello: I'm asking you—who's on first?

Abbott: That's the man's name!

Saying you are asking does not make it a request for information; saying you are telling does not make it an act of informing.

As an attempted solution to this problem, Clark and his colleagues proposed that language users coordinate meaning via joint action (e.g., Clark 1996; Clark and Carlson 1982; Clark and Marshall 1981; Clark and Schaefer 1989). Language users can be perceived as engaging in joint projects to accomplish goals, and the meanings of what they say are grounded in these activities. They are like dancers who coordinate their steps on the dance floor. In this dance, Costello is leading:

Costello: Have you got a first baseman on first?

Abbott: Certainly.

Costello: Then who's playing first?

Abbott: Absolutely.

Costello: (pause) When you pay off the first baseman every month, who gets the money?

Abbott: Every dollar of it. And why not, the man's entitled to it.

Costello: Who is?

Abbott: Yes.

The interesting thing about this exchange is that although the joint activity of coordinating understanding requires the speakers to work together, their beliefs set them apart. They have different beliefs regarding what their actions are about—beliefs that are not mutual.

In this chapter we consider the role of action and belief in conversation. Over the last twenty years, the theory of joint action and language use that Clark and colleagues put forth has been very influential in psychology, pragmatics, and computational linguistics. This theory assumes that mutual belief is central to almost any aspect of the conversational act. We will call this the *mutuality assumption*. Though this assumption was challenged early on (e.g., Johnson-Laird 1982; Sperber 1982; Sperber and Wilson 1982), it has become widely accepted among researchers on language use. We present arguments and evidence against different instantiations of this assumption, and show how language users coordinate meaning in a variety of settings without the mutuality of belief.

Belief, Mutual Belief, and Basic Assumptions

It is crucial to distinguish between shared and mutual belief. When you take money out of a cash machine and put it in your pocket, you believe you have cash in your pocket. If a thief saw you do that, then he also believes that. The belief that you have cash in your pocket is now shared in the sense that you both hold it. But only if you noticed that he saw you put the money in your pocket, and that he saw that you noticed, does it become mutual belief. So sharing a belief is not sufficient to make it mutual; you both must also believe that you both believe that it is mutual. Mutual belief, mutual knowledge, and common ground all basically refer to kinds of knowledge that have this criterial attribute of mutuality—that is, of being known to be shared.

The mutuality assumption appears in different forms in the literature. It can be described as a set of strong assumptions about the role of mutuality of belief in the coordination of language use, at both the level of the dyad and the level of the language community. If one takes seriously the idea that mutual belief pervades central aspects of comprehension and production, these assumptions follow:

1. Mutual knowledge is essential for the development of conventions in language communities and underlies their use in conversation.

2. Any joint action requires mutual knowledge; therefore the coordination of meaning in conversation requires mutual knowledge.

3. Language users *should* rely on mutual knowledge to coordinate meaning.

4. Comprehension is constrained to mutual knowledge.

5. Conversation relies on "conceptual pacts," a form of mutual agreement among the members of a dyad.

We challenge these basic assumptions and argue that interlocutors rely on simpler mechanisms, which do not require the routine use of mutual information. Instead, we suggest that language users might opportunistically use mutual knowledge to diagnose and correct coordination problems.

Mutual Knowledge and the Evolution of Conventions: The Coordination of Meaning in Language Communities

Conversation constantly relies on conventions. Any time a word is used, a convention is invoked. Conventions are arbitrary; there is no "natural" relationship between the word *dog* and its meaning. Such conventions must therefore be known by the individuals in the community; they are typically also mutually known in the community. If we mutually know that we know English, we can infer that we mutually know the conventions of the language.

It is assumed that conventions are established and sustained by mutual knowledge (Lewis 1969). It is also assumed that in order for language users to rely on a convention in conversation, they must realize that it is mutually known with their interlocutor (Clark and Marshall 1981; Clark 1996). We suggest that both assumptions are incorrect. We first present the argument concerning the establishment of conventions and later address the role of mutual knowledge during conversation.

The creation of a linguistic convention requires coordination by community members. A new word is not a convention until knowledge of the word has disseminated throughout the community. But is it necessary that community members represent it as mutually known for this process to take place? Barr (chapter 16, this volume; 2003) shows that conventions can evolve in a linguistic community even without the benefit of mutual knowledge.

Barr demonstrates this with a community of agents simulated in a computer program. The agents pair up into dyads and play a simple communication game, in which one agent attempts to communicate four meanings to an addressee. The problem is, they start with no conventional meanings. Although each agent has four forms and four meanings, every agent starts with random mappings between the forms and meanings. This should make for difficult communication, so the agents also have a very simple update function that tells them how to change their mappings based on the successes or failures of their past interactions with other members of the community (see Barr 2003 for details).

Just as with any other linguistic community where many individual conversations take place simultaneously, pairs of agents interacted in parallel during each "round," and then broke off to seek out new partners for the next round. Agents were most likely to interact with other agents who lived in their "neighborhood," but could also interact with agents who lived farther away.

Barr's simulation shows that even with these limited skills, a community of 1,000 agents established conventions that mapped forms onto meanings, either in the form of "dialects" or a single accepted system. The convergence on the conventionalized system was highly efficient; for agents who lived in a neighborhood of nine other agents, it took an average of 280 rounds to establish a single conventional system. The striking thing is that no agent had any representation of what was mutually known in their neighborhood or in the larger community. This simulation is analogous to an entire city converging on the use of a new slang term only because people use it with their neighbors. They start by using it in different ways, but over time they end up using it the same way, all without ever thinking about what other city residents believe the term means.

Of course, one might argue that when members of a community adopt a new slang term, most believe that almost everyone knows it. It is likely to be mutually known for many reasons, one of which is the mass media, which could nearly instantaneously make it so. This is true, but the fact that the evolution of a typical convention is accompanied by mutual knowledge of that convention does not mean that this higher-level mutual knowledge played any role in its establishment. It might have been simply an epiphenomenon. Barr's simulation shows that such knowledge of mutuality is certainly not a necessary ingredient in a community converging on a common set of conventions.

Mutual Knowledge and Conversation: The Coordination of Meaning in Dyads

While mutual knowledge may not be necessary for coordination to take place in a community, perhaps it is necessary in the dyad. We consider this possibility in three different ways. First, we ask if the coordination of understanding in conversation requires mutual knowledge by virtue of requiring a joint action; next, we consider the role of mutual knowledge in the use of linguistic precedents during conversation; and finally, we address the more general question of when people rely on mutual knowledge in comprehending language.

Joint Actions in General and the Coordination of Meaning in Particular

There is no question that the coordination of meaning in conversation requires a joint action. Abbott and Costello's dialogue will not hold if they were not collaborating to pin down who's on first. The question is, does all such coordination, even when a bit more successful than that of Abbott and Costello, require that each participant consider what is mutually believed by both? The mutuality assumption provides several ways of answering this question, all of which result in an unequivocal yes. One in-principle answer is an implied deduction:

All joint actions require mutual knowledge.

The coordination of meaning is a joint action.

Therefore the coordination of meaning requires mutual knowledge.

We argue against the conclusion because, we suggest, the first premise is false.

Though it seems reasonable that all joint action would depend on mutual knowledge, the premise is demonstrably false. If it were true, then any agent who is unable to represent mutual information would be unable to perform joint actions. But there are plenty of examples to suggest otherwise. When you change the clothes of a newborn it is clearly an individual action. You might as well be changing the clothes of a soft-limbed doll. But parents know that as their babies develop minimal motor control over their limbs in the first few months of life, they can, if they are in a good mood, coordinate with the parent and transform the changing of the clothes into a joint activity. Babies as young as 2 months help their parents by stiffening their arm to allow the sleeve to slide over it. Babies younger than 1 year can easily give a high five, a coordination feat analogous to adults' achievement of the prototypical joint action, the handshake. Playing peek-a-boo is a joint activity, because it requires coordination to lock eye gaze at the right moment and avert it at others. While babies as young as a couple of months can coordinate a joint action, no one would suggest that they have the ability to represent mutual belief. Only around 3 years of age do toddlers develop the ability to distinguish between what they believe and what others believe (e.g., Astington, Harris, and Olson 1988; Wellman 1990). Even if this is a conservative estimate, clearly babies who are several months old cannot represent what they believe that the other person believes about what they believe to be mutual.

One might suggest that perhaps the coordination between an adult and a baby is not truly a joint action because perhaps the adult is the one doing all the coordination. The young baby might simply learn to lift up a hand to a "give me high five" cue while the adult does all the work of coordinating with that otherwise uncooperative hand. Yet there are plenty of other examples that are unlikely to be so easily explained away. For example, young babies can jointly attend to an object with an adult, establish mutual gaze, and so on (Corkum and Moore 1995; Dunham and Moore 1995). Young babies use mutual attention to aid understanding (Bruner 1978), and they even have a notion of intention (Baldwin 1991, 1995), but they can hardly be said to be able to represent mutual knowledge of the sort required by the mutuality assumption.

There are also examples of joint activities by mature agents who cannot represent, or are unlikely to have a representation of, mutual knowledge. Just as it takes two to perform the conversational dance, it takes two male deer to lock horns in a well-coordinated, joint struggle. Any two street cats can jointly lock eye gaze in a highly coordinated joint action that requires the cooperation of both cats, though it is unlikely that cats would pass the false-belief test, a hallmark of possessing a theory of the other's mind (Perner, Leekam, and Wimmer 1987). Closer to our species, nonhuman primates who can clearly perform joint actions do not seem to have a theory of mind that distinguishes between what they believe and what others believe (Povinelli, Bering, and Giambrone 2000; Povinelli and Giambrone 2001).

With examples from young babies and animals, we can safely conclude that mutual knowledge or belief is by no means a necessary ingredient in joint action. Even fine-tuned mental operations such as engaging in joint attention need not require mutual knowledge. Therefore, there is no reason to believe that the coordination of meaning requires mutual knowledge simply because it is a joint action.

Coordinating Meaning without Mutual Knowledge

The mutuality assumption holds that mutual belief permeates every layer of the coordination of meaning. Every conversation you have in English involves the consideration that you mutually know that you know English, that you mutually know the meanings of its words, the rules of its syntax, and so on. While this might make sense, it is not necessarily true. Conversations in English could just as well be carried out without any regard to the fact that English is mutually known to the interlocutors.

An incident that one of us was once involved in illustrates this point. BK, a native speaker of Hebrew, had his arm twisted to join colleagues from the United States in a visit to the Arab market in the Old City of Jerusalem. BK attempted to blend in with his friends as an American tourist, carrying the required tourist gear and speaking only English. After a long negotiation in a carpet store that took place completely in English, the merchant said to BK, "You should come over for tea sometime." To which BK replied, unreflectively, "Thank you." This short conversational exchange is a prime example of an adjacency pair (Schegloff and Sacks 1973)—a kind of miniconversation. By the merchant making the offer and BK accepting, they successfully performed the joint action of coordinating meaning, not a minor achievement for an Israeli and a Palestinian.

Though the exchange was a success, it occurred without the benefit of mutual belief of the language it took place in. The merchant did not really say, "You should come over for tea sometime." He said "Tavo paam lishtot te," which is the same thing in Hebrew. And BK did not really say "Thank you," he said, "Toda," which is Hebrew for "thank you." Only after BK had replied did it hit home that the merchant had tricked him into blowing his own cover. Clearly, BK participated in a short conversational exchange in Hebrew without recognizing that Hebrew was mutually known to him and the merchant—in fact, not even fully realizing that they were speaking Hebrew. The merchant succeeded in tricking BK because he suspected that BK knew Hebrew and that BK believed that he, the merchant, believed that BK did not speak Hebrew. Perhaps he also believed that such a lack of *mutual* knowledge of Hebrew was not going to stand in the way of the perfect execution of an adjacency pair. The merchant's trick was to unveil the sharing of Hebrew, make it mutual, and thereby reveal BK's true identity, but because that mutual knowledge was itself a *product* of BK's participation in the adjacency pair, it could not have been its ingredient.

Meaning Coordination and Linguistic Precedents

Mutual knowledge of the language is a function of membership in the general language community. A different source of mutual knowledge comes from the history of interaction of specific individuals (Clark and Marshall 1981). The coordination of meaning often requires much back-and-forth effort to jointly pin down meaning and reference. This process is often called *grounding* (Clark and Brennan 1991). Once something is "grounded" it could become part of the specific common ground between the interlocutors, part of their mutual knowledge. As such, it could serve as a precedent that facilitates their future coordination. The mutual-belief assumption would hold that such grounded precedents are specific to the dyads that originally participated in the grounding. We suggest that grounded precedents are an instantiation of a much more general mechanism of language use, which operates independently of the history of specific partners.

Conceptual Pacts and the Partner-Specificity View   Consider the partner-specificity view in the context of naming. Any choice of words entails a particular conceptualization of a referent (Brown 1958). We can refer to this contribution as *the chapter*, suggesting that it is part of a book; *the essay*, suggesting that it is nonfiction; *the file*, conceiving of it as a digital entity; and so on. In choosing a name, we choose a particular conceptualization. The naming choice becomes grounded between interlocutors and could become part of their common ground. Brennan and Clark (1996) argue that when interlocutors ground a particular conceptualization, this becomes a partner-specific "conceptual pact" between a speaker and an addressee—that is, an agreement about a conceptualization that should not extend beyond the original dyad that grounded it.

To support this claim, Brennan and Clark presented speakers with photographs of objects and asked them to name the objects so that a listener could identify them. For example, speakers were supposed to identify one of two shoes. When the shoe was presented in the context of the other shoe, speakers' conceptual choice was to use the subordinate-level term *loafer* as opposed to the basic-level term *shoe*. When the speakers later received the same shoe without the context of another shoe, they still tended to refer to it as *the loafer*, even though there was no need to distinguish it from any other shoe. In producing this overinformative name, speakers violated Grice's (1975) maxim of quantity, which states that speakers should provide no more and no less information than is necessary to achieve their conversational goals. This is interesting because it suggests that conceptual pacts can override the conventions of cooperative conversation.

Brennan and Clark suggest that the reason speakers chose to keep using *loafer* was the establishment of a conceptual pact. After referring to the shoe as a loafer several times in the context of another shoe, they came to conceptualize that shoe at a subordinate level, causing them to continue to use the term even when it was more specific than necessary. But Brennan and Clark's claim is more sweeping than this; they argue that the reason speakers continued to use the overly specific term was that they knew they had a history of using the term with *that specific partner*. This is because according to the partner-specificity view, "Speakers choose their wording . . . for the specific addressees they are now talking to" (p. 1484).

Using a clever design, Brennan and Clark suggested that if the name choice is indeed partner specific, then speakers should stop using the term with a new partner. To test this, they had speakers name the same pictures as before in a context requiring only basic-level description. Half of the speakers did this with a completely new partner while the other half continued with the same one. They found evidence that speakers who continued with the same partner were more likely to continue to use the term *loafer*, while those who went on with a new partner tended to revert to the basic-level term *shoe* with new partners. Because speakers did not have a conceptual pact with the new listener to call the shoe a *loafer*, they had to revert to the contextually appropriate term, *shoe*. This was taken to support the partner specificity of conceptual pacts.

This argument reflects the mutuality assumption, that meaning coordination relies on mutual knowledge or common ground. The choice of words in reference depends on the specific history of reference between interlocutors, down to the decision to call an object either a shoe or a loafer.

However, our research suggests otherwise. We propose that word choice of the sort investigated by Brennan and Clark, while important to the coordination of meaning, does not involve partner-specific pacts or mutual expectations. Instead, the coordination of naming at this level relies on precedents that are independent of the specific individuals with whom they were established.

Grounding and Comprehension without Partner Specificity   Just as the mutuality assumption predicts that speakers should choose words based on their history with the addressees they are talking to, it also predicts that addressees should develop partner-specific expectations about what speakers will say. Thus, addressees' expectations about conceptual pacts should be exclusive to the particular partner with whom the pact was established and should not generalize to new partners. We tested this prediction of the mutuality assumption in a series of experiments (Barr and Keysar 2002), one of which used the logic of Brennan and Clark (1996).

In this experiment, we presented addressees with pairs of pictures on a computer screen. Addressees heard a speaker name one of the two pictures, and selected the corresponding picture with a computer mouse. We used an eye tracker to index comprehension processes by examining the latency to fixate the target object from the onset of the referring phrase (see Eberhard et al. 1995; Tanenhaus et al. 1995).

Figure 3.1 presents the three phases of the experiment with an example item. Consider phase 1, where the addressee views a screen with a picture of a car and a flower. At this point, addressees should expect to hear the general, basic-level names *car* and *flower* because no specific precedents exist. Thus, on hearing *car* we would expect addressees to quickly fixate on the car. In phase 2, addressees saw the same two pictures, but now they were in a context where the speaker would need to use more specific names. Here, the speaker used the specific terms *carnation*, to pick out the carnation from the set of two flowers, and *sports car* to pick out the sports car from the set of two cars. These trials were repeated several times to allow addressees to entrain on these specific precedents. Now consider phase 3; this is the critical phase of the experiment. Here, the two pictures are presented back in their original context, such that speakers should, according to Grice, again use the general terms *car* and *flower*. On the other hand, listeners may still expect speakers to use the specific precedents *sports car* and *carnation*. What they actually did hear was the basic-level term *car*. If they expected to hear *carnation* instead, then they might take the sound *car* to be the beginning of the word *carnation*. Thus, expectation of the precedent should cause temporary interference as they initially consider the flower and realize that though they heard *car . . . ,* *. . . nation* is not coming. The pretest, which was identical in all respects except that the

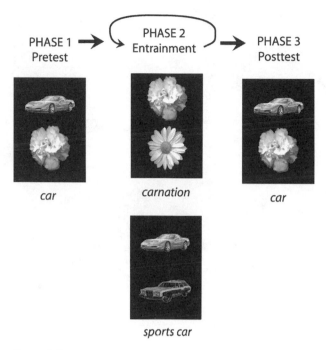

Figure 3.1
Design of experiment 3 in Barr and Keysar 2002.

specific precedents had not yet been established, provided a baseline to assess potential interference.

The results presented in figure 3.2 are averaged over eight items that were designed analogously to the *car/carnation* item. As the top panel of figure 3.2 clearly shows, expectation of the precedent interfered with addressees' comprehension of the basic-level term. The *x*-axis represents time from the onset of the word *car*, and the *y*-axis is the probability that the addressee is looking at a particular picture. In the pretest, for up to about 300 ms addressees were equally likely to look at the target car (represented by the black squares) or the competitor flower (the black circles), but then their eye started to favor the car over the flower. The same happened during the posttest, but the preference for the target occurred about 200 ms later. Addressees considered the carnation (white circles) longer and showed a preference for the car (white squares) later than in the pretest, suggesting that they indeed were likely to take the sound *car* as the beginning of *carnation*—that is, they expected the speaker to use the subordinate-level term.

But was this expectation partner specific, or would addressees have expected to hear *carnation* even from a speaker who had not established the precedent? To test this, half

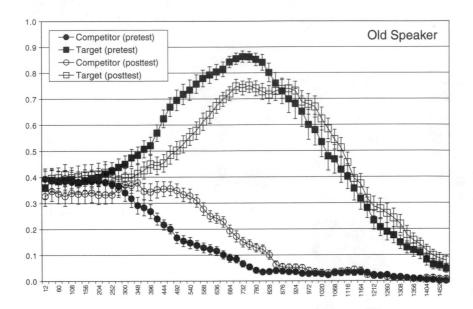

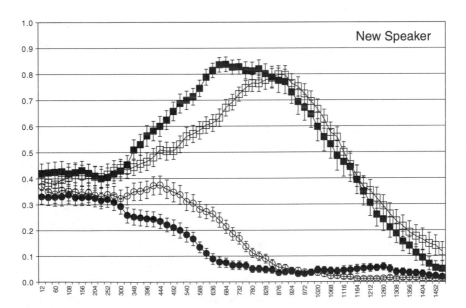

Figure 3.2
Figure 4 from Barr and Keysar 2002. The x-axis represents elapsed time from the onset of the word (0 ms). The y-axis represents the probability of fixating the different regions (see the legend).

the addressees received a completely new speaker for the posttest while the other half continued on with the same speaker. The experiment was designed so that it would seem obvious to addressees that this new speaker had never seen the pictures before and did not know the old speaker's precedents. It should be clear that according to Grice and the mutuality assumption, addressees who listen to the new speaker should have a lower expectation for the precedent *carnation* than the conventional, basic-level terms *car* or *flower*. At the very least, they should exhibit less interference from the precedent than addressees who continued on with the same person who established the precedent. But, as figure 3.2 demonstrates, on hearing *car* these addressees (bottom panel) exhibited precisely the same pattern of interference from the precedent *carnation* as addressees who continued on with the old speaker (top panel). The delay in eye movements to the car relative to the pretest was no shorter than for the old-speaker addressees. They also looked at the carnation much longer relative to the pretest. The interference caused by the precedents was not diminished, even though addressees had little reason to expect those precedents from this new speaker.

This experiment clearly shows that addressees develop strong expectations about precedents that are partner independent. These expectations are not tied to the common ground that accumulates with specific speakers.

The carnation experiment is surprising only if you truly believe in the existence of partner-specific conceptual pacts. But if you do not already believe in the theory, then your reaction is probably less enthusiastic. After all, you might think, the pictures had conventional names that are clearly known to all native English speakers. The flower is a perfectly good *flower* and also a perfectly good *carnation*; the shoe is just as much a *shoe* as it is a *loafer*. So possibly the expectations of the addressees were generalized because the choice of words reflected conventional ways of construing the referent. Perhaps if the precedents were more idiosyncratic and less conventional, addressees would have developed expectations that were partner specific.

To evaluate this possibility, consider an experiment that used nonconventional precedents (Barr and Keysar 2002, experiment 2). In that experiment we first wanted to demonstrate that grounding benefits future comprehension; that once a naming precedent had been established, the term would be more easily understood when it was used again later. We explain how we demonstrated this grounding benefit, and then describe how we evaluated whether it is partner specific.

Listeners played a referential communication game with a speaker (e.g., Glucksberg, Krauss, and Higgins 1975; Krauss and Glucksberg 1977; Wilkes-Gibbs and Clark 1992). They sat in front of a 4×4 grid of objects and the speaker (who was a confederate) gave them instructions to move objects around in the grid. We used eye movements to the target objects as a measure of comprehension difficulty. Unlike the carnation experiment, the target objects did not have conventional names. Instead, we used objects that elicited a large variety of names from speakers in a norming study, such as a piece of paper folded in half (an "upside down V," an "A-frame," a "roof," a "pyramid," and so on). In a typical trial, a name for the object would first be grounded by the speaker, who said something like "Now put the apple above the thing that looks like a tent." Then, after moving other objects, the speaker would say, "Now move the tent one slot down." We measured how quickly the addressee identified the tent in the second reference, after it had been initially grounded. As a baseline we used identical trials that were not preceded by the first grounding reference.

Indeed, when the term had been grounded earlier, addressees were much faster to identify the referent than when it was not grounded—about a second and a half faster. This should not be very surprising to anyone, irrespective of their theoretical biases. If the director christened that odd object a *tent*, then next time the director referred to it, it should be easier for the listener to know what she was talking about. This illustrates the benefit of grounding for comprehension. But is this benefit specific to the grounding partner? Is it a result of a conceptual pact between the dyad that the folded paper shall be called a *tent*, especially given that someone else is very likely to conceive of the folded paper in an entirely different way (e.g., the "paper," the "upside down V," and so on)?

If grounding results in a partner-specific conceptual pact, then the comprehension benefit that comes with a previously grounded exchange should not fully generalize to a speaker who was not in on the original grounding. To test this, we manipulated the identity of the speaker that originally grounded the referent. In half the cases, it was the same speaker who would refer to it in the second utterance. In the other half, it was a different speaker from the one who would later refer to it in the second utterance. Surprisingly, the grounding benefit was identical regardless of whether the original grounding had been performed by the same speaker who delivered the test utterance or by another speaker who clearly did not share mutual knowledge of the precedent. Even when the person who said *tent* the second time was different from the one who said it the first time, listeners benefited equally from having heard the term previously. This suggests that listeners' expectations of precedents that are developed in the process of grounding, such as that of calling a piece of paper a *tent*, are not partner specific but partner independent.

Malt and Sloman (2003) report converging evidence for the idea that naming precedents are generalized beyond particular partners. In their experiment, directors and matchers played a referential communication game. Directors identified pictures of objects for matchers. For example, they referred to an object as either a tube or a container, creating a conceptual precedent. The matchers then played as directors with new matchers, and these new matchers, in turn, later played the role of directors with a different set of new matchers. Interestingly, if the original director referred to the object as a *tube*, then the final director tended to prefer *tube* over *container* as well, even though the final directors had not interacted with the original director and had not directly established any such earlier pact with their new matchers. Such carryover is consistent with our assumption that when precedents are introduced in conversation, they function in a partner-independent way. This has the added benefit of allowing a community of individuals to converge on a conventionalized form.

A strange picture emerges from experiments on grounding and conceptual pacts. On the one hand, Brennan and Clark present some evidence that speakers or directors use terms they grounded with the specific partner. On the other hand, we find that their partners do not seem to care who grounded terms with them; comprehension seems to benefit from the existence of a precedent independent of the identity of its source. This seems like an unusual asymmetry between speakers and addressees, especially given that interlocutors constantly alternate between the roles of a speaker and an addressee. Yet Brennan and Clark report that speakers' reversion to basic-level terms with new listeners was not immediate but gradual. In other words, they did not find the partner specificity they had predicted, namely, that "speakers *choose* their wording . . . for the specific addressees they are *now* talking to" (p. 1484; emphasis added), but instead they found that "the references in our task *emerged* not from solitary choices on the part of the director, but *from an interactive process* by both director and matcher" (p. 1491; emphasis added). Thus speakers initially continued using the precedents with the new addressees, who probably expressed some surprise at these overly specific terms. The speakers could have sensed the addressees' surprise, which would cause them to revert to the basic-level terms. This pattern of results for speakers seems quite consistent with our results for addressees.

The Coordination of Meaning and the Process of Comprehension

Referring in conversation is a prototypical joint action. It requires the coordination of one person to name or describe a referent and another to pick that referent out of the set of alternatives. Grounding is often part of a successful act of referring, but sometimes objects can become part of common ground in other ways. For example, when objects are mutually visible, they become part of the mutual knowledge of interlocutors (e.g., Clark 1996; Clark, Schreuder, and Buttrick 1983). When you sit at a table for dinner, the salt and pepper between you and your companion are part of your mutual knowledge. So when you ask your companion to pass the salt, she can simply restrict her search to the objects that are mutually visible to the two of you and zoom into the intended referent. She need not consider another saltshaker that is on the counter behind you.

We conducted a series of experiments to test if meaning coordination benefits from such focus on mutually visible information. In one experiment subjects played a communication game with a partner (Keysar et al. 2000). There were objects on the table between the players, and the director, a confederate, gave the addressee instructions to move these objects around. The objects were clearly part of the common ground of the two because they were mutually visible. We distinguished between the perspectives of the two by occluding some objects so that they were invisible to the director. So while most objects were mutually visible, the identities of the occluded objects were privy only to the addressee. Those objects were obviously not part of the common ground with the director and could not have been referred to by the director. The central question was, would the addressee consider as potential referents only objects that were mutually visible? Would the process of jointly coordinating the meaning, of jointly identifying referents, be restricted to mutual knowledge, or would addressees consider the occluded referents that were not part of this set?

To test this, occluded spaces sometimes contained objects that fit speakers' descriptions of mutually visible objects. For example, the director told the matcher to "put the tape next to the truck." The corresponding grid contained both an audiotape that was mutually visible and a roll of Scotch tape that was visible only to the matcher. When searching for a referent for *tape*, would the addressee simply search for a tape exclusively among the objects that the director can see, in which case they should select the audiotape and not consider the hidden Scotch tape? To address this question, we used an eye tracker to monitor addressees' eye movements as they listened to a speaker's instructions to move objects.

Surprisingly, our results showed that addressees behaved quite egocentrically—they showed a strong tendency to consider hidden objects, such as the Scotch tape, as potential referents. In fact, a full quarter of the time they reached for it or attempted to move it. In general, we found that addressees searched among objects visible to them, even if those objects were clearly not accessible to the director, and therefore not part of common ground.

Even though addressees eventually selected the audiotape, sometimes only with the help of the director who had to correct them, the presence of hidden Scotch tape interfered with comprehension. Compared to the control condition, in which the occluded Scotch tape was replaced with an object that could not be a referent for *tape*

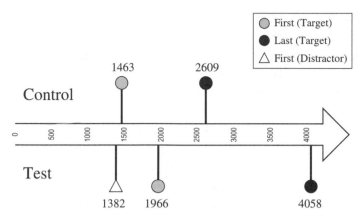

Figure 3.3
Timeline of eye fixations in experiment 1 from Keysar et al. 2000. Average latencies following the critical noun phrase (point 0). The difference between first fixation on the shared object (i.e., noticing it) and the last fixation on it (i.e., selecting it) is the decision lag. This decision took longer in the test than in the control condition.

(e.g., a toy monkey), it took subjects on average almost 2 seconds longer to select the tape as indicated by the last fixation before reaching for it (see figure 3.3). Clearly, even when people know exactly what is mutually believed, they do not restrict their search of referents to this set.

The experiment shows that a search for referents in the world is quite egocentric, in that objects visible only to the addressee are still considered referents. But this phenomenon is not unique to identifying referents in the world; it even happens when addressees search for referents in their own minds. In Keysar et al. 1998, we found that addressees who searched their memory for referents to a speaker's utterances considered information that was clearly not mutual. Just like in the tape experiment, they interpreted utterances egocentrically.

In our experiment the hidden object was always a better referent for the instructions than the target object. So while the cassette tape was a fine referent of *tape*, the hidden Scotch tape tends to be better. Consequently, even if people consider both tapes, the instruction *tape* need not be ambiguous but can yield a unique referent. This design allowed us to test a strong version of the mutuality assumption, namely, that people will spontaneously restrict comprehension to mutual information. Because the hidden referents were more typical, listeners were able to arrive at a unique referent from their own perspective, such that if they ignored mutual knowledge, they would make systematic mistakes. The design, then, allowed us to detect cases when people considered objects beyond common ground.

Although people clearly do not fully restrict comprehension to mutual knowledge, our experiment does not allow us to determine whether mutuality partially constrains comprehension from the earliest moments of comprehension. Some studies provide evidence for such a possibility (e.g., Hanna et al. 1997; Nadig and Sedivy 2002). For instance, Nadig and Sedivy (2002) found early effects of mutual knowledge in situations where an egocentric interpretation would not yield a unique referent (e.g., in response to the instruction "pick up the glass" when there were two identical glasses, one visible and one hidden). Because the ambiguity was egocentrically unresolvable, this would trigger a search for other sources of information (such as mutual knowledge) that could further circumscribe the set of potential referents. This finding is not wholly inconsistent with our view, and seems to indicate that there is some flexibility in the deployment of mutual knowledge. This raises the question of under what conditions comprehension is more or less egocentric. Our experiments have important implications for theories of language use. The prevalent mutuality assumption holds that people should restrict their comprehension to mutually known information, and that if they do not, they will make systematic errors (Clark and Carlson 1981). Subjects in the tape experiment made precisely such errors, identifying an occluded object as a referent only to later recognize their mistake and correct it. So clearly, people do not do what they "should" when comprehending language (Keysar and Barr 2002).

In fact, in contrast to the mutuality assumption, an egocentric component might not be detrimental for comprehension. Restricting comprehension to common ground would be advantageous if the most important consideration is to avoid errors. But routinely considering the other person's perspective might be too costly for the cognitive system. Therefore, a relatively egocentric interpretation process might make more sense given that people typically have limited attentional resources (Baddeley 1986; Shiffrin 1976; Wickens 1984).

Meaning coordination could be quite compatible with a relatively egocentric comprehension process. Much of interlocutors' own context is also part of their mutual context. So often when people use their own context they are also inadvertently using information that is mutual (Keysar 1997; Keysar, Barr, and Horton 1998). In this way, interlocutors could benefit from most of the advantages of a mutual perspective without having to consider the mutuality of the information they are using. They exploit the fact that their own perspective tends to be serendipitously mutual, and avoid the extra cognitive work involved in computing the mutuality of information.

For example, a typical conversation has a topic and an ongoing "record." Interlocutors know both what they are talking about and what each has said so far. They know this information individually as well as mutually. But when they rely on the conversational record, they need not consider the fact that it is mutual; they could just use it because it is known to them. The fact that a typical conversation tends to keep its topic also makes the mutuality of the topic relatively redundant. I know the topic, I do not need to also think about the fact that you know it too or that we mutually know it. It is possible that in most cases we could manage to coordinate meaning jointly with our individual knowledge.

Success and Perceived Success of Meaning Coordination

A joint action has a goal, and a central goal in conversation is the successful coordination of meaning. To increase the chances that they will be successful, interlocutors typically go back and forth in checking their understanding. Abbott and Costello realize that their joint action is incomplete as they keep coming back to the *who* in the "who's on first." Their exchange does not end because they realize they have not completely succeeded in coordinating their individual intentions. This illustrates the difficulty in coordinating mental entities such as beliefs or intentions.

It is easier when the goal of the enterprise is to pick out a referent in the world. When our subjects selected the hidden tape as the intended referent, they either realized their mistake because they eventually took into account the obvious occlusion, or because their partner corrected them. The success or failure of the joint action of identifying that referent can be objectively verified. This allows interlocutors to know when they have finished their joint project and can move on to the next one.

But when there is no objective evidence for the success of meaning coordination, interlocutors can only rely on their perception of its successful completion. This opens up the possibility that interlocutors can experience an illusion of mutual understanding. Here is a case where Abbott and Costello seem to experience just such an illusion:

Abbott: Well, that's all you have to do . . .

Costello: is to throw it to first base.

Abbott: Yes.

Costello: Now who's got it?

Abbott: Naturally.

Costello: Naturally.

Abbott: Naturally.

Costello: OK.

Abbott: Now you've got it.

Costello now believes that *Naturally* is the name of the first baseman, a false belief that goes undetected. Because Abbott and Costello now individually feel satisfied with their understanding, they will attempt to move on and may never realize their error.

One might want to know how frequently language users experience this illusion of mutuality. No one knows, mainly because we lack an objective way of verifying success; thus we cannot tell if what seems like successful coordination actually is. A major element in determining the prevalence of illusory coordination is how interlocutors perceive the success of their joint action. Our research suggests two tendencies that could substantially contribute to the illusion. One is the egocentric component in comprehension, which we have already discussed. The other is the tendency of speakers to overestimate their ability to convey their intentions (Keysar and Henly 2002).

Keysar and Henly gave subjects ambiguous sentences such as "Angela killed the man with the gun," and asked them to convey one particular reading of this sentence to an addressee. Speakers were instructed to attempt to convey either that Angela used the gun to kill the man, or that she killed the man that had the gun. After the speakers said the sentence, addressees selected, from the two different readings, the meaning they thought their speakers intended. Speakers, in turn, selected the meaning they thought their addressees would select. This permitted a comparison of how well speakers gauged their addressees' understanding.

Overall, speakers exhibited a tendency to overestimate how well their addressees understood them. While addressees were only slightly better than chance in detecting the speaker's intention (61 percent accuracy), speakers believed that, on average, they would understand them 72 percent of the time. When addressees did not understand the speakers' intention, in 46 percent of the cases speakers thought they had. Only 12 percent of the time did speakers think their addressees had not understood them when in fact they had. The vast majority of speakers (80 percent) systematically overestimated how well they were understood, while only 10 percent underestimated it; the remaining 10 percent were well calibrated. This study discovered speakers' overestimation with particular kinds of syntactic and lexical ambiguities. Given the abundance of ambiguities in language, it would be interesting to see whether other ambiguities such as pragmatic ones result in a smaller tendency to overestimate or perhaps lead speakers to overestimate their effectiveness even more.

Our findings lead us to the somewhat disheartening conclusion that, if speakers overestimate how well they are understood, while addressees comprehend egocentrically, many coordination problems may not be detected immediately. However, all hope may not be lost, because undetected misunderstandings have a tendency to surface over the course of the conversation. The multimodal feedback present in face-to-face situations, as well as the way conversation tends to build on itself, may provide language users with much-needed, perhaps even redundant, checks on their understanding. In fact, the interactive nature of conversation, with its abundant feedback and other checks on understanding, might in itself account for why speakers do not seem to expend valuable resources tailoring utterances to mutual knowledge, and why listeners do not always use mutual information when comprehending these utterances.

The Moral

To summarize, we have argued that while the coordination of meaning in conversation is a joint action, it does not necessarily require interlocutors to resort to their mutual beliefs. Simply because meaning coordination is a joint action does not mean that it requires mutual belief; many other types of joint actions do not. We showed that in order for a community to evolve an accepted convention, its members need not represent the convention as mutually known. We argued that the joint action of grounding and the use of the resulting conversational precedent do not necessarily involve mutual belief. Addressees seem to make use of a conversational precedent irrespective of the identity of the person who established the precedent with them. We also showed that understanding reference need not rely on mutually believed information. Instead, language users often rely on their own beliefs and their own perspective. Thus, to explain the action of meaning coordination, one always needs "belief," but not always "mutual belief." Interlocutors take a conversational exchange as successful not when they manage to coordinate their intentions, but when they individually believe they did. Whether they are mutually right or individually wrong is beside the point.

Note

The writing of this chapter was supported by a PHS grant R01 MH49685-06A1 to Boaz Keysar. Dale Barr was supported by a postdoctoral fellowship funded by the Beckman Foundation.

Correspondence concerning this chapter should be addressed to Boaz Keysar, Department of Psychology, The University of Chicago, 5848 South University Avenue, Chicago, IL 60637; boaz@uchicago.edu.

References

Astington, J., Harris, P., and Olson, D., eds. 1988. *Developing Theories of Mind*. New York: Cambridge University Press.

Austin, J. L. 1962. *How to Do Things with Words*. Oxford: Clarendon Press.

Baddeley, A. 1986. *Working Memory*. Oxford: Clarendon Press.

Baldwin, D. 1991. Infants' contribution to the achievement of joint reference. *Child Development, 62*, 875–890.

Baldwin, D. 1995. Understanding the link between joint attention and language. In C. Moore and P. Dunam, eds., *Joint Attention: Its Origins and Role in Development*, 131–158. Hillsdale, NJ: Erlbaum.

Barr, D. J. 2003. Distributed design: How communities establish shared communication systems. Unpublished manuscript.

Barr, D. J., and Keysar, B. 2002. Anchoring comprehension in linguistic precedents. *Journal of Memory and Language, 46*, 391–418.

Brennan, S. E., and Clark, H. H. 1996. Conceptual pacts and lexical choice in conversation. *Journal of Experimental Psychology: Learning, Memory, and Cognition, 22*, 1482–1493.

Brown, R. 1958. How shall a thing be called? *Psychological Review, 65*, 14–21.

Bruner, J. 1978. From communication to language: A psychological perspective. In I. Markova, ed., *The Social Context of Language*, 255–287. New York: Wiley.

Clark, H. H. 1969. Linguistic processes in deductive reasoning. *Psychological Review, 76*, 387–404.

Clark, H. H. 1996. *Using Language*. Cambridge, UK: Cambridge University Press.

Clark, H. H., and Brennan, S. E. 1991. Grounding in communication. In L. B. Resnick, J. Levine, and S. D. Teasley, eds., *Perspectives on Socially Shared Cognition*. Washington, DC: American Psychological Association.

Clark, H. H., and Carlson, T. B. 1981. Context for comprehension. In J. Long and A. Baddeley, eds., *Attention and Performance IX*, 313–330. Hillsdale, NJ: Erlbaum.

Clark, H. H., and Carlson, T. B. 1982. Hearers and speech acts. *Language, 58*, 332–373.

Clark, H. H., and Marshall, C. R. 1981. Definite reference and mutual knowledge. In A. H. Joshi, B. Webber, and I. A. Sag, eds., *Elements of Discourse Understanding*, 10–63. Cambridge, UK: Cambridge University Press.

Clark, H. H., and Schaefer, E. F. 1989. Contributing to discourse. *Cognitive Science, 13*, 259–294.

Clark, H. H., Schreuder, R., and Buttrick, S. 1983. Common ground and the understanding of demonstrative reference. *Journal of Verbal Learning and Verbal Behavior, 22*, 245–258.

Corkum, V., and Moore, C. 1995. Development of joint visual attention in infants. In C. Moore and P. Dunam, eds., *Joint Attention: Its Origins and Role in Development*, 61–83. Hillsdale, NJ: Erlbaum.

Dunham, P. J., and Moore, C. 1995. Current themes in research on joint attention. In C. Moore and P. Dunam, eds., *Joint Attention: Its Origins and Role in Development*, 15–28. Hillsdale, NJ: Erlbaum.

Eberhard, K. M., Spivey-Knowlton, M. J., Sedivy, J. C., and Tanenhaus, M. K. 1995. Eye movements as a window into real time spoken language comprehension in natural contexts. *Journal of Psycholinguistic Research*, *24*, 121–135.

Glucksberg, S., Krauss, R. M., and Higgins, E. T. 1975. The development of referential communication skills. In F. E. Horowitz, ed., *Review of Child Development Research*, 305–345. Chicago: University of Chicago Press.

Grice, H. P. 1975. Logic and conversation. In P. Cole and J. Morgan, eds., *Syntax and Semantics 3: Speech Acts*, 41–58. New York: Academic Press.

Hanna, J. E., Trueswell, J. C., Tanenhaus, M. K., and Novick, J. M. 1997. Consulting common ground during referential interpretation. Paper presented at *the Thirty-Seventh Annual Meeting of the Psychonomic Society*, November, Philadelphia.

Johnson-Laird, P. N. 1982. Mutual ignorance: Comments on Clark and Carlson's paper. In N. V. Smith, ed., *Mutual Knowledge*. London: Academic Press.

Keysar, B. 1997. Unconfounding common ground. *Discourse Processes*, *24*, 253–270.

Keysar, B., and Barr, D. J. 2002. Self anchoring in conversation: Why language users don't do what they "should." In T. Gilovich, D. W. Griffin, and D. Kahneman, eds., *Heuristics and Biases: The Psychology of Intuitive Judgment*, 150–166. Cambridge, MA: Cambridge University Press.

Keysar, B., Barr, D. J., Balin, J. A., and Brauner, J. S. 2000. Taking perspective in conversation: The role of mutual knowledge in comprehension. *Psychological Sciences*, *11*, 32–38.

Keysar, B., Barr, D. J., Balin, J. A., and Paek, T. S. 1998. Definite reference and mutual knowledge: Process models of common ground in comprehension. *Journal of Memory and Language*, *39*, 1–20.

Keysar, B., Barr, D. J., and Horton, W. S. 1998. The egocentric basis of language use: Insights from a processing approach. *Current Directions in Psychological Science*, *7*, 46–50.

Keysar, B., and Henly, A. S. 2002. Speakers' overestimation of their effectiveness. *Psychological Science*, *13*, 207–212.

Krauss, R. M., and Glucksberg, S. 1977. Social and nonsocial speech. *Scientific American*, *236*, 100–105.

Lewis, D. 1969. *Convention: A Philosophical Study*. Cambridge, MA: Harvard University Press.

Malt, B. C., and Sloman, S. A. 2003. Beyond conceptual pacts: Enduring influences on lexical choice in conversation. Unpublished manuscript.

Nadig, A. S., and Sedivy, J. C. 2002. Evidence for perspective-taking constraints in children's on-line reference resolution. *Psychological Science, 13,* 329–336.

Perner, J., Leekam, S., and Wimmer, H. 1987. Three-year-olds' difficulty with false belief: The case for a conceptual deficit. *British Journal of Developmental Psychology, 5,* 125–137.

Povinelli, D. J., Bering, J. M., and Giambrone, S. 2000. Toward a science of other minds: Escaping the argument by analogy. *Cognitive Science, 24,* 509–541.

Povinelli, D. J., and Giambrone, S. 2001. Reasoning about beliefs: A human specialization? *Child Development, 72,* 691–695.

Schegloff, E. A., and Sacks, H. 1973. Opening up closings. *Semiotica, 8,* 289–327.

Shiffrin, R. M. 1976. Capacity limitations in information processing, attention, and memory. In W. K. Estes, ed., *Handbook of Learning and Cognitive Processes,* vol. 4. Hillsdale, NJ: Erlbaum.

Sperber, D. 1982. Comments on Clark and Carlson's paper. In N. Smith, ed., *Mutual Knowledge,* 46–51. London: Academic Press.

Sperber, D., and Wilson, D. 1982. Mutual knowledge and relevance in theories of comprehension. In N. Smith, ed., *Mutual Knowledge,* 61–87. London: Academic Press.

Tanenhaus, M. K., Spivey-Knowlton, M. J., Eberhard, K., and Sedivy, J. C. 1995. Integration of visual and linguistic information in spoken language comprehension. *Science, 268,* 1632–1634.

Wellman, H. M. 1990. *The Child's Theory of Mind.* Cambridge, MA: MIT Press.

Wickens, C. D. 1984. Processing resources in attention. In R. Parasuraman and D. R. Davies, eds., *Varieties of Attention,* 63–102. Orlando, FL: Academic Press.

Wilkes-Gibbs, D., and Clark, H. H. 1992. Coordinating beliefs in conversation. *Journal of Memory and Language, 31,* 183–194.

4 How Conversation Is Shaped by Visual and Spoken Evidence

Susan E. Brennan

When two people communicate successfully, they each come to the belief that they are talking about the same things, and their individual mental representations seem to converge. How does this happen? Perhaps the simplest explanation is that as long as both speaker and addressee are rational, cooperative, and following the same linguistic conventions, understanding emerges serendipitously. As Sperber and Wilson (1986, 41) have stated, "Clearly, if people share cognitive environments, it is because they share physical environments and have similar cognitive abilities." This explanation for how speakers and addressees come to believe they are talking about the same thing emphasizes the ways their abilities, environments, and language processes are similar. Not only are two individuals in conversation likely to share some of the same biases, but the processes of production and comprehension themselves likely share the same resources. That is, what is easy for an individual to understand is often easy for that individual to produce (Brown and Dell 1986; Dell and Brown 1991).

A second sort of explanation of how people achieve shared mental representations emphasizes the interactive *coordination* of meaning, above and beyond speakers using encoding rules that match addressees' decoding rules. In other words, successful communication depends not only on conventions about the content of messages, but also on a metalinguistic process by which conversational partners interactively exchange evidence about what they intend and understand. This is *not* to say that similar abilities and biases play no role in successful communication, but that these are often not *sufficient* to achieve shared mental representations. Consider this episode of a spontaneous face-to-face conversation:

Susan: You don't have any nails, do you?

Bridget: ⟨*pause*⟩
          Fingernails?

Susan: No, nails to nail into the wall.

⟨*pause*⟩

When I get bored here I'm going to go put up those pictures.

Bridget: No.

The two people in this example spoke the same native language. They lived in the same town, were members of the same university community, and in fact were both psycholinguists. They shared the same graduate advisor, interests, social milieu, and office. In this conversation they were talking about something concrete, using simple, high-frequency English words. But similarity alone did not guarantee that Bridget would immediately understand what Susan meant. It turns out that Bridget had a different meaning in mind for "nails" than Susan did, but Susan did not discover this until after Bridget tested her hypothesis with "fingernails?" What Bridget may have had in mind during the pause after Susan's "no, nails to nail into the wall" seems less clear. Was Bridget trying to recollect the state of her toolbox? Was she wondering whether Susan was just being sarcastic and really *did* mean fingernails? After a pause during which Bridget did not take up the attempted explanation, Susan offered a further rationale for why she needed the nails. Then Bridget's hypothesis about what Susan meant by "nails" appeared to converge with Susan's, and she provided a relevant answer. At this point, but not before, Susan could conclude that she had succeeded in asking her question.

Clearly, similarity between two conversational partners can get them part of the way toward converging mental states. And the fact that, within the same mind, the processes of speech production and comprehension share some of the same resources increases the odds that what is easy to say (e.g., high-frequency words) will be easy to understand. But similarity is not enough. Rather than simply delivering and receiving messages, speakers and addressees jointly construct and negotiate meanings in conversation. This is necessary because natural languages afford a generativity and a flexibility that formal languages do not. For instance, the possible mappings from word to referent change from situation to situation and from speaker to speaker (see, e.g., Brennan and Clark 1996), and speakers routinely create new words when the need arises (see, e.g., Clark 1983; Clark and Gerrig 1983). Moreover, speakers and addressees process language in the face of potential noise, distractions, and limited cognitive resources.

What ensures successful communication is that speakers and addressees engage in a process of *grounding*, in which they continually seek and provide evidence that they understand one another (Brennan 1990; Clark and Brennan 1991; Clark and Schaefer

1987, 1989; Clark and Wilkes-Gibbs 1986; Isaacs and Clark 1987; Schober and Clark 1989). According to Clark (1994, 1996), language use is concerned with two sorts of signals: those in *Track 1*, having to do with the primary, "official business" of the conversation, and those in *Track 2*, the secondary, often paralinguistic signals that are used to ground or coordinate the understanding of the material in Track 1 (Clark 1994, 1996). Repairs like the one between Bridget and Susan can be accounted for by considering how Track 2 signals aid in disambiguating Track 1 signals.

Much research on language can be characterized as fitting either a *language-as-product* tradition (where the focus is on utterances and their processing in a generic or "default" context and where comprehension is considered apart from production) or a *language-as-action* tradition (where utterances are seen as emerging from both intra- and interpersonal processes, embedded in a physical context). Many psycholinguists work squarely in the first tradition, whereas some, along with ethnographers and conversation analysts, work in the second. A goal of this book is to bridge these traditions, in part by presenting research on spontaneous, interactive language use in carefully chosen contexts, using online measures that afford some degree of experimental control and reliability. This chapter reports previously unpublished details of an experiment that attempted to do this, before unobtrusive head-mounted eye trackers were available for measuring moment-by-moment processing (Brennan 1990). In this introduction, I will describe a framework from the language-as-action tradition with which to view both *intra*personal and *inter*personal processes of language use.

Seeking and Providing Evidence for Mutual Understanding

The Contribution Model

Clark and Wilkes-Gibbs (1986) originally proposed (but did not test directly) a *principle of mutual responsibility*, stating that people in conversation try to establish the mutual belief that the addressee understands a speaker's utterance to a criterion sufficient for current purposes before they move the conversation along. This proposal contrasts with theories of communication that assume that the responsibilities of conversational participants are fixed and that speakers bear all responsibility for avoiding misunderstanding (e.g., Sperber and Wilson 1986, 43). The principle of mutual responsibility and the process of grounding extend Grice's cooperative principle (Grice 1975) to the unfolding of a conversation over time.

Mutual responsibility was formalized in Clark and Schaefer's *contribution model*. According to this model, a contribution to a conversation is achieved jointly in two phases: a *presentation* phase and an *acceptance* phase. Every utterance or turn in a conversation represents a presentation, as when, in our example, Susan said to Bridget, "You don't have any nails, do you?" But a presentation cannot be presumed to be part of a speaker and addressee's common ground until its acceptance phase is complete—that is, until there is enough evidence for the speaker to conclude that the addressee has understood. An acceptance phase can be longer than a single utterance, with additional contributions nested inside it, as with Susan's first attempt at a question and the exchange that followed. Evidence of understanding can be explicit, as when a partner provides a backchannel response, a clarification question, or a demonstration, or it can be implicit, as when a partner continues with the next relevant utterance (as when Bridget finally answered, "No"). Participants set higher or lower *grounding criteria* for the form, strength, and amount of evidence necessary at any particular point (Clark and Wilkes-Gibbs 1986; Wilkes-Gibbs 1986, 1992). Grounding criteria vary depending on the current purposes of the conversation (Clark and Brennan 1991; Wilkes-Gibbs 1986; Russell and Schober 1999) and also on the resources available within a communication medium (Clark and Brennan 1991; see also Whittaker, Brennan, and Clark 1991).

Clark and Schaefer supported the contribution model with examples from the London-Lund corpus of British English conversation (Svartvik and Quirk 1980). They showed how the contribution model could result in data structures (contribution trees) that emerge as the *product* of conversations. However, as they themselves pointed out, transcripts are only products, and the data from the Lund corpus do not capture the moment-by-moment *processes* by which speaker and addressee coordinate their individual knowledge states (Clark and Schaefer 1989, 273–274). In the next section, I will highlight why it is that language transcripts alone are inadequate for testing these predictions.

Conversation Online

A text transcript and the recording it originated from contain clues about what happened in a conversation. But the previous gloss of Bridget and Susan's misunderstanding is ultimately not very satisfying as a window into their processing, for at least three reasons. First, there is ample evidence that overhearers, addressees, and side participants experience a conversation differently (Kraut, Lewis, and Swezey 1982; Schober and Clark 1989; Wilkes-Gibbs and Clark 1992). Discourse analysts are, ordinarily, only overhearers.

A second problem is that a post hoc account based on a transcript does not enable predictions about why, at each juncture, Bridget and Susan would do what they did.

Although some aspects of conversation seem routine, there are in fact many options at every point. For instance, Susan could have first said "Do you have any nails?" without the tag question. Bridget could have held up the back of her hand so that Susan could see for herself. Or, after the second pause, Susan could have waited longer for an answer from Bridget, rather than providing a justification for her question. Sometimes conversants opt to provide more evidence about their own beliefs, and sometimes they opt to seek more evidence about their partner's. Are these choices systematic? How do conversants know when to stop seeking and providing evidence and conclude that they understand each other well enough? While a transcript provides some information about a conversation's product, it says little about the process from which the product emerges.

A third problem with relying on transcripts in the study of discourse is that they give no independent evidence of what people actually do understand or intend at different points in a conversation. Many referential communication studies have addressed this problem by collecting task-oriented dialogues using a variant of the card-matching task developed by Krauss and his colleagues (Clark and Wilkes-Gibbs 1986; Isaacs and Clark 1987; Krauss and Glucksberg 1969; Krauss and Weinheimer 1964, 1966, 1967; Schober and Clark 1989). The assumption is that by observing a task in which pairs of people have to move objects into some preset configuration, we can tell when they are talking about the same object and when they have misunderstood one another. However, the typical referential communication task manages to document outcomes of matching trials without uncovering much about the time course by which two people get their individual hypotheses to converge.

What is needed, then, is a way to study the grounding process *online*, as it unfolds. A classic referential communication study in the language-as-action tradition that took steps in this direction videotaped participants in a matching task (Schober and Clark 1989). Schober and Clark observed that addressees sometimes picked up a card and held it for a while before placing it in the target location described by their partners; they proposed that these addressees had reached an individual "conjecture point" prior to the "completion point" by which both partners could conclude that they understood one another and move on to the next card. That study served as the inspiration for the one reported here, which documents the online processing of evidence during conversation in greater detail. More recently, the use of head-mounted eye trackers (e.g., Tanenhaus et al. 1995) has enabled the precise and unobtrusive tracking of eye gaze, providing a nuanced measure of what people intend and understand in conversation.

Language Use as Hypothesis Testing

Consider what individuals need to do in order to achieve shared meanings with their conversational partners. In the case of addressees, this seems straightforward; the addressee (like the reader) forms possible interpretations or *meaning hypotheses* (Krauss 1987) and then tests and revises them as evidence accrues (Berkovits 1981; Kendon 1970; Krauss 1987; Rumelhart 1980). Meaning hypotheses involve smaller hypotheses (some conscious, some not) that concern many dimensions of the utterance, such as who is being addressed, what word to retrieve, how best to resolve lexical or syntactic ambiguity, where the speaker's attention is, what is presupposed, what schema to evoke, what part of an utterance is new and what is given, and how the utterance is relevant to the situation. The addressee can set his criterion for rejecting a meaning hypothesis conservatively or liberally, depending on what is at stake. He has the option of pursuing more evidence if the intention behind an utterance or word is unclear.

Addressees are not the only ones doing hypotheses testing; speakers do it too. An utterance embodies a speaker's hypothesis about what might induce her addressee to recognize and take up her intention at a particular moment. The speaker monitors the addressee's responses such as eye gaze, nods, verbal acknowledgments, and other backchannels (Yngve 1970), relevant next turns and actions, and clarification questions (Bruner 1985; Clark and Schaefer 1989; Goodwin 1979; Heath 1984); these responses provide evidence of attending and understanding. The speaker evaluates the response she observes against the response she expected; she can then refashion her utterance and re-present it, or even revise her original intention so that it now converges with the one her addressee seems to have recognized.[1] So the speaker's hypothesis, as expressed in her utterance, plays a dual role by providing the evidence against which the addressee tests his hypothesis, while his response in turn enables the speaker to test hers.

Note that there is a built-in temporal asymmetry with respect to the speaker's and the addressee's hypothesis testing (Brennan 1990; Cahn and Brennan 1999). When Susan said, "You don't have any nails, do you?", Bridget recognized there might be a problem before Susan did. When Bridget replied, "fingernails?", Susan realized that Bridget had misunderstood her question before Bridget did. Because neither partner is omniscient with respect to the other's mental state, and because of this asymmetry between their distinct mental states, the computation of common ground is not determinate, but is made in the face of uncertainty. Since mutual knowledge cannot be proven, people rely on copresence heuristics in order to assume that they understand one another well enough for current purposes (Clark and Marshall 1981).

The rest of this chapter presents an experiment on the time course of how pairs of people in conversation get their meaning hypotheses to converge. Two partners' hypotheses should not converge steadily, but in phases that correspond roughly to the presentation and acceptance phases of contributions. Moreover, these phases—particularly the acceptance phase—should differ depending on the modality of the evidence available for grounding, as predicted by Clark and Brennan (1991). For this experiment, I developed a computerized spatial task that recorded two partners' mouse movements in order to provide continuous, moment-by-moment estimates of how the speaker's and addressee's meaning hypotheses were converging. This information was then synchronized with the transcript of their utterances. After describing the experiment and results I will compare this sort of behavioral measure to that of eye tracking, because each measure has something different to contribute to the study of conversation online.

Predictions

In this section I develop four specific predictions about moment-by-moment coordination that follow from the contribution model and indicate how these predictions were tested (additional detail can be found in Brennan 1990). These predictions are contrasted with some alternatives that arise from other assumptions or proposals about language use in conversation. These four predictions concern (1) how quickly and closely two partners' meaning hypotheses come to converge, (2) how having visual evidence about a partner's beliefs affects the time course of convergence, (3) how prior knowledge affects the time course of convergence, and (4) how the modality of evidence affects the grounding criterion, and in turn, how closely two meaning hypotheses can be made to converge. I will outline plans for testing each prediction.

Prediction 1: Addressees Form Early Meaning Hypotheses That They Then Ground with Their Partners   The first prediction from the contribution model is that in spoken conversation, addressees should form meaning hypotheses relatively early in an exchange. Then it should take significant additional time and effort for addressees and speakers to determine and signal to each other that their hypotheses have converged, especially if they are limited to exchanging evidence via verbal utterances that have been linearized (more or less) as a sequence of speaking turns. Alternative possibilities are that an exchange could end shortly after the addressee forms a correct meaning hypothesis, or that any additional time after having formed a correct meaning hypothesis could be spent in silent deliberation. This could be the case if people in conversation did not ground or coordinate their mental states with input from their partners—that is, if addressees and speakers tested their hypotheses individually without taking an active role in each other's hypothesis testing. This is what would be expected if convergence was achieved from simply having the same biases and using the same system for encoding and decoding utterances.

I tested these predictions using a collaborative matching task in which twelve pairs of same-sex strangers who could not see each another discussed locations on identical maps displayed on networked computer screens. One person, the *director*, saw a car icon in a preprogrammed target location, and the other person, the *matcher*, used a mouse to move his own car icon to the same location. This task enabled moment-by-moment tracking of how closely the matcher's and director's hypotheses converged over time, synchronized with what they said.

Prediction 2: The Modality of Evidence Shapes the Grounding Process   Many studies have found differences in conversations or tasks conducted over different media (e.g., Chapanis et al. 1972; Cohen 1984; Ochsman and Chapanis 1974; Williams 1977); the evidence available for grounding and the contribution model provide a framework for explaining these differences (Clark and Brennan 1991). The next prediction about the time course of reaching shared hypotheses concerns the impact, moment by moment, of having both visual and spoken evidence of a partner's understanding, as opposed to only spoken utterances and backchannels.

Clark and Schaefer (1989, 267) stated that it is generally up to the addressee to initiate the acceptance phase for an utterance. Typically in spoken conversation (especially when participants are not visually copresent), the addressee is in the best position to judge the goodness of his own hypothesis and to propose to the speaker that he understands what she meant. But if the distribution of responsibility is flexible, the acceptance phase should be initiated by whichever partner first amasses strong-enough evidence that the addressee's hypothesis is a good one.

In the current task, on half of the trials the director saw the matcher's icon superimposed on her[2] own screen (visual evidence condition), and on half she did not (verbal-only evidence condition). Having visual evidence in addition to verbal evidence may speed up the presentation phase somewhat, if the director is able to adapt her descriptions of the target location moment by moment to what she can see of the matcher's attempts to move there. However, visual evidence should have its strongest impact *late* in a contribution. When the director could see the matcher's icon, both partners should expect the director to take over the responsibility for proposing that their hypotheses had converged. This should shorten the acceptance phase considerably by providing strong evidence of convergence to the director and by saving the matcher at least one speaking turn.

A more specific expectation about the effect of evidence involves addressees' verbal backchannels. According to the contribution model, backchannels are specific, relevant signals intended for grounding (Brennan 1990; Clark and Brennan 1991; Clark and Wilkes-Gibbs 1986; Clark and Schaefer 1989). If this is the case, then matchers should take into account the changing modality of evidence available *to their partners* at any given moment and adapt their own responses accordingly, even when the evidence available to the matchers themselves stays the same. An alternative possibility is that backchannels are general, diffuse responses to speech, regulating the "flow of information" (Rosenfeld 1987), serving "to organize and to direct the stream of communication" (Duncan 1973, 29), or acting as reinforcers to encourage the speaker to continue talking (Duncan 1975; Wiemann and Knapp 1975). As such, the particular form that backchannels take may be simply a practiced, automatic response to the rate of information presented within a particular communication medium as experienced by an addressee; people unfamiliar with a particular medium may need to learn to produce appropriate backchannels in that medium (as Cook and Lalljee (1972) and Williams (1977) have proposed). If this is the case, then a matcher's verbal backchannel behavior should be difficult to modify; he should provide about the same number and kinds of verbal responses regardless of whether his partner has visual evidence about what he understands. This would also be expected if the main purpose of addressee responses is to reinforce a social relationship or to show general engagement in a conversation, as some analysts have proposed. I tested this set of predictions by comparing the distributions of acknowledgments in the visual and verbal conditions.

Prediction 3: Prior Shared Knowledge Has an Early Impact   It is reasonable to expect that having more shared and relevant prior knowledge—which includes having more similarity in knowledge and experiences—should enable two people to understand one another more quickly, thereby shortening an exchange. The contribution model enables more specific predictions as to when and how both prior shared knowledge and type of evidence affect the grounding process. Prior shared knowledge should have its strongest effects early, during the presentation phase, where it may help the director tailor her description to the matcher's needs, enabling the matcher to form a reliable meaning hypothesis sooner. The alternative to this prediction is that prior shared knowledge should shorten all parts of an exchange roughly equally. I tested these possibilities by varying the knowledge that two partners could assume they shared at the outset of the task: the pairs (who were Stanford University graduate students recruited from thirteen academic departments) discussed locations half the time on maps of the Stanford campus and half the time on maps of Cape Cod (a locale with which they were unfamiliar).

Prediction 4: Grounding Is Only as Precise as It Needs to Be   Some have assumed that having more evidence or copresence should lead to greater convergence in understanding than having less (see, e.g., Karsenty 1999). If this is so, we might expect that people's hypotheses (and their corresponding icon locations) would converge more closely when the director could see where the matcher's icon is located (visual evidence) than when she could not (verbal-only evidence). But according to the contribution model and the grounding framework, people in conversation do not try to get their hypotheses to converge perfectly—in fact, since neither party is omniscient, this is not even feasible. Instead, they try to reach a level of convergence that is sufficient for current purposes, *satisficing* in Simon's (1981) terms. Efforts at convergence are guided by the grounding criteria people set and by how effectively they can use the evidence available in a communication medium.

So when visual evidence is readily available, people should be only as detailed and persistent in their evidence-providing and evidence-seeking as they need to be to satisfy current purposes. When evidence of a partner's understanding is weaker or less direct, as in the verbal condition, they will have to set their grounding criteria higher to ensure the same level of performance, causing them to be more accurate on average (that is, more convergent) than they need to be and less efficient overall. This yields the specific and somewhat counterintuitive prediction that two people's meaning hypotheses about a spatial location may come to converge *less* closely when they have visual evidence than when they do not. I tested this prediction by giving pairs a criterion for the task: they were to get their car icons parked in the same spot so that if their two screens (each measuring 1024×768 pixels) were superimposed, at least part of their icons (each measuring 16×12 pixels) would overlap.

Language-Action Transcripts: Design and Analysis

Each of the twelve pairs described a total of eighty different preprogrammed target locations. Within a pair, one person acted as director for four blocks of ten trials (where a trial involved describing one location on a map) and then switched roles with the partner in order to act as matcher for the subsequent four blocks. After each block, either the evidence condition or the map changed. The evidence condition alternated between visual and verbal-only evidence; in the verbal-only condition, the director could not see where the matcher's icon was, and they had to do the task entirely by conversing aloud, whereas in the visual condition, the director could, in addition, monitor the position and movement of the matcher's icon on her own screen, with the matcher's icon appearing in a different color than her own. The maps, both in black and white and equally legible and detailed, alternated every two blocks between one of the Stanford campus and one of Cape Cod. These two locales varied in their familiarity to participants, and the maps were therefore intended to vary in the amount of prior knowledge the participants were likely to share. Map, evidence condition, director-matcher roles, and presentation order were completely counterbalanced for a repeated-measures design both within pairs and within locations. Directors and matchers were explicitly informed at the outset of each block as to whether the director would be able to see the matcher's icon.

The director began a trial by clicking on her icon, which then moved automatically to a preprogrammed target location and stopped. Whenever the matcher was ready, he selected his icon by clicking on it and then freely moved it over the map. Once the matcher believed his icon to be in the target location, he then parked it by clicking again. This concluded the trial; once the icon was parked, it could not be moved again until the director initiated the next trial. Conversation during each trial was audiotaped in stereo, and a time-stamped log file of both partners' mouse clicks and the x- and y-coordinates of their icons was generated automatically. This log began when the director initiated the trial, continued through when the matcher picked his icon up, and ended when he finally parked it.

Action Transcripts

The log files were reduced by a filtering program that automatically identified and timed all trial durations, pauses, and intervals during which the matcher stopped moving within a specified radius of the target location. There was some "jitter" associated with pausing the mouse, so a pause in the action was considered to be any period of time when the matcher moved his icon by two pixels or fewer. After the data were reduced, the distance between the director's and matcher's icons was calculated for each time increment; these data were the basis for the action transcript, which was represented as the plot of the distance between their icons over time. Figure 4.1 displays a prototypical time-distance plot generated by one matcher during one trial.

Analysis of the action transcripts was based on the assumption that the matcher's icon movements provided an estimate of what he understood at that point. Of course, icon location did not always correspond precisely to the matcher's hypothesis about

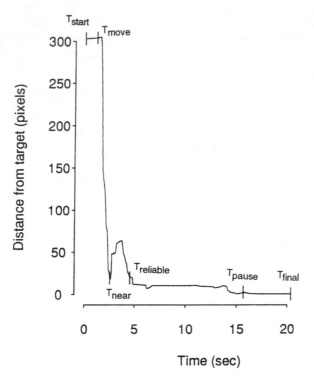

Figure 4.1
Time-distance plot and points of interest for one typical trial.

the target, since at times he may have had only a vague location (or set of locations) in mind, or he may have been temporarily "stuck." But at any particular moment, the icon location constituted an observer's best estimate of the matcher's hypothesis about what the director had presented so far. When the matcher's icon was motionless and when the distance between the matcher's and the director's icons was equal to zero, the matcher was assumed to have a perfectly convergent hypothesis of where the target location was.

The time-distance plots show to what extent the matcher's overall progress toward the target was monotonic. A steep negative slope indicates movement directly toward the target. An abrupt change in slope indicates one of three things. First, an acute angle where the slope changes its sign from negative to positive indicates that the matcher moved on a continuous path that went right by the target. His close approach might have been due not to a precise, correct hypothesis, but to chance. Second, when the slope changes from positive to negative, the matcher has gone from moving away from the target to moving toward it. Finally, a change from a sloped line to a horizontal one indicates that the matcher has stopped moving altogether or else has moved at a consistent distance from the target (essentially circling it). These possibilities are distinguished by the star-shaped points on the plot, which correspond to moments when the experiment software detected a movement from the mouse; a horizontal region with few points on it indicates that the matcher's icon was stationary or nearly so. Points located close together on a slope indicate slower movement than points located farther apart.

Several moments of interest during the time course of a trial were identified automatically and are labeled on figure 4.1: T_{start}, T_{move}, T_{near}, $T_{reliable}$, T_{pause}, and T_{final}. T_{start} was the moment the matcher first clicked to pick up his icon. T_{move} was the moment he started to move it. Presumably, at that point he must have had some idea where to move it (even if only in which general direction). Sometimes there was initial movement away from the target at the very beginning of a trial. This initial movement was probably not a reliable indicator of where a matcher thought the target was; some individuals seemed to make a large movement right after they clicked to select their icons, perhaps just to see if the click had taken effect. Apart from this difference in mouse technique at the very beginning of some trials, icon movement was assumed to provide an index into the matcher's understanding of the director's verbal presentation of the target location.

T_{final} was the moment when the matcher parked his icon, ending the trial. This point corresponds to the "completion point" in the referential communication study of Schober and Clark (1989). Our window into a matcher's understanding, then, consists of the period of time from the matcher's first icon motion, or T_{move}, to when he finally decided to park. If the matcher paused along the way, the locations where he paused were taken to approximate his intermediate meaning hypotheses. T_{near} was between T_{move} and T_{final}, when the matcher first arrived within close radius of the target location. This was the earliest location where the matcher would have been correct, or very nearly so, had he parked the icon there. Of course, chance movements could also have led the matcher closer to the target, so to properly identify the moment when the matcher had a *reliable* hypothesis, not only did his icon need to be overlapping the director's icon, but it should not move out of range of the target again before T_{final}. So $T_{reliable}$ was determined as the moment when the center of the matcher's icon arrived within a 20-pixel range of the center of the target icon, thereafter staying within this range. It was by definition equal to or later than T_{near}. It corresponded to the best estimate of when the matcher reached a meaning hypothesis that turned out to be correct.[3] T_{pause} was the moment when the matcher finally stopped moving, just before parking his icon (T_{final}). This is where, presumably, he had the opportunity to perform any final processing or checking before concluding that he and the director had the same target location in mind.

In figure 4.1, the matcher's icon began about 300 pixels away from the target (T_{start}). After about a second and a half (T_{move}), he moved very slightly away and then rapidly toward the target. He passed within 20 pixels of the target (T_{near}) and then moved right by it. About 2 seconds later, he came back within 20 pixels of the target ($T_{reliable}$). At this point there is an abrupt "elbow"—that is, a change in slope from steep to nearly flat. After this point, progress toward the target is more gradual, and the plot shows a long, flat "tail." T_{pause} represents our closest estimate for the point at which he reached his final meaning hypothesis, and the time between T_{pause} and T_{final} indicates how long it took to conclude hypothesis testing and complete the trial.

Language Transcripts

Six of the twelve pairs of subjects were chosen at random and their conversation was transcribed.[4] This yielded a corpus of 480 conversational interchanges about the eighty map locations. These language transcripts were coded for level of description of the target location (general, specific, and detailed), acknowledgments, deictic cues, questions, and instances where speakers truncated their own utterances or interrupted their partner's.

Language-Action Transcripts

During each trial, there was a .5-second audible beep when the matcher clicked to make his icon movable and a .25-second audible beep when he clicked to park it. The beeps were marked in the language transcripts with #'s; the first # indicated where in the speech the beep began, and the second #, where it ended. The beeps were used to synchronize[5] the language transcripts with the action transcripts for a subset of forty-eight trials performed by the six pairs whose speech was transcribed. These forty-eight trials included eight different map locations, half on each map and half in each evidence condition. Within these constraints, the forty-eight trials were chosen randomly. For these trials, language-action transcripts were generated, where superscripts on the language transcripts correspond to numbered labels on the time-distance plots.

Findings

Next I will discuss the findings[6] with respect to each of the four predictions.

Early vs. Late Meaning Hypotheses

The contribution model, with its presentation and acceptance phases, led to the expectation that the distance between the matcher's and the director's icons would not decrease at a steady rate over time, but relatively rapidly at first (as they established a description from which the matcher could derive a meaning hypothesis), followed by at least one elbow in the time-distance plot (an estimate of the point during which the matcher had formed a promising meaning hypothesis) and then a relatively horizontal phase (during which the description continued to be grounded—that is, the matcher's meaning hypothesis was tested and accepted). As expected, the time-distance plots in the verbal-only evidence condition at the left of figures 4.2 and 4.3 show this pattern. Both T_{near}, the point at which the matcher's icon managed to approach the target closely enough to touch it, and $T_{reliable}$, the point at which the matcher appeared to have a reliable hypothesis (one that not only turned out to be correct, but after which any further approach to the target was monotonic), occurred relatively early, especially in the verbal-only evidence condition. This pattern contrasted with the possibility of a more gradual progression to the target that would have been expected if grounding did not occur—that is, if the matcher's icon were to have reached the correct location just before the end of the exchange, without an apparent acceptance phase before continuing to the next trial.

Impact of Visual vs. Verbal Evidence on Grounding

Elsewhere we have predicted (without systematically testing) that the evidence available for grounding shapes both the conversations and task performance (Clark and Brennan 1991). Consistent with that prediction, this task was most efficient with visual evidence. A trial, measured from the matcher's first icon movement (T_{move}) to when he parked (T_{final}), was more than twice as long with verbal-only evidence than with visual evidence, 20.68 seconds to 9.03 seconds, $min\, F'(1, 35) = 125.86$, $p < .001$.[7] Consistent with this finding, fewer than half as many words were spoken in the visual condition as in the verbal-only condition (for the 480 transcribed trials, $min\, F'(1, 13) = 45.51$, $p < .001$). It is not surprising that a spatial task proceeds faster when there is visual evidence available; what is of particular interest, however, is that this evidence did not facilitate convergence evenly over the whole time course of a trial.

There was a striking qualitative difference in the shape of the time-distance plots in the two evidence conditions; compare the left-hand versus right-hand plots in figures 4.2 and 4.3. In the verbal-only condition, after the matcher reached the target location the plots showed a relatively long, nearly horizontal tail before he parked his icon, whereas in the visual condition, trials ended shortly after he reached the target. This

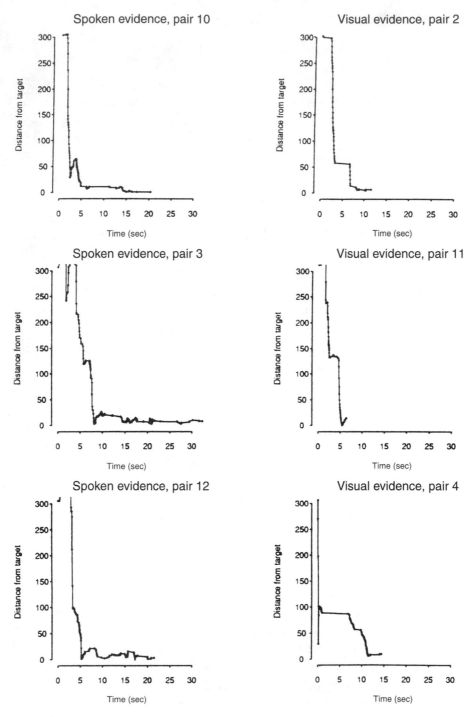

Figure 4.2
Time-distance plots for six matchers' progress toward the same target on the unfamiliar (Cape Cod) map. Those on the left were generated in the verbal-only evidence condition, and those on the right, in the visual evidence condition.

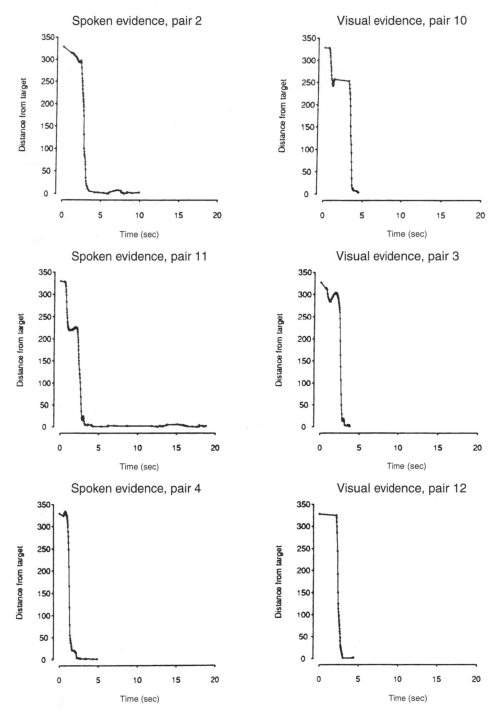

Figure 4.3

Time-distance plots for six matchers' progress toward the same target on the familiar (Stanford) map. Those on the left were generated in the verbal-only evidence condition, and those on the right, in the visual evidence condition.

shows that it took the matcher less time to conclude he was correct when the director had visual evidence. Consider the interval after the elbow, between $T_{reliable}$ and T_{final}. This is the interval in which the matcher already held and was testing the hypothesis that he ultimately accepted. For the randomly chosen subset of forty-eight trials, it took the matcher nearly four times longer to conclude that his location at $T_{reliable}$ was correct with verbal-only evidence alone than with visual evidence, 8.40 to 2.12 seconds, $min\ F'(1, 17) = 14.37$, $p < .005$.

The interval from $T_{reliable}$ to T_{final} was where I predicted the director and matcher would reciprocally test their final meaning hypotheses; if this is so, then in the verbal-only evidence condition, this interval should include speech by not only the director, but also the matcher. Alternatively perhaps the director would just speak until she finished what she thought was an appropriate description and then wait while the matcher silently searched for the target (testing his hypothesis autonomously) before he eventually parked his icon. For the random subset of forty-eight trials, I examined the number of words spoken by the matcher from $T_{reliable}$ (the moment when the matcher reliably reached the target location without moving away again) to T_{final}. Matchers uttered a mean of 6.33 words from $T_{reliable}$ to T_{final} in the verbal-only evidence condition (different from zero at $t(12) = 5.28$, $p < .001$). So in the verbal-only condition, the matcher was far from silent after reaching the target, just before parking his icon. In the visual condition, matchers took less responsibility, uttering only 2.13 words in the interval after $T_{reliable}$.

Even a highly accurate hypothesis at $T_{reliable}$ often did not stay *exactly* the same but got refined as the matcher made the final decision to park his icon. So it made sense to examine the impact of visual evidence after that, near the very end of a trial. In the contribution model, this point would correspond approximately to the end of the acceptance phase of a contribution. Consider the interval between T_{pause} and T_{final}, when (by definition) the matcher was motionless just before parking his icon. Here, the matcher could provide a final acknowledgement to the director, or perhaps even seek a final bit of evidence. This interval should be shorter in the visual condition than in the verbal-only condition because partners could use visual evidence for grounding. Indeed, it was less than half as long in the visual condition as in the verbal-only condition, 1.22 seconds to 3.00 seconds, $min\ F'(1, 45) = 17.30$, $p < .001$. As it turns out, the matcher was far from silent during this interval in the verbal-only condition, uttering three times as many words as in the visual condition, 3.83 to 1.08.

Another way to look at this is by counting how many trials ended with verbal acknowledgments by the matcher. Clark and Wilkes-Gibbs's (1986) principle of mutual responsibility leads to the prediction that when directors do not have visual evidence,

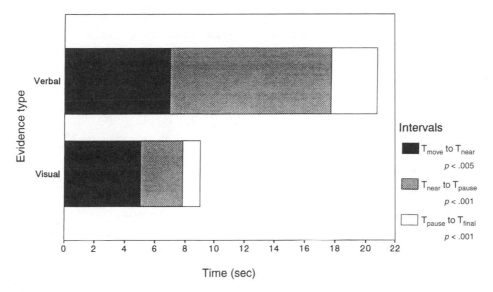

Figure 4.4
Effects of evidence on the time course of the action transcripts (955 trials).

matchers should give verbal acknowledgments, and when directors have visual evidence, matchers should withhold them. Every one of the verbal-only trials in the sample of forty-eight contained an acknowledgment by the matcher immediately before, during, or immediately after the moment he parked his icon, whereas only 29 percent of the ones in the visual condition contained such an acknowledgment, $min\, F'(1, 17) = 32.00$, $p < .001$. That matchers adapted their own acknowledgments according to the perceptual evidence available *to their partners* supports the idea that backchannels are precise signals used for grounding (Brennan 1990), as opposed to responses emitted automatically or at a particular rate (as suggested by Duncan (1973) and Rosenfeld (1987)).

The type of evidence also affected the time course of the matcher's understanding during the presentation of the target-location description early in the trial (although not as dramatically as it did at the end of the trial, in the acceptance phase). With visual evidence, it took 5.0 seconds for the matcher's icon to first arrive within 20 pixels of the target (the interval from T_{move} to T_{near}); without visual evidence, it took 6.9 seconds, $min\, F'(1, 42) = 9.48$, $p < .005$. The effect of the type of evidence on these intervals is summarized in figure 4.4.

How do these effects of evidence arise? Although the ultimate responsibility for parking the icon and ending the trial rested with the matcher (since the next trial could not be initiated until he parked his icon), the director was the one who took the responsibility for proposing to the matcher that his hypothesis was correct whenever she could see his icon. Sometimes the director did this by cutting herself off in mid-presentation as soon as she could see that the matcher had arrived:

D: ok,
     now we're gonna go over to
     M-Memorial Church?
     and park right in Memor-
     right there.
     that's good.

The corresponding language-action transcript in figure 4.5 confirms that this matcher had just arrived at the target and stopped there at the moment the director cut herself off at "Memor-." In the smaller sample of forty-eight trials, twenty-two of the twenty-four trials in the visual condition ended with a deictic cue from the director, such as "You're there," which the matcher acknowledged simply by clicking to park his icon. Then the director initiated the next trial.

Impact of Familiar vs. Unfamiliar Maps on Grounding

Consider the familiar and unfamiliar maps. When the director and matcher mutually believed they were members of the same relevant community (in this case, Stanford), it should have taken them less time to establish a referent because they could make assumptions about each other's knowledge and build on their common ground. Indeed, the mean time it took to complete a trial was less for the Stanford map than for the Cape Cod map, 13.00 seconds to 16.71 seconds ($min\ F'(1, 100) = 14.97$, $p < .001$). As predicted, this difference was particularly strong very early in the trial, in the interval from T_{move} to T_{near}. The matcher got within 20 pixels of the correct target 2.26 seconds faster on the Stanford map than on the Cape Cod map ($min\ F'(1, 101) = 14.36$, $p < .001$). So most of the timing advantage of discussing a Stanford location happened within the first 5 seconds, as the director designed and presented a description. In contrast, the type of map made no difference at all at the end of each trial in the interval between T_{pause} and T_{final} ($min\ F'(1, 61) = 0.36$, n.s.). The moment-by-moment effects of maps on these intervals is summarized in figure 4.6.

The early advantage with the familiar (Stanford) map appears to have been due to the director's ability to present intelligible definite references earlier than with the unfamiliar (Cape Cod) map. Whenever the director began to describe a target location to a matcher, she had to choose a level of detail for the description, a choice that may

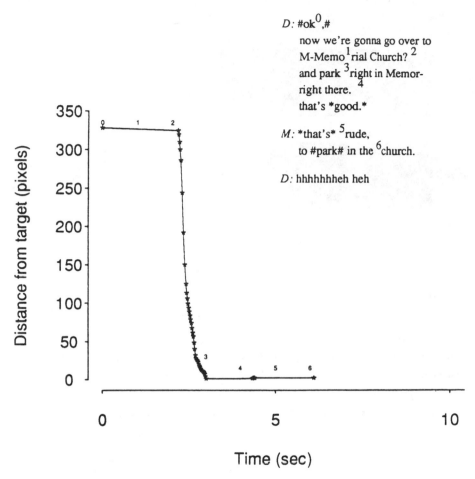

Figure 4.5
Using a deictic cue (*right there*) in the visual evidence condition to propose that hypotheses have converged. Superscripts in text correspond to points directly below numbers on the plot. Audible beeps at beginning and end of trial are represented within ##s. Stretches of overlapping speech are marked by pairs of **s.

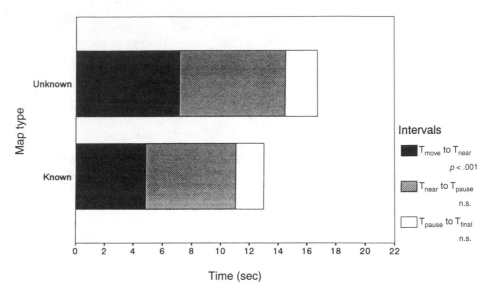

Figure 4.6
Mean effects of map on the time course of the action transcripts (955 trials).

have been guided by her estimation of the knowledge she shared with the matcher. The sooner she was able to present a detailed description, the sooner the matcher could form a good hypothesis about the target and move there. Consider this initial description of a target on the Cape Cod map (the levels of description are categorized at the right):

D: uhh
    go northeast   (*general level*)
    up to the corner,   (*definite level*)
    there's a little tiny street that has a three-letter name   (*detailed level*)

This presentation starts with a general directive, then increases in detail with a definite description and then a description of a more detailed landmark, which may have helped the matcher "zoom in" on the target. This strategy was common. In the sample of forty-eight trials, directors began with descriptions that were more specific for Stanford than for Cape Cod locations (in a sign test of the median, $p < .05$).

In contrast to map type, the *evidence* type a director had made no difference in the initial level of description, but it did affect subsequent descriptions. Closer inspection of the forty-eight individual language-action transcripts showed that directors "zoomed out" again when they had visual evidence that matchers were having trouble. Consider this description of a location on the Stanford map in the visual evidence condition:

D: we're movin:g
     south,   (*general level*)
     we're in Mem Chu,   (*definite level*)
     right in the center of Mem Chu,   (*detailed level*)
     which is right on the Quad,   (*definite level*)
     right there.   (*deictic*)
     stop.

Here, the director got to a relatively high level of detail with "right in the center of Mem Chu" and then zoomed out or backed off a level by mentioning "the Quad" as a landmark relative to Memorial Church. At the moment the detailed description was uttered, the matcher had actually just gone past the target (see figure 4.7); the director may have changed her level of description in response to this direct evidence about the matcher's understanding. Finally, the director let the matcher know when his icon reached the target with a deictic cue.

Impact of Evidence on How Precisely Speakers' and Addressees' Hypotheses Converged

As predicted, the grounding process involves satisficing; directors and matchers actually got their hypotheses to converge more closely when the director *lacked* visual evidence of what the matcher was doing. Without visual evidence, matchers were, on average, 4.6 pixels off from dead center on the target, whereas with visual evidence, they were 5.6 pixels off ($min\ F'(1, 73) - 4.00$, $p < .05$). This supports the prediction from the contribution model that people set their grounding criteria to ensure the desired degree of convergence, rather than the simple intuition that more evidence yields more convergence (see Karsenty 1999). How *precisely* two people could set their grounding criteria depended on how well they could use the available evidence. With visual evidence, they were only as accurate as they needed to be. Without visual evidence, they needed to adopt a higher criterion in order to be sure to reach an equivalent level of performance, and this took more effort overall.

What is remarkable is how flexible each pair was able to be, adjusting their grounding criteria whenever the evidence available to the director changed.

There were no more errors without visual evidence than with visual evidence; performance in both evidence conditions was nearly at ceiling. An error was counted whenever a pair failed to reach the criterion described in the task instructions—that is,

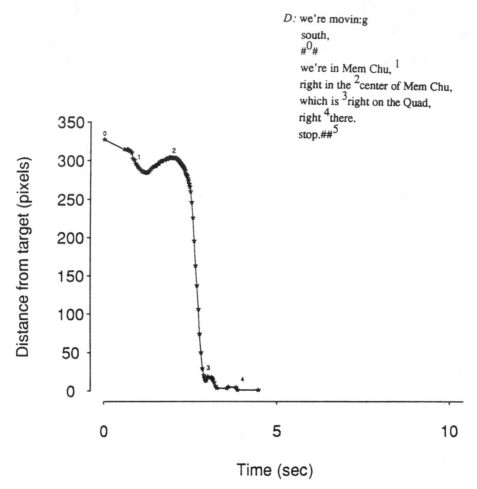

Figure 4.7

Levels of description, synchronized with the matcher's icon movements (visual condition). Just before point 3, the matcher goes past the target and the director responds by issuing a more general locative.

whenever the matcher's parked icon would not have overlapped the director's, if the two screens were superimposed. There were only 11 errors in 955 trials, made by 9 different matchers and distributed evenly across the verbal-only condition (5 errors) and the visual condition (6 errors). So even though they were doing a spatial task in which visual evidence was highly relevant, people did just as well at reaching the task criterion when directors could not see matchers' icons as when they could; it just took more than twice as long when the director lacked visual evidence.

Discussion

These data serve two broad purposes. First, they exemplify a technique—earlier than eye tracking and more precise than the videotaped card-matching task used by Schober and Clark 1989—for measuring, moment by moment, what people understand and intend during task-oriented conversation (see also Clark and Krych 2002 for a later version of a task that generated a language-action transcript). This sort of evidence aims to combine the control and reliability valued by researchers in the language-as-product tradition with the ecological validity valued by those in the language-as-action tradition. Both are necessary in order to understand the intra- and interpersonal processing that underlies human language ability.

Second, and more specifically, these data are consistent with the contribution model and shed light on the time course by which two individuals in conversation coordinate their processing. The shapes of the language-action transcripts showed, on average, a distinct phase between the time when a matcher first had a correct meaning hypothesis and the time when he accepted it by ending the trial. This grounding or acceptance phase was shortened considerably when the director had visual evidence of the matcher's progress toward the target. The documentation of a distinct phase after the matcher arrives at an adequate meaning hypothesis suggests that the mental representations of two individuals in conversation do not converge simply because of similarity between the individuals or between the processes of speaking and listening.

These findings also confirm that backchannels are specific, timely signals for coordinating individuals' mental states, as opposed to habitually or automatically emitted signals showing a general level of engagement in the conversation. Even though what the matcher saw on his display was exactly the same in both evidence conditions, he provided verbal acknowledgments when the director could not see his icon movements and withheld them when she could. He rapidly adapted this behavior as the experimental conditions alternated between visual and verbal-only evidence.

The difference between the two evidence conditions concerning which of the two partners took responsibility for concluding that their individual hypotheses had converged is consistent with Clark and Wilkes-Gibbs's (1986) principle of mutual responsibility. When the only possible evidence from the matcher was in spoken form, the director typically relied on the matcher's judgment that their hypotheses had converged. With ostensive visual evidence from the matcher, the director could judge the likelihood of convergence for herself. The responsibility for concluding that their hypotheses had converged fell to whoever was in a position to have the strongest evidence. In a task-based conversation such as this one, seeing the matcher's icon counts as strong evidence, and so the director in the visual condition took on most of that responsibility. This saved not only the matcher's effort, but their collective effort as well. The distribution of responsibility between partners in conversation turned out to be quite flexible.

Trials with visual evidence and with the familiar map were fastest, but these advantages were distributed quite differently over the course of a trial. The mutually familiar Stanford map led to an advantage early in the trial, while the bulk of the descriptions of the target locations were being presented, but not late in the trial. In contrast, visual evidence led to an advantage throughout the trial that was especially large late in the trial, during the phase in which the descriptions were being grounded.

It is striking that so many of the exchanges in the visual evidence condition contained no speech at all by the matcher. In these cases, what the matcher did with icon movements substituted for what he did with speaking turns in the verbal-only condition. Obviously, icon moves are instrumental to doing the task. So did the matcher really intend certain icon moves to function, in addition, like utterances? That is, did he use ostensive actions deliberately, intending the director to recognize this? Ostensive evidence can function in two ways: as a mere *symptom* of what was understood (as "natural" evidence in the sense that "smoke means fire") or *intentionally* where one person expects the other to recognize it as communicative, in the sense of nonnatural meaning or *meaning$_{nn}$* (Grice 1957, 1989). When the matcher and the director were mutually aware that the director could see the matcher's icon, the matcher adapted by withholding verbal acknowledgments, and his icon move counted as his turn or presentation in the conversation. This enabled the matcher's presentations (in the form of icon moves) to overlap the director's (in the form of verbal descriptions), so that they could ground continually instead of by discrete turns, coordinating their meaning hypotheses in finer increments.

Consider the interchange in figure 4.8, during which the director presented a description in many installments separated by pauses (indicated by new lines). As we see

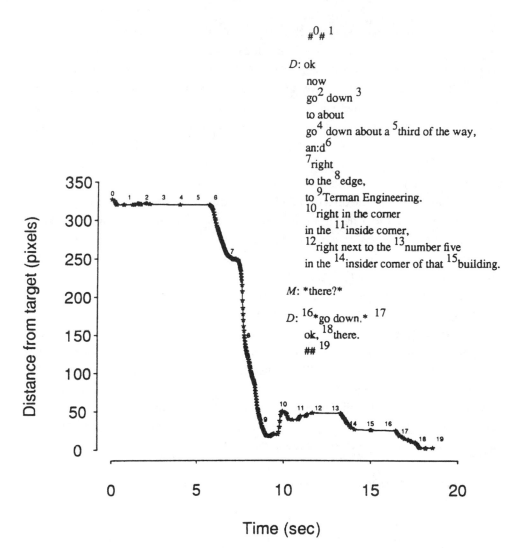

Figure 4.8
Repairing a matcher's incorrect meaning hypothesis between points 14–18 (visual evidence condition).

from figure 4.8, the matcher reached a location about 30 pixels above the target after 14 seconds and stopped. The director did not respond explicitly to this evidence, but kept on presenting installments. The matcher did not say anything at first, seemingly waiting for the possibly inattentive director to stop talking and notice his icon. After the director produced quite a few descriptive phrases, there was a pause. Then the matcher made an explicit verbal proposal that their hypotheses had converged: "there?" (superscripts 15–16). This suggests that he may have originally intended for the director to accept his icon position as an intentional presentation. As it turned out, the director was not being inattentive; the matcher's hypothesis was simply *not* close enough. It appears that the director had been responding to the incorrect icon position by continuing to present descriptions. When the matcher finally demanded to know whether his position was correct, the director opted, at the same time, to provide explicit deictic evidence in the form of an overlapping utterance, "go down—ok, there." This exchange demonstrates that collaborative hypothesis testing requires positive evidence (of convergence) as well as negative evidence (of misunderstanding). A lack of response will not do when positive evidence is expected.

It particularly interesting that directors were so attuned to the evidence of understanding from matchers that they sometimes interrupted themselves midword or mid-constituent in order to provide a timely deictic cue (as in the exchange in figure 4.5). We are currently investigating such self-interruptions by directors who can monitor matchers' eye movements in a referential communication task, in order to understand how closely the processes of speech planning and monitoring may be attuned to feedback from addressees (Brennan and Lockridge 2004).

Tracking Eye-Gaze vs. Mouse Movements in a Referential Communication Task

The online measure developed for this study presents both advantages and disadvantages in comparison to head-mounted eye tracking, an important new technique in the study of spoken-language use (see, e.g., Metzing and Brennan 2003 and chapters 1, 3, 5, and 6 in this volume). The usefulness of eye tracking is based on the "eye-mind assumption"—that the object a person is looking at reflects what is being processed at that moment. Eye movements to locations in space are ordinarily accompanied by shifts in attention to those locations (Deubel and Schneider 1996; Hoffman and Subramaniam 1995; Kowler et al. 1995); however, the reverse is not necessarily true—one may shift attention without shifting gaze (Posner 1980).

For studying online processing in conversation, how does eye tracking compare to the spatial technique used in this study? Tracking eye gaze is obviously far more temporally precise as an indicator of mental processes because the time to plan and launch a saccade is shorter than the time to plan and execute the motor movements for positioning a cursor with a mouse. Unlike mouse movements, eye movements need not be intentional. Eye tracking is also more spatially precise than mouse tracking; note that in my task, when the mouse was still (reflected in the time-distance plots as a perfectly flat horizontal line), the matcher may have been searching the display for the referent of the director's description, and this evidence is not recorded in the action transcripts.

On the other hand, the precision afforded by eye tracking may actually present disadvantages for answering the sorts of questions I have asked here. Not all eye fixations represent a hypothesis about what a speaker is referring to in a task like this one. People often make irrelevant saccades, as well as fixations whose purpose it is to take in information while searching for a potential referent. The map displays in my task were complex enough that they were not completely encoded by matchers before the task, so any eye fixations to a location could have represented information gathering about what was in the display rather than a likely hypothesis about its status as a potential referent. In this spatial task, mouse movements were instrumental in dragging the icon to the target, and so these movements were actually more directly coupled to the matcher's intentions and hypotheses than eye movements would have been. The matcher's mouse movements indicated at least some level of confidence that he had narrowed down his hypothesis about the target location. For a location-finding task such as this one, the language-action transcripts provide a useful window into the time course by which two people's beliefs converge.

Implications for Mediated Communication

Although theories of discourse structure have focused mainly on linguistic utterances, visual evidence can be as much a part of discourse as can verbal evidence. As Grice (1957, 388) argued, "linguistic intentions are very like nonlinguistic intentions." A theory of discourse should be able to account not only for a conversation's linguistic structure, but also for its visually presented elements. Of particular interest in the current study was how conversations in the two evidence conditions differed in their turn-taking structure. Within the visual condition, grounding did not have to be done in discrete verbal turns, but was done *continuously* and in parallel, because the expression of one partner's hypothesis provided the other partner's evidence. People in this experiment appeared to adjust quite flexibly and rapidly to the degree of perceptual copresence they had. Similarly, in another study of remote communication using a shared electronic whiteboard, we found that utterances produced by typing were sometimes presented and accepted in parallel, and that when they lacked spoken evidence and had *only* visual evidence, people used spatial rather than temporal contiguity to ground utterances (Whittaker, Brennan, and Clark 1991).

Understanding the process of grounding in the detail presented here enables us to better predict how a medium will shape conversation and collaboration. Many studies have described differences in tasks conducted over different media without any theoretical framework to explain these differences (e.g., Chapanis et al. 1972; Cohen 1984; Ochsman and Chapanis 1974; Williams 1977). For instance, Cohen studied telephone and keyboard conversations in which one person directed another to assemble a pump. On the telephone, people would first get their partners to identify a part, and only then tell them what to do with it, whereas with keyboards, they would do all this in a single turn. He concluded that "speakers attempt to achieve more detailed goals in giving instructions than do users of keyboards" (Cohen 1984, 97). The reason this should be so follows logically from the grounding framework, in which people make different trade-offs in different media in order to minimize their collective effort (Clark and Brennan 1991). Acquiring evidence about an addressee's understanding is less costly in spoken conversation than with text messages (which lack prosodic cues and take more time and effort to produce), so speakers take more frequent turns and ground smaller constituents than do typists in chat conversations. Also, the fact that speech is ephemeral and text is not makes grounding larger constituents easier for text messages and grounding small constituents more cost-effective for speech, particularly when there is visual copresence between partners.

In closing, when people are physically copresent, actions can stand in for utterances, and one partner's feedback and task-related actions can affect another's utterance planning, moment by moment. In this way, the techniques that a medium affords for grounding shape both the products and the processes of spontaneous language use.

Notes

This chapter presents previously unpublished data from Brennan 1990. I thank Herbert Clark for his insights at all stages of this project and many other colleagues, including Richard Gerrig, Michael Schober, Joy Hanna, and Eric Stubbs, for helpful input on earlier drafts. Thanks also to Stephen Lowder for software assistance, to Kathryn Henniss for coding assistance, and to Caroline Collins, Martin Kay, and Peter Sells for loaning their equipment. This material is based on work supported by the National Science Foundation under grants 0082602, 9980013, and 9202458. Any opinions, findings, and conclusions or recommendations expressed in this material are those of the author and do not necessarily reflect the views of the National Science Foundation. Address correspondence to Susan Brennan at the Department of Psychology, State University of New York, Stony Brook, NY 11794-2500.

1. Understanding is not the same as agreement or uptake. When speakers and addressees have incompatible intentions, they might understand one another perfectly well but "agree to disagree" (see Bly 1993). The task I present here provides speakers and addressees with a shared goal, so this study focuses on cases where speakers and addressees with shared goals attempt to make their hypotheses converge.

2. For expository convenience, I will refer to the director as female and the matcher as male, even though subjects were run in single-sex pairs and they switched director/matcher roles halfway through the session.

3. Note that these points provide more detail about the time course of a contribution than does Schober and Clark's (1989) "conjecture point". A particular "conjecture point" could ambiguously correspond to when the matcher *first* reached a correct hypothesis (T_{near}), when the matcher *reliably* reached a correct hypothesis ($T_{reliable}$), or when the matcher reached a *final* hypothesis ($T_{completion}$).

4. Speech was transcribed in segments that corresponded roughly to one phonemic clause per line—that is, a short sequence of words separated by a pause, and generally containing one primary pitch accent (Rosenfeld 1987; see also Boomer 1978; Dittman and Llewellyn 1967). Each line was punctuated according to its clause-final prosody: "." for final pitch lowering, "?" for final rising, "," for the end of a tone unit (if midclause) or else for listlike intonation (when at the end of a clause), "-" for a sudden self-cutoff on a level pitch, and no punctuation for level pitch. Slowed speech or drawled syllables were denoted by ":" following the letter that most closely matched the sound being drawn out (ye:s for "yeeees," versus yes: for "yesss"). Overlapping speech was transcribed using single or double asterisks to enclose the beginning and ending of the simultaneous talk. Unintelligible speech was enclosed in "⟨ ⟩". All transcripts were checked for accuracy.

5. A linguistics graduate student naive to the experimental hypotheses listened to the videotapes of each trial with the language transcripts in front of her, using a videotape player equipped with a counter and a shuttle knob. For each trial she zeroed the counter at the start of the initial beep and recorded an integer at every 1.0-second interval over the text version of its corresponding spoken syllable on the transcript. It took many passes over the tapes to record these intervals and to check the synchronization of each trial.

6. Five action trials were eliminated because matchers inadvertently clicked twice while picking up the icon, inadvertently parking it and ending the trial early. The results presented here are based on the 955 automatically logged trials, unless otherwise stated. There was more variability in elapsed time for trials with verbal-only evidence alone than with visual evidence added (in a standard ratio-of-variances test, $F(2, 78) = 5.81$, $p < .01$), so I transformed all time-interval lengths as a function of log(time). I then analyzed the transformed data using two-way ANOVAs with map and evidence condition as fixed factors, treated pairs of subjects and items (map locations) as random factors, and computed the statistic *min F'* as recommended by Clark (1973). There were no interactions between map and evidence.

7. *Min F'* combines into a single statistic the by-subjects and by-items ANOVAS (F_1 and F_2) traditionally reported in psycholinguistics and memory studies, but in a more conservative fashion (if a result is significant by *min F'*, then it is significant by both F_1 and F_2). The degrees of freedom are recalculated as a combination of those for F_1 and F_2 (see Clark 1973).

References

Berkovits, R. 1981. Are spoken surface structure ambiguities perceptually unambiguous? *Journal of Psycholinguistic Research, 10,* 41–56.

Bly, B. 1993. Uncooperative Language and the Negotiation of Meaning. Unpublished doctoral dissertation, Stanford University.

Boomer, D. S. 1978. The phonemic clause: Speech unit in human communication. In A. W. Siegman and S. Feldstein, eds., *Nonverbal Behavior and Communication.* Hillsdale, NJ: Erlbaum.

Boyle, E., Anderson, A., and Newlands, A. 1994. The effects of visibility on dialogue and performance in a cooperative problem solving task. *Language and Speech, 37,* 1–20.

Brennan, S. E. 1990. Seeking and Providing Evidence for Mutual Understanding. Unpublished doctoral dissertation, Stanford University.

Brennan, S. E., and Clark, H. H. 1996. Conceptual pacts and lexical choice in conversation. *Journal of Experimental Psychology: Learning, Memory and Cognition, 6,* 1482–1493.

Brennan, S. E., and Lockridge, C. B. 2004. How visual copresence and joint attention shape speech planning. Unpublished manuscript.

Brown, P. M., and Dell, G. S. 1986. Adapting production to comprehension: The explicit mention of instruments. *Cognitive Psychology, 19,* 441–472.

Bruner, J. S. 1985. The role of interactive formats in language acquisition. In J. P. Forgas, ed., *Language and Social Situations,* 31–46. New York: Springer-Verlag.

Cahn, J. E., and Brennan, S. E. 1999. A psychological model of grounding and repair in dialog. *Proceedings, AAAI Fall Symposium on Psychological Models of Communication in Collaborative Systems,* 25–33. North Falmouth, MA: American Association for Artificial Intelligence.

Chapanis, A., Ochsman, R. B., Parrish, R. N., and Weeks, G. D. 1972. Studies in interactive communication: I. The effects of four communication modes on the behavior of teams during cooperative problem-solving. *Human Factors, 14,* 487–509.

Clark, H. H. 1973. The language-as-fixed-effect fallacy: A critique of language statistics in psychological research. *Journal of Verbal Learning and Verbal Behavior, 12,* 335–359.

Clark, H. H. 1983. Making sense of nonce sense. In G. B. Flores d'Arcais and R. Jarvella, eds., *The Process of Language Understanding,* 297–331. New York: Wiley.

Clark, H. H. 1994. Managing problems in speaking. *Speech Communication, 15,* 243–250.

Clark, H. H. 1996. *Using Language*. Cambridge, MA: Cambridge University Press.

Clark, H. H., and Brennan, S. E. 1991. Grounding in communication. In L. B. Resnick, J. Levine, and S. D. Behrend, eds., *Perspectives on Socially Shared Cognition*, 127–149. Washington, DC: American Psychological Association Books.

Clark, H. H., and Gerrig, R. J. 1983. Understanding old words with new meanings. *Journal of Verbal Learning and Verbal Behavior, 22*, 591–608.

Clark, H. H., and Krych, M. A. 2004. Speaking while monitoring addressees for understanding. *Journal of Memory and Language, 50*, 62–81.

Clark, H. H., and Marshall, C. R. 1981. Definite reference and mutual knowledge. In A. K. Joshi, B. Webber, and I. A. Sag, eds., *Elements of Discourse Understanding*, 10–63. Cambridge, UK: Cambridge University Press.

Clark, H. H., and Schaefer, E. F. 1987. Collaborating on contributions to conversations. *Language and Cognitive Processes, 2*, 19–41.

Clark, H. H., and Schaefer, E. F. 1989. Contributing to discourse. *Cognitive Science, 13*, 259–294.

Clark, H. H., and Wilkes-Gibbs, D. 1986. Referring as a collaborative process. *Cognition, 22*, 1–39.

Cohen, P. R. 1984. The pragmatics of referring and the modality of communication. *Computational Linguistics, 10*, 97–146.

Cook, M., and Lalljee, M. 1972. Verbal substitutes for visual signals in interaction. *Semiotica, 6*, 212–221.

Dell, G. S., and Brown, P. 1991. Mechanisms for listener adaptation in language production. In D. J. Napoli and J. A. Kegl, eds., *Bridges between Psychology and Linguistics: A Swarthmore Festschrift for Lila Gleitman*, 105–129. Hillsdale, NY: Erlbaum.

Deubel, H., and Schneider, W. 1996. Saccade target selection and object recognition: Evidence for a common attentional mechanism. *Vision Research, 36*, 1827–1837.

Deutsch, W., and Pechmann, T. 1982. Social interaction and the development of definite descriptions. *Cognition, 11*, 159–184.

Dittman, A. T., and Llewellyn, L. G. 1967. The phonemic clause as a unit of speech decoding. *Journal of Personality and Social Psychology, 6*, 341–349.

Duncan, S. D. 1973. Toward a grammar for dyadic conversation. *Semiotica, 9*, 29–47.

Duncan, S. 1975. Interaction units during speaking turns in dyadic, face-to-face conversations. In A. Kendon, R. M. Harris, and M. R. Key, eds., *Organization of Behavior in Face-to-Face Interaction*. The Hague: Mouton.

Goodwin, C. 1979. *Conversational Organization: Interaction between Speakers and Hearers*. New York: Academic Press.

Grice, H. P. 1957. Meaning. *Philosophical Review, 66*, 377–388.

Grice, H. P. 1975. Logic and conversation (from the William James lectures, Harvard University, 1967). In P. Cole and J. Morgan, eds., *Syntax and Semantics 3: Speech Acts*, 41–58. New York: Academic Press.

Grice, H. P. 1989. Meaning revisited. In *Studies in the Way of Words*, 283–303. Cambridge, MA: Harvard University Press.

Heath, C. 1984. Talk and recipiency: Sequential organization in speech and body movement. In J. M. Atkinson and J. Heritage, eds., *Structures of Social Action*, 247–265. Cambridge, UK: Cambridge University Press.

Hess, L. J., and Johnston, J. R. 1988. Acquisition of back channel listener responses to adequate messages. *Discourse Processes, 11*, 319–335.

Hoffman, J., and Subramaniam, B. 1995. The role of visual attention in saccadic eye movements. *Perception and Psychophysics, 57*, 787–795.

Isaacs, E. A., and Clark, H. H. 1987. References in conversation between experts and novices. *Journal of Experimental Psychology: General, 116*, 26–37.

Karsenty, L. 1999. Cooperative work and shared visual context: An empirical study of comprehension problems in side-by-side and remote help dialogues. *Human-Computer Interaction, 14*, 283–315.

Kendon, A. 1970. Movement coordination in social interaction: Some examples described. *Acta Psychologica, 32*, 101–125.

Kowler, E., Anderson, E., Dosher, B., and Blaser, E. 1995. The role of attention in the programming of saccades. *Vision Research, 35*, 1897–1916.

Krauss, R. M. 1987. The role of the listener: Addressee influences on message formulation. *Journal of Language and Social Psychology, 6*, 81–98.

Krauss, R. M., and Fussell, S. R. 1991. Constructing shared communicative environments. In L. B. Resnick, J. Levine, and S. D. Behrend, eds., *Perspectives on Socially Shared Cognition*, 172–200. Washington, DC: American Psychological Association Books.

Krauss, R. M., and Glucksberg, S. 1969. The development of communication: Competence as a function of age. *Child Development, 40*, 255–256.

Krauss, R. M., and Weinheimer, S. 1964. Changes in reference phases as a function of frequency of usage in social interaction: A preliminary study. *Psychonomic Science, 1*, 113–114.

Krauss, R. M., and Weinheimer, S. 1966. Concurrent feedback, confirmation, and the encoding of referents in verbal communication. *Journal of Personality and Social Psychology, 4*, 343–346.

Krauss, R. M., and Weinheimer, S. 1967. Effect of referent similarity and communication mode on verbal encoding. *Journal of Verbal Learning and Verbal Behavior, 6*, 359–363.

Kraut, R., Lewis, S., and Swezey, L. 1982. Listener responsiveness and the coordination of conversation. *Journal of Personality and Social Psychology*, *43*, 718–731.

Ochsman, R. B., and Chapanis, A. 1974. The effects of 10 communication modes on the behavior of teams during co-operative problem-solving. *International Journal of Man-Machine Studies*, *6*, 579–619.

Posner, M. 1980. Orienting of attention. *Quarterly Journal of Experimental Psychology*, *32*, 3–25.

Rosenfeld, H. M. 1987. Conversational control functions of nonverbal behavior. In A. W. Siegman and S. Feldstein, eds., *Nonverbal Behavior and Communication*, 563–601. Hillsdale, NJ: Erlbaum.

Rumelhart, D. E. 1980. *Understanding Understanding*. Technical Report No. 100. San Diego: Center for Human Information Processing, University of California.

Russell, A. W., and Schober, M. F. 1999. How beliefs about a partner's goals affect referring in goal-discrepant conversations. *Discourse Processes*, *27*, 1–33.

Schober, M. F., and Clark, H. H. 1989. Understanding by addressees and overhearers. *Cognitive Psychology*, *21*, 211–232.

Simon, H. 1981. *The Sciences of the Artificial* 2nd ed. Cambridge, MA: MIT Press.

Sperber, D., and Wilson, D. 1986. *Relevance*. Cambridge, MA: Harvard University Press.

Svartvik, J., and Quirk, R. 1980. *A Corpus of English Conversation*. Lund, Sweden: Gleerup.

Tanenhaus, M. K., Spivey-Knowlton, M. J., Eberhard, K. M., and Sedivy, J. 1995. Integration of visual and linguistic information in spoken language comprehension. *Science*, *268*, 1632–1634.

Whittaker, S. J., Brennan, S. E., and Clark, H. H. 1991. Coordinating activity: An analysis of interaction in computer-supported cooperative work. *Proceedings, CHI '91, Human Factors in Computing Systems*. 361–367. New Orleans, LA: Addison Wesley.

Wiemann, J. M., and Knapp, M. L. 1975. Turn-taking in conversations. *Journal of Communication*, *25*, 75–92.

Wilkes-Gibbs, D. 1986. Collaborative Processes of Language Use in Conversation. Unpublished doctoral dissertation, Stanford University.

Wilkes-Gibbs, D. 1992. Individual goals and collaborative actions: Conversation as collective behavior. Unpublished manuscript.

Wilkes-Gibbs, D., and Clark, H. H. 1992. Coordinating beliefs in conversation. *Journal of Memory and Language*, *31*, 183–194.

Williams, E. 1977. Experimental comparisons of face-to-face and mediated communication. *Psychological Bulletin*, *84*, 963–976.

Yngve, V. H. 1970. On getting a word in edgewise. In *Papers from the Sixth Regional Meeting of the Chicago Linguistic Society*, 567–578. Chicago: Chicago Linguistic Society.

II Speakers and Listeners as Participants in Conversation

5 The Use of Perspective during Referential Interpretation

Joy E. Hanna and Michael K. Tanenhaus

To communicate successfully, conversational partners must coordinate their individual knowledge and actions with one another in order to create and interpret linguistic expressions. However, relatively little is known about how this joint activity affects the moment-by-moment processes central to real-time language production and comprehension. Until recently, models of the time course of language processing have tended to ignore the effects of being engaged in conversation (cf. Clark 1997), focusing instead on core processes that were viewed as rapid, encapsulated, and autonomous. Part of the problem has been methodological. Studying interactive conversation requires creating controlled yet natural situations in which participants can engage in face-to-face communication, all within an environment where the communication can be monitored on the millisecond time scale at which real-time processing effects are seen. Only with the relatively recent advent of head-mounted eye trackers have researchers been able to explore the fine-grained time course of language use in conversational settings. This chapter presents an important step in combining research in online language comprehension with research in face-to-face interactive conversation. We monitored eye movements with a head-mounted eye tracker in two different referential communication tasks (cf. Krauss and Weinheimer 1966). Our purpose was to examine how perspective taking in a joint task affects the initial interpretation of referential expressions, focusing primarily on definite reference.

We investigated definite reference for two reasons. First, the resolution of referential expressions, especially those involving definite noun phrases, has long been viewed as a central component of real-time language processing, and it interacts with other basic processes such as syntactic-ambiguity resolution. Second, definite noun phrases are used to refer to or introduce uniquely identifiable entities, but only with respect to a particular context or *referential domain of interpretation* (e.g., Searle 1969; Barwise 1989). Without a restricted domain—for example, the set of objects in a kitchen workspace— the set of potential referents for a definite noun phrase, such as *the glass*, would be unlimited. In light of this, two important questions arise: (1) What determines or constitutes the appropriate referential domain for an addressee in interactive conversation? (2) What is the time course with which this domain has its restrictive effects?

One proposal, perhaps most notably made by Clark and his colleagues, is that a particular kind of context, the "common ground" or mutual knowledge, beliefs, and assumptions among conversational participants, has a primary role in defining the domain of interpretation (e.g., Clark 1992, 1996; Clark and Brennan 1989; Clark and Marshall 1981; Clark and Schaefer 1987; Clark and Wilkes-Gibbs 1986). We know that the process of collaboratively establishing and maintaining common ground plays a crucial role in determining many aspects of reference, from whether it will be definite or indefinite (Clark and Haviland 1977), to the linguistic form it will take (e.g., Brennan 1990; Brennan and Clark 1996; Clark and Clark 1979; Clark and Wilkes-Gibbs 1986; Lockridge and Brennan 2002). Viewing language as a type of joint action that is performed by people who cooperate in order to achieve particular goals, Clark and colleagues argue that interlocutors will only be successful if they monitor what is mutually known about a situation and use that knowledge effectively (Clark 1996). However, while common ground might ultimately determine the appropriate context for interpretation in cooperative conversation, the precise timing with which it is used to constrain referential interpretation remains an open empirical question.

Work using the head-mounted eye-tracking methodology has addressed the question of timing by focusing on how early common ground can restrict referential interpretation. This work has employed designs with a common- versus privileged-ground logic in referential communication experiments. Participants act as the addressee, interpreting instructions produced by a confederate speaker to manipulate real objects in a display. Some of the objects in the display are in common ground because they are physically visible to both the addressee and the speaker, or because they have been talked about. In contrast, some of the objects are in privileged ground because they are only visible or known to the addressee, and are kept hidden or secret from the speaker. The critical question is what happens when a definite referring expression matches both an object that is in common ground and an object that is in the addressee's privileged ground. If common ground has immediate effects, addressees should be relatively able to ignore information that is privileged to them and pay more attention to objects that are mutually known. If common ground does not operate immediately, then addressees should initially consider objects in common and privileged ground equally often.

An experiment conducted by Keysar et al. (1996, 2000; see also Keysar, Barr, and Horton 1998) provided striking evidence that common ground does not initially restrict referential domains in real-time comprehension. The results showed that in the earliest moments of processing, addressees considered objects in both privileged and common ground as possible interpretations for referring expressions; initial fixation launches were often to the privileged object, and addressees even selected this object in some cases. Initially, Keysar et al. (1996; Keysar, Barr, and Horton 1998) took this pattern of results as evidence that addressees first pursue interpretations based on an egocentric perspective, a perspective that in this task included both the privileged- and common-ground objects since they were all equally visible to the addressee. They further argued that these interpretations are monitored and then adjusted in a later stage to take into account common ground only when necessary, as when the privileged object was selected by mistake. However, as Keysar et al. (2000) acknowledge, the design of this experiment does not allow one to draw strong inferences about whether common ground influences initial processing. This is because the critical instructions always favored reference resolution to the object in privileged ground on the basis of typicality. For example, if the reference was to *the tall candle*, the tallest candle was the one in privileged ground, while a medium candle and a short candle were in common ground. Thus, while the results of Keysar et al. (2000) demonstrate that common ground does not completely restrict the initial domain of interpretation, it does not necessarily support the stronger claim that common ground is a late-stage filter.

We and our colleagues conducted a similar common-ground experiment (Hanna 2001; Hanna, Tanenhaus, and Trueswell 2003; Hanna et al. 1998), which did find evidence for the early influence of common ground. In this experiment, the objects in common and privileged ground were equally good matches for the critical referring expressions (they were identical colored shapes such as yellow triangles and red squares). The results showed that, consistent with the Keysar et al. (2000) finding, objects in an addressee's privileged ground were considered potential referents some of the time. Importantly, however, the results also showed a clear advantage for objects in common ground from the earliest moments of processing. We have argued from these results that common ground can be used by addressees immediately to constrain the domain of interpretation in a graded, probabilistic manner.

However, while it is possible that information about what was mutually known acted as an immediate constraint, it is also possible that the task did not require addressees to take into account common ground to restrict the domain of interpretation. In fact, any task employing the common-ground/privileged-ground logic described above is subject to an ambiguity of interpretation. In both the Keysar et al. (2000) studies and those by Hanna, Tanenhaus, and Trueswell (2003), the common-ground objects were, by necessity, more likely to be referred to by the speaker; they were also more recently referred to in cases where the privileged objects were referred to at all (e.g., with a written reference at the beginning of each trial in the study by Hanna and colleagues). Therefore, it is unclear whether addressees' preference for referents in common ground in the Hanna, Tanenhaus, and Trueswell (2003) study arose because the common ground object was more likely to be mentioned or was more salient, or whether addressees were actually taking into account the perspective of the speaker. In other words, addressees could have been performing a relatively simple form of probability matching in order to complete the task. This is not to say that the representation of common ground, or the mechanism by which it could exert its effects, is fundamentally distinct from any form of probability matching; rather, the point is that this simple form of probability matching is a computation that can be done egocentrically.

To avoid this problem, the experiments presented in this chapter used two tasks that manipulated the perspectives of the conversational participants such that the referential domain was clearly different from each conversant's perspective, and was not confounded with the likelihood or recency of reference. The experiments explored the time course with which an addressee can take the perspective of the speaker when it conflicts with perceptually salient information available to the addressee, either due to the speaker being misled as to the real state of a set of display objects (experiment 1), or due to differences in the ability to physically reach various objects in order to perform an action (experiment 2). If addressees are able to take into account the speaker's perspective in the initial moments of interpretation, then referential expressions that are misleading or ambiguous from the addressee's perspective, but unambiguous from the speaker's perspective, should cause no processing difficulty. This would provide further support for an account in which common ground is a source of information that is integrated with other constraints during the earliest moments of processing.

Experiment 1

The goal of this experiment was to determine the time course with which an addressee can utilize information from a speaker's perspective when it conflicts with perceptually salient information in their privileged ground. To avoid the possibility of probability matching or salience differences, all of the task objects were mentioned equally frequently and recently.

Participant addressees (A) were seated across a table from a (female) confederate speaker (C) who was completely hidden from view behind a vertical divider. On each trial, unseen by C, the experimenter placed four objects on a shelf on A's side of the table, and then named them in order to inform C of their identity. C repeated the object names in order to ground them and firmly establish her perspective, and then instructed A to pick one of them up and place it in one of two areas on the table surface. The displays always contained two sets of two identical objects, except that all the objects in a single display could be modified in the same manner to be either empty/containing something, open/closed, or opened/unopened. Fillers contained different adjectival modification.

We manipulated the precise point in the spoken instructions where the referent of a noun phrase became unambiguous with respect to the visual display. This *point of disambiguation* was varied by taking advantage of two linguistic factors: the uniqueness conditions carried by definite descriptions, and the contrastive property of adjectives. To give an example, consider a display such as the middle array of objects in figure 5.1, in which there are two empty jars and two martini glasses, one with olives and one without. As the instruction *Pick up the empty martini glass* unfolds, the addressee can begin to identify the referent as the martini glass without olives as soon as the words *the empty* are encountered. The definite article *the* signals that there is a uniquely identifiable referent, eliminating the set of jars as potential referents and locating the referent within the set of martini glasses, and the adjective *empty* uniquely identifies the martini glass without olives. However, consider the same instruction in combination with a display such as the top array of objects in figure 5.1, in which there are two jars, one with olives and one without, and two martini glasses, one with olives and one without. In this case, the intended referent would not be disambiguated until the word *martini* because the determiner and adjective *the empty* could refer to either the empty jar or the empty martini glass. Studies by Eberhard et al. (1995), Sedivy et al. (1998), and Chambers et al. (2002) have demonstrated that listeners assign reference incrementally, such that this type of point-of-disambiguation manipulation affects the time course of reference resolution.

For this experiment we created situations where the point of disambiguation was either early or late (e.g., *the empty* versus *martini*) and where the perspectives of the participant addressee and the confederate speaker either matched or mismatched. To create mismatching perspectives, the experimenter described the early disambiguation displays inaccurately (from A's perspective) to C. This was done by switching the modification between the two sets of objects. For example, for the instruction *Pick up the empty martini glass*, the objects were described as two empty jars, an empty martini glass, and a martini glass with olives in it, but the group really consisted of an empty jar, a jar with olives in it, and two empty martini glasses. See the bottom array of objects in figure 5.1 for the mismatching-perspective condition. In addition to

Late Disambiguation/Matching Perspective Description:
There's an empty jar, a jar with olives in it,
and an empty martini glass,
and a martini glass with olives in it.

Late/Matching Instruction:
*Pick up the empty **martini** glass and put it in area 2.*

Early Disambiguation/Matching Perspective and Mismatching
Perspective Description:
There are two empty jars,
and an empty martini glass,
and a martini glass with olives in it.

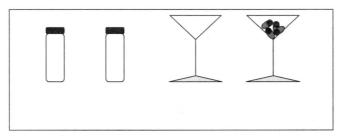

Early/Matching Instruction:
*Pick up **the empty** martini glass and put it in area 2.*

Mismatching Instruction:
Pick up the empty martini glass and put it in area 2.

Figure 5.1
Example descriptions, displays, and critical instructions for the definite late disambiguation/
matching-perspective, early disambiguation/matching-perspective, and mismatching-perspective
conditions in experiment 1. Points of disambiguation in the instructions are indicated in bold.

instructions containing definite descriptions, the experiment also contained conditions with indefinite referring expressions (e.g., *Pick up one of the empty martini glasses*) along with displays that created the same point-of-disambiguation manipulation. In the interest of space, however, only the results from the definite conditions will be addressed.

Under matching conditions, we expected to see a clear point-of-disambiguation effect. In the early disambiguation/matching-perspective condition, addressees should identify the target relatively quickly; fixations to the target set of objects (e.g., the set of martini glasses) should begin soon after the onset of the article and adjective, and there should be few looks to the competitor set of objects (e.g., the set of jars). In the late disambiguation/matching-perspective condition, it should take longer to identify the target; early fixations should be equally distributed to both the target and competitor set of objects, and looks to the target should rise reliably only after the onset of the object name. This condition is a baseline since under all circumstances the latest point at which disambiguation can occur is at the object name—that is, uniqueness conditions aside, there is always at least one object that matches the description of the intended referent.

The crucial question was what would happen when there was a mismatch between C's and A's perspectives in the context of a display that would, under matching conditions, normally provide an early point of disambiguation. Taking the speaker's perspective in these conditions requires remembering what C thinks the set of objects are like. If addressees act egocentrically, they should initially experience interference from their own perceptual perspective, which conflicts with what the speaker believes. Thus, there should be early looks to the competitor set of objects (e.g., to the single empty jar in response to the referring expression *the empty*), and a delay in the identification of the intended referent. In contrast, if addressees are able to quickly adopt the speaker's perspective when interpreting an utterance, then reference resolution should still show an advantage compared to the late disambiguation condition.

Eighteen participant addressees' eye movements were monitored using an Applied Sciences Laboratories E5000 eye tracker. A's were told, in the absence of C, that sometimes the experimenter would make a mistake during the object description, just as people sometimes do in conversation, but that they were in the condition where they could not communicate with C to fix the mistake. A's were trained to fixate a cross on the vertical divider at the beginning of each trial until C began speaking.

Examining the late disambiguation condition first, we see in figure 5.2 the proportion of time that A's were fixating on the four objects in the display: the target empty

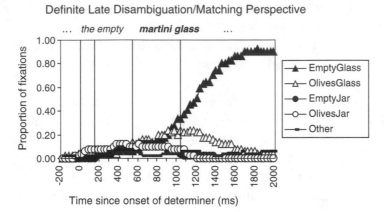

Figure 5.2

Proportion of fixations to each object type over time in the late disambiguation/matching-perspective condition, including the target (EmptyGlass), the other object in the target set (OlivesGlass), the two objects in the competitor set (EmptyJar, OlivesJar), and any other place (Other).

martini glass (EmptyGlass), the martini glass with olives in it (OlivesGlass), the empty jar (EmptyJar), and the jar with olives in it (OlivesJar). The onset of the determiner is at 0, and the light bars mark the average duration of the definite article *the*, the modifying adjective, and the object name. Statistical analyses were performed on the proportion of time spent looking at the target, either of the competitor objects, and the other object in the target set within ten 200 ms windows beginning at the onset of the determiner. Early on in the late disambiguation condition there was a rise in looks to both the martini glasses and the jars, and A's did not begin looking significantly often at the target martini glass until the 800–1,000 ms window of time after the onset of the determiner. Taking into account that it takes about 200 ms for an eye movement to be launched after it is programmed (Matin, Shao, and Boff 1993), it is clear that these eye movements to the target object were not being programmed until after the onset of the object name, which was expected.

Turning to the early disambiguation condition, recall that only the target set of martini glasses had a single empty one. In figure 5.3 we see that A's began to look at one of the martini glasses significantly earlier, within the 400–600 ms window, meaning the eye movements were programmed toward the end of the adjective. Comparing the late and early disambiguation conditions, we see the predicted point-of-disambiguation effect.

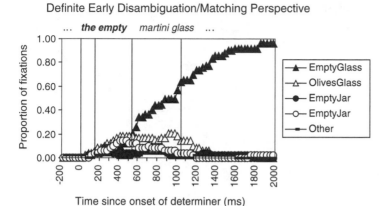

Figure 5.3

Proportion of fixations to each object type over time in the early disambiguation/matching-perspective condition, including the target (EmptyGlass), the other object in the target set (OlivesGlass), the two objects in the competitor set (EmptyJar), and any other place (Other).

Critically, figure 5.4 shows that in the mismatching-perspective condition, A's were quickly able to take into account the perspective of the speaker, even though it conflicted with their egocentric perceptual information. There was no early preference for the competitor set of objects, indicating that addressees were not confused by, for example, seeing a single empty jar in the display as they heard *the empty*. There was some cost associated with perspective taking, because this condition patterned later than the early disambiguation/matching-perspective condition. Most importantly, however, A's identified the target empty martini glass in this condition faster than in the late disambiguation condition, showing a significant rise in target fixations within the 600–800 ms window, meaning the eye movements were programmed before the object name.[1] Results for the indefinite referring-expression conditions showed the same pattern of results.

These results indicate that it is possible for addressees to quickly use a perspective other than their own to restrict reference resolution. This was the case even though they had to remember that the speaker thought the objects were different than they really were. In fact, addressees took the speaker's perspective even when it was not necessary. Examining the mismatching-perspective condition (figure 5.4), either of the two empty martini glasses could have been chosen, but we see a clear preference for the martini glass that had also been *described* as the empty one, with addressees choosing this glass 72 percent of the time. This advantage for the speaker's perspective

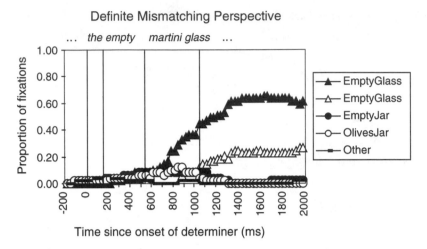

Figure 5.4

Proportion of fixations to each object type over time in the mismatching-perspective condition, including the two objects in the target set (EmptyGlass), the single empty object in the competitor set (EmptyJar), the full object in the competitor set (OlivesJar), and any other place (Other).

occurred without a bias arising from frequency or recency of mention. Perceptual information was not ignored, however; the other empty martini glass was chosen 28 percent of the time. This pattern of results argues against a strictly egocentric account, and provides evidence in favor of an account in which information from another person's perspective, a component of the information in common ground, can play an immediate role during comprehension along with other conversationally based sources of information.

Experiment 2

The goal for this experiment was to further investigate the time course with which an addressee can take into account the speaker's perspective, this time in a setting where changes in perspective arose from task-relevant goals and physical abilities (as opposed to differing beliefs about the characteristics of a display), and where we could more naturally incorporate the necessary scripted control over the speaker's utterances. Thus, in this experiment we had participants follow a recipe in a cooking simulation. A (female) confederate speaker (C) played the role of the cook who read a recipe, and participant addressees played the role of the helper (H). Since reading a recipe aloud is quite common during cooking, C's utterances could be scripted without appearing

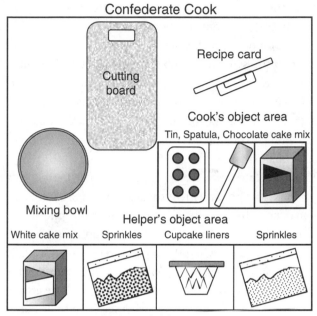

Confederate Cook

Recipe card

Cutting board

Cook's object area

Tin, Spatula, Chocolate cake mix

Mixing bowl

Helper's object area

White cake mix   Sprinkles   Cupcake liners   Sprinkles

Helper Addressee

Cook's critical instructions (Hands-empty/Hands-full)
I need to put liners in the cupcake tin.   (Finishes.)
*And could you put the **cake mix** next to the mixing bowl? /*
I need to put liners in the cupcake tin.   (Doesn't finish.)
*Oh, first could you put the **cake mix** next to the mixing bowl?*

Figure 5.5
Example display and instruction sequence for the two-objects conditions in experiment 2. In the one-object conditions the chocolate cake mix was replaced with frosting. This recipe was for cupcakes.

unnatural, and instructions could be directed to herself or to H to move and manipulate objects in a particular order.

Figure 5.5 shows a schematic of the setup and a sample instruction sequence. C and H were seated across a table from each other, and had spatially separate and easy-to-remember sets of objects that they were responsible for. H was told that most of the time he would be asked to move objects from his own area because C clearly could not reach them, but that if C was in the middle of something and had her hands full, he might be asked to move an object from C's area, which he could reach. A cutting board was present for every trial, and on most trials either a mixing bowl or a burner was also present. C had a vertical mount for the recipe cards, placed so that she could easily see them by turning her head, but so that H could not see them.

Recipes were groups of instructions for doing such things as making cupcakes, tea, or bread. The set of objects present, and the sequence of object movement and manipulation, were arbitrary so that object references were not predictable. The objects were everyday kitchenware and food items, such as bowls, measuring cups, spices, and pasta. All the objects were named by C before beginning the recipe instructions, and the critical objects were modified along either a kind or size dimension—for example, skim or 2 percent milk, or a big or small spatula.

The critical instructions to H manipulated two factors. The first was whether only one object on the table matched the critical definite referring expression, in H's object space, or whether two objects matched the definite referring expression, one in H's space and one in C's space. To create definite references that could apply equally well to either of two objects, modification was used when the objects were named initially but not in the critical referring expression. For example, in figure 5.5 there is a white cake mix in H's object area and a chocolate cake mix in C's object area, and the critical instruction referred to the *cake mix*. The second factor was whether C had her hands full when she produced the instruction. On those trials, C began but did not finish the preceding instruction, which required her to manipulate two to three objects that had already been moved, such as to put a teabag in a mug. In addition, hands-full trials began with the expression *Oh, and first could you put* (in contrast to *And could you put*) to help draw attention to the fact that C was in the middle of something.

Each stimulus item included a filler set of two objects that varied along a kind or size dimension, and references to these objects included the modifying adjective. Filler trials also contained fully specified references, and, along with two practice trials, had the cook reach for her own objects if her hands were empty. C varied noncritical instructions slightly to appear natural, and she wore mirrored sunglasses and stayed relatively still to avoid providing referential cues with her eye-gaze or body movements.

The ability of the cook to reach the various objects provides a potential referential domain restriction, one that requires the helper to take into account information from her perspective as to what objects are and are not relevant. When C's hands are empty, H should only consider objects in his own area as possible referents. If H can take C's empty hands and reaching ability into account, this restriction should persist even when there is another object that matches the referring expression in C's area, since C could reach for that object herself if that was the intended referent. Examining figure 5.5, if H's are able to restrict the domain of interpretation to their own area when C's hands are empty, there should be no interference from the chocolate cake mix when C refers to the *cake mix*, and H's should not ask which one was intended. In contrast, when C's hands are full, the domain should widen to include the objects in C's area, since C can no longer reach those objects on her own. H's should consider the chocolate cake mix at least as often as the white cake mix, perhaps asking which was meant. Importantly, this change in the domain of interpretation requires the helper addressee to both attend to and understand which objects the cook can reach moment by moment.

Twelve participant helpers' eye movements were monitored using an Applied Sciences Laboratories E5000 eye tracker. On each trial, the experimenter placed objects on the table and handed C a recipe card. C named the recipe, asked the experimenter for either the mixing bowl or the burner if necessary, and listed the objects in her own area and in H's area, looking between the recipe card and the objects to make it clear that she was becoming familiar with them. C then read aloud the recipe instructions. In the two object conditions, the target was the one in H's area when C's hands were empty, and was designated as the one in C's area when C's hands were full. If H chose the wrong object in these conditions, or asked which object was meant, C responded with the fully specified object name.

Examining the one-object conditions first, figure 5.6 presents the proportion of time that H's were fixating on the target cake mix in their own area (H-Cake), the other object in their area (H-Sprinkles), an unrelated object in C's area (C-Frosting), and the cook, in the hands-empty and hands-full conditions. The onset of the object name is at 0, and the light bars mark the average duration of the critical instruction preamble and the object name. Clearly, and not surprisingly, when there was only one object on the table that matched the referring expression, H's rapidly identified the target. Fixations to the single cake mix diverged quickly from other referents within 100 ms after the offset of the object name, meaning these eye movements were programmed during the object name. This was true regardless of whether C's hands were full or empty. The only difference is that in the hands-full condition there were frequent looks to C and C's area during the preamble, indicating that H's were anticipating that C might need help with something in her area.

In contrast, when the cook's hands were full and there was an additional object in C's area (C-Cake) that matched the referring expression (figure 5.7, bottom graph), H's expanded the domain of reference to include C's objects, and were equally likely to look at both object areas. There was an initial bias toward C's area, presumably because attention was focused on C, but in this condition the chocolate cake mix clearly competed with the white cake mix during reference resolution. Critically, the cake mix in C's area did not compete to this degree when C's hands were empty; while there is a

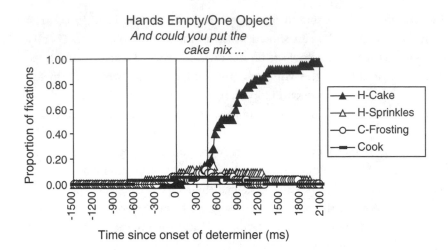

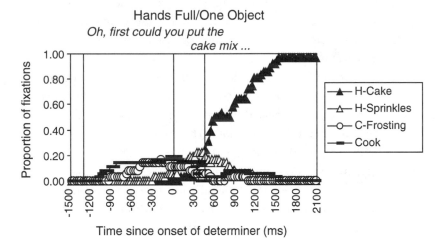

Figure 5.6
Proportion of fixations to each object type over time in the hands-empty/one-object condition (top graph) and the hands-full/one-object condition (bottom graph), including the single target object in the helper's area (H-Cake), any other object in the helper's area (H-Sprinkles), the unrelated object in the cook's area (C-Frosting), or the cook.

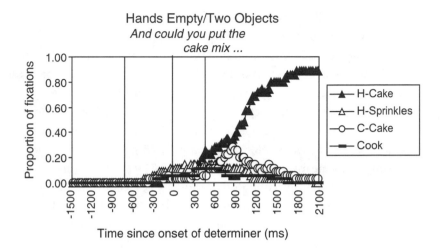

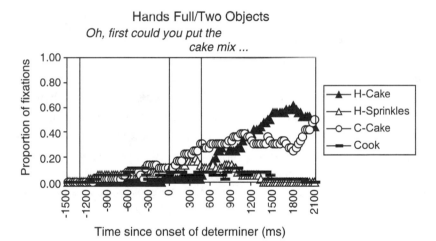

Figure 5.7
Proportion of fixations to each object type over time in the hands-empty/two-objects condition (top graph) and the hands-full/two-objects condition (bottom graph), including the target object in the helper's area (H-Cake), any other object in the helper's area (H-Sprinkles), the critical object in the cook's area (C-Cake), or the cook.

later rise in looks to C's object, H's show an immediate preference for their own object, just as quickly as they did in the one-object conditions.

Statistical analyses of the initial and total proportion of fixations on the objects in H's area and the object in C's area (these areas defined the two domains of interpretation) confirmed these observations. The percentage of initial and total looks to the objects in H's area were statistically equivalent in the one-object and hands-empty/two-objects conditions (hands-empty/one-object means = 78 percent initial, 79 percent total; hands-full/one-object means = 89 percent initial, 75 percent total; hands-empty/two-objects conditions means = 68 percent initial, 71 percent total), and were greater than the hands-full/two-objects condition (means = 45 percent initial, 56 percent total). There were also significantly more initial (mean = 36 percent) and total (mean = 41 percent) fixations on the object in the cook's area when the cook's hands were full in comparison to the other three conditions (all means ≤ 18 percent). In addition, in the hands-empty/two-objects condition H's never chose C's object, asking which one was meant 8 percent of the time and overwhelmingly choosing their own object 92 percent of the time, a percentage that differed significantly from the low 39 percent choice of their own object in the hands-full/two-objects condition.

These results show that the helper's referential domain was dynamically modified by information about the cook's abilities. When the cook's hands were empty, helpers quickly and overwhelmingly interpreted a request containing a definite noun phrase as referring to the referent in their own area, even when the perceptual environment included a second potential referent in the cook's area. Their own object was the single plausible referent given the cook's reaching ability and goals. In contrast, when the cook's hands were full, helpers considered the object in the cook's area as a potential referent. Thus, the referential domain within which the addressee's uniqueness constraints were interpreted was modulated by an awareness of the speaker's perspective, as defined by the task structure and signaled by a nonverbal cue.

Discussion

The results presented here provide insight into the dynamics of reference resolution, and contribute support for the argument that the common ground between interlocutors, including the ability to take the perspective of a speaker, has immediate, probabilistic effects on the referential domain of interpretation. We did see interference from privileged and egocentric information during reference resolution, where this information was defined by the perceptually available referents. However, we also saw that there was an immediate advantage for interpretations based on the speaker's perspective, where this information was defined by either a conflicting belief or changing physical abilities. This counters the claim that addressees initially pursue interpretations based solely on an egocentric perspective.

These results taken together with those of the study by Hanna, Tanenhaus, and Trueswell (2003) are in line with the increasing evidence for constraint-based accounts of language processing. Constraint-based models at a general level propose that alternative interpretations with some degree of likelihood are evaluated in parallel, based on the simultaneous and continuous integration of probabilistic evidence provided by multiple constraints. These constraints include discourse context and within-sentence structural and lexical biases, taking into account the frequencies and contingent (conditional) frequencies associated with words, categories, and structures (Jurafsky 1996; MacDonald 1994; Spivey-Knowlton, Trueswell, and Tanenhaus 1993; Tanenhaus and Trueswell 1995; Trueswell 1996; Taraban and McClelland 1988). From a constraint-based perspective, common ground can be thought of as another kind of contextual constraint that has immediate and probabilistic effects on interpretation.

The constraint-based view also helps reconcile the current results with the different pattern of results found by Keysar et al. (2000). Recall that in the Keysar et al. experiment, the competitor in privileged ground was a better perceptual match to the referential description than the object in common ground. Under these conditions one would expect relatively weak effects of common ground. In contrast, in our experiments the objects in privileged and common ground were equally good referential matches, or the use of a different perspective was integral to the task and the cues to the perspective differences were perceptually salient, allowing for stronger effects of context. These results are consistent with head-mounted eye-tracking findings by Arnold, Trueswell, and Lawentmann (1999) and Nadig and Sedivy (2000), who used equally good referential matches with fewer display objects and found that attentive adults and children showed early and strongly restrictive effects of common ground.

While the particular cues available in these experiments were clearly made salient by the task instructions, our finding is nonetheless of central theoretical importance for two reasons. First, it complements demonstrations that pragmatic constraints can determine whether perceptually salient entities are included in the domain relevant for computing the uniqueness conditions of definite reference (e.g., Chambers et al. 2002). It also complements studies showing that interlocutors can and do adjust their utterances to take into account addressee- and speaker-specific information (e.g., Horton and Gerrig 2002; Lockridge and Brennan 2002; Metzing and Brennan 2001, 2003). Second, and most importantly, goal-based domain restrictions, especially those signaled by relatively simple nonverbal cues, are likely to provide an important source of information that allows participants to coordinate their perspectives and to use common ground without requiring resource-demanding models of each other's mutual beliefs. Exploring the effects of this type of information, in conjunction with other constraints, will contribute fundamentally to our understanding of what constitutes common ground and how it is used during communication.

Notes

This material is based on work supported by the National Institutes of Health under National Research Service Award 1F32MH1263901A1 and grant HD-27206, and by the National Science Foundation under SBR grant 95-11340 as well as grants 0082602 and 9980013. Any opinions, findings, and conclusions or recommendations expressed in this material are those of the authors and do not necessarily reflect the views of the National Science Foundation.

We are very grateful to Ellen Hogan, Craig Chambers, and Katie Schack for all their help in running the experiments. Correspondence concerning this chapter should be addressed to Joy E. Hanna, Department of Psychology, SUNY Stony Brook, Stony Brook, NY 11794. Electronic mail may be sent to jhanna@sunysb.edu.

1. A reviewer suggested that participants in the mismatching-perspective condition might be simply adopting the linguistic precedent established by the experimenter's having (mis)labeled one of the empty martini glasses as *a martini glass with olives*. This makes the implausible prediction (see Metzing and Brennan 2003 for a study on partner effects in comprehension) that a participant would have been confused if the experimenter had asked him to give back the jar with olives, since it had been labeled *an empty jar*, or to give back one of the empty glasses, since one of them had been labeled *a martini glass with olives*. Although we did not conduct such a test, the fact that the perceptual mismatch had small but immediate effects rules out the possibility that perceptual information was being ignored in favor of a linguistic precedent.

References

Arnold, J. E., Trueswell, J. C., and Lawentmann, S. M. 1999, November. Using common ground to resolve referential ambiguity. Paper Presented at the Fortieth Annual Meeting of the Psychonomic Society, Los Angeles.

Barwise, J. 1989. *The Situation in Logic*. Stanford, CA: Center for the Study of Language and Information, Stanford University.

Brennan, S. E. 1990. Seeking and Providing Evidence for Mutual Understanding. Unpublished doctoral dissertation, Stanford University, Stanford, CA.

Brennan, S. E., and Clark, H. H. 1996. Conceptual pacts and lexical choice in conversation. *Journal of Experimental Psychology: Learning, Memory and Cognition, 22*, 482–493.

Chambers, C. G., Tanenhaus, M. K., Eberhard, K., Filip, H., and Carlson, G. 2002. Circumscribing referential domains in real-time language comprehension. *Journal of Memory and Language, 47*, 30–49.

Clark, E. V., and Clark, H. H. 1979. When nouns surface as verbs. *Language, 55,* 430–477.

Clark, H. H. 1992. *Arenas of Language Use.* Chicago: University of Chicago Press.

Clark, H. H. 1996. *Using Language.* New York: Cambridge University Press.

Clark, H. H. 1997. Dogmas of understanding. *Discourse Processes, 23,* 567–598.

Clark, H. H., and Brennan, S. E. 1989. Grounding in communication. In L. Resnick, J. Levine, and S. Teasley, eds., *Perspectives on Socially Shared Cognition.* Washington, DC: American Psychological Association.

Clark, H. H., and Haviland, S. 1977. Comprehension and the given-new contract. In R. Freedle, ed., *Explaining Linguistic Phenomena.* Washington, DC: Hemisphere Publication Corporation.

Clark, H. H., and Marshall, C. R. 1981. Definite reference and mutual knowledge. In A. H. Joshe, B. Webber, and I. A. Sag, eds., *Elements of Discourse Understanding,* 10–63. Cambridge, UK: Cambridge University Press.

Clark, H. H., and Schaefer, E. F. 1987. Collaborating on contributions to conversations. *Language and Cognitive Processes, 2(1),* 19–41.

Clark, H. H., and Wilkes-Gibbs, D. 1986. Referring as a collaborative process, *Cognition, 22,* 1–39.

Eberhard, K. M., Spivey-Knowlton, M. J., Sedivy, J. C., and Tanenhaus, M. K. 1995. Eye movements as a window into spoken language comprehension in natural contexts. *Journal of Psycholinguistic Research, 24,* 409–436.

Hanna, J. E. 2001. The Effects of Linguistic Form, Common Ground, and Perspective on Domains of Referential Interpretation. Unpublished doctoral dissertation, University of Rochester, Rochester, NY.

Hanna, J. E., Tanenhaus, M. K., and Trueswell, J. C. 2003. The effects of common ground and perspective on domains of referential interpretation. *Journal of Memory and Language, 49,* 43–61.

Hanna, J. E., Tanenhaus, M. K., Trueswell, J. C., and Novick, J. M. 1998, March. Consulting common ground during referential interpretation. Paper Presented at the Eleventh Annual CUNY Conference on Human Sentence Processing, Rutgers, NJ.

Horton, W. S., and Gerrig, R. J. 2002. Speakers' experiences and audience design: Knowing when and knowing how to adjust utterances to addressees. *Journal of Memory and Language, 47,* 589–606.

Horton, W. S., and Keysar, B. 1995. When do speakers take into account common ground? *Cognition, 59,* 91–117.

Jurafsky, D. 1996. A probabilistic model of lexical and syntactic disambiguation. *Cognitive Science, 20,* 137–194.

Keysar, B., Barr, D. J., Balin, J. A., and Brauner, J. S. 1996, November. Common ground: An error correction mechanism in comprehension. Paper Presented at the Thirty-Seventh Annual Meeting of the Psychonomic Society, Chicago.

Keysar, B., Barr, D. J., Balin, J. A., and Brauner, J. S. 2000. Taking perspective in conversation: The role of mutual knowledge in comprehension. *Psychological Science, 11(1)*, 32–37.

Keysar, B., Barr, D. J., and Horton, W. S. 1998. The egocentric basis of language use: Insights from a processing approach. *Current Directions in Psychological Science, 7*, 46–50.

Krauss, R. M., and Weinheimer, S. 1966. Concurrent feedback, confirmation, and the encoding of referents in verbal communication. *Journal of Personality and Social Psychology, 4*, 343–346.

Lockridge, C. B., and Brennan, S. E. 2002. When do speakers adjust to addressees? Effects of visual co-presence on the planning of utterances. *Psychological Bulletin and Review, 9*, 550–557.

MacDonald, M. C. 1994. Probabilistic constraints and syntactic ambiguity resolution. *Language and Cognitive Processes, 9(2)*, 157–201.

Matin, E., Shao, K. C., and Boff, K. R. 1993. Saccadic overhead: Information processing time with and without saccades. *Perception and Psychophysics, 53(4)*, 372–380.

Metzing, C. A., and Brennan, S. E. 2001. When conceptual pacts are broken: Partner effects in comprehending referring expressions. Paper Presented at the Forty-Second Annual Meeting of the Psychonomic Society, Orlando, FL.

Metzing, C. A., and Brennan, S. E. 2003. When conceptual pacts are broken: Partner effects in comprehending referring expressions. *Journal of Memory and Language, 49*, 201–213.

Nadig, A., and Sedivy, J. C. 2000, August. Finding common ground in children's referential communication. Poster Presented at the Twenty-Second Annual Conference of the Cognitive Science Society, Philadelphia.

Searle, J. R. 1969. *Speech Acts: An Essay in the Philosophy of Language.* Cambridge, UK: Cambridge University Press.

Sedivy, J. C., Tanenhaus, M. K., Chambers, C., and Carlson, G. N. 1998. Achieving incremental processing through contextual representation: Evidence from the processing of adjectives. *Cognition, 71*, 109–147.

Spivey-Knowlton, M. J., Trueswell, J. C., and Tanenhaus, M. K. 1993. Context effects in syntactic ambiguity resolution: Discourse and semantic influences in parsing reduced relative clauses. *Canadian Journal of Experimental Psychology: Special Issue, 37*, 276–309.

Tanenhaus, M. K., and Trueswell, J. C. 1995. Sentence comprehension. In J. Miller and P. Eimas, eds., *Handbook of Cognition and Perception.* San Diego, CA: Academic Press.

Taraban, R., and McClelland, J. L. 1988. Constituent attachment and thematic role assignment in sentence processing: Influences of context-based expectations. *Journal of Memory and Language, 27*, 597–632.

Trueswell, J. C. 1996. The role of lexical frequency in syntactic ambiguity resolution. *Journal of Memory and Language, 35*, 566–585.

6 Real-Time Reference Resolution by Naive Participants during a Task-Based Unscripted Conversation

Sarah Brown-Schmidt, Ellen Campana, and Michael K. Tanenhaus

In characterizing work in language performance, Clark (1992) pointed out that the field has been largely divided into two traditions. One tradition, the language-as-action tradition, emphasizes interactive conversation as the most basic form of language use. According to this tradition the principles of language performance and language design cannot be understood without taking into account the interactive collaborative processes that are embedded in conversation. A central tenet of work in this tradition is that utterances can only be understood within a particular *context*, which includes the time, place, and participants' conversation goals. Thus researchers in this tradition have focused primarily on investigations of interactive conversation using natural tasks, typically with real-world referents.

A second tradition, the language-as-product tradition, focuses primarily on the processes by which listeners decode (and speakers encode) linguistic utterances. Psycholinguistic work on language comprehension in this tradition typically examines moment-by-moment processes in real-time language processing using fine-grained reaction-time measures. The rationale for using these measures is that comprehension processes are closely time-locked to the linguistic input, which, for spoken language, unfolds over time. Until recently, the real-time response measures in the psycholinguist's toolkit required the use of decontextualized language, typically prerecorded sentences presented in impoverished contexts. This constraint ruled out real-time investigations of natural, interactive conversation. Moreover, a dominant theoretical perspective in the product tradition was that initial "core" processes (e.g., lexical access and syntactic processing) are informationally encapsulated from contextual influences (e.g., Fodor 1983).

A striking difference between work in these two traditions is the type of stimuli used. The "stimuli" in the action tradition are typically naturally produced, or embedded in a conversation. Anyone familiar with the painstaking process of transcribing a conversation knows that interactive conversation is quite different from written language.

Speakers frequently (if not usually) use incomplete sentences, interrupt one another, are disfluent (e.g., the speech contains *um*'s, *uh*'s, and extended pauses), and produce speech errors. Despite this imperfect signal, listeners often have the illusion of continuous, fluent speech.

In contrast, the "stimuli" used in the experiments of the product tradition are scripted and often abstract away from many typical properties of natural spoken utterances. The participant tends to be isolated in time and space from the speaker, and is responding to language stimuli in a noninteractive setting. Use of scripted utterances allows experimenters to manipulate the linguistic properties of primary theoretical interest, while avoiding the variability associated with spontaneous conversation, which necessarily introduces many extraneous variables that the experimenter has little control over. Implicit in the use of text and prerecorded stimuli is the assumption that the use of scripted language does not affect the way language is processed in ways that would alter theoretical conclusions about the processes under investigation.

The advent of lightweight head-mounted eye-tracking systems has made it possible to investigate real-time comprehension in more natural tasks, such as tasks where participants follow spoken instructions to manipulate objects in a task-relevant "visual world" (Tanenhaus et al. 1995; Tanenhaus and Trueswell, chapter 1, this volume). Fixations to task-relevant objects are closely time-locked to the unfolding utterance, providing a continuous real-time measure of comprehension processes at a temporal grain fine enough to track the earliest moments of lexical access, parsing, and reference resolution (Cooper 1974; Tanenhaus et al. 2000). In the present research, we have taken advantage of the fine temporal grain and relative unobtrusiveness of the eye-tracking methodology in order to apply it to a highly unconstrained experimental situation, more similar to the type used in the language-as-action tradition.

A growing body of research employing eye-tracking techniques demonstrates clear and immediate effects of contextual constraints. For example, syntactic-ambiguity resolution is influenced by referential constraints provided by the visual context, including the number of potential referents and their properties (Tanenhaus et al. 2000; Spivey et al. 2002; Tanenhaus and Trueswell, chapter 1, this volume). Moreover, work using confederates in constrained tasks suggests that under some circumstances information provided by knowledge of the speaker's perspective and intentions can affect even the earliest moments of comprehension (Hanna 2001; Hanna and Tanenhaus, chapter 5, this volume).

However, a limitation of previous work is that all of the language has been prescripted, ruling out spontaneous collaborative processes that likely influence circumscription of referential domains, and ruling out interpretation of referential expressions in natural interactive settings. Additionally, even though tasks that employ confederates are a closer approximation of natural conversation, there is reason to believe that naive participants may interact with confederates and naive speakers differently. Schober and Brennan (2003) review two different papers using the same technique, one employing a confederate (Brown and Dell 1987; Dell and Brown 1991), and one using a naive listener (Lockridge and Brennan 2001). In both studies, speakers retold stories to listeners. The comparison of central interest, as highlighted by Schober and Brennan, was whether speakers would choose to explicitly mention the instrument used in a critical action (e.g., whether speakers mentioned *knife* as the instrument when describing a "stabbing" event) when listeners could or could not see a picture of the event. Instruments were either typical (e.g., inferrible, such as knife stab) or atypical (e.g., uninferrible, such as icepick stab) for that action. While Brown and Dell only found a marginal effect for presence versus absence of the picture, Lockridge and Brennan found that naive speakers were 10 percent more likely to mention the instrument when it was atypical, and the listeners did *not* have access to a picture of the event. While these studies have a major advantage over work in which the second person is not present, it is important to note the change in results with a true listener. The fact that speakers were more sensitive to a naive listener suggests, first, that the presence of a conversational partner matters, and second, that people are sensitive to the naturalness of that person. Employing confederates or not even using a second participant may alter experimental results, as in these experiments.

A second piece of evidence comes from Clark and Wilkes-Gibbs (1986), who investigated conversational partners' use of collaborative processes to refer to low-codability shapes in a referential communication task (Krauss and Weinheimer 1966). In their study, pairs of participants worked together to arrange different abstract shapes. During the conversation they converged on shared names for the shapes, dramatically increasing the efficiency of their communication over the course of the interaction. In Brennan and Clark's (1996) words, conversational partners develop "conceptual pacts" during the course of a conversation. The mere action of participating in the development of conversational pacts facilitates the efficiency of the conversation; overhearers privy to the entirety of the conversation are unable to perform as well in these natural tasks (Schober and Clark 1989). Taken together, these results support two conclusions. First, the act of participating in a natural conversation contributes to efficient communication. Second, eliminating conversational interaction from language comprehension may remove an important component of natural-language processing.

There is also a more general methodological concern about results from experiments with scripted utterances that motivates the importance of developing complementary paradigms with unscripted language. Despite the best efforts of experimenters to avoid creating predictable contingencies between the referential world and the form of the utterances, most controlled experiments are likely to draw attention to some feature of the language being studied. Sentences or utterances of a particular type are likely to be overrepresented in the stimulus set, and the participants' attention is likely to be drawn to small differences in structure or usage that are being investigated in the experiment. Thus it would be desirable to be able to replicate results from experiments with scripted utterances using more natural unscripted utterances.

Consider, for example, a study conducted in our laboratory by Chambers and colleagues (Chambers et al. 2002). In that study, participants followed instructions such as *Pick up the cube. Now put the cube in the/a can.* On critical trials there were two cans, one of which was large and the other small. The cube was either small enough to fit inside either can or too big to fit in the smaller of the cans. Use of a definite noun phrase was confusing to participants when the cube would fit into both cans because the definite noun phrase *the can* did not uniquely identify a single referent. However, confusion was dramatically reduced when the cube would fit into only one can, demonstrating that referential domains are circumscribed on the fly, taking into account task-relevant real-world properties of objects. Crucially, the opposite pattern of results was found for instructions with indefinite articles (e.g., *a can*), providing striking evidence that listeners make immediate use of information about definiteness. The problem is that the design may have called attention to the potentially contrastive uses of *a* and *the*, causing listeners to rely more heavily on information about definiteness than they normally would.

The goal of the present study was to explore the feasibility of examining real-time comprehension processes during natural, unscripted, interactive conversation. We focused on the comprehension of definite referring expressions, such as *the red block* and *the cloud*. Definite reference is a promising domain for a first investigation for several reasons. First, definite reference is one of the most ubiquitous and central components of natural language. Second, use of definite reference assumes that a referent will be uniquely identifiable within a circumscribed referential domain. Third, much of the strongest evidence for the collaborative model of language processing comes from demonstrations that people collaborate to define referential domains. Finally, an important theoretical issue in computational models of reference resolution is whether non-discourse-based conversational goals and task constraints should be used in conjunction with discourse history to determine the saliency of potential referents, or whether saliency should be based primarily on discourse history. If the goal of these models is to approximate human-human interaction, evaluation of these two strategies will rely on our ability to assess the time course of human reference resolution in natural collaborative tasks containing clear goal structures that develop over the course of the conversation.

Work with scripted utterances has established two clear empirical results that allow one to track the time course of reference resolution: cohort (lexical competitor) effects and "point-of-disambiguation" effects. Cohort effects are observed during the course of understanding a single word. When listeners are instructed to pick up or move an object, such as a picture of a cloud, stimulus-driven fixations to the target object begin as early as 200 ms after the onset of the noun (Allopenna, Magnuson, and Tanenhaus 1998). Eye movements launched at this point in the speech stream are equally likely to be directed to the eventual referent as other objects with names that are also consistent with the speech signal, such as a clown. However, looks to these competitors, hereafter *cohort competitors*, are reduced or eliminated when context creates a referential domain that makes the cohort an implausible referent (Dahan and Tanenhaus 2002; Dahan, Tanenhaus, and Chambers 2002; Arnold, Fagnano, and Tanenhaus 2003). Thus we can use cohort effects to infer the degree to which conversation restricts initial referential domains.

The second source of evidence for rapid restriction of referential domains, point-of-disambiguation effects, can be observed during understanding of a full noun phrase. For example, Eberhard et al. (1995) presented subjects with displays containing a variety of differently colored shapes, as they listened to instructions such as *Click on the red triangle*. In a subset of trials the color of the target item was not shared with any other items in the referential domain. In these trials the referentially disambiguating information was the color, which was conveyed in the prenominal adjective. In the remaining trials, the target item was the same color as another item in the referential domain. For example, the display accompanying the instruction *Click on the red triangle* might contain a red circle and a red triangle. In these trials the referentially disambiguating information came at the noun. Eye movements to the target were again closely time-locked to the speech. Looks to the target increased dramatically immediately following the point of disambiguation, whether it came at the adjective or the noun.

In the present experiment we monitored eye movements as pairs of participants, separated by a curtain, worked together to arrange blocks in matching configurations and confirm those configurations. The characteristics of the blocks afforded comparison with findings from scripted experiments investigating language-driven eye movements, specifically those demonstrating cohort effects and point-of-disambiguation effects during reference resolution. We investigated (1) whether these effects could be

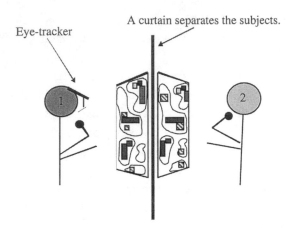

Figure 6.1

Schematic of the setup for the referential communication task. Solid colored regions represent blocks; striped regions represent stickers (which will eventually be replaced with blocks). The scene pictured is partway through the task, so some portions of the partners' boards match, while other regions are not completed yet.

observed in a more complex domain during unrestricted conversation, and (2) under what conditions the effects would be eliminated, indicating that factors outside of the speech itself might be operating to circumscribe the referential domain.

Method

We tested four pairs of undergraduates, who were paid for their participation in the study. The discourse partners each had an array of blocks and a board on which to place them. Figure 6.1 presents a schematic of the experimental setup. In order to encourage participants to divide up the workspace (e.g., the board) into smaller referential domains, we divided participants' boards into five physically distinct subareas. Initially, subareas contained fifty-six stickers representing blocks. While partners' boards were identical with respect to subareas, partners' stickers differed: where one partner had a sticker, the other had an empty spot. The participants' task was to replace each sticker with a matching block and instruct their partner to place a block in the same location in order to make their boards match. No other restrictions were placed on the interaction. The entire experiment lasted approximately 2.5 hours. For each pair we recorded the eye movements of one partner and the speech of both partners.

The fifty-six stickers (and corresponding blocks) that the subjects described were of two types. Thirty-seven of the blocks were of assorted shapes (square or rectangle) and colors (red, blue, green, yellow, white, or black). The initial configuration of the stickers was such that the color, size, and orientation of the blocks would encourage the use of complex noun phrases and grounding constructions. The remaining nineteen stickers (and corresponding blocks) contained pictures similar to those used by Allopenna and colleagues (1998), which could be easily described by naming the picture (e.g., "the candle"). Seventeen of the pictures were from a full-color version (Rossion and Pourtois 2001) of a large corpus of normed pictures, balanced for their linguistic codablilty (Snodgrass and Vanderwart 1980), and the remaining two were similar, easily nameable clip-art pictures. We selected pairs of these pictures that referred to objects with initially acoustically consistent names (cohort competitors). Half of the cohort-competitor stickers were arranged such that both cohort-competitor blocks would be placed in the same subarea of the board. The other half of the cohort-competitor stickers were arranged such that the cohort-competitor blocks would be placed in different subareas of the board. All of the cohort-competitor pairs were separated by approximately 3.5 inches.

Eye movements were monitored using an ISCAN visor-mounted system (for details see Trueswell et al. 1999). The image of the eye-tracked partner's board, and their superimposed eye position, along with the entirety of the conversation (both participants' voices), were recorded using a frame-accurate digital videorecorder (a SONY DSR-30).

Results

The conversations for each of the four pairs were transcribed, and eye movements associated with definite references to blocks were analyzed. The non-eye-tracked partner of each pair generated approximately 100–150 definite references to blocks during the course of the conversation. Fixations were analyzed from the onset of the definite reference until 2,000 ms after the end of the definite noun phrase.

Cohort Trials

Each pair generated approximately 75 references to blocks that had cohort competitors. Looks to cohorts were rare; a preliminary analysis of a subset of these references revealed that looks to cohorts and unrelated blocks were equivalent at all time windows analyzed (p's $> .6$). The absence of cohort effects cannot be attributed to poor choice of materials. Most of the items and pictures were taken from previous studies that demonstrated clear cohort competition. Moreover, we did observe cohort competition when the referential domain was not constrained by the task-related conversation. Periodically, subjects needed to remove the eye tracker to take a break. On one occasion when we put the tracker back on and recalibrated, we tested the calibration by asking the subject to look at different items on the board, using instructions like *Look at cloud, look at the lamb, look at the seal.* Here we saw clear cases of the subject initially looking at the cohort competitor (e.g., clown, lamp) before looking at the intended referent (e.g., cloud, lamb). The fifteen trials of this sort did not give us enough statistical power to replicate a standard cohort effect, but the pattern of fixations and mean differences between cohorts and targets are similar to those found in Allopenna, Magnuson, and Tanenhaus 1998.

The lack of a cohort effect during the actual task suggests that the referential domain was so tightly circumscribed that cohort competitors, which were only 3.5 inches away from the target, were not in the same referential domain. Further evidence that referential domains were restricted to small spatial regions will be presented when we examine "proximity" effects for the point-of-disambiguation manipulation. The fact that we did see looks to cohorts during less constrained instructions opens up the possibility of manipulating distance between cohort competitors to investigate how the size of the referential domain varies as a function of task and discourse.

Point-of-Disambiguation Effects

The non-eye-tracked partners generated a total of 436 definite references to colored blocks. An analysis of these definite references demonstrated that just over half (55 percent) contained a linguistic point of disambiguation, while the remaining 45 percent were technically ambiguous with respect to the subarea in which the referent was located (e.g., *the red one* uttered in a context of multiple red blocks). Two researchers coded the noun phrases for their point of disambiguation (POD), defined as the point at which the noun phrase uniquely identified a referent, given the visual context at the time. Average POD was 864 ms following the onset of the noun phrase. Eye movements elicited by noun phrases with a unique linguistic POD were analyzed separately from those that were never fully disambiguated linguistically. The eye-tracking analysis was restricted to cases where at least one competitor block was present. This left 74 linguistically disambiguated trials and 192 ambiguous trials.

Eye movements elicited by disambiguated noun phrases are pictured in figure 6.2. Before the POD, subjects showed a preference to look at the target block, but the proportion of fixations to targets rose dramatically after the POD. Separate planned comparisons were performed on 600 ms epochs for ambiguous and disambiguated noun phrases. The target bias for disambiguated noun phrases was present at all three 600 ms epochs analyzed. Significant repeated measures (rm) ANOVAs at each epoch

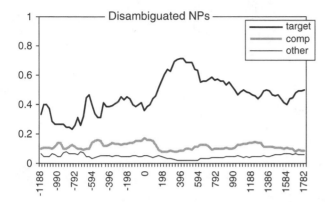

Figure 6.2
Relative proportion of fixations to targets, competitors, and other blocks by time (ms) for disambiguated noun phrases. Graph is centered by item with 0 ms = point-of-disambiguation onset.

(F's > 5.90, p's < .01) were due to a higher relative proportion of fixations to targets than competitors and unrelated blocks (p's < .0001). During a 460 ms baseline epoch, a significant rmANOVA ($F(2, 36) = 5.94$, $p < .01$) was due to increased looks to targets compared to unrelated blocks ($p < .01$) and competitors ($p = .052$). Additionally, an analysis including all four epochs revealed that participants were more likely to look at competitors than unrelated blocks ($p < .001$), but this did not interact with epoch.

Crucially, the dramatic rise in looks to targets following the POD was reliable; within 200 ms of the onset of the word in the utterance that uniquely specified the referent, looks to targets rose substantially. A rmANOVA for looks to targets revealed a significant effect of epoch ($F(3, 68) = 3.77$, $p < .05$). Bonferroni posttests revealed significantly more looks to the target in the epoch beginning 200 ms after the POD in comparison to the baseline, $p < .001$ (see figure 6.2). In contrast, looks to competitors remained the same at all four epochs ($F(3, 68) = .27$, $p = .89$). This POD effect for looks to the target is similar to that seen by Eberhard et al. (1995), demonstrating that we were successful in using a more natural task to investigate online language processing. The persistent target bias and lack of a significant increase in look to competitors are likely due to additional pragmatic constraints that we will discuss shortly.

Most remarkably, while we found clear POD effects for disambiguated noun phrases, for ambiguous utterances (see figure 6.3) fixations were primarily restricted to the referent. Thus the speaker's underspecified referential expressions did not confuse listeners, indicating that referential domains of the speaker and the listener were closely coordinated.

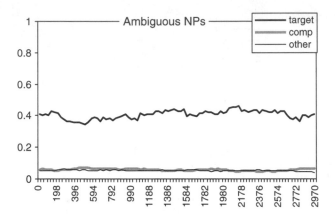

Figure 6.3
Relative proportion of fixations to targets, competitors, and other blocks by time (ms) for ambiguous noun phrases. 0 ms = noun-phrase onset.

We observed significantly more looks to targets than competitors within the first 200 ms of noun-phrase onset. The significant effect of condition ($F(2, 176) = 60.08$, $p < .0001$) was due to significant differences between target and both competitor and other blocks (p's $< .0001$). This effect persisted in the second 600 ms window. Moreover, participants were no more likely to look at competitors than at unrelated blocks ($p = .5$). The early preference for the target suggests that listeners were privy to an early cue as to the likely referent of these ambiguous noun phrases.

The eye-tracking analysis clearly suggests listeners were rarely confused by these ambiguous noun phrases. This was confirmed by examining how often the participant asked for clarification. Not surprisingly, listeners never asked for clarification about linguistically disambiguated utterances. Following ambiguous utterances, they only asked for clarification on 8 percent of the trials. Of the fifteen ambiguous references where listeners did ask for clarification, only seven were explicit questions about the ambiguous reference, whereas the remaining eight questions were vague (e.g., *what*?). Taken together, these results suggest that (1) speakers systematically use less specific utterances when the referential domain has been otherwise constrained, (2) the attentional states of speakers and addressees become closely tuned, and (3) utterances are interpreted with respect to referential domains circumscribed by contextual constraints.

Factors Determining the Specificity of the Referential Expression
To identify what factors led speakers to choose underspecified referring expressions, and enabled addressees to understand them, we performed a detailed analysis of all of

the definite references, focusing on factors that seemed likely to be influencing the generation and comprehension of referential expressions. Our general hypothesis was that speakers would choose to make a referential expression more specific when the intended referent and at least one competitor block were each salient in the relevant referential domain.

Guided by our intuitions, we focused on *recency, proximity,* and *compatibility with task constraints*. These constraints are similar to those identified by Beun and Cremers (1998) using a "construction" task in which participants, separated by a screen, worked together in a mutually copresent visual space to build a structure out of blocks. Unlike our task, in which both participants manipulated objects in their own visual space, only the "instructor" had a view of the building model, and only the "builder" had access to the blocks with which to build a replica. The instructor told the builder how to arrange the blocks to recreate the building in the mutually copresent space. In analyzing the conversation, the authors found that defining a spatial locus of attention (see also Grosz 1977; Grosz and Sidner 1986) aided interpretation of referential expressions by limiting the referential domain. As with our findings with ambiguous noun phrases, in these discourses noun phrases that would be ambiguous with respect to the entire scene, were felicitous definite noun phrases within this restricted domain. The spatial locus of attention was combined with recency and task constraints to create a linguistic focus hierarchy that best predicted the pattern of reference resolution and modification that they found.

The Beun and Cremers (1998) results were extended by Krahmer and Theune (2002) for use in a natural-language generation system (see also Dale and Reiter 1995). Krahmer and Theune's implemented model uses the proximity of potential referents to the last-mentioned referent as a metric to predict likelihood of mention. In production, this constraint can be thought of as providing the language generator with a halo of accessibilities (or activation levels) with which to make decisions about the degree of specification necessary. In comprehension, these same accessibilities provide the listener with information on how to interpret a potentially ambiguous noun phrase with respect to the visual environment.

Recency We assumed that recency would influence the saliency of a referent, with the most recently mentioned entities being more salient than other (nonfocused) entities. Thus, how recently the target block was last mentioned should predict the degree of specification, with references to the most recently mentioned block of a type, resulting in ambiguous referring expressions. For example, if *the green block* is uttered in the context of a set of ten blocks, two of which are green, recency would predict that the referent should be the green block most recently mentioned.

An example of a segment of discourse from the experiment in which recency might circumscribe the referential domain is shown below. This exchange, and other examples we will present, occurred partway through the task, so participants are familiar with the task and have developed many collaborative terms.

2.   OK. RIGHT directly next to the cloud?

1.   mm-hmm.

2.   Just throw in <u>a red piece</u>, line it up evenly.

1.   Just <u>a red</u>, little *square*.

2.   Yup.

1.   K, got it.

2.   OK.

1.   Now, I got an easy one, so I wanna *give it* to you.

2.   *OK*.

1.   Directly ... ABOVE **the red**, grab your lamp.

The first description of the target block (first underlined) is unambiguous, because there is only one red block to be placed. In contrast, the third reference to the block (bolded) is ambiguous given the visual context (there are five other red blocks in that subarea of the board). The linguistic ambiguity in this situation can be resolved by taking recency into account, unifying the referents of the three referring expressions.

Proximity   We examined the proximity of each block to the last-mentioned block, because partners seemed to adopt a strategy of focusing their conversation on small regions within each subarea. In the following segment of the discourse, we see an example where the referent of an otherwise ambiguous noun phrase is constrained by proximity:

2.   OK, so it's four down, you're gonna go over four, and then you're gonna put the piece right there.

1.   OK ... how many spaces do you have between this green piece and <u>the one to the left of it, vertically up</u>?

As before, the referring expression (underlined) is ambiguous given the visual context; there are approximately three green blocks up and to the left of the previously focused block (the one referred to as *this green piece*). In this case the listener does not have difficulty dealing with the ambiguity because she considers only the block closest to the last-mentioned block.

Task Compatibility   Task compatibility refers to constraints on block placement due to the size and shape of the board, as well as the idiosyncratic systems that partners used to complete the task. In the following exchange, compatibility circumscribes the referential domain as the participants work to agree where the clown block should be placed:

1.   OK, you're gonna line it up ... it's gonna go ⟨pause⟩ one row ABOVE the green one, directly next to it.

2.   Can't fit it.

1.   Cardboard?

2.   Can't yup, cardboard.

1.   Well, tell it too bad.

2.   The only way I can do it is if I move, all right, should the green piece with the clown be directly lined up with thuuh square?

Again, the referring expression (underlined) is ambiguous given the visual context. While the general task is to make their boards match, the current subtask is to place the clown piece (which they call *the green piece with the clown*). To complete this subtask, speaker 2 asks whether the clown should be lined up with the target, *thuuh square*. The listener does not have difficulty dealing with this ambiguous reference because, although there are a number of blocks one could line up with *the green piece with the clown*, only one is task relevant. Given the location of all the blocks in the relevant subarea, the target block is the easiest block to line up with the clown. The competitor blocks are inaccessible because of the position of the other blocks or the design of the board.

For all ambiguous and disambiguated trials, each colored block in the relevant subarea was coded for recency (number of turns since last mention), proximity (ranked proximity to last mentioned item), and task constraints (whether the task predicted a reference to that block). Targets consistently showed an advantage for all three constraints, establishing their validity (see figure 6.4; for all three constraints, low scores = larger advantage).

Planned comparisons revealed that target blocks were more recently mentioned and more proximal than competitor blocks; additionally, target blocks best fit the task constraints (p's < .001). However, neither recency, proximity, nor task compatibility

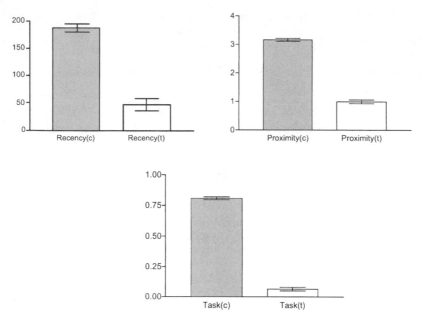

Figure 6.4

Ratings of recency, task and proximity constraints for competitor (c) versus target (t) blocks (ambiguous and disambiguated trials are grouped together). For all three constraints, lower scores indicate higher accessibility. Error bars indicate standard error of the mean.

of target blocks predicted speaker ambiguity. Instead, the relative degree to which *competitor* blocks were predicted by *proximity* and *task compatibility* predicted speaker ambiguity; the more that competitor blocks that were predicted (e.g., the more competitive), the more likely speakers were to disambiguate. Surprisingly, recency of competitors was equivalent for ambiguous and disambiguated utterances ($t(190) = -.585$, $p > .5$), suggesting that recency of competitors does *not* play a role in speakers' choice of specificity of the referring form. A logistic regression model supported these observations: noun-phrase ambiguity was significantly predicted by a model that included recency, task, and proximity effects (-2 log likelihood $= 835.2$, $\chi^2(G) = 46.31$, $p < .001$). However, the contributions of the constraints to the model were not equivalent: task and proximity both contributed significantly to the model (p's $< .05$), whereas recency did not ($p = .83$). A second model with only recency as a predictor was not significant (-2 log likelihood $= 878.81$, $\chi^2(G) = 2.71$, $p = .1$), whereas a third model containing only task and proximity was (-2 log likelihood $= 835.25$, $\chi^2(G) = 46.27$, $p = < .001$).

Discussion

Our results demonstrate that it is possible to study real-time language processing in a complex domain during unrestricted conversation. In particular, we show that when a linguistic expression is temporarily ambiguous between two or more potential referents, reference resolution is closely time-locked to the word in the utterance that disambiguates the referent. This result replicates effects found in controlled experiments with less complex displays and prescripted utterances (Eberhard et al. 1995; Sedivy et al. 1999; Chambers et al. 2002). Thus it contributes to the growing literature that referential domains are dynamically circumscribed during language comprehension, and demonstrates that these results scale up to less constrained situations. Most importantly, our results provide a striking demonstration that participants in a task-based or "practical dialogue" (Allen et al. 2001) closely coordinate their referential domains as the conversation develops, as hypothesized by Clark and his colleagues (e.g., Clark 1996). Evidence comes from the fact that speakers often generated utterances whose referents would be ambiguous if one took into account only the local visual context and the utterance. However, the speaker's choice of referential description was not random. Speakers were more likely to choose a more specific referential expression when both the referent and a competitor were salient in the immediate task-relevant environment (saliency of competitors was predicted by task and proximity constraints). When only the referent was salient, speakers were less likely to add additional modification. While recency is an important component of models of reference, recency of competitors did not predict speaker ambiguity. This may be due to the fact that the dialogues were highly structured by the task. Modifying the analysis by taking into account task-defined discourse segments may improve the predictiveness of this constraint.

Clearly, speakers chose referential expressions with respect to a circumscribed task-relevant referential domain. This by itself makes sense and is unremarkable, though the degree of ambiguity is perhaps surprising. What *is* remarkable is that the eye movements and the small number of clarification requests demonstrated that listeners were rarely even temporarily confused by underspecified referential expressions. This demonstrates that the participants in the conversation had developed closely matching referential domains, suggesting that referential domains become closely aligned as proposed by Pickering and Garrod (forthcoming). Moreover, reference resolution appeared to be affected by collaborative constraints that developed during the conversation. Our participants spontaneously created collaborative terms for troublesome words (such as *horizontal* and *vertical*), and tuned their utterances and comprehension systems for such details as the recency of mention of each particular kind of block, proximity of blocks to one another, and task constraints idiosyncratic to our block game. These observations suggest that the attentional states of the speaker and listener become closely tuned during the course of interaction.

Three important topics for future research include investigating how this tuning develops over the course of a conversation, exploring the use of pronominals in the discourse, and examining how the factors that we identified (recency, task constraints, and proximity) differentially affect speakers and addressees. One cautionary note is that the functional properties of the proximity constraint are likely to vary with respect to the task. Our task, the Beun and Cremers task, and Krahmer and Theune's generation system are similar in that they are all concerned with object reference in a construction-type domain. The notion of proximity we developed (namely, a reference at time $t + 1$ is likely to refer to a referent that is physically close to the referent at time t) is likely to be reinforced by two properties of construction domains. First, construction of structures or patterns on a board, is likely to be completed most efficiently by starting in one area, and then proceeding to adjacent areas. This bias (which we need to verify) would tend to cause speakers to refer to objects close to the last referent, and also within the spatial focus of attention. Whether the proximity constraint is due to these task-based factors, or to a more general spatial focus of attention, is a question we would like to address in the future.

Second, our domain is largely visual, and thus, the dimension within which focus of attention is defined (or most explanatory) is likely to be the visual domain. One could imagine that in other task arenas—dimensions such as similarity of function, size, and object type—would be more useful in defining the attentional space. A multidimensional saliency map, probabilistically combining proximity and task-based information, may allow for a successful extension of our findings to other domains. A final observation is that while spatial locus of attention was a useful predictor of speaker ambiguity, we did find that speakers often modified noun phrases by using references to past actions and proprietary issues (such as which block belongs to whom), which are clearly not part of the visual domain at the time of reference. This observation adds to our interest in exploring other types of constraints that operate to constrain reference.

Conclusion

To summarize, we successfully replicated a standard psycholinguistic effect, the POD effect, in unscripted interactive conversation with naive participants. We also obtained results suggesting that reference selection and comprehension are modulated by discourse-based factors, such as recency, and by task-specific pragmatic constraints. This result is important because it suggests that discourse-based reference resolution strategies that ignore task constraints are unlikely to be successful. Although discourse history is clearly important for reference resolution, non-utterance-based constraints appear to influence the earliest moments of reference resolution. This has important implications for computational models of reference resolution.

To our knowledge, this is the first demonstration of online circumscription of referential domains in a natural interactive task with naive participants. Our experiment demonstrates the feasibility of rigorously analyzing the online processing of interactive conversation "in the wild." As we continue to develop more explicit models of online language processing, a critical part of this process should be to inform these models with observations made in natural situations. We believe that pairing methodologically rigorous laboratory studies with naturalistic studies is essential for a more complete understanding of the mechanisms underlying language processing.

Note

This research was partially supported by NIH grant HD 27206. Thanks to Jesseca Aqui, Anne Tanenhaus, Theresa Pucci, and Sanjukta Sanyal for help transcribing and coding data, and to Joy Hanna for helpful comments on the manuscript.

References

Allen, J. F., Byron, D. K., Dzikovska, M., Ferguson, G., Galescu, L., and Stent, A. 2001. Towards conversational human-computer interaction. *AI Magazine, 22*, 27–35.

Allopenna, P. D., Magnuson, J. S., and Tanenhaus, M. K. 1998. Tracking the time course of spoken word recognition: Evidence for continuous mapping models. *Journal of Memory and Language, 38*, 419–439.

Arnold, J. E., Fagnano, M., and Tanenhaus, M. K. Disfluencies signal theee, um, new information. *Journal of Psycholinguistic Research, 32(1)*, 25–36.

Beun, R.-J., and Cremers, A. H. M. 1998. Object reference in a shared domain of conversation. *Pragmatics and Cognition, 6(1/2)*, 121–152.

Brennan, S., and Clark, H. 1996. Conceptual pacts and lexical choice in conversation. *Journal of Experimental Psychology: LMC, 22*, 482–493.

Brown, P. M., and Dell, G. S. 1987. Adapting production to comprehension: The explicit mention of instruments. *Cognitive Psychology, 19*, 441–472.

Chambers, C. G., Tanenhaus, M. K., Eberhard, K. M., Filip, H., and Carlson, G. N. 2002. Circumscribing referential domainsin real-time sentence comprehension. *Journal of Memory and Language*, *47*, 30–49.

Clark, H. H. 1992. *Arenas of Language Use*. Chicago: University of Chicago Press.

Clark, H. H., and Wilkes-Gibbs, D. 1986. Referring as a collaborative process. *Cognition*, *22*, 1–39.

Clark, H. H. 1996. *Using Language*. Cambridge: Cambridge University Press.

Cooper, R. M. 1974. The control of eye fixation by the meaning of spoken language: A new methodology for the real-time investigation of speech perception, memory, and language processing. *Cognitive Psychology*, *6*, 84–107.

Dahan, D., and Tanenhaus, M. K. 2002. Continuous integration of phonetic and semantic constraints on spoken-word recognition: Evidence from eye movements. Unpublished manuscript.

Dahan, D., Tanenhaus, M. K., and Chambers, C. G. 2002. Accent and reference resolution in spoken language comprehension. *Journal of Memory and Language*, *47*, 292–314.

Dale, R., and Reiter, E. 1995. Computational interpretations of the Gricean maxims in the generation of referring expressions. *Cognitive Science*, *19*, 233–263.

Dell, G. S., and Brown, P. M. 1991. Mechanisms for listener-adaptation in language production: Limiting the role of the "model of the listener." In D. J. Napoli and J. A. Kegl, eds., *Bridges between Psychology and Linguistics: A Swarthmore Festschrift for Lila Gleitman*, 105–129. Hillsdale, NJ: Erlbaum.

Eberhard, K. M., Spivey-Knowlton, M. J., Sedivy, J. C., and Tanenhaus, M. K. 1995. Eye-movements as a window into spoken language comprehension in natural contexts. *Journal of Psycholinguistic Research*, *24*, 409–436.

Fodor, J. A. 1983. *Modularity of Mind*. Cambridge, MA: Bradford Books.

Grosz, B. J. 1977. The representation and use of focus in a system for understanding dialogs. In *Proceedings of the Fifth International Joint Conference on Artificial Intelligence*, 67–76. Cambridge, MA.

Grosz, B. J., and Sidner, C. L. 1986. Attention, intentions, and the structure of discourse. *Computational Linguistics*, *12(3)*, 175–204.

Hanna, J. 2001. The Effects of Linguistic Form, Common Ground, and Perspective on Domains of Referential Interpretation. Unpublished doctoral dissertation, University of Rochester.

Krahmer, E., and Theune, M. 2002. Efficient context-sensitive generation of referring expressions. In K. van Deemter and R. Kibble, eds., *Information Sharing: Reference and Presupposition in Language Generation and Interpretation*, 223–264. Stanford, CA: CSLI Publications.

Krauss, R. M., and Weinheimer, S. 1966. Concurrent feedback, confirmation, and the encoding of referents in verbal communication. *Journal of Personality and Social Psychology*, *4*, 343–346.

Lockridge, C. B., and Brennan, S. E. 2001. Addressees' needs affect speakers' syntactic choices. Paper Presented at the Eleventh Annual Meeting of the Society for Text and Discourse, UC Santa Barbara.

Pickering, M., and Garrod, S. (Forthcoming). Toward a mechanistic psychology of dialogue. *Behavioral Brain Sciences*.

Rossion, B., and Pourtois, G. 2001. Revisiting Snodgrass and Vanderwart's object database: Color and texture improve object recognition. Paper Presented at the First Vision Conference, Sarasota, FL.

Schober, M. F., and Brennan, S. E. 2003. Processes of interactive spoken discourse: The role of the partner. In A. C. Graesser and M. A. Gernsbacher, eds., *Handbook of Discourse Processes*. Mahwah, NJ: Erlbaum.

Schober, M. F., and Clark, H. H. 1989. Understanding by addressees and overhearers. *Cognitive Psychology, 21*, 211–232.

Sedivy, J. C., Tanenhaus, M. K., Chambers, C., and Carlson, G. N. 1999. Achieving incremental semantic interpretation through contextual representation. *Cognition, 71*, 109–147.

Snodgrass, J. G., and Vanderwart, M. 1980. *Journal of Experimental Psychology: Human Learning and Memory, 6(3)*, 174–215.

Spivey, M. J., Tanenhaus, M. K., Eberhard, K. M., and Sedivy, J. C. 2002. Eye movements and spoken language comprehension: Effects of visual context on syntactic ambiguity resolution. *Cognitive Psychology, 45(4)*, 447–481.

Tanenhaus, M. K., Magnuson, J. S., Dahan, D., and Chambers, C. G. 2000. Eye movements and lexical access in spoken language comprehension: Evaluating a linking hypothesis between fixations and linguistic processing. *Journal of Psycholinguistic Research, 29*, 557–580.

Tanenhaus, M. K., Spivey-Knowlton, M. J., Eberhard, K. M., and Sedivy, J. E. 1995. Integration of visual and linguistic information in spoken language comprehension. *Science, 268*, 632–634.

Trueswell, J. C., Sekerina, I., Hill, N., and Logrip, M. 1999. The kindergarten-path effect: Studying on-line sentence processing in young children. *Cognition, 73*, 89–134.

7 Referential Form, Word Duration, and Modeling the Listener in Spoken Dialogue

Ellen Gurman Bard and Matthew P. Aylett

Speakers are said to design their utterances to suit the needs of their listeners, insofar as those needs can be known (Ariel 1990; Clark and Marshall 1981; Gundel, Hedberg, and Zacharski 1993; Lindblom 1990). Certainly, there is variation in form. Clarity of pronunciation varies with predictability from local context (Hunnicutt 1985; Lieberman 1963) and with repeated mention (Fowler and Housum 1987). Referential forms are syntactically simpler the more readily interpreted or "accessible" their antecedents are (*a blacksmith's cottage* versus *it*) (Ariel 1990; Fowler, Levy, and Brown 1997; Gundel et al. 1993; Vonk, Hustinx, and Simmons 1992), and they appear to be adjusted for the history of a dialogue with a particular addressee (Brennan and Clark 1996; Isaacs and Clark 1987). There is some doubt, however, that these differences in form should always be taken as evidence for tailoring.

Even with texts in front of them, normal adults show limitations in their ability to draw inferences (Estevez and Calvo 2000; McKoon and Ratcliff 1992; Singer and Ritchot 1996) or even to find referents for anaphors (Garrod, Freudenthal, and Boyle 1993; Levine, Guzman, and Klin 2000). Tracking a listener's knowledge as a spoken conversation unfolds should be more demanding than reading texts. It would seem to entail maintaining an incrementally updated model of what the listener knows, what is established as common ground between speaker and hearer, and what the listener needs to know, while at the same time planning and producing coherent speech. Tracking the listener's knowledge is not just a matter of brute-force memory but of intricate strings of inferences. Clark and Marshall (1981) have pointed out that since it may be impossible to assess the listener's knowledge accurately, speakers can make use of the fact that their own knowledge usually overlaps with the listener's: speakers may default to an account of their own knowledge as a proxy for the listener's. In fact, many studies simply assume that the two are the same, for they manipulate the speaker's knowledge without independently manipulating the listener's (see Keysar 1997).

Recently, studies of interpretation of referring expressions have used online techniques of some delicacy to determine how far listeners take the interlocutors' perspective into account in finding referents for expressions that do not refer uniquely to an item in the common ground (Hanna, Tanenhaus, and Trueswell 2003; Hanna and Tanenhaus, chapter 5 this volume; Keysar et al. 2000) or that, as labels, have a history of use by a particular interlocutor (Barr and Keysar 2002). The question in each case is whether perspectives of interlocutors are instantaneously effective in limiting the listeners' candidate referents or whether later processes sort the conversationally likely from the unlikely interpretations. In no case is exclusion from common ground effective in eliminating a potential referent or object label, though in some cases the experimental manipulations induce the listeners to favor the shared alternative quickly. In all these studies, however, the subjects were not full participants in dialogue in the sense that they made few, if any, contributions of their own.

In contrast, this chapter addresses the question of how fully participatory speakers might manage the cognitive burdens involved in listener modeling. To do this, we compare two instantiations of the hypothesis that referring expressions are genuinely tailored to their addressee. One deals with the articulation of individual words, the other with the syntactic form of referring expressions.

We distinguish the two potential means of tailoring, because under current models of language production, noun-phrase structure and articulation are generated within units of different sizes, intonational or syntactic phrases on the one hand and phonological words, lexical words, or syllables on the other (Levelt and Wheeldon 1994; Smith and Wheeldon 1999; Wheeldon and Lahiri 1997). Moreover, speech appears to be produced in a cascade, with a sequence of smaller units being prepared for articulation even as the succeeding larger unit is being designed. Figure 7.1 illustrates this model. Time runs from left to right, whereas planning operates from the top to the bottom of the diagram.

To adjust referential expressions appropriately, the speaker must consult a listener model at least once per intonational phrase (e.g., as seen in the middle layer of figure 7.1) to permit correct tailoring of the syntactic form of any references in the phrase. The speaker must then update the listener model incrementally with a record of the referring expressions in the phrase so as to gauge the appropriate format for the expressions in the next phrase. Assuming that even the largest of the wordlike units, the phonological word (seen in the lowest level of figure 7.1), is the site for important stages in the planning of articulation, tailoring articulation to the listener's needs would be a faster-cycling process imposing a much heavier computational burden on

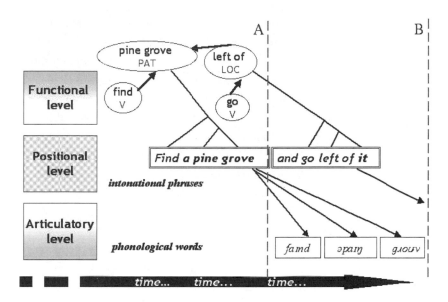

Figure 7.1
Levels and units in a cascaded model of language production.

the speaker, who must update and consult the listener model much more often. Moreover, the cascading quality of this model imposes an even more demanding task. Before time A in figure 7.1, the form of the referring expression (*a pine grove*) is set at the positional level within the intonational phrase *Find a pine grove*. The form chosen is suitable for discourse-New entities. Between times A and B, the appropriate articulation for the phonological words corresponding to *a pine* and *grove* is planned sequentially and presumably in a way that also indicates a New entity. At the same time, however, the speaker is planning the syntactic form of the later coreferential noun phrase *it*, a very reduced expression suitable for a Given entity. Insofar as the two layers of planning overlap temporally, the listener model would have to operate both in the state appropriate to the word being produced and in the state appropriate to the phrase being designed. Thus, the entity is simultaneously both New and Given. In the light of natural uncertainty about what the addressee has noticed or understood, the model makes very heavy demands on the speaker, who must monitor and update these two different knowledge states simultaneously while continuing to formulate later parts of the message (top level of figure 7.1) and to utter the early phases. Yet such demands appear to follow if listener modeling is intercalated with the online production of speech.

There are a number of proposals in the literature for how speakers manage the tasks involved in modeling listeners while planning and producing speech. We will first develop these existing hypotheses. Then we will report four studies that test these hypotheses on materials from a single corpus. They follow the comparisons that Bard et al. (2000) made for a balanced sample of excised spoken words, using a psychological measure of clarity, the recognition rate, or intelligibility to naive listeners. The present chapter, in contrast, reports a phonetic measure of clarity, word duration, and a syntactic measure of referential form for all suitable cases in the identical corpus. Finally, we will discuss the implications of our studies for the notion of listener modeling within a model of language production.

Modeling Listeners While Speaking

Existing accounts of tailoring to listeners' needs appear to make different computational demands on speakers. Some of these accounts do not originate within the language-production framework. Some are intended to explain the forms produced rather than the cognitive load assumed by speakers in online processing. Hence, we will have to interpret the implications of those models for processes perhaps not considered by their authors. We will attempt conservative interpretations.

One well-known account of tailoring, Lindblom's *H-and-H hypothesis* (1990), makes the heaviest computational demands. To explain the variability of pronunciations given to the same words by the same speakers, it posits that speakers adjust the articulation of spoken words incrementally to the knowledge that the listener can currently recruit to the task of decoding the speech signal. Thus, speakers should hyperarticulate when listeners lack such auxiliary information and hypoarticulate when redundancy is high. More redundant linguistic environments do contain word tokens articulated with greater speed and less precision (Bard and Anderson 1983, 1994; Fowler and Housum 1987; Hunnicutt 1985; Lieberman 1963; Samuel and Troicki 1998). The question is whether this relationship depends on the speaker's consulting an up-to-date model of the listener's current knowledge each time she or he prepares the prosodic character of a phonological word or the articulation of its syllables. H-and-H does not preclude defaulting to the speaker's own knowledge, which, as we have noted, can be a convenient proxy for the listener's. Nonetheless, the hypothesis is framed in terms of genuine listener knowledge and so implies that the speaker should observe the listener continuously for signs of misunderstanding or disagreement. Wherever the speaker's and listener's knowledge differ, the latter should take precedence.

In contrast, Brown and Dell (1987) propose a modular division between the initial formulation of utterances and the revision of any output that does not adequately convey the intended concepts. The listener's knowledge is implicated only in revision (Dell and Brown 1991, 119–120; see also Carletta and Mellish 1996), though some revision can take place in the course of framing an utterance. Called the monitor-and-adjust hypothesis (Horton and Keysar 1996), this model defaults to speaker knowledge first and pays later—if necessary. As originally formulated, monitor-and-adjust does not explain how the hitherto speaker-driven processes assess the adequacy of an utterance from the listener's point of view. We assume, however, that during a dialogue, each interlocutor's knowledge will include some record of what the other has actually said. Listeners' occasional explicit feedback, properly interpreted, could constitute a minimal listener model. This feedback could therefore influence a modular system that revises inadequate utterances. Under what we should in fairness call the *extended monitor-and-adjust hypothesis*, postfeedback utterances could reflect any listener knowledge that the feedback has conveyed. Otherwise, listener knowledge should be irrelevant to production at any level.

The third proposal deals with copresence, characteristics of listeners that affect the likely overlap with speakers' own knowledge (Brennan and Clark 1996; Fussell and Krauss 1992; Isaacs and Clark 1987; Schober 1993). The manifestations of copresence in the dialogue literature are many, but the notion was originally directed at reducing the computation a speaker must perform to determine the unknown component of mutual knowledge—that is, what the listener knows. As kinds of copresence, Clark and Marshall (1981) list shared community membership, the physical copresence of the interlocutors and the objects under discussion, and knowledge both of the dialogue and of real-world scenarios. Since much of copresence is long lasting, it can reduce both the depth and the frequency of listener modeling. To exploit these economies, however, speakers should attend to evidence for and against copresence, and they should maintain copresence defaults for some time after positive evidence. We will call this the *copresence default hypothesis*.

Finally, Bard et al. (2000) develop a suggestion of Brown and Dell (1987), which we will call the *dual-process hypothesis*. It proposes a division between fast, automatic processes, which have no computational cost, and slower, more costly processes requiring inference or attention. The former include priming (see Balota, Boland, and Shields 1989; Mitchell and Brown 1988), the change in the likelihood or speed of a response as a result of the responder's own recent experience. Pertinent experience includes the kind of complex reasoning usually implicated in constructing a model of the listener.

An essential feature of this view is that listener modeling competes for cognitive resources with the activities that support planning a dialogue or tracking a shared task. When there is competition for time and attention (Horton and Keysar 1996), inferential processes may suffer, leaving the speaker with only cost-free defaults in the form of his or her own knowledge. Thus the dual-process hypothesis assumes that listener modeling is not obligatory and that if it takes place anywhere, it will affect the slower-cycling positional level rather than the faster-cycling articulatory level.

Studies of Referring Expressions

Givenness and Referring Expressions

Nothing in the hypotheses above limits their application to referring expressions. We have examined repeated mentions of landmark names, largely because there is a well-developed literature on referring expressions and the status of their referents and because it is relatively easy to arrange for interlocutors to have different knowledge about potential referents. We examine two correlates of Given status broadly defined. First, spoken words making the first mention of an entity in a discourse are longer and clearer than those in repeated mentions (Fowler and Housum 1987), but only when the two tokens are coreferential (Bard, Lowe, and Altmann 1989; Fowler 1988). In effect, the first mentions are introductions of New entities and the second coreferential tokens are mentions of the same entities at a point where they are Given. Initial mentions of items uttered without visible referents (Prince's (1981) "brand new") are also longer and clearer than those with visible referents (Prince's "situationally" Given) (Bard and Anderson 1994). Second, referring expressions simplify with repeated mention (*a blacksmith's cottage.... it*) as their antecedents become more accessible (Ariel 1990; Gundel, Hedberg, and Zacharski 1993). To compare the two systems, we used a single coded corpus of spontaneous speech whose design provided items that were Given to one or both interlocutors on the basis of what each saw, said, or heard in the dialogue.

Method

Materials   All materials came from the HCRC Map Task Corpus (Anderson et al. 1991), 128 unscripted dialogues in which pairs of Glasgow University undergraduates ($N = 64$) communicated routes defined by labeled cartoon landmarks on schematic maps of imaginary locations. Though one player, on whose map the route was pre-printed, was designated the Instruction Giver and the other the Instruction Follower, no restriction was placed on what either could say. The Giver and Follower maps for any dialogue matched only in alternate landmarks, with other landmarks mismatched in a variety of ways. Participants knew that their maps might differ but not where or how. Players could not see each other's maps. Familiarity of participants and ability to see the interlocutor's face were counterbalanced. Each participant served as Instruction Giver for the same route to two different Followers and as Instruction Follower for two different routes. At the end of their map session, participants read a list of landmark names that serve as control tokens. The majority were longer than the running speech tokens by the same speakers.

Channel-per-speaker stereo digital recordings were word-segmented. All words of any expression referring to a landmark were coded for the landmark. The entire corpus was tagged for part of speech, parsed (McKelvie 1998), and coded for disfluency (Lickley 2001). Interrupted or disfluent items were excluded from the present studies. All remaining expressions making repeated reference to a landmark and meeting the design criteria were used. Duration was measured only if both mentions included the same words. All repeated mentions were assessed for syntactic form.

Dependent Variables

K-reduction   Normalized duration (Campbell and Isard 1991) assigns each word token a standardized value, here called *k*, representing its position in the expected log length distribution for words of its dictionary phoneme composition and stress pattern. *K*-reduction is the difference between the *k*-lengths of the read control form and of the corresponding item as uttered by the same speaker in running speech. Faster articulation with repeated mention would enhance *k*-reduction.

Form of Referring Expression   The twenty-seven items with relative clauses in their first mentions were excluded because of a conflict in coding schemes. All other first and second mentions of landmarks ($N = 1,136$) were classed on the scale displayed in table 7.1, where 0 indicates least simplified/accessible. Simplification of form with repeated mention should make accessibility scores rise.

Experiment 1: Inferable Listener Knowledge

Design   Experiment 1 used only first encounters with particular maps and compared repeated mentions of landmarks appearing on both players' maps under two conditions: self-repetition and other-repetition. The key to the design is the fact that a

Table 7.1
Simplification or accessibility scale for referring expressions

Code	Definition	Example
0	$\left.\begin{array}{l}\text{numeral}\\\text{indef art}\end{array}\right\}$ + noun sequence	*one mountain* *a mountain*
1	$\left.\begin{array}{l}\text{def art}\\\text{poss}\end{array}\right\}$ + nominal	*the mountain* *my one*
2	possess pro deictic pro deictic adj + nominal	*mine* *that* *this mountain*
3	other pro	*it*

speaker who first mentions a landmark must have it on his or her own map, for there is no other way to know that these imaginary objects exist. Thus, in an other-repetition the repeater can easily infer that the introducer can see the landmark. The second token, therefore, refers to an object that is Given both to the repeater, who has just heard it mentioned and can see it, and to the current listener, who has also heard it mentioned, who can see it, and who has mentioned it before. In self-repetitions, however, the repeater introduced the landmark, and, therefore, cannot be sure that the listener has the same landmark on his or her map. In this case, the repeater can see the landmark, has heard it mentioned, and can see it on his or her map. The listener to whom the repetition is addressed can be assumed to have heard it mentioned, but has not mentioned it and cannot be assumed to have it in view. Thus, the design contrasts a case where the listener can easily be concluded to have more knowledge of the referent with a case where the listener's knowledge is in doubt. The inference about shared visual resource is both simple and important to the task. Since visibility can affect clarity of mention (Bard and Anderson 1994), tailoring to the listener here should enhance change across mentions where the listener has more information: more *k*-reduction and greater simplification of expression should be found for other-repetitions than for self-repetition.

The listener-modeling hypotheses discussed earlier make a variety of predictions for this study. H-and-H makes the most straightforward prediction—that articulation at least will be sensitive to the listener's needs. Copresence should also predict effects of what the listener can see, but predicts no difference between articulation and referential form. Extended monitor-and-adjust makes no special prediction because it supposes that speakers are not obliged to model listeners continuously to conduct dia-

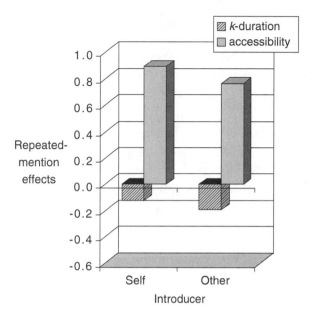

Figure 7.2
Effects of inferred knowledge: changes in articulation (additional loss of *k*-duration) and referential form (accessibility code) in self-repetitions (less listener knowledge) and other-repetitions (more listener knowledge).

logues. Dual process predicts instead that any effect will be found in referential form, which is designed over intervals long enough to allow for completing the necessary inference.

Results   For articulation, the *k*-duration of each word token in relevant landmark names was compared to the *k*-duration of the corresponding citation form as read by the same speaker. The difference can be thought of as the degradation of articulation with use of a word in running speech. Statistics performed on degradation or on *k*-durations themselves give the same results here. Figure 7.2 shows repetition effects in terms of differences between the degradation of first and second tokens. Because second tokens are even shorter than first, these numbers are negative.

For referential form, a code (on the 0-to-3 scale described in table 7.1) was given to each referring expression. Because accessibility rises with repetition, the code for the first mention was subtracted from the code for the second, giving positive repetition effects.

As in Bard et al. 2000, repetition effects here were robust. Words were said faster on repeated mention ($F_2(1,691) = 63.75$, $p < .0001$) and referential form simplified with repeated mention ($F_2(1,269) = 177.12$, $p < .0001$). These main effects are represented in figure 7.2 as differences from 0. Critically, however, there was no effect of the listener's inferable knowledge. There was no significant difference in temporal reduction between the 263 other-repetitions and the 430 self-repetitions (mention × prior speaker: n.s.). Nor was there any significant difference between the referential form changes in the 90 other-repetitions and those in the 430 self-repetitions (mention × prior speaker: n.s.). Contrary to the H-and-H predictions, the listener's experience was not critical. Contrary to copresence, the listener's ability to see what the speaker can see is unimportant. Repetitions of any mentions of visible objects that the repeater had heard were treated alike.

Experiment 2: Listener Feedback

Design Experiment 2 provides a more direct test of the effects of listener knowledge. When one speaker introduces an unshared landmark, the listener, who lacks it, may provide corrective feedback indicating the discrepancy between the players' maps. Sometimes, however, the listener fails to do this. We compare the effects of self-repetition in these two cases. In both, the repeater has said and heard the initial mention and can see the object. When the listener denies having it, the repeater knows that the listener has heard the word but cannot see the object. Otherwise, the repeater can assume that the listener has heard the word but cannot tell if that listener can see the landmark.

Tailoring to the listener would yield a more restricted effect of repetition where the listener has denied ability to find the object. This comparison is important for the extended version of monitor-and-adjust, which allows feedback to affect design of a subsequent mention. Only dual process holds that pronunciation must and syntactic form may be designed without regard to the listener's comments.

Results Figure 7.3 represents repetition effects measured in the way described above. Figure 7.3 shows that both articulation and form of referring expression were unaffected by feedback. Both the 73 repeated words with intervening denial and the 122 without any such feedback abbreviated with repetition significantly and equally ($F_2(1,193) = 9.45$, $p = .0024$; mention × denial: n.s.). The simplification of referring expressions on second mention was similar for the 44 cases with intervening denials

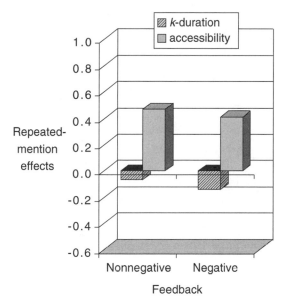

Figure 7.3
Effects of overt feedback about listener knowledge: changes in articulation (additional loss of *k*-duration) and accessibility of referential form (code values 0–3) in self-repetitions after listener has denied (less listener knowledge) and/or not denied (more listener knowledge) ability to see an unshared landmark.

and the 86 without ($F_2(1, 128) = 18.49$, $p < .0001$; mention × denial: n.s.). Feedback that should block defaulting under monitor-and-adjust does not do so. Only what the repeater has seen, heard mentioned, and said seems to play a role.

Experiment 3: Listener Identity

Design Experiment 3 examines introductory mentions of the same shared landmarks in Instruction Givers' two trials with the same map. In the first trial, the landmark is New for both players. In the second, it is Given for the speaker—an Instruction Giver who has mentioned it before, heard that mention, and seen the landmark. However, it is equally New to each successive listener, who has not heard it mentioned before. Adjustment to the new listener should block any tendency to utter a second introduction as a shorter, more accessible Given item.

In fact, this experiment offers the classic test of copresence. Mentions to new listeners should be geared to their ignorance. Accordingly, forms of referring expression

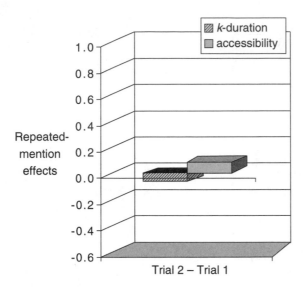

Figure 7.4

Effects of listener identity: changes in articulation (additional loss of *k*-duration) and referential form (accessibility code) from first to second introductory mentions to different listeners.

are generally found to revert from less to more elaborate versions when addressees change. Note that this is not exactly the same as the prediction we make here. The hypothesis that is usually tested compares late mentions to one addressee with early mentions to another. Instead, we are testing the prediction that the forms will be equally elaborate on each introductory mention.

Of the other models, H-and-H also posits that listener modeling will block at least articulatory change. Monitor-and-adjust, in contrast, predicts changes in both articulation and form, because the speaker's knowledge controls language production, and the referent is speaker-Given at its second introduction. Dual process predicts a loss of clarity because articulation depends on the speaker's experience, rather than on the listener's knowledge. According to this model, only form of referring expression may reflect the listener's ignorance and remain unchanged across mentions.

Results   In this case the critical comparison is between first and second trial introductory mentions. Figure 7.4 shows a repetition effect across these first mentions: second introductions are significantly shorter than first for 239 pairs of words ($F_2(1, 238) = 12.48$; $p < .0005$). In contrast, simplification of referring expression does not significantly increase over 116 pairs of introductory mentions ($F_2(1, 115) < 1$). Thus, word reduction appears to reflect the Given status of the item for the speaker, while referential form reflects the fact that the freshly introduced landmark is New for each listener. Tailoring of referring expressions without tailoring of articulation is predicted only by the dual-process hypothesis.

Experiment 4: Speaker Knowledge

Design In contrast to the earlier studies, experiment 4 holds listener knowledge constant. To achieve this, we again used other-repetitions, but now the landmark in question was either shared by both speakers (as it was in experiment 1) or absent from the repeater's map. In both cases, the original introducer, who is the listener at the point of second mention, can see the item, has mentioned it, and has heard it mentioned. The repeater has also heard it mentioned, but has not mentioned it and may (referent present) or may not (referent absent) be able to see it.

Since listener knowledge is constant across conditions, adjustment to the listener cannot yield any differences between them. If the speaker's visual surroundings are important, changes across repeated mentions will be greater where the speaker has more knowledge—that is, for the shared landmarks, which are present on the repeater's own map, as compared to the unshared, which are not.

H-and-H does not predict an effect of what the speaker can see. Copresence does not appear to make any particular prediction for speaker-knowledge effects. Monitor-and-adjust allows speaker knowledge to drive both articulation and referential form, and so should predict effects of what the speaker can see on both. Dual process claims that articulatory effects are driven by auditory priming, which, as experiment 1 illustrated, operates in other-repetitions. Like monitor-and-adjust, however, dual process claims that referential form is geared by default to the speaker's own knowledge, and that knowledge is more extensive where the speaker can see the referent. Hence both models predict speaker-knowledge effects on referring expressions.

Results Figure 7.5 shows the usual reduction of word tokens with repeated mention ($F_2(1, 224) = 12.37$, $p < .0005$) but no significant difference between the outcome for the 144 shared landmarks, which the repeater can see, and the 82 unshared (mention $\times$ visibility: n.s.), which are not visible on the speaker's map. Referential form, however, is speaker-centric here. Second mentions are more simplified than first overall ($F_2(1, 138) = 24.67$, $p < .0001$), and the change is greater for the 90 shared items than for the 50 unshared (mention $\times$ visibility: $F_2(1, 138) = 6.48$, $p < .02$).

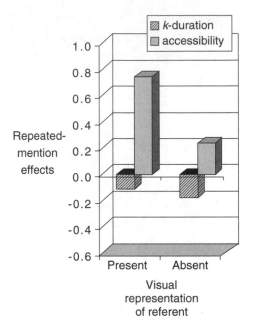

Figure 7.5
Effects of speaker knowledge: changes in articulation (additional loss of *k*-duration) and referential form (accessibility code) in other-repetitions of names of landmarks that repeater can (more speaker knowledge) or cannot (less listener knowledge) see.

This outcome is not consistent with adjustment to listeners alone or with overall use of speakers' knowledge as a proxy for listeners'. It conforms best to the notion that referential form is sensitive to a wider range of information than articulatory clarity.

Discussion

The experiments reported here and in Bard et al. 2000 test for effects on repeated mentions of several aspects of speaker or listener knowledge. Table 7.2 summarizes the studies in terms of the knowledge manipulated. Experiment 1 pitted the speaker's own experience in seeing and hearing against the listener's under two conditions, when it could and could not readily be inferred that those listeners could see the landmark. Experiment 2 pitted the speaker's experience of seeing, saying, and hearing against the listener's declared inability to see the item in question. Experiment 3 pitted the speaker's experience in having seen the mentioned landmark, mentioned it, and heard it mentioned against the new listener's ignorance of the item as the landmark was

Table 7.2
Summary of results by source of speaker and listener knowledge and by dependent variable

Experiment	Condition	How given status achieved						Repeated mention effects	
		By speaker of token 2			By listener to token 2			Articulatory clarity	Referential form
		Said	Sees	Heard	Said	Sees	Heard		
1. Inferable listener knowledge	self-repetition	+	+	+	−	?	+	**yes**	yes
	other-repetition	−	+	+	+	+	+	**yes**	yes
2. Direct feedback on listener knowledge	no denial	+	+	+	−	?	+	**yes**	yes
	denial	+	+	+	−	−	+	**yes**	yes
3. Listener identity	reintroduction	+	+	+	−	−	−	**yes**	no
4. Speaker knowledge	unshared landmark	−	−	+	+	+	+	**yes**	less
	shared landmark	−	+	+	+	+	+	**yes**	more

introduced in a second trial. Experiment 4 kept the listener's knowledge constant as well as the speaker's experience in hearing a prior mention, but manipulated the speaker's ability to see the landmark.

In all these cases, the repeating speaker had heard the original mention. In all, clarity of articulation was sensitive only to what the speaker had heard. These are exactly the results found by Bard et al. (2000) for a balanced but restricted sample of materials and with intelligibility to naive listeners directly measuring clarity. Thus, faster, less intelligible speech is conditioned in a simple way by the repeater's experience. There is no indication that models of the listener are consulted.

Referential form showed a different pattern. Like articulation, it was insensitive to some information that should have entered a model of the listener: an indication of what the listener could or could not see (experiments 1 and 2). Yet it did show a listener effect that articulation did not: referential form did not simplify on reintroduction to new listeners (experiment 3).[1] In this case, form of referring expression was tailored to the listener's needs. However, referential form also showed an extra speaker effect: the change in accessibility score across repeated mentions was enhanced when the speaker could see the named landmark (experiment 4). Thus, referential form is more sensitive than articulation but to both interlocutors' knowledge.

Why should form have these characteristics? It does not respond online to aspects of copresence delivered via feedback or inference. It shows neither the complete insensitivity to listeners that monitor-and-adjust predicts for initial design, nor the sensitivity to feedback that should guide redesign. We would argue that Map Task participants juggled competing demands on their attention, as the dual-process hypothesis predicts. Unlike the fast automatic processes through which speaker memory affects articulation, slower processes can compete for attention with the communicative task in hand. In this task, however, listener modeling does not take precedence. Only the listener factor most grossly related to the task—who is participating—affects the design of referring expressions. It shares that honor with an equally basic speaker factor— what is on the speaker's own map.

None of what we have shown here implies that speakers never model listeners or never consult those models. Hence, the present claims do not conflict with the results of the studies of referring-expression interpretation that suggest that, at least under restricted task demands, listeners can sooner or later display appreciation of the difference between shared and privileged knowledge. The present results do imply that interlocutors' natural behavior as speakers does not rely on maintaining and consulting an elaborate, incrementally updated model of the listener. Much of the time, it would seem, other tasks are more pressing (see Horton and Keysar 1996). It may prove worthwhile now to examine what speakers' priorities are and how they rearrange their tasks to meet them. Speakers could be more sensitive to listener knowledge if some kind of external record keeping were to ease the computational burden. In a sense, a speaker who uses his or her own knowledge as a proxy for the listener's is consulting a convenient, if approximate, record of this kind.

Notes

This work was supported by the ESRC (UK)–funded Human Communication Research Centre. The first author is grateful for the support of CNRS Laboratoire Parole et Langage, Université de Provence, during the preparation of this chapter.

Correspondence concerning the chapter should be addressed to Dr. E. G. Bard, School of Philosophy, Psychology, and Language Sciences, University of Edinburgh, Adam Ferguson Building, George Square, Edinburgh EH8 9LL, U.K. Electronic mail may be sent to ellen@ling.ed.ac.uk.

1. While Jurafsky et al. (2001) have reported less reduction for reintroduction to new listeners than to old, they find significant reduction to both. Their results can thus not attribute duration directly to the listener's knowledge.

References

Anderson, A., Bader, M., Bard, E. G., Boyle, E., Doherty, G., Garrod, S., Isard, S. D., Kowtko, J., McAllister, J., Miller, J., Sotillo, C., Thompson, H. S., and Weinert, R. 1991. The H.C.R.C. Map Task Corpus. *Language and Speech, 34*, 351–366.

Ariel, M. 1990. *Accessing Noun-Phrase Antecedents.* London: Routledge/Croom Helm.

Balota, D. A., Boland, J. E., and Shields, L. W. 1989. Priming in pronunciation: Beyond pattern-recognition and onset latency. *Journal of Memory and Language, 28*, 14–36.

Bard, E. G., and Anderson, A. 1983. The unintelligibility of speech to children. *Journal of Child Language, 10*, 265–292.

Bard, E. G., and Anderson, A. 1994. The unintelligibility of speech to children: Effects of referent availability. *Journal of Child Language, 21*, 623–648.

Bard, E. G., Anderson, A., Sotillo, C., Aylett, M., Doherty-Sneddon, G., and Newlands, A. 2000. Controlling the intelligibility of referring expressions in dialogue. *Journal of Memory and Language, 42*, 1–22.

Bard, E. G., Lowe, A., and Altmann, G. 1989. The effects of repetition on words in recorded dictations. In J. Tubach and J. Mariani, eds., *Proceedings of EUROSPEECH '89*, vol. 2, 573–576. Paris: European Speech Communication Association.

Barr, D. J., and Keysar, B. 2002. Anchoring comprehension in linguistic precedents. *Journal of Memory and Language, 46*, 391–418.

Brennan, S., and Clark, H. H. 1996. Conceptual pacts and lexical choice in conversation. *Journal of Experimental Psychology: Learning Memory and Cognition*, *22*, 1482–1493.

Brown, P., and Dell, G. 1987. Adapting production to comprehension—the explicit mention of instruments. *Cognitive Psychology*, *19*, 441–472.

Campbell, W. N., and Isard, S. D. 1991. Segment durations in a syllable frame. *Journal of Phonetics*, *19*, 37–47.

Carletta, J., and Mellish, C. 1996. Risk-taking and recovery in task-oriented dialogue. *Journal of Pragmatics*, *26*, 71–107.

Clark, H. H., and Marshall, C. R. 1981. Definite reference and mutual knowledge. In A. K. Joshi, B. Webber, and I. Sag, eds., *Elements of Discourse Understanding*. Cambridge, UK: Cambridge University Press.

Dell, G., and Brown, P. 1991. Mechanisms for listener-adaptation in language production: Limiting the role of the "model of the listener." In D. J. Napoli and J. A. Kegl, eds., *Bridges between Psychology and Linguistics*. Hillsdale, NJ: Erlbaum.

Estevez, A., and Calvo, M. 2000. Working memory capacity and time course of predictive inferences. *Memory*, *8*, 51–61.

Fowler, C. 1988. Differential shortening of repeated content words produced in various communicative contexts. *Language and Speech*, *31*, 307–319.

Fowler, C., and Housum, J. 1987. Talkers' signaling of "new" and "old" words in speech and listeners' perception and use of the distinction. *Journal of Memory and Language*, *26*, 489–504.

Fowler, C., Levy, E., and Brown, J. 1997. Reductions of spoken words in certain discourse contexts. *Journal of Memory and Language*, *37*, 24–40.

Fussell, S., and Krauss, R. 1992. Coordination of knowledge in communication: Effects of speakers' assumptions about what others know. *Journal of Personality and Social Psychology*, *62*, 378–391.

Garrod, S., Freudenthal, D., and Boyle, E. 1993. The role of different types of anaphor in the online resolution of sentences in a discourse. *Journal of Memory and Language*, *33*, 39–68.

Gundel, J. K., Hedberg, N., and Zacharski, R. 1993. Cognitive status and the form of referring expressions in discourse. *Language*, *69*, 274–307.

Hanna, J. E., Tanenhaus, M. K., and Trueswell, J. 2003. The effects of common ground and perspective on domains of referential interpretation. *Journal of Memory and Language*, *49*, 43–61.

Horton, W., and Keysar, B. 1996. When do speakers take into account common ground? *Cognition*, *59*, 91–117.

Hunnicutt, S. 1985. Intelligibility vs. redundancy—conditions of dependency. *Language and Speech*, *28*, 47–56.

Isaacs, E., and Clark, H. H. 1987. References in conversation between experts and novices. *Journal of Experimental Psychology: General*, *116*, 26–37.

Jurafsky, D., Bell, A., Gregory, M., Raymond, W., and Girand, C. 2001. Probabilities in the mental grammar: Evidence from language production in natural conversation. *Proceedings of CUNY2001*, Philadelphia. Institute for Research in Cognitive Science, University of Pennsylvania, Philadelphia, PA.

Keysar, B. 1997. Unconfounding common ground. *Discourse Processes, 24*, 253–270.

Keysar, B., Barr, D. J., Balin, J. A., and Brauner, J. S. 2000. Taking perspective in conversation: The role of mutual knowledge in comprehension. *Psychological Science, 11*, 32–38.

Levelt, W., and Wheeldon, L. 1994. Do speakers have access to a mental syllabary? *Cognition, 50*, 239–269.

Levine, W., Guzman, A., and Klin, C. 2000. When anaphor resolution fails. *Journal of Memory and Language, 43*, 594–617.

Lickley, R. J. 2001. Dialogue moves and disfluency rates. *Proceedings of DISS-01*, University of Edinburgh, Edinburgh, U.K., 93–96.

Lieberman, P. 1963. Some effects of the semantic and grammatical context on the production and perception of speech. *Language and Speech, 6*, 172–175.

Lindblom, B. 1990. Explaining variation: A sketch of the H and H theory. In W. Hardcastle and A. Marchal, eds., *Speech Production and Speech Modeling*. Dordrecht: Kluwer.

McKelvie, D. 1998. SDP—Spoken Dialogue Parser. HCRC Research Paper, University of Edinburgh.

McKoon, G., and Ratcliff, R. 1992. Inference during reading. *Psychological Review, 99*, 440–466.

Mitchell, D. B., and Brown, A. S. 1988. Persistent repetition priming in picture naming and its dissociation from recognition memory. *Journal of Experimental Psychology: Learning, Memory, and Cognition, 14*, 213–222.

Prince, E. 1981. Toward a taxonomy of given-new information. In P. Cole, ed., *Radical Pragmatics*. New York: Academic Press.

Samuel, A., and Troicki, M. 1998. Articulation quality is inversely related to redundancy when children or adults have verbal control. *Journal of Memory and Language, 39*, 175–194.

Schober, M. 1993. Spatial perspective taking in conversation. *Cognition, 47*, 1–24.

Singer, M., and Ritchot, K. 1996. The role of working memory capacity and knowledge access in text inference processing. *Memory and Cognition, 24*, 733–743.

Smith, M., and Wheeldon, L. 1999. High level processing scope in spoken sentence production. *Cognition, 73*, 205–246.

Vonk, W., Hustinx, L., and Simmons, W. 1992. The use of referential expressions in structuring discourse. *Language and Cognitive Processes, 7*, 301–333.

Wheeldon, L., and Lahiri, A. 1997. Prosodic units in speech production. *Journal of Memory and Language, 37*, 356–381.

8 Lexical Repetition and Syntactic Priming in Dialogue

Janet F. McLean, Martin J. Pickering, and Holly P. Branigan

There are good reasons to assume that dialogue is the most natural or basic form of language use. For instance, children acquire language through dialogue, and all normal adult speakers can take part in a dialogue. In contrast, the production and comprehension of monologue is much harder and is far from being a universal skill. Dialogue is of course used in a range of very different situations and in very different ways. For example, it is used in casual conversation and for very clear purposes (e.g., asking for information, negotiating deals), in different settings (e.g., face to face or by telephone), and can be formal (e.g., in interviews or interactions between shop assistants and customers) or informal. Thus types of dialogue differ from each other to a great extent, perhaps as much as dialogue differs from monologue.

However, a striking fact about experimental psycholinguistics is that research on any type of dialogue has been very limited in comparison with research on monologue, as Clark (1992) in particular has pointed out. Typical experimental methods explore language use by investigating how a single speaker produces or comprehends isolated words and sentences. Thus they have investigated language use as an individual process. One reason for this may be that in experiments it is easier to control the variables of interest. In contrast, in a dialogue there are many other variables that may have an impact on how language is produced: when turn taking should take place, how much shared knowledge there is between the listener and speaker, the use of interruptions and gestures, and so on (Clark 1996; Clark and Marshall 1981; Horton and Keysar 1996). However, it is possible to devise experimental methods for studying language use in dialogue under controlled circumstances. In this chapter, we will describe one such method, which we call *confederate scripting* (cf. Branigan, Pickering, and Cleland 2000). We show how this method can be used to study syntactic processing in dialogue, and then outline a number of studies that we have conducted using this method.

Dialogue is intrinsically an interactive process, a joint action that emerges when speakers and listeners perform their individual actions in coordination (Clark 1996). Many studies have demonstrated that dialogue should not be regarded as the sum of two monologues, and that language processing in dialogue cannot be explained in terms of the actions of two autonomous cognitive systems. Both production and comprehension in dialogue are sensitive to the communicative context and in particular to the behavior of other participants. For example, the way speakers describe objects depends in part on their assumptions about their listeners' knowledge (e.g., Fussell and Krauss 1992; Isaacs and Clark 1987). Equally, comprehension in dialogue is a far from passive process: listeners' comprehension is seriously impaired when they are unable to interact with the speaker (Schober and Clark 1989). It should be clear that any account of language processing that relies solely on evidence from experiments in monologue will be inadequate to account for dialogue. Instead, any complete account of language processing must be based at least in part on evidence from research on dialogue.

In this chapter, we explore syntactic processing in dialogue, and specifically the way speakers construct syntactic structure. We are particularly concerned with the interplay between lexical and syntactic processing. To do this, we exploit one of the most striking and pervasive aspects of naturalistic language production: its repetitiveness. We argue that this repetitiveness is tied in with the fact that interlocutors tend to become aligned during dialogue—if interlocutors come to understand each other, they must develop representations that are very similar in ways that are central to the dialogue. For example, if two people are discussing a particular topic, they can only understand each other if much of their knowledge of that topic is shared. This partly means that they will share knowledge of the "facts" being discussed, but also means, for instance, that they will generally use similar language to refer to the topic (e.g., referring expressions).

Of course, both monologue and dialogue can be repetitive, but repetitiveness is particularly apparent in dialogue, as demonstrated by both corpus studies (e.g., Aijmer 1996; Schenkein 1980; Tannen 1989; Weiner and Labov 1983) and experiments (Brennan and Clark 1996; Garrod and Anderson 1987; Garrod and Doherty 1994; Levelt and Kelter 1982; Wilkes-Gibbs and Clark 1992). One aspect of linguistic repetition is the tendency for individual speakers to repeat particular words, phrases, or semantic structures. As an example, Garrod and Anderson (1987) found a tendency for speakers describing mazes to reuse particular types of description—for instance in terms of paths between nodes or as row-column indices. In addition to such within-speaker repetition, there is also substantial evidence of between-speaker repetition in dialogue. In particular, speakers seem to converge on common patterns of linguistic behavior through the course of a dialogue. For example, just as individual speakers tend to repeatedly use the same type of descriptions in maze descriptions, pairs of speakers gradually converge on the same descriptions.

Experimental demonstrations of these convergence effects have focused on semantic and lexical alignment (Brennan and Clark 1996; Clark and Schaefer 1989; Clark and Wilkes-Gibbs 1986; Garrod and Anderson 1987; Garrod and Clark 1993; Garrod and Doherty 1994; Schober and Clark 1989). These studies have been particularly interested in alignment with respect to the repetition of referring expressions. Brennan and Clark (1996) showed that speakers come to use the same term to refer to the same object. For instance, a shoe might come to be commonly described by one pair of speakers as a *pennyloafer*, whereas another pair of speakers will end up calling it a *docksider*. Garrod and Anderson (1987) showed that speakers tend to converge on common interpretations for a particular word. For example, in the context of a maze, pairs of speakers came to use the word *square* in the same way, to mean either an individual node or a configuration of multiple nodes.

Garrod and Anderson (1987) explained such convergence in terms of a principle that they called *input-output coordination*. Essentially, they argued that there are functional benefits to be gained from speakers reusing the principles of interpretation that were required to interpret the most recent input, whenever they formulate an utterance. This minimizes computational load, by reducing the number of decisions that must be made from scratch. In more mechanistic terms, both within- and between-speaker lexical repetition can be interpreted as a lexical priming effect (Scarborough, Cortese, and Scarborough 1977). Prior access of a particular lexical item raises its activation; residual activation from this initial activation then facilitates subsequent access, raising the probability of its use in subsequent production. The same type of account could explain semantic repetition effects.

Although most research has concentrated on lexical, and to a lesser extent, semantic repetition, there is also good evidence that speakers in dialogue repeat syntactic structure. Corpus studies noted an apparent tendency for the repetition of syntax (Schenkein 1980; Tannen 1989), and Levelt and Kelter (1982) presented an experimental demonstration of syntactic convergence in question-answer pairs. We would expect syntactic repetition in dialogue as well, because there is good evidence that it occurs in monologue. Under the guise of a memory test, Bock (1986) had speakers alternate between repeating prime sentences and describing semantically unrelated target pictures. She manipulated the syntactic forms of the sentences that speakers repeated. For example, the prime sentence might use the *prepositional-object* (PO) form of an alternating dative verb in one condition (e.g., *A rock star sold some cocaine to an undercover agent*) and the *double-object* (*DO*) form in the other condition (e.g., *A rock star sold an undercover agent some cocaine*). The target pictures could be described using either form. Participants tended to produce a PO target-picture description after a PO prime, a DO target-picture description after a DO prime, and so on. Bock also found similar effects for active/passive sentences. In other studies, Bock and colleagues provided good evidence that the effects were truly syntactic and could not be entirely explained at other levels of syntactic structure (Bock 1989; Bock and Loebell 1990). There are many other demonstrations of syntactic priming in monologue, using different paradigms, different constructions, and different languages (Hartsuiker and Westenberg 2000; Pickering and Branigan 1998). Potter and Lombardi (1998) found priming between comprehension and production in a monologue context. These experiments therefore suggest that syntactic repetition is at least partly due to priming of representations and processes associated with syntactic rules that underlie language production (see Pickering and Branigan 1999 for a review). It therefore seems likely that the corpus evidence for syntactic repetition in dialogue is likely to hold in experimental contexts.

More recently, Branigan, Pickering, and Cleland (2000) provided an explicit experimental demonstration of syntactic repetition in dialogue. Using a confederate-scripted method (described in more detail below), they asked pairs of participants (a subject and a confederate) to take turns describing pictures to each other, including ditransitive events. Branigan and colleagues found that subjects tended to produce descriptions that had the same syntactic structure as that of an immediately prior description. For example, after hearing a *Prepositional-Object* (*PO*) description like *the chef giving the cake to the swimmer*, subjects tended to produce another PO description for an immediately subsequent picture (e.g., *the nun handing the apple to the doctor*). Conversely, after hearing a *Double-Object* (*DO*) description like *the chef giving the swimmer the cake*, subjects tended to produce another DO description (e.g., *the nun handing the doctor the apple*). Of particular interest for the current chapter was the finding that, although such syntactic alignment occurred in the absence of any open-class lexical overlap, it was considerably enhanced when both the prime and target cards involved the same verb (e.g., *the chef giving the cake to the swimmer* and *the nun giving the apple to the doctor*). In such cases, speakers produced 55 percent more syntactically aligned than nonaligned descriptions, compared to 26 percent when the prime and target cards involved different verbs. The effects of manipulating verb repetition were comparable to the effects reported by Pickering and Branigan (1998) for isolated sentence production (though the overall magnitude of priming is much larger in dialogue).

This finding is striking in that it suggests some interaction between syntactic and lexical levels of processing. It raises the question of whether the prevalence of repetition effects in dialogue at different levels of structure might reflect not only residual activation of representations at each of those levels, but also interactions between different levels. In particular, interaction between lexical and syntactic processing might explain why syntactic repetition effects have been noted in corpus studies (there is presumably much lexical repetition in corpora).

Unlike experimental studies of monologic production, where great care is taken to exclude lexical and semantic relationships between adjacent utterances, dialogue inherently involves the repeated use of particular lexical and semantic representations. This is not simply because those representations are primed: more fundamentally, topics of conversation in normal dialogue are introduced and maintained across a number of turns. Hence the same concepts (and labels for those concepts) occur repeatedly across utterances. A dialogue in which each speaker introduced a new (unrelated) topic of conversation in each utterance would be unnatural and incoherent in the extreme. Thus lexical and semantic repetition arises naturally in dialogue.

What are the consequences for syntactic repetition? Dialogue does not intrinsically require the repetition of syntactic structure: the maintenance of particular topics of conversation does not in itself need the reuse of particular sentence forms, because it is normally possible to convey a particular message using more than one sentence form. In that case, one might expect syntactic repetition in dialogue to be less prevalent than corpus evidence suggests. Certainly, it would be difficult to explain why syntactic priming appears stronger in dialogue than in monologue (Branigan, Pickering, and Cleland 2000).

However, syntactic repetition is likely to occur in dialogue at least in part for the same reasons that it occurs in monologue—because particular syntactic representations are primed. But if lexical and syntactic processing interact, syntactic repetition might be enhanced in natural dialogue. Syntactic repetition might be highly prevalent both because syntactic structures can be primed by prior use, and because the particular lexical items that appear in those structures also occur repeatedly (through topic maintenance and lexical priming), resulting in an enhanced syntactic repetition effect.

As we have noted, Branigan, Pickering, and Cleland (2000) found some evidence for enhanced syntactic repetition between sentences where the verb was repeated. Because the topic was not maintained between sentences, the effect can be localized to a specific effect of lexical repetition on syntactic repetition. There was no evidence concerning repetition of nouns, perhaps a more likely source of lexical repetition in dialogue, because topic maintenance normally involves talking about the same entities and not talking about the same actions. This was the focus of a series of studies reported fully in Pickering, McLean, and Branigan 2002. The studies examined whether repetition of noun-phrase arguments influenced the repetition of syntactic structure. All of the experiments used the same experimental technique, the confederate-scripted dialogue (Branigan, Pickering, and Cleland 2000). We begin by giving a full account of the method.

Confederate-Scripted Dialogue Technique

The confederate-scripted dialogue technique employs a picture-matching task, in which two participants alternate in describing pictures to their partner and finding cards from the set on the table that match their partner's descriptions. One of the participants is a confederate of the experimenter and reads picture descriptions from a script. The other participant is a naive subject. Throughout the experiment, the experimenter and the confederate act as if the confederate is a genuine subject and the subject believes that they are taking part in a genuine dialogue. We are interested in whether the subject is influenced in syntactic structure by the structure used by the confederate.

Figure 8.1 shows the experimental setup. In the experimental room the confederate and subject sit on opposite sides of a table with a divider between them. Throughout the experiment they cannot see each other. On each side of the table, there are two boxes and an array of piles of cards. One box contains a set of cards that are to be described to the other participant (description set) and the other box is for cards that have been selected. The cards on the table include the cards that are to be selected. The verb is written on the bottom of all the cards and the cards are stacked in piles alphabetically by verb. There is also one distractor card per verb pile. These are included to ensure that the subject has to look carefully at all the cards before they identify the prime card.

To begin the experiment, the confederate takes the first card from their box to be described (the confederate's description set). They read from a script a sentence that is appropriate for the card. For example, for the card in figure 8.1 this could be a PO sentence (e.g., *the chef giving the jug to the swimmer*), or a DO sentence (e.g., *the chef giving the swimmer the jug*).[1] Once they have described the card, they place it at the back of the box. The subject hears the description and turns to the array of cards on their table. Because this card uses the verb *give*, they turn to the *give* pile and select the card that matches the description. Once they find the card, they put the card in the empty box for selected cards. It is then the subject's turn to describe a card. They select the first card in their "to be described" box (the subject's description set), look at the picture and the verb, and produce a sentence to describe the card. The confederate finds the

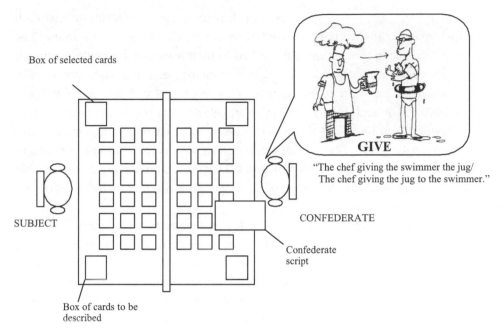

Figure 8.1
An overhead diagram of the confederate-scripted dialogue technique.

card and places it in their selection box. The confederate then describes their next card. The experiment continues until all the cards had been described. The cards are arranged so that the confederate always produces a prime card before the subject produces a target card. The experimenter instructs the subject and the confederate that the experiment investigates how well people communicate when they cannot see each other. They are told that they can say their descriptions and "Please repeat," to request repetition of a description, but nothing else.

Most of our studies have investigated the dative alternation, involving verbs like *give*. The first response the subject produces is coded as PO (if the patient of the action immediately follows the verb and is followed by the preposition *to* and the beneficiary); as DO (if the beneficiary immediately follows the verb and is followed by the patient); or Other (other response).

We believe the task mirrors natural dialogue in a number of ways. It involves a picture-matching game in which participants have to gain information from one another to attain a goal. This means that the task is interactive. It is a joint activity in which the participants take turns being the speaker and the listener and the result is dependent on them both doing this. Thus it incorporates turn taking so that each participant has to listen to the "speaker" in order that the correct card is found. The timing of turn taking is much more fixed than in most (casual) conversations (though clearly some forms of dialogue involve rigid turn taking—e.g., some interviews, meetings, and games). Furthermore, unlike many other studies of dialogue (e.g., Clark and Wilkes-Gibbs 1986), each participant has an equally important role and neither dominates. However, this form of dialogue is manifestly more restrictive than many forms of "free" dialogue, such as casual conversation. Our view is that this task is representative of one form of comparatively structured dialogue. It is an open question whether our results can generalize to other forms of dialogue, and whether such differences impact the mechanisms underlying alignment.

The task also differs from many natural dialogues in that the participants cannot see each other during the task. This means that they are not able to take into account any facial expressions or gestures that a participant may use. However, it is very similar to a telephone conversation, where each participant uses auditory cues alone. In our experiment, the participants are copresent in the same room so they can hear when the other participant places the card in the selected card box.

In an initial experiment (experiment 1), Pickering, McLean, and Branigan (2002) used the confederate-scripted technique to examine whether priming was enhanced by repetition of all three noun phrases in the prime and target. Participants described to each other sets of cards that included cards depicting ditransitive actions involving an agent, a patient, and a beneficiary. The cards involved a variety of verbs (e.g., *give*, *show*). Other cards depicted transitive actions and these were included as fillers. For all the cards, the appropriate verb was printed below each picture. So this experiment (like the others discussed here) was similar to the experiment reported by Branigan, Pickering, and Cleland (2000) except that repetition of noun-phrase arguments rather than verbs was manipulated.

Prime-target pairs were created by pairing ditransitive cards from the confederate's description set (prime card) and ditransitive cards from the subject's description set (target card). The identity of the depicted entities was manipulated so that they were either all the same on the prime and target cards, or all differed. The verb always differed between prime and target. Each target was paired with the four different prime conditions: PO all entities the same (PO-same), DO all entities the same (DO-same), PO all entities different (PO-diff), DO all entities different (DO-diff). The prime conditions were assigned in a Latin square. In each script, half the primes were assigned PO descriptions, and half were assigned DO descriptions. To analyze the results, only the proportions of PO target responses were calculated because there were very few Other

Table 8.1
Mean proportion of PO target responses for experiment 1

Prime description	Mean PO target response
PO-same	.94
DO-same	.18
PO-diff	.80
DO-diff	.43

sentences produced. Therefore, the proportion of DO target responses is approximately 1 − (proportion of PO target responses).

Pickering, McLean, and Branigan (2002) found that having overlapping entities did affect the sentence structure that the subjects used to describe their target card. The proportions of PO target responses for each prime condition are shown in table 8.1. This table shows that subjects produced more PO target descriptions after the PO prime conditions than the DO prime conditions (87 versus 31 percent). However, the proportion of PO targets was higher when the entities remained the same than when they were all different. The different-entities part of this experiment provides a replication of Branigan and colleagues' (2000) findings. The same-entities part involves no repetition of the verb, but there is a great deal of lexical repetition overall, because all three nouns are repeated.

In combination with the findings of Branigan and associates (2000), the results suggest open-class lexical repetition tends to increase syntactic repetition. Obviously, the repetition of verbs and the repetition of noun-phrase arguments only constitute two possible types of open-class lexical repetition, but the results lend support to a general class of account in which repetition at one linguistic level leads to increased priming at an associated level (Pickering and Garrod, in press). However, Cleland and Pickering (2003) report three experiments concerned with the repetition of noun-phrase structure using the confederate-scripting technique. In these experiments, subjects produced descriptions like *the red sheep* or *the sheep that's red*. Subjects produced the relative-clause construction after a relative-clause prime (e.g., *the book that's red*), whereas they almost never produced it after a simple noun-phrase prime (e.g., *the red book*). Most interestingly, however, the tendency to repeat syntactic structure was enhanced if the head noun was repeated between prime and target (e.g., *the sheep that's red*), or even if the prime and target were only semantically related (e.g., *the goat that's red*). These results allow us to conclude that priming is enhanced by repetition of verbal and nominal heads, and nominal arguments.

Table 8.2
Mean proportion of PO target responses for experiments 2 and 3

Prime description		Mean PO target response
Experiment 2	PO	.83
	DO	.70
	PO-for	.67
	HA	.69
	INT	.72
Experiment 3	PO	.95
(all entities repeated)	DO	.15
	PO-for	.91
	INT	.70

Two further experiments explored prepositional object sentences in which the preposition was *for* instead of *to* (e.g., *the witch making the sandwich for the knight*). Bock (1989) found priming between *to* and *for* PO structures, which suggests that different closed-class words in the prepositional phrase do not affect priming. Pickering, McLean, and Branigan (2002) decided to investigate whether this result could be replicated using the confederate-scripted dialogue technique.

In the first closed-class experiment (experiment 2), none of the entities between the prime and target were repeated. Thus the experiment was similar to Bock 1989. This experiment also included a high-attached (HA) prime condition (e.g., *the skier hitting the juggler in the forest*). This sentence has the same constituent order as the PO condition but a different syntactic structure, in that the prepositional phrase is an adjunct rather than an argument. An intransitive (INT), baseline condition (e.g., *the witch crying*) was also included because this would give an indication of the number of PO sentences that subjects produced without priming, and hence we would be able to gauge the amount of priming each condition elicited. Thus in this experiment there were five prime conditions (PO-to, DO, PO-for, HA, and INT).

The proportions of PO target responses are shown in table 8.2. Pickering and colleagues found that the PO-for prime structure did not prime a PO-to target structure. Subjects produced fewer PO-to target responses after a PO-for prime than after a PO-to prime. Furthermore, the proportion of PO target responses for the PO-for condition was no different than those after the intransitive condition. The HA prime condition was also no different from the baseline. This result was in contrast to Bock's (1989) study and suggested that priming is only found if exactly the same structure is used in the prime and the target and if the same closed-class items are used, when open-class words differed. However, the effects in general were fairly small.

In the second closed-class experiment (experiment 3), all the entities between the prime and target overlapped. In this experiment the high-attached condition was not included because this prime condition was not part of this research. Thus, there were four prime conditions (PO-to, DO, PO-for, and INT). Across the pairings, the prime and target card involved the same three entities (agent, patient, beneficiary), though obviously the intransitive only contained one entity (the agent). In all the pairings, the prime and target cards had different verbs to describe the action taking place.

The proportions of PO target responses for each prime condition are shown in table 8.2. Pickering, McLean, and Branigan (2002) found that when the entities overlapped between prime and target, there was priming between PO-to and PO-for structures. Thus when there are overlapping entities between the prime and target, the proportions of PO target responses after PO-to prime and PO-for prime are very similar. The PO-for prime was also different from the intransitive prime condition. This suggests that PO-for structures do prime as strongly as PO-to structures when all the entities overlap. In addition, the level of priming after the PO-to prime with all entities overlapping was similar to those found in the first experiment.

A series of experiments also investigated low-attached sentences that use the preposition *to*, as a prime condition (e.g., *the witch burning the letter to the princess (LA-to)*), where the prepositional phrase modifies the noun (here, *letter*) rather than the verb (*burning*). These sentences have the same constituent order but vary in syntactic structure. Three experiments were conducted that investigated whether it was possible to prime ditransitive sentences using a low-attached sentence structure and whether any particular phrase within the sentence was essential for priming.

In the first low-attached experiment (experiment 4), there were four prime conditions (PO-to, DO, LA-to, and INT). Across the pairings, the prime and target card involved the same three entities (agent, patient, beneficiary). For the low-attached pairings, the agent and the patient were the same, but the beneficiary was not present in the picture. The beneficiary was indicated by their name printed in an entity occurring in the picture (e.g., for *the witch burning the letter to the princess*, the letter was addressed to the princess). In the intransitive prime-target pairing only the subject was the same. In all the pairings, the prime and target cards had different verbs to describe the action taking place.

Pickering, McLean, and Branigan (2002) report that when the all the entities between the prime and target overlap, the level of priming is the same for the PO and LA-to prime conditions. The proportions of PO target responses for each prime condition are shown in table 8.3. The LA-to prime was also different from the intransitive prime condition. This suggests that LA-to structures prime as strongly as PO-to

Table 8.3
Mean proportion of PO target responses for experiments 4–6

Prime description		Mean PO target response
Experiment 4	PO	.93
(all entities repeated)	DO	.17
	LA	.90
	INT	.64
Experiment 5	PO	.97
(patient repeated)	DO	.68
	LA	.90
	INT	.80
Experiment 6	PO	.88
(beneficiary repeated)	DO	.45
	LA	.73
	INT	.70

structures when all the entities are repeated. When all the entities are the same, priming remains whether or not the same constituent structure is repeated. This suggests that priming in not due to enhancing syntactic rules but to placing phrases in the same position.

In each of the experiments with overlapping entities described so far, all the entities between the prime and target have been repeated. However, it may be possible that partial repetition of the entities could lead to similar results. Two further experiments looked at particular phrases within the verb phrase. In a second low-attached experiment (experiment 5), only the postverbal noun phrase was repeated. The materials for this experiment were very similar to those described in the experiment above. The only change to the cards was that the only overlapping entity between the prime and target was the patient.

Pickering and colleagues (2002) report that when the only overlapping entity is the patient, the level of priming is the same for the PO and LA-to prime conditions. The proportions of PO target responses for each prime condition are shown in table 8.3. The PO and the LA-to prime conditions were not different from each other. Furthermore, both the PO and LA-to prime sentences elicit many more PO target responses than does the intransitive prime condition. Therefore, it appears that having the same patient (postverbal noun phrase for PO and LA-to conditions) does lead to similar levels of priming as having all entities the same.

In the third low-attached experiment (experiment 6), only the prepositional phrase (in the PO structure) was repeated. In this experiment, the cards described above were altered so that the prime and target card involved the same beneficiary. The agent and patient were different. Pickering and associates (2002) report that when the only over-lapping entity is the beneficiary, the only priming occurs when the prime and target have the exact structure. The proportions of PO target responses for each prime condi-tion are shown in table 8.3. Following a LA-to prime, the proportion of PO target responses was much lower than the proportion produced after a PO prime. The level of priming after a LA-to prime is similar to the situation with the intransitive. This suggests that when only the beneficiary is repeated, priming is not increased and hence the LA-to sentence does not prime.

Thus the three experiments show that when there is overlap of the entities, priming can occur even when the target produced does not have the exact syntactic structure of the prime. However, it appears that some entities have a stronger influence on the priming. When the patient is repeated, priming remains the same. The experiments discussed above and in Pickering, McLean, and Branigan 2002 suggest that syntactic priming occurs with or without repetition of noun arguments. However, when all nominals are repeated there is increased priming. This effect does not appear to be dependent on the preposition in the prime structure or be tied to exact repetition of syntactic structure.

An interesting question is the extent to which the results might be affected by the tendency for repeated entities to occur early in utterances or in subject position be-cause they are treated as given. This tendency—proposed in centering theory (Grosz, Joshi, and Weinstein 1995)—has been found in dialogue by Brennan (1998). However, the main effect of such a tendency would be to affect the production of the subject, not to affect the choice of PO or DO construction. It is hard to see how any difference between PO and DO primes in terms of their focusing properties would affect the form produced as target, especially given the complex pattern of results that we found in our complete set of experiments.

These experiments have allowed us to separate out lexical and syntactic effects of repetition in dialogue and provide some evidence for why corpus data provide strong evidence that syntactic structure is regularly repeated in natural dialogue. The effect of repeating lexical items seems to be additional to the priming found when the same type of verb is used in subsequent sentences.

One reason why participants in a dialogue repeat lexical items and syntax when producing sentences is that it allows them to develop aligned situation models (Zwaan and Radvansky 1998). Previous studies have shown that there are different linguistic levels at which this alignment occurs. The studies described above show that these levels appear to be interrelated, such that lexical repetition can enhance syntactic alignment. We suspect that increased syntactic alignment also leads to increased alignment of situation models, and that the effects of repetition discussed here serve as a mechanism that leads to semantic alignment and hence mutual understanding during dialogue (Pickering and Garrod in press).

The confederate-dialogue technique allows us to study dialogue effectively. The participants are able to converse naturally while the lexical, semantic, and/or syntactic elements can be controlled. We are able to use this method to help determine how people use different outputs of the production process to communicate effectively.

Note

1. The confederate always described all the entities on their card with definite noun phrases. Entities were not explicitly labeled as definite noun phrases prior to the experiment, but the experimenter also used them in her instructions.

References

Aijmer, K. 1996. *Conversational Routines in English: Convention and Creativity*. London: Longman.

Bock, J. K. 1986. Syntactic persistence in language production. *Cognitive Psychology, 18*, 355–387.

Bock, J. K. 1989. Closed class immanence in sentence production. *Cognition, 31*, 163–186.

Bock, J. K., and Loebell, H. 1990. Framing sentences. *Cognition, 35*, 1–39.

Branigan, H. P., Pickering, M. J., and Cleland, A. A. 2000. Syntactic co-ordination in dialogue. *Cognition, 75*, B13–B25.

Brennan, S. E. 1998. Centering as a psychological resource for achieving joint reference in spontaneous discourse. In M. A. Walker, A. K. Joshi, and E. F. Prince, eds., *Centering Theory in Discourse*. New York: Oxford University Press.

Brennan, S. E., and Clark, H. H. 1996. Conceptual pacts and lexical choice in conversation. *Journal of Experimental Psychology: Learning, Memory and Cognition, 22*, 1482–1493.

Clark, H. H. 1992. Arenas of language use. Chicago: University of Chicago Press.

Clark, H. H. 1996. *Using Language*. Cambridge, UK: Cambridge University Press.

Clark, H. H., and Marshall, C. R. 1981. Definite reference and mutual knowledge. In A. H. Joshi, B. Webber, and I. Sag, eds., *Elements of Discourse Understanding*. Cambridge, UK: Cambridge University Press.

Clark, H. H., and Schaefer, E. F. 1989. Contributing to discourse. *Cognitive Science, 13*, 259–294.

Clark, H. H., and Wilkes-Gibbs, D. 1986. Referring as a collaborative process. *Cognition, 22*, 1–39.

Cleland, A. A., and Pickering M. J. 2003. The use of lexical and syntactic information in language production: Evidence from the priming of noun-phrase structure. *Journal of Memory and Language*, *49*, 214–230.

Fussell, S. R., and Krauss, R. M. 1992. Coordination of knowledge in communication: Effects of speakers' assumptions about what others know. *Journal of Personality and Social Psychology*, *62*, 378–391.

Garrod, S. C., and Anderson, A. 1987. Saying what you mean in dialogue: A study in conceptual and semantic coordination. *Cognition*, *27*, 181–218.

Garrod, S. C., and Clark, A. 1993. The development of dialogue co-ordination skills in school-children. *Language and Cognitive Processes*, *8*, 101–126.

Garrod, S. C., and Doherty, G. 1994. Conversation, coordination and convention: An empirical investigation of how groups establish linguistic conventions. *Cognition*, *53*, 181–215.

Grosz, B. J., Joshi, A. K., and Weinstein, S. 1995. Centering: A framework for modeling the local coherence of discourse. *Computational Linguistics*, *2*, 203–225.

Hartsuiker, R. J., and Westenberg, C. 2000. Word order priming in written and spoken sentence production. *Cognition*, *75*, B27–B39.

Horton, W. S., and Keysar, B. 1996. When do speakers take into account common ground? *Cognition*, *59*, 91–117.

Isaacs, E. A., and Clark, H. H. 1987. References in conversation between experts and novices. *Journal of Experimental Psychology: General*, *116*, 26–37.

Levelt, W., and Kelter, S. 1982. Surface form and memory in question answering. *Cognitive Psychology*, *14*, 78–106.

Pickering, M. J., and Branigan, H. P. 1998. The representation of verbs: Evidence from syntactic persistence in written language production. *Journal of Memory and Language*, *39*, 633–651.

Pickering, M. J., and Branigan, H. P. 1999. Syntactic priming in language production. *Trends on Cognitive Science*, *3*(4), 136–141.

Pickering, M. J., and Garrod, S. In Press. Toward a mechanistic psychology of dialogue. Behavioral and Brain Sciences.

Pickering, M. J., McLean, J. F., and Branigan, H. P. 2002. Lexical influences on syntactic activation in dialogue. Unpublished manuscript.

Potter, M. C., and Lombardi, L. 1998. Syntactic priming in immediate recall of sentences. *Journal of Memory and Language*, *38*, 265–282.

Scarborough, D. L., Cortese, C., and Scarborough, H. S. 1977. Frequency and repetition effects in lexical memory. *Journal of Experimental Psychology: Human Perception and Performance*, *3*, 1–17.

Schenkein, J. 1980. A taxonomy for repeating action sequences in natural conversation. In B. Butterworth, *Language Production*, vol. 1, 21–47. London: Academic Press.

Schober, M. F., and Clark, H. H. 1989. Understanding by addressees and overhears. *Cognitive Psychology*, *21*, 211–232.

Tannen, D. 1989. *Talking Voices: Repetition, Dialogue and Imagery in Conversational Discourse.* Cambridge, UK: Cambridge University Press.

Weiner, J. E., and Labov, W. 1983. Constraints on the agentless passive. *Journal of Linguistics*, *19*, 29–58.

Wilkes-Gibbs, D., and Clark, H. H. 1992. Coordinating beliefs in conversation. *Journal of Memory and Cognition*, *31*, 183–194.

Zwaan, R. A., and Radvansky, G. A. 1998. Situation models in language comprehension and memory. *Psychological Bulletin*, *123*, 162–185.

9 Prosodic Influences on the Production and Comprehension of Syntactic Ambiguity in a Game-Based Conversation Task

Amy J. Schafer, Shari R. Speer, and Paul Warren

There is now considerable evidence that listeners are sensitive to prosodic structure in their syntactic analysis of spoken language (for reviews see Cutler, Dahan, and Donselaar 1997; Warren 1999). Some research suggests that the prosodic contrasts investigated in comprehension research are not produced consistently by speakers, but may directly depend on ambiguity levels in the discourse situation. When naive untrained speakers produced disambiguating prosody in situations where two or more syntactic parses were plausible, they did so less reliably if the discourse context contained other disambiguating information (Allbritton, McKoon, and Ratcliff 1996; Snedeker and Trueswell 2003; Straub 1997). Earlier studies similarly demonstrated stronger prosodic disambiguation when speakers were explicitly instructed to disambiguate (Cooper, Paccia, and LaPointe 1978; Lehiste 1973), as well as situational dependence, with speakers reducing the length of a description with repeated mention (Clark and Schober 1992), or producing reduced forms of words on repetition in discourse context (Fowler and Housum 1987).

However, these studies showing variable prosodic disambiguation may not be representative of typical speech situations. In most of these studies, the speakers read sentences aloud in paragraph contexts or as (imagined) instructions to listeners who provided no spoken response.[1] Reading tasks—and the prosody produced in them—may differ from spontaneous speech, not least because the pragmatic goals and production constraints of reader-listener pairs differ markedly from those of interacting speaker-listener pairs. Production studies (Ayers 1994; Butterworth 1975) have highlighted some of the differences between the prosodic structures of read speech and those of spontaneous speech: read speech tends to have fewer and shorter pauses, and fewer prosodic phrases. Thus, reading studies might provide a poor guide to the distribution and size of prosodic boundaries in spontaneous speech and therefore to the extent and nature of disambiguation in spontaneous speech (Mazuka, Misono, and Kondo 2001). Studies of conversational language have shown sharp differences in production and comprehension between conversing speaker-hearer pairs and noninteracting speakers or overhearers. Speakers in conversation designed their utterances to reflect the knowledge they had in common with their listeners and to accommodate feedback from listeners about how well they were being understood (Brennan 1990; Clark and Wilkes-Gibbs 1986). Overhearers were less accurate than conversing listeners in identifying speakers' intended referents, even when these were visually available objects (Clark and Schober 1992). Conversational effects such as these are strengthened when speaker-listener pairs are aware of the need to cooperate (Schober, Conrad, and Fricker 2000).

An advantage of using scripted tasks to study correspondences between prosodic and syntactic structure is that they allow experimenter control of lexical and syntactic content, and make it possible to carefully compare alternative resolutions of ambiguous utterances. Some spontaneous speech tasks have been designed to give a certain degree of control over the range of utterances produced, such as map tasks (Anderson et al. 1991), route descriptions (Levelt and Cutler 1983), or tangram tasks (Clark and Wilkes-Gibbs 1986). However, even these tasks do not elicit multiple renditions from the same speaker of a targeted syntactic contrast.

The current research employed a cooperative game task, involving a set of predetermined expressions that were used to negotiate the movement of gamepieces around a board. These expressions contained a range of syntactic ambiguities, although not every expression was ambiguous. In this chapter we focus on PP attachments, as in the sentence *I want to change the position of the square with the triangle.* Depending on whether the PP attaches high (to modify the verb) or low (to modify the noun *square*), the utterance might mean "use the triangle to move the square" or "move the combined square + triangle piece," corresponding to two legitimate commands in our games.

Previous small-scale studies of PP ambiguities with read materials have revealed more pausing and prepausal lengthening before the PP when it attaches high (Lehiste, Olive, and Streeter 1976; Straub 1997; Warren 1985). Of interest to our discussion above, production studies that have included disambiguating contexts have shown evidence of both the maintenance of prosodic contrasts (Price et al. 1991) and their reduction (Cooper and Paccia-Cooper 1980; Snedeker and Trueswell 2003; Straub 1997), as have listener judgments from these studies. Studies of prosodic boundary location in PP ambiguities have shown that low attachment interpretations were most likely when a prosodic boundary preceded the direct-object NP, and high attachments when one followed the NP (Pynte and Prieur 1996; Schafer 1997).

Our game task allowed manipulation of the degree of contextual determination of one meaning of an ambiguity over another. Straub (1997), for instance, has proposed that the production system will allocate resources to prosodic disambiguation when other sources of disambiguating information would not be available for the listener in the resulting utterance. This comports with findings that prosodic disambiguation is less marked when utterances are read with disambiguating contexts. In our task, a number of information sources potentially helped disambiguate between the different PP attachments (see Warren et al. 2000). Here, we examine two types of variation of situational ambiguity. One reflects the configuration of gamepieces on the playing boards and the preceding discourse. The other is linked to players' potential awareness of the PP attachment contrast, which might result in increased disambiguation as time spent playing the game increased.

Two experiments provide the relevant data for PP utterances. Experiment 1 presents acoustic and intonational analyses of productions by naive speakers. Experiment 2 considers the categorization by a second set of naive listeners of utterances isolated from the game context. The combination allows us to investigate separately the extent to which speakers alter their prosody to reflect syntactic and situational factors, and the extent to which listeners use whatever prosodic cues are present to recover the intended syntactic form. The transcriptions generated in experiment 1, encoding phonological distinctions such as the presence or absence of a prosodic boundary, allow us to relate production patterns to claims made in the comprehension literature. We can also evaluate whether any given token, considered in isolation, is one that we would expect to bias comprehension, on the basis of claims about the prosody-syntax interface (e.g., Schafer 1997; Selkirk 1984; Carlson, Clifton, and Frazier 2001).

Our combined analyses allow us to evaluate three aspects of situational effects on prosodic form. As situational ambiguity increases,

• Does the proportion of utterances pronounced with disambiguating prosody rise, as determined by categories of prosodic transcriptions?

• Does the strength of the acoustic cues for disambiguation rise, regardless of phonological categorization?

• Do speakers' productions become more effective in helping listeners recover the intended syntactic structure?

Prosodic Assumptions

We assume the analysis of prosodic structure in American English proposed in Beckman and Pierrehumbert 1986 (following Pierrehumbert 1980). Each utterance is composed of one or more intonation phrases, each made up in turn of one or more intermediate phrases. We collectively refer to intonation phrases and intermediate phrases as prosodic phrases. The ends of prosodic phrases in American English carry edge tones, typically associated with changes in fundamental frequency. They also show *final lengthening*—increased duration for the final syllable of the phrase—and can be followed by a silent interval. These durational effects tend to be more extreme for intonation phrases than for intermediate phrases (Wightman et al. 1992). The edges of prosodic phrases are also associated with changes in segmental articulation (e.g., Keating et al. 2004), and with resetting of the pitch range.

Experiment 1

Our production study included both phonological and acoustic phonetic analyses of utterances such as (1) to (4), exploring the syntactic and situational determination of the prosodic realization of PP ambiguities by naive speakers in our game task.

(1)   I want to change the position of the square with the triangle.

(2)   I am able to confirm the move of the square with the triangle.

(3)   I want to change the position of the square with the cylinder.

(4)   I am able to confirm the move of the square with the cylinder.

We conducted our experiments with the following hypotheses in mind.

1. *Syntactic determination.* We predicted a difference in the realizations of high (VP) and low (NP) attachments of the PP. The high attachment was predicted to be reflected in a stronger prosodic boundary before the PP than found in the low-attachment sentences.

2. *Illocutionary force.* In our game task, one speaker (the driver) issued instructions, such as (1), while another (the slider) followed these instructions and confirmed that moves had taken place, using utterances such as (2). Disambiguation was potentially more crucial in driver utterances, since the incorrect move could otherwise have been chosen. If prosodic realization is sensitive to such pragmatic factors, disambiguation should be greater for driver than for slider utterances.

3. *Level of situational ambiguity 1: gamepiece contrast.* Our game included *square with the cylinder* sequences, in which the only interpretation in the context of the game was that of a high attachment, since there was no combined square + cylinder piece. Situational sensitivity predicts that the features that indicate high attachment would not be as clearly marked in the *cylinder* utterances as in the *triangle* utterances.

4. *Level of situational ambiguity 2: gameboard configuration.* In the game there were configurations of the pieces on the board that resulted in the driver's use of (1) being truly ambiguous, biased toward one interpretation or the other, or unambiguous, as

defined below. If speakers are sensitive to situational constraints, then we should expect greater disambiguation for ambiguous situations than for biased or unambiguous ones.

Method

In our cooperative game task two players used scripted sentences to negotiate moves of gamepieces from starting positions to goals. By observing gamepiece moves, the experimenter was able to identify each PP utterance as an intended high- or low-attachment utterance. Neither player could see the board used by the other, although they knew they had identical gamepieces. The design of the boards and the rules of the game encouraged negotiation and the strategic use of moves. The driver's role was to tell the slider which piece to move, to inform the slider when he or she had moved incorrectly, and to indicate when a gamepiece had reached its goal. The slider's role was to choose directions to move in and to report moves back to the driver, but the slider was also required to ask the driver for more information when necessary. Players were restricted to uttering sentences from a provided list, but chose freely from this list to best match their communicative needs. Through repeated use of the sentences over the course of the experiment, players became increasingly familiar with the sentence forms and less dependent on reading processes. Further information about the methodology is provided in Warren et al. 2000.

Situational-Ambiguity Levels for Gameboard Configurations   We defined three levels of situational ambiguity for the gameboard configurations. *Ambiguous*—Disregarding prosody and any underlying syntactic or lexical preferences, sentence (1) could with equal likelihood be interpreted with high or low attachment. *Unambiguous*—The global ambiguity could refer to only one legal move. For example, the square was in its goal and no triangle could be used to move it out. *Biased*—Both interpretations of the utterance were possible, but one was more likely. For instance, the players had just moved a triangle next to a square, so that using the triangle to move the square would be an obvious next move.

Subjects   Eight pairs of subjects, all native speakers of American English naive to the purposes of the experiment, were recorded at the University of Kansas. All subject pairs played as many games as they could within two hours, using multiple boards, and exchanging driver/slider roles between games. Subjects wore head-mounted microphones, and their utterances were recorded. Further details of the participants, excluded participants, and excluded productions appear in Warren et al. 2000.

Transcription Methods   All PP sentences were excised from the game context, placed in separate audiofiles, and assigned coded filenames that masked the speaker's intended syntactic structure. The prosody was transcribed by a team of five transcribers, trained to use the English ToBI (Tones and Break Indices) transcription system (Beckman and Ayers 1997). All were native speakers of English. Each transcriber analyzed a subset of the utterances, using auditory information and visual inspection of waveform displays, F0 tracks, and if desired, spectrograms. Reliability across transcribers was determined on the basis of a subset on which all five overlapped, using the reliability metric of Pitrelli, Beckman, and Hirschberg (1994). There was at least 94 percent agreement on the presence of pitch accents, phrase accents (indicating an intermediate phrase boundary), and boundary tones (indicating an intonational phrase boundary).

Results

As mentioned above, this chapter focuses on the effect of the gameboard configuration manipulation. Therefore, in this section we report only the results for driver utterances containing the phrase *the square with the triangle*, returning to the driver-versus-slider comparison and triangle-versus-cylinder comparison in the general discussion.

Transcription Results   There was substantial variation in the intonational and durational patterns that were produced for the sequence *the position of the square* in sentence (1), both within and across speakers. In data from 13 speakers, we found 63 distinct patterns on 79 high-attached utterances, and 87 distinct patterns on 101 low-attached utterances. This indicates that the exact prosodic form cannot be predicted solely on the basis of morphosyntactic structure.

We assigned the transcribed utterances to three groups to evaluate the relationships among syntactic structure, situational ambiguity, and prosodic disambiguation. The first group contained all utterances with a stronger prosodic boundary at the end of *square* (i.e., immediately prior to the PP) than at any other location in the sentence. Boundary strength was determined by the phonological category of the boundary (i.e., word, intermediate phrase, or intonation phrase boundary). The second group had been pronounced with the strongest boundary at a location other than at the end of *square*. The third group contained utterances in which the boundary at the end of *square* and at least one other boundary were of equal strength, and these were the strongest boundaries in the sentence.

Previous production results have shown longer duration for the prosodic boundary preceding high PP attachments than low ones (e.g., Warren 1985). In the comprehen-

Table 9.1
Boundary strength patterns by gameboard ambiguity level

	Discourse situation		
	Ambiguous	Biased	Unambiguous
Strongest boundary at the end of:			
square	14 (52%)	12 (48%)	19 (70%)
square and some other word(s)	7 (26%)	8 (32%)	4 (15%)
Some other word than *square*	6 (22%)	5 (20%)	4 (15%)
Total number of tokens	27	25	27

sion domain, Schafer (1997) and Carlson, Clifton, and Frazier (2001) have argued that prosodic disambiguation is influenced by the pattern of prosodic boundary strengths in the preceding material. Both proposals predict that pronunciations of (1) should be biased toward high attachment when the strongest prosodic boundary in the sentence is located at the end of *square*.[2]

Our transcription results suggest that the pattern of relative boundary strengths was strongly influenced by the intended syntactic structure. The strongest boundary followed *square* for 57 percent of the high-attachment utterances, versus 7 percent for low attachment. There is a potential concern that the "low-attached" utterances could have been produced with lexicalization of the phrase *the square with the triangle*.[3] The prosodic evidence concerning lexicalization is complex (Liberman and Sproat 1992) and beyond the scope of this chapter. However, the existence of lexicalized utterances would not affect the hypotheses for the high-attached sentences, which are our focus for the assessment of effects of situational ambiguity on prosody.

The distribution of transcription patterns for high-attached tokens by level of gameboard ambiguity is given in table 9.1.[4] Similar percentages of tokens were pronounced with the strongest boundary following *square* in ambiguous, biased, and unambiguous game situations, with the highest percentage in the unambiguous situation. The results indicate that speakers pronounced the PP sentence with a variety of prosodic structures, which ranged across prosodies expected to be more and less indicative of the syntactic structure. A substantial portion of the variability in boundary-strength patterns can be explained by the intended syntax, but none of it seems to be explained by the level of situational ambiguity.[5]

Duration Results   The transcription patterns in table 9.1 do not exclude the possibility of significant effects of situational ambiguity on prosodic disambiguation, since

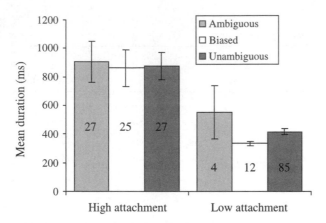

Figure 9.1

Mean *square* + pause durations (with standard error bars) for high- and low-attached *triangle* tokens, by situational ambiguity level (see text for details). Data are from thirteen speakers. Number of tokens for each mean are indicated.

matching phonological structures may have systematically differing phonetic realizations. For example, the silent interval of an intonation phrase boundary in a critical position could be reliably longer in utterances produced in ambiguous situations than unambiguous ones. Using digitized speech waveforms, we compared the durations of the word *square*, of any following pause, and of the combined *square* + pause sequence. Each was significantly longer for high-attached versions of (1) (Warren et al. 2000), providing clear support for the prediction that, in general, speakers would reflect the intended interpretation of the PP sentences in their prosody.

To examine whether the syntactic effect on prosody was modulated by situational ambiguity we looked at durational data in the three ambiguity levels described above. The overall mean durations of *square* + pause for these ambiguity levels for each of the high- and low-attachment conditions for thirteen speakers in the driver role are shown in figure 9.1.

The variable number of tokens making up these data (see figure 9.1) made the comparison of overall means rather unreliable. In particular, the breakdown by ambiguity level left some speakers with very small or empty cells for some conditions. Therefore, we restricted our statistical analysis to those speakers with at least one instance in each ambiguity × attachment condition. The resulting ANOVAs were consequently for high-attachment data only, from just eleven of our speakers. They showed no effect of ambiguity level on the duration of *square*, of the following pause, or of *square* + pause (Warren et al. 2000).

Thus, the duration results, like the transcription results, show that speakers in our task marked the syntactic difference between high and low attachments of PPs with some consistency. Yet the lengthening of the word and pause before the PP in high attachments, compared with low attachments, did not depend on the level of situational ambiguity.

Experiment 2

In the second experiment, game task materials collected in the production study were presented to listeners in a categorization task in order to determine whether the prosodic patterns identified in the production study would be useful to listeners faced with interpreting the utterances. High- and low-attachment tokens of sentence (1) were presented to listeners as complete sentences in a forced-choice task in which they selected between paraphrases indicating high versus low attachment. Nineteen native speakers of Midwestern American English from the University of Kansas took part in this experiment. None of them had previously taken part in the production experiment described above.

Hypotheses

If speakers produce prosodic structures that reflect syntactic structure, and that are useful to listeners, then percentages of correct classification in the comprehension experiment should be above chance for both high- and low-attachment sentences.

Further, if speakers increase prosodic disambiguation to reflect situational need, then correct categorization should be higher for tokens produced in the ambiguous condition than in the biased condition, and higher for tokens produced in the biased condition than in the unambiguous condition. Note that this would imply the use of further prosodic cues to disambiguation than just the boundary-strength and durational differences measured in experiment 1, which did not reliably distinguish levels of ambiguity.

Results

The percentages of correct classifications are given in figure 9.2. The overall classification was greater than chance, showing that listeners were able to make use of distinctions that reflect syntactic structure. The percent correct scores for each condition and for each individual participant were subjected to an arcsine transformation, (2 arcsine $\div$ p), and entered into an ANOVA with attachment and ambiguity level as factors. This revealed a significant main effect of attachment type ($F[1, 18] = 5.80$,

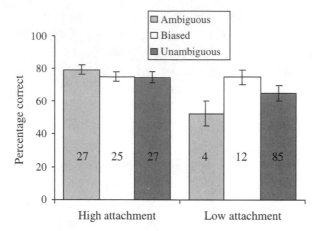

Figure 9.2
Percentages of correct classifications of tokens as high- or low-attached sentences, by level of situational ambiguity. The percentages are averages of the values obtained for nineteen subjects listening to thirteen speakers. The numbers of tokens heard in each condition are indicated.

$p < 0.027$), with more correct classifications for high than for low attachments (76 percent versus 64 percent overall). This main effect may reflect a slight overall bias toward high attachments of the PP.

There was also a significant interaction of attachment type and ambiguity level ($F[2, 36] = 5.133$, $p < 0.011$), reflecting the fact that there was no effect of ambiguity for the high-attachment condition, but a significant effect for the low-attachment condition. This latter effect resulted from the *lower* correct score for ambiguous than for biased or unambiguous items. That is, it was low attachments produced in the ambiguous situation that showed the least evidence of prosodic disambiguation.[6] The absence of a main effect of ambiguity level fails to support the hypothesis that speakers produce different degrees of prosodic disambiguation according to differences in situational ambiguity. It supports the conclusion from the production experiment that our speakers tended to disambiguate the PP structure, and they did so regardless of the ambiguity of the situation.

Production Sequence Analysis
Given the extent to which interacting speakers can alter their productions over the course of some tasks (e.g., Clark and Schober 1992), we might expect that speakers in the game task would have changed their use of prosody across the experiment. They presumably became more aware of the contrast between high and low PP attachments

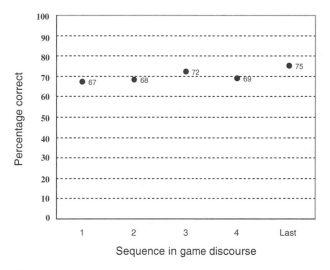

Figure 9.3
Percentages of correct classifications of tokens as high- or low-attached PP sentences, by sequence within high- or low-attached utterances in the game discourse. The percentages are averages of the values obtained for nineteen subjects listening to thirteen speakers. Sequence positions were assigned separately for the two attachment conditions; the figure shows the average of the high- and low-attached mean for each position.

as play continued, especially since the design of the games elicited the first production of each attachment in an unambiguous configuration. They also received evidence, directly after each PP production, of whether their conversation partner had interpreted the sentence correctly. Each of these factors might result in a tendency toward stronger disambiguation at the end of the task than at the beginning. Therefore, we reanalyzed the listener categorization results to examine whether categorization improved across the production sequence of experiment 1. Since each speaker produced at least five utterances for each attachment, the percentage of correct categorizations was determined for the first through fourth and last utterance for each of the attachment sequences.

The results are shown in figure 9.3. ANOVAs revealed only a marginal effect of utterance sequence on categorization (nor were there any systematic effects with a breakdown into ambiguity classes). We wish to emphasize that the lack of a significant effect cannot be attributed to a high degree of consistency within each speaker's prosodic productions. Each speaker produced utterances that received high percentages of correct categorizations and ones that received low percentages. The average difference across speakers between the utterance with the highest percentage of correct categorization and that with the lowest was 35 percent for high attachments and 49 percent for low attachments. As with the other results, there was considerable variation within each speaker, but this variation does not appear to be explained by situational ambiguity, as determined by either the gameboard configuration or a presumed rising awareness of the PP contrast across the course of the game.

General Discussion and Conclusions

Our analyses found strong and consistent evidence that prosodic structure reflected syntactic structure, at least in the majority of productions, but no evidence that prosodic disambiguation was modulated by situational need. Transcription, duration, and listener categorization results all showed syntactic effects, but gave no indication that prosodic disambiguation increased with situational ambiguity. Similarly, the investigation of sequence effects demonstrated that speakers' productions at the beginning of the task were as biasing as those from the end of the task.

Other analyses from our game have produced similar results (Schafer et al. 2000; Warren et al. 2000). Speakers strongly disambiguated an early/late closure contrast in our game, which was produced with quite limited situational ambiguity. The durational pattern for *cylinder* PP sentences, which in our game received referential support for only the high-attached interpretation, matched the durational pattern for high-attached *triangle* PP sentences. There was no apparent reduction of disambiguation for the *cylinder* sentences, even though the intended interpretation was unambiguous throughout the game. We also found equally strong durational effects of syntax in PP utterances by sliders, who were confirming a move, as in utterances by drivers, who were introducing a move. Thus, across two syntactic ambiguities and multiple types of analyses our results consistently show prosodic reflections of syntactic attachment, unaffected by situational ambiguity.

These results contrast sharply with those from previously published research on prosodic disambiguation and other tests of situational effects on production (but see also Ferreira and Dell 2000). We believe there are several reasons to be cautious in generalizing from the previous prosody results to spontaneous discourse situations. As noted in the introduction, the previous studies either did not include a conversation partner or allowed very limited interaction, and most relied much more heavily than our task on reading processes. Although our task did not elicit fully spontaneous speech, we believe that the utterances we collected are much more similar to spontaneous speech than those in other studies.[7] In addition, we believe our task was extremely effective in clearly establishing a syntactic interpretation of the ambiguous sentence for the speaker in a manner that did not have unintended consequences for the prosodic structure of the utterance. The use of biasing linguistic contexts in some of the previous work might not have always resulted in the speaker recovering the syntactic structure intended by the experimenter. In our study, the speaker's intended meaning was always unambiguously demonstrated to the experimenter by an associated move of a gamepiece. Further, it is quite likely that certain discourse contexts can induce focal structures that impact the prosody-syntax correspondences. Schafer and Jun (2001) have demonstrated that prosodic reflections of PP attachment in English can be affected by changes in focal structure. We believe that such factors were minimized in our task, but may have had significant effects in some of the previous studies.

In this chapter we have been most concerned with effects of situational ambiguity on prosody. We looked for its effects with an experimental design that we hoped would be quite representative of everyday speech. The levels of situational ambiguity in the game fluctuated because of the preceding discourse and because of actions performed on objects in the discourse context. Some of the experimental materials received referential support for both PP interpretations (the *triangle* utterances), and others received referential support for just one interpretation throughout the game (the *cylinder* utterances). We believe that discourse situations such as these should be highly informative with respect to the relative strengths of grammatical constraints on prosodic form (such as prosody-syntax correspondences) and tendencies in speakers to alter the prosodic disambiguation they provide in response to situational needs in nonexperimental contexts. Nevertheless, much research remains to be done in this area, and there is a particular need to analyze the prosody found in truly spontaneous speech produced for a range of sentence forms and a range of discourse contexts.

Although we did not find effects of situational ambiguity on prosodic disambiguation in any of our comparisons, we did see an effect of the discourse situation on utterance form. Speakers tended to have faster rates of speech when playing the game in the slider role than in the driver role (Warren et al. 2000), suggesting that they may have been more deliberate when they were directing the course of action than when they were confirming it. (Recall that players switched roles after each game.) However, as mentioned above, this difference did not seem to affect the degree of prosodic disambiguation in the driver-versus-slider role.

There are certainly cases—including some in research cited above—in which speakers employ a disambiguating prosodic structure in an attempt to indicate one interpretation over another. Speakers also make conscious and unconscious choices to be generally clearer in certain speech situations, and may therefore do such things as alter their rate of speech in response to the audience. Such changes may have indirect effects on prosodic disambiguation—for instance, the inclusion of stronger prosodic boundaries in several positions within a sentence when it is uttered in a more deliberate style. Nevertheless, we believe that the production of sentence prosody is primarily controlled by grammatical factors, such as phonosyntactic constraints relating prosodic form to syntactic form, phonological constraints governing the length or weight of prosodic units, and semantic/pragmatic constraints relating information/discourse structure and prosody. Under this view, most prosodic disambiguation of syntax in everyday speech is not disambiguation per se, but the regular application of grammatical constraints. In such a model, we should expect that the degree of prosodic disambiguation found in most speech depends very little on the degree of situational ambiguity, but very much on the grammatical structures involved, as found in our game task.

Acknowledgments

This research was supported by NIH research grants DC-00029 and MH-51768, NZ/USA Cooperative Science Programme grant CSP95/01, and Marsden Fund grant VUW604.

Notes

1. Snedeker and Trueswell (2003) employed a task in which the speaker uttered a series of commands involving the manipulation of a set of toys to a listener separated by a screen. Interaction between the two participants was limited to the speaker asking if the listener was ready. In this task the experimental materials were presented as printed text and acted-out toy manipulations. The textual stimulus was then removed and the command produced by the speaker from memory.

2. Schafer (1997) and Carlson, Clifton, and Frazier (2001) differ in their predictions about several boundary-strength patterns, such as a pattern with intonation phrase boundaries at the end of both *position* and *square*. In Schafer's proposal, this pronunciation would bias listeners toward high attachment; in the proposal by Carlson and colleagues, it would not. Since more finely graded analyses are beyond the scope of this chapter, we focus on the cases where there is consensus.

The location of prosodic boundaries is likely influenced by several other factors than the intended attachment site. For example, there is some tendency to produce a prosodic boundary at the midpoint of an utterance (e.g., Gee and Grosjean 1983). Utterances with the strongest prosodic boundary at the end of *square* are unlikely to be showing the influence of this tendency alone, given the late location of the boundary.

3. We thank Gary Dell for first mentioning this possibility to us, as well as Jesse Snedeker, Michael Tanenhaus, and John Trueswell.

4. In addition to being unaffected by the possibility of lexicalization, the high-attached tokens were more evenly distributed across the three gameboard configurations and had the widest distribution across our three boundary-pattern groups.

5. The high-attached utterances with strong prosodic breaks located prior to the end of *square* may reflect the pressure to balance the lengths of prosodic phrases and to avoid long prosodic phrases (e.g., Gee and Grosjean 1983; Nespor and Vogel 1986). Phonological factors such as these likely account for some of the remaining variability in prosodic boundary location.

6. It is possible that this reflects a choice by the speakers to produce more deliberate pronunciations in the low-attachment ambiguous-situation condition. See Warren et al. 2000 for further discussion of this possibility. We note, though, that very few tokens were produced in this condition in experiment 1. Therefore, the stimuli tested in this condition in the comprehension study might not accurately reflect the range of prosodic patterns that would be found in a larger sample.

7. The task of Snedeker and Trueswell (2003), like our task, produced speech that was less dependent on reading processes than that of previous tasks. However, our task involved greater interaction between participants than theirs, seems to have included a greater range of syntactic structures in the discourse situation, and required more varied interaction with the objects in the discourse situation.

References

Allbritton, D. W., McKoon, G., and Ratcliff, R. 1996. Reliability of prosodic cues for resolving syntactic ambiguity. *Journal of Experimental Psychology: Learning, Memory, and Cognition, 22,* 714–735.

Anderson, A. H., Bader, M., Boyle, E., Bard, E. G., Doherty, G., Garrod, S., Isard, S. D., Kowtko, J., McAllister, J., Miller, J., Sotillo, C., Thompson, H. S., and Weinert, R. 1991. The HCRC map task corpus. *Language and Speech, 34,* 351–366.

Ayers, G. 1994. Discourse functions of pitch range in spontaneous and read speech. *OSU Working Papers in Linguistics, 44,* 1–49.

Beckman, M. E., and Ayers, G. 1997. Guidelines for ToBI labeling. Unpublished manuscript, Ohio State University, Columbus.

Beckman, M. E., and Pierrehumbert, J. B. 1986. Intonational structure in Japanese and English. *Phonology, 3,* 255–309.

Brennan, S. E. 1990. Seeking and Providing Evidence for Mutual Understanding. Unpublished doctoral dissertation, Stanford University.

Butterworth, B. 1975. Hesitation and semantic planning in speech. *Journal of Psycholinguistic Research, 4,* 57–87.

Carlson, K., Clifton, C., and Frazier, L. 2001. Prosodic boundaries in adjunct attachment. *Journal of Memory and Language, 45,* 58–81.

Clark, H., and Schober, M. F. 1992. Understanding by addressees and overhearers. In H. Clark, ed., *Arenas of Language Use,* 176–197. Chicago: University of Chicago Press.

Clark, H. H., and Wilkes-Gibbs, D. 1986. Referring as a collaborative process. *Cognition, 22,* 1–39.

Cooper, W. E., and Paccia-Cooper, J. 1980. *Syntax and Speech.* Cambridge, MA: Harvard University Press.

Cooper, W. E., Paccia, J. M., and LaPointe, S. G. 1978. Hierarchical coding in speech timing. *Cognitive Psychology, 10,* 154–177.

Cutler, A., Dahan, D., and Donselaar, W. van 1997. Prosody in the comprehension of spoken language: A literature review. *Language and Speech, 40,* 141–201.

Ferreira, V. S., and Dell, G. S. 2000. The effect of ambiguity and lexical availability on syntactic and lexical production. *Cognitive Psychology, 40,* 296–340.

Fowler, C., and Housum, J. 1987. Talkers' signaling of "new" and "old" words in speech and listeners' perception and use of the distinction. *Journal of Memory and Language, 26,* 489–504.

Gee, J., and Grosjean, F. 1983. Performance structures: A psycholinguistic and linguistic appraisal. *Cognitive Psychology, 15,* 411–458.

Keating, P., Cho, T., Fougeron, C., and Hsu, C.-S. 2004. Domain-initial articulatory strengthening in four languages. In J. Local, R. Ogden, and R. Temple, eds., *Phonetic Interpretation: Papers in Laboratory Phonology VI.* Cambridge, UK: Cambridge University Press.

Lehiste, I. 1973. Phonetic disambiguation of syntactic ambiguity. *Glossa, 7,* 103–122.

Lehiste, I., Olive, J. P., and Streeter, L. A. 1976. Role of duration in disambiguating syntactically ambiguous sentences. *Journal of the Acoustical Society of America, 60,* 1199–1202.

Levelt, W. J. M., and Cutler, A. 1983. Prosodic marking in speech repair. *Journal of Semantics, 2,* 205–217.

Liberman, M., and Sproat, R. 1992. The stress and structure of modified noun phrases in English. In I. Sag and A. Szabolcsi, eds., *Lexical Matters,* 131–181. Stanford, CA: CSLI.

Mazuka, R., Misono, Y., and Kondo, T. 2001, March. Differences in levels of informativeness of prosodic cues to resolve syntactic ambiguity. Paper presented at the Fourteenth Annual CUNY Conference on Human Sentence Processing, University of Pennsylvania, Philadelphia.

Nespor, M. A., and Vogel, I. 1986. *Prosodic Phonology.* Boston: Kluwer.

Pierrehumbert, J. B. 1980. The Phonology and Phonetics of English Intonation. Unpublished doctoral dissertation, MIT.

Pitrelli, J., Beckman, M., and Hirschberg, J. 1994, September. Evaluation of prosodic transcription labeling reliability in the ToBI framework. In *Proceedings of the International Conference on Spoken Language Processing*, Yokohama, Japan, 123–126.

Price, P., Ostendorf, M., Shattuck-Hufnagel, S., and Fong, C. 1991. The use of prosody in syntactic disambiguation. *Journal of the Acoustical Society of America*, *90*, 2956–2970.

Pynte, J., and Prieur, B. 1996. Prosodic breaks and attachment decisions in sentence parsing. *Language and Cognitive Processes*, *11*, 165–192.

Schafer, A. J. 1997. Prosodic Parsing: The Role of Prosody in Sentence Comprehension. Unpublished doctoral dissertation, University of Massachusetts.

Schafer, A. J., and Jun, S.-A. 2001, July. Effects of focus on prosodic reflections of phrase structure in American English. Paper presented at the Prosody in Processing Workshop, Utrecht University, Utrecht, Netherlands.

Schafer, A. J., Speer, S. R., Warren, P., and White, S. D. 2000. Intonational disambiguation in sentence production and comprehension. *Journal of Psycholinguistic Research*, *29*, 169–182.

Schober, M. F., Conrad, F. G., and Fricker, S. S. 2000. Listeners often don't recognize when their conceptions differ from speakers'. Paper presented at the Annual Meeting of the Psychonomics Society, New Orleans.

Selkirk, E. O. 1984. *Phonology and Syntax: The Relation between Sound and Structure*. Cambridge, MA: MIT Press.

Snedeker, J., and Trueswell, J. 2003. Using prosody to avoid ambiguity: Effects of speaker awareness and referential context. *Journal of Memory and Language*, *48*, 103–130.

Straub, K. A. 1997. The Production of Prosodic Cues and Their Role in the Comprehension of Syntactically Ambiguous Sentences. Unpublished doctoral dissertation, University of Rochester.

Warren, P. 1985. The Temporal Organisation and Perception of Speech. Unpublished doctoral dissertation, University of Cambridge.

Warren, P. 1999. Prosody and language processing. In S. Garrod and M. Pickering, eds., *Language Processing*, 155–188. Hove: Psychology Press.

Warren, P., Schafer, A. J., Speer, S. R., and White, S. D. 2000. Prosodic resolution of prepositional phrase ambiguity in ambiguous and unambiguous situations. *UCLA Working Papers in Phonetics*, *99*, 5–33.

Wightman, C. W., Shattuck-Hufnagel, S., Ostendorf, M., and Price, P. J. 1992. Segmental durations in the vicinity of prosodic phrase boundaries. *Journal of the Acoustical Society of America*, *92*, 1707–1717.

III Language-Scene Interactions

10 The Time Course of Constraint Application during Sentence Processing in Visual Contexts: Anticipatory Eye Movements in English and Japanese

Yuki Kamide, Gerry T. M. Altmann, and Sarah L. Haywood

In this chapter, we explore the processes by which aspects of forthcoming lexical items can be anticipated or *predicted* even before those items are encountered in the linguistic sequence. We will focus in particular on the types of information that can drive prediction, and on the time course of their application during the prediction process.[1] The idea that the human sentence processor can predict upcoming information is not new. Even in some of the earliest formulations of the architecture of the human sentence processor (e.g., Frazier and Fodor 1978), it was hypothesized that the processor could use its knowledge of syntactic structure to project structure that dominates the current lexical items, and to project any obligatory daughters of that dominating node. Thus, encountering the subject of a sentence would enable the projection of a dominating S (sentence) node and the daughter VP (verb phrase) node, for example. Similarly, at an obligatorily monotransitive verb in an English sentence, the processor could project a sister NP (noun phrase) node using the syntactic constraints conveyed by the verb with respect to its permissible argument structure. Thus, prediction—or expectation-based language processing—has been discussed widely in both psycholinguistics (e.g., mainly by Tanenhaus and his colleagues within a constraint-satisfaction framework; Boland et al. 1995; Tanenhaus, Garnsey, and Boland 1990; also more traditionally, Frazier and Fodor 1978; Taraban and McClelland 1988) and computational linguistics (e.g., Elman 1990; Christiansen and Chater 1999; Jurafsky 1996). However, the literature on empirical data in support of such predictive processing is sparse, at best.

In one of the few previous studies on this topic, Altmann and Kamide (1999) demonstrated that semantic constraints on the potential arguments of a verb (*selectional restrictions*) can be used at the verb to narrow down the semantic domain of forthcoming arguments. Altmann and Kamide (1999) used a *visual-world paradigm* initiated by Cooper (1974) and further developed by Tanenhaus and colleagues (e.g., Tanenhaus et al. 1995). In one of their experiments, Altmann and Kamide (1999) presented participants with an auditory sentence such as *The boy will eat the cake* and,

Figure 10.1
An example of a visual stimulus in Altmann and Kamide 1999.

concurrently, a visual scene containing a boy, a cake, a toy train, a toy car, and a ball (figure 10.1).

The manipulation relied on the fact that the cake (the target object) was the only object that, in the *selective* condition above, satisfied the selectional restrictions of the verb (something edible). A second condition, the *nonselective* condition, used sentences in which verbs' selectional restrictions did not exclusively select the target object. For example, the nonselective condition for the picture in figure 10.1 was *The boy will move the cake*. In this case, other objects in the scene, and not just the cake, could function as the potential Theme of the verb *move*. The experiment revealed that the probability of launching a saccadic eye movement to the target object was significantly higher in the selective condition than in the nonselective condition. This difference was found to be statistically significant in the region between verb onset and noun (*cake*) onset, and also even as early as in the region between verb onset and verb offset. These data were interpreted as suggesting that the processor anticipates at the verb a forthcoming postverbal argument, applies to this argument the semantic constraints afforded by the verb's selectional restrictions, and evaluates the result against, in this case, the visual context.

Although Altmann and Kamide's (1999) data are robust enough to be regarded as evidence for predictive processing in *some* environments, their study does not, naturally, cover all possible linguistic circumstances in which prediction might occur.

The present chapter describes two further experiments using the same experimental paradigm as used in the Altmann and Kamide (1999) study. Whereas the Altmann and Kamide (1999) study established that the verb in a simple transitive sentence can drive *anticipatory eye movements*—eye movements toward the referent of a yet-to-be-encountered referring expression—the emphasis here will be on the conditions under which such anticipatory eye movements can be observed.

In the present chapter, the first experiment asks whether the verb is the only information source for predicting the semantic domain of potential direct objects (Themes) in English active monotransitive constructions. In particular, it asks whether only the verb is used, or whether the verb *in combination with* its subject (Agent) can drive the prediction. For instance, encountering *The cat will eat . . .* and *The man will eat . . .* should lead the processor to predict different classes of edible objects if semantic constraints associated with the subject are combined with the verb's selectional restrictions in order to arrive at a predicted (semantic) class of object that could be referred to in direct-object position. Although not specifically designed to do so, this experiment may also identify the timing with which constraints from different sources are combined as the sentence unfolds. It is conceivable, for example, that constraints associated with the subject (in terms of likely associates) could be applied as soon as the subject is encountered (in the case of *The cat will . . .* , this may include associates such as milk, mice, and so on). When the verb is encountered, the selectional restrictions conveyed by that verb might then be applied independently of the subject, before the intersection of the two sets of objects (those associated with cats, and those associated with eating) is identified. Alternatively, and possibly more likely, there may be no independent application of the verb's selectional restrictions—rather, information associated with the verb may be combined immediately with information associated with the verb's subject, and this combined information may then form the basis for predicting the class of object that may be referred to in direct-object position.

The second experiment takes advantage of the fact that Japanese is a head-final language in which the thematic roles of preverbal arguments are indicated by postpositional case markers. For example, Japanese native speakers would interpret a sentence *girl-nominative cat-dative milk-accusative gave* as indicating that the girl is the Agent, the cat is the Goal, and the milk is the Theme (*The girl gave the milk to the cat*), based on syntactic knowledge about the typical roles that the head nouns of each case marker play in the language (nominative—Agent, dative—Goal, accusative—Theme). Within our experimental and theoretical frameworks, the experiment will explore the question of whether a subsequent argument is predicted after a sequence of arguments with certain head nouns and case markers. For instance, will *the milk* be predicted as a potential Theme after the sequence *girl-nominative cat-dative* in the context of a scene depicting a girl, a cat, and a bowl of milk? If it is, the data would suggest two crucial aspects of prediction that the previous English experiments did not allow us to explore. First, such anticipatory eye movements would indicate that syntactic information (case-marking information) on NP arguments that have been encountered so far triggers access to nonsyntactic information (real-world knowledge), which leads to prediction of a further argument. In our example, looks to the milk after the sequence *girl-nominative cat-dative* would show that the nominative and dative case markers in the first two NP arguments not only assign an Agent and Goal roles to their respective head nouns, but also indicate that the next argument should fill the Theme slot after having the Agent and Goal slots filled. This information would then trigger a search for the most plausible Theme in the context scene given the situation where the girl is the Agent and the cat is the Goal in the event, which would result in anticipating the milk as the most plausible Theme based on real-world knowledge. The second issue to be addressed in the Japanese experiment concerns the extent to which these predictive processes are verb driven. Because the verb constrains both syntactically and semantically the arguments that it may take, and because the verb determines the roles that define the relationships between the participants in the event described by the sentence, there is a sense in which the verb can be considered the "glue" that binds the elements within the sentence. Consequently, the verb may therefore be a necessary element in the sentence that can serve as the basis for predicting its internal arguments. Such an account would be compatible with linguistic formalisms that assume that the lexical head (e.g., the verb) is the information source on which basis the sentential structure and semantics can be formulated (e.g., Chomsky 1965, 1981, 1995; Pollard and Sag 1994). However, anticipatory eye movements toward the milk after *girl-nominative cat-dative* would undermine such head-driven approaches to prediction (and indeed processing): the data would indicate that the prediction of preverbal arguments can be achieved in absence of the head (the verb).

To recap, experiment 1 will, like Altmann and Kamide (1999), focus on semantic information and pragmatic real-world knowledge as the information source underpinning prediction. However, unlike in Altmann and Kamide's (1999) materials, the sentence structure used in experiment 1 will enable us to investigate whether such an information source could be spread across multiple constituents in the sentence (subject and verb). Experiment 2, on the other hand, will establish whether such a prediction can be accomplished on the basis of structural information also, since one extreme interpretation of the Altmann and Kamide (1999) experiments could

Figure 10.2
A sample visual stimulus in experiment 1.

be that a purely semantics-driven processor could achieve prediction in any linguistic environment.[2]

Experiment 1

As mentioned above, in experiment 1 we explore whether the semantics of the verb's subject (Agent) are combined with the verb's selectional restrictions when predicting a potential Theme. Sentences (1) and (2) were presented to participants in the context of the visual scene shown in figure 10.2.

(1) The man will ride the motorbike.

(2) The girl will ride the carousel.

The selectional restrictions of the verb *ride* are satisfied by the two Themes *motorbike* and *carousel* (both can be ridden) and by the two Agents *man* and *girl* (both are animate). However, real-world knowledge suggests that the man is more likely to ride the motorbike than is the little girl, who is more likely to ride the carousel. If combinatory information guides anticipatory eye movements, there should be more anticipatory eye movements to the motorbike when the Agent is the man than when it is the girl. Similarly, there should be more anticipatory eye movements to the carousel when the Agent is the girl than when it is the man.

One complicating factor in the design of experiment 1 is whether anticipatory eye movements to the "appropriate" Themes could be driven by *low-level associations* between the Agent and the Theme. For example, the man who will ride the motorbike is shown wearing a motorcycle helmet, and that information alone, independently of real-world knowledge regarding the plausibility of men (rather than little girls) riding motorbikes, might drive eye movements toward the motorbike. To rule out the possibility that anticipatory eye movements in experiment 1 might be guided by such associations (lexical, conceptual, or perceptual), the experimental material set also includes the following control conditions (presented with the picture in figure 10.2).

(3)   The man will taste the toffee apple.

(4)   The girl will taste the toffee apple.

In these cases, the motorbike and carousel are no longer the most plausible Themes. However, if low-level, noncombinatory information drives the eye movements from the motorcyclist to the motorbike, we should see more eye movements toward the motorbike in (3) than in (4). For the purposes of analysis, we will label the motorbike as the "appropriate" object when the Agent is the man, and the carousel as the "inappropriate" object. Conversely, when the Agent is the girl, we will label the carousel "appropriate" and the motorbike "inappropriate." These labelings ignore the verb— thus, even in the case of *The man will taste the toffee apple*, we label the motorbike "appropriate." The rationale is that we should observe an interaction between appropriateness and verb if eye movements are launched to the appropriate objects only when the Agent *and* the verb support such movements—there should be no difference in appropriateness when the verb is *taste*, for example. Finally, we refer to the toffee apple as the "control" Theme, because it is the Theme of the control conditions (e.g., (3) and (4)).

One last methodological point: the scenes were modified so that the Agent of the sentence was always in the same physical location relative to the other objects in the scene. Thus, the motorcyclist and the girl swapped location as a function of which was the Agent. This was to ensure that low-level distributional properties of the objects relative to one another did not contaminate the results.

Sixty-four native speakers of English took part in the experiment, during which their eye movements were recorded by a head-mounted SMI EyeLink eye tracker. Twenty-four scenes such as that shown in figure 10.2 were constructed. Pretesting ensured that the motorbike (or its equivalent across the different scenes) was the most plausibly ridden object when the man was the Agent, and the carousel was most plausibly rid-

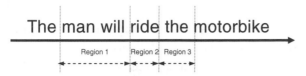

Figure 10.3
Regions for data analyses in experiment 1.

Table 10.1
Percentages of trials with a fixation onto the appropriate objects, inappropriate objects, and control themes in regions 1, 2, and 3 in each condition in experiment 1

Region	Condition	Appropriate objects	Inappropriate objects	Control themes
Region 1	Test (ride)	13	13	15
	Control (taste)	15	11	12
Region 2	Test (ride)	12	12	7
	Control (taste)	13	12	11
Region 3	Test (ride)	11	6	4
	Control (taste)	5	4	13

den object when the girl was the Agent. Further twenty-four scenes and accompanying sentences were constructed that served as filler items. These used ditransitive verbs. Each trial consisted of a visual presentation that coincided with the auditory sentence. Each scene was presented for 5 seconds, and thus lasted approximately 2 or 3 seconds beyond the offset of the sentence. Participants were asked simply to look at the scene and listen to the concurrent sentence. They were told that we would monitor their eye movements as they listened and looked, but other than that, there was no further task for them to perform.

We analyzed data in three different temporal regions, as shown in figure 10.3. The mean duration for each region was as follows: from Agent onset to Verb onset (region 1): 745 ms; from Verb onset to Verb offset (region 2): 480 ms; from Verb offset to Theme onset (region 3): 233 ms.[3] We calculated the percentage of trials in which eye movements were launched toward the various objects within each of these temporal regions, and statistical analyses were performed on the arcsine-transformed data. All reported differences were significant at $p < .05$ (with one exception—see below) and on both subject and item analyses. A summary of the results, broken down by condition and target object, is given in table 10.1.

Region 1

There were no significant effects in this region. The lack of a main effect of Appropriateness suggests that objects with strong low-level (lexical, conceptual, perceptual) associations to the subject nouns were looked at no more often than any other object, indicating that low-level associations did not guide eye movements toward certain objects (toward the motorbike given the motorcyclist as Agent, for example) before the verb information became available, at least as far as our materials were concerned.

Region 2

There were again no significant main effects in this region. Note that this is the earliest possible region where a main effect of Verb (*ride* versus *taste*) or Appropriateness could first be significant. The lack of a Verb effect suggests that verbs' selectional restrictions were not used while the verb was being recognized, and consequently, that combinatory information was not used to drive any predictive processing during the verb itself. Similarly, the interaction between Verb and Appropriateness was not significant. However, the analysis of looks to the control Theme (the toffee apple) revealed that it was looked at significantly more often in the control conditions (examples (3) and (4) above) than in the test conditions (examples (1) and (2) above).

Region 3

Analysis of the data in this region (between verb offset and Theme onset) yielded a very different pattern compared to the previous two regions. First, main effects of both Appropriateness and Verb were found. Second, the interaction between these two factors was also significant (by subjects; by items, it was only marginally significant: $p = .055$). Planned comparisons confirmed that the appropriate objects were looked at more often than the inappropriate objects in the test conditions, although there was no difference in the control conditions. It was also found that the appropriate objects were looked at more often in the test conditions than in the control conditions. Analysis of fixations on the control Themes confirmed that there were more looks in the control condition than in the test condition, as in the previous region.

Overall, the data suggest that anticipatory eye movements were directed toward the most plausible object that could serve as a Theme. Information extracted from the verb (selectional restrictions) was combined with information about the Agent (of the action denoted by the verb) in order to predict, in conjunction with the visual context, whatever would be referred to by the forthcoming lexical items.

Figure 10.4
A sample visual stimulus in experiment 2.

Experiment 2

The second experiment uses the same visual-world paradigm to examine prediction processes in Japanese sentence processing. As mentioned above, the purposes of the experiment were to see whether the verb must have been encountered to make prediction possible (i.e., whether the verb is necessary for prediction), and whether syntactic information (e.g., case-marking information) can be used for prediction, as well as semantic information and real-world knowledge.

The experimental materials were as follows, and were presented in the context of the scene shown in figure 10.4.

(5) *Dative condition:* ウェイトレスが客に楽し気にハンバーガーを運ぶ。
     waitress-nom customer-dat merrily hamburger-acc bring.
     The waitress will merrily bring the hamburger to the customer.

(6) *Accusative condition:* ウェイトレスが客を楽し気にからかう。
     waitress-nom customer-acc merrily tease.
     The waitress will merrily tease the customer.

At issue is whether, after hearing *waitress-nom customer-dat* in (5), the processor will anticipate that the third argument will refer to whatever could plausibly be transferred by the waitress to the customer, namely, the hamburger. In this dative condition,

NP-acc is obligatory after the sequence *NP1-nom NP2-dat*, although NP-dat could be interpreted as the Theme of one of very few monotransitive verbs that take an NP-dat as its Theme (e.g., *aisatu-suru*, "greet"), or as the Goal/Location after an intransitive verb (e.g., *iku*, "go"). Either way, the most frequent structure is the one in which an accusative would follow. In the accusative condition (6), there are two alternative ways the fragment *NP1-nom NP2-acc* can continue—either as part of a monotransitive construction, in which case no further arguments will be anticipated (*NP1-nom NP2-acc verb*), or as part of a scrambled ditransitive construction (*NP1-nom NP2-acc NP3-dat verb*). In the latter case, the scene contains no plausible object that could be referred to as Goal (neither the hamburger nor the dustbin is a plausible Goal). Thus, if the first two NPs provide enough information to enable the prediction of forthcoming material, there should be more anticipatory looks toward the hamburger in the dative condition, when it can plausibly fulfill the Theme function, than in the accusative condition, when it cannot plausibly fulfill any function that might be anticipated on the basis of the sequence *NP1-nom NP2-acc*. Moreover, any difference between these conditions that manifested itself before the verb could only be attributed to the different case marking on the first two NP arguments. This in turn would suggest that syntactic information, as distinct from the semantic constraints manipulated in experiment 1, could be a vital information source in the predictive process. Therefore, the implication is that the predictive operations we have observed in our previous studies need not be attributed solely to semantic processes operating independently of the establishment of syntactic dependencies during sentence processing.

The same experimental technique and procedure were used as in experiment 1. Twenty-two native speakers of Japanese took part in experiment 2. We constructed sixteen experimental items such as the one described above, and these were embedded amongst sixteen foils (ditransitive items using scrambled structures) and a further sixteen fillers.

The eye-movement data were collected and analyzed in the same way as in experiment 1. The region between the offset of the second NP (e.g., the offset of *customer-dat* or *customer-acc*) and the onset of the forth constituent (e.g., the onset of *hamburger-acc* or *tease*) was regarded as the critical period (the mean duration of the critical region was 1,150 ms).[4] As before, the data consisted of the percentage of trials in which at least one saccadic eye movement was initiated to the target object within the critical period (as shown in table 10.2), and statistical analyses were performed on the arcsine-transformed data. There were significantly more looks in both the subject and item analyses to the target objects in the dative condition than in the accusative condition during the critical period. The pattern of fixations, therefore, suggests that people

Table 10.2
Percentages of trials with a fixation onto the target objects in each condition in experiment 2

Dative condition	Accusative condition
43	31

anticipated that the object in the picture would be most likely to follow as the most plausible Theme before hearing the onset of the corresponding referring expression (NP3).

Thus, the results suggest that prediction of a verb's arguments is achievable prior to the verb, using information extracted from the case markers on the existing NPs and combined with real-world knowledge regarding the thematic-role information provided by those case markers. Thus, the experimental paradigm used here does not reflect eye movements driven only by semantic processing, but also driven by the construction of *syntactic structure* during the processing of the concurrent sentence input (see Kamide, Scheepers, and Altmann 2003; they drew a similar conclusion using a German verb-initial structure in a visual-world experiment).

General Discussion

The two experiments reported above explored predictive processes in sentence processing. Experiment 1 demonstrated that the prediction of a postverbal Theme can be based on more than just the selectional restrictions associated with the verb: the processor is capable of combining information about the Agent of the action denoted by the verb with information about the verb's selectional restrictions, and is able to base its predictions regarding the likely semantic properties of the postverbal object on this combined information. Our finding is further evidence that the processor accrues constraints incrementally as each word is encountered, and rapidly deploys those constraints to narrow down the domain of subsequent reference. Experiment 2 focused on the fact that the anticipatory eye movements reported both in Altmann and Kamide 1999 and in experiment 1 took place during or after the matrix verb. It explored whether the verb is necessary for the purpose of anticipating semantic properties of its arguments. Using Japanese, experiment 2 revealed that information extracted from preverbal arguments (NP1 NP2) drove anticipatory eye movements to the object in the visual scene that could most plausibly serve as the head of a subsequent preverbal argument (NP3). Thus, a verb's arguments can be predicted on the basis of information not directly conveyed by the verb. The data indicated that syntactic factors, such as case marking, play a key role in the prediction process, in addition to the semantic/ pragmatic factors explored in Altmann and Kamide 1999 and in experiment 1.

Taken together, our results suggest that many different sources of information can contribute to the content of the predictions that are made as a sentence unfolds in time. The Japanese data, for example, demonstrate that syntactic factors, which define the roles played by each head noun (or its referent), trigger the evaluation of plausible event scenarios given the constraints imposed by the visual scene. This evaluation process takes into consideration real-world knowledge and the plausibility of "who-in-the-scene" could do "what" to "whom-in-the-scene." The English data demonstrate that such evaluation takes into consideration also what is known thus far about the protagonists in the event and the action that they, as causal agents, effect. Thus, information about the Agent is combined with information about the action denoted by the verb, and this combined information drives the prediction of what kinds of object, given the concurrent visual scene, will plausibly be referred to next. In fact, the Japanese and English data are not so different: the case marking on the first two arguments (NP1-nominative and NP2-dative) determines, with a high likelihood, that the sentence-final verb will denote an action of transference, from the referent of NP1 to the referent of NP2. This information, in combination with knowledge of what NP1 and NP2 actually refer to, drives the prediction of the kind of object that, given the concurrent scene, will be referred to next (in NP3 position).

Although our data are robust enough to serve as evidence for anticipation during sentence processing, there are a few methodological issues to take into consideration. First, the visual-world methodology does not permit us to draw conclusions one way or another about the nonsemantic content of whatever is anticipated. For example, in the Japanese experiment, it is not clear whether the anticipation of NP3 includes information about its likely case marking (it will most likely be accusative, denoting a Theme, but the methodology cannot demonstrate it). Second, another methodologically oriented question concerns the role of the visual contexts in these experiments. In all the experiments, the linguistic stimuli were accompanied by relevant visual scenes that restricted the range of potential candidates that could be predicted. This methodology certainly enables us to simulate situations in which there are potential objects in view of the listener. However, the technique does not necessarily apply to other situations in which there are no relevant objects in view of the listener. Thus, it is unclear at present whether, in the absence of a concurrent visual (or linguistic) context, the fragment *The boy will eat* . . . causes the anticipation of a subsequent direct object that will refer to something edible. Other methodologies are required to establish the generalizability of our results to other linguistic situations. After all, a defining feature of language is that it can be used to refer to things even in their absence. Whether our data generalize to this situation is unclear. Nonetheless, we believe it would be extremely unlikely, if not implausible, for the processor not to use information conveyed by a verb such as *eat* to anticipate that the subsequent direct object will refer to something edible. Although such a prediction could not be evaluated with respect to any concurrent visual context, it could be evaluated with respect to a mental model constructed on the basis of linguistic context (see Altmann 1999 for an example of such predictive processing), or with respect to general world knowledge.

Finally, why does the processor predict subsequent arguments, and evaluate its predictions against the context? Why not simply wait until those arguments are encountered? We speculate that the answer to this question lies in the nature of incremental processing. Although, in principle, an incremental processor does not have to have a predicting mechanism, we do believe that our findings suggest the possibility that the human sentence-processing mechanism is most likely to be incremental, and furthermore they imply that prediction of a forthcoming item may contribute to full interpretation of the items that have been already encountered. Thus, interpreting a sentence incrementally, word by word, requires the partial interpretation of what has been encountered so far. Crucially, this might include the interpretation at each moment in time of the consequences of what has been encountered so far for what may come next (both in the language and in the mental or real world described by that unfolding language). That is, the fullest possible interpretation may entail prediction.

Notes

We appreciate very helpful comments from Michael Tanenhaus, Michael Spivey, and an anonymous reviewer on an earlier version of the present chapter. We also thank Vicki White, Lynne Weighall, and Matthew Smelt-Webb for helping us recruit the participants in the experiments reported here. The present research was supported by grants from the Medical Research Council (G9628472N and G0000224), the Economic and Social Research Council (R000222798), and the Royal Society (all awarded to GTMA). The materials used in the experiments can be obtained from YK on request.

1. In this chapter, we use the term *prediction*, in the context of thematic-role assignment, to refer to the process by which thematic dependencies can be established prior to the point at which those dependencies are unambiguously signaled within the linguistic input. Whether this process in fact involves the projection of structure (syntactic or otherwise) that is explicitly tagged as representing future input, or whether it does not, is less relevant to the present discussion than the fact that thematic dependencies can be computed in advance of their corresponding grammatical dependencies.

2. Kamide, Altmann, and Haywood (2003) provide a fuller version of a report on experiment 2, and also a report on a follow-up experiment to experiment 1.

3. The relatively long regions were due to a number of properties of our stimuli used in this experiment. For example, pauses between the words at intonational boundaries might have been unusually long (note that some regions contain pauses), and some items contained a particle verb (e.g., *dig up*) in the Verb region (region2). Although the main purpose of the present research is to explore whether prediction can be achieved in the processing of sentences with *certain* linguistic structures (and *arbitrary* physical properties), we acknowledge the importance of further investigation into the effect of the rate of speech on anticipatory eye movements.

4. Similar to experiment 1, the critical region might appear to be relatively long. This is presumably because some adverbs in the critical region consisted of relatively large numbers of morae (the mean number of morae: 5.125).

References

Altmann, G. T. M. 1999. Thematic role assignment in context. *Journal of Memory and Language, 41*, 124–145.

Altmann, G. T. M., and Kamide, Y. 1999. Incremental interpretation at verbs: Restricting the domain of subsequent reference. *Cognition, 73*, 247–264.

Boland, J. E., Tanenhaus, M. K., Garnsey, S. M., and Carlson, G. 1995. Argument structure and the parsing of sentences with long-distance dependencies. *Journal of Memory and Language, 34*, 774–806.

Chomsky, N. 1965. *Aspects of the Theory of Syntax*. Cambridge, MA: MIT Press.

Chomsky, N. 1981. *Lectures on Government and Binding*. Dordrecht: Foris.

Chomsky, N. 1995. *The Minimalist Program*. Cambridge, MA: MIT Press.

Christiansen, M. H., and Chater, N. 1999. Toward a connectionist model of recursion in human linguistic performance. *Cognitive Science, 23*, 157–205.

Cooper, R. M. 1974. The control of eye fixation by the meaning of spoken language: A new methodology for the real-time investigation of speech perception, memory, and language processing. *Cognitive Psychology, 6*, 84–107.

Elman, J. L. 1990. Finding structure in time. *Cognitive Science, 14*, 179–211.

Frazier, L., and Fodor, J. D. 1978. The sausage machine: A new two-stage parsing model. *Cognition, 6*, 291–326.

Jurafsky, D. 1996. A probabilistic model of lexical and syntactic access and disambiguation. *Cognitive Science, 20*, 137–194.

Kamide, Y., Altmann, G. T. M., and Haywood, S. L. 2003. The time course of prediction in incremental sentence processing: Evidence from anticipatory eye movements. *Journal of Memory and Language*, *49*, 133–156.

Kamide, Y., Scheepers, C., and Altmann, G. T. M. 2003. Integration of syntactic and semantic information in predictive processing: Cross-linguistic evidence from German and English. *Journal of Psycholinguistic Research*, *32*, 37–55.

Pollard, C., and Sag, I. A. 1994. *Head-driven phrase structure grammar*. Chicago Stanford: University of Chicago Press CSLI.

Tanenhaus, M. K., Garnsey, S. M., and Boland, J. E. 1990. Combinatory lexical information and language comprehension. In G. T. M. Altmann, ed., *Cognitive Models of Speech Processing: Psycholinguistic and Computational Perspectives*. Cambridge, MA: MIT Press.

Tanenhaus, M. K., Spivey-Knowlton, M. J., Eberhard, K. M., and Sedivy, J. C. 1995. Integration of visual and linguistic information in spoken language comprehension. *Science*, *268*(5217), 1632–1634.

Taraban, R., and McClelland, J. L. 1988. Constituent attachment and thematic role assignment in sentence processing: Influences of content-based expectations. *Journal of Memory and Language*, *27*, 597–632.

Trueswell, J. C., Tanenhaus, M. K., and Kello, C. 1993. Verb-specific constraints in sentence processing: Separating effects of lexical preferences from garden-paths. *Journal of Experimental Psychology: Learning, Memory and Cognition*, *19*, 528–553.

11   Rapid Relief of Stress in Dealing with Ambiguity

Silvia Gennari, Luisa Meroni, and Stephen Crain

In the literature on formal semantics, there has been considerable discussion of the influence of phonological stress on sentence interpretation (Jackendoff 1972; Rooth 1992, 1996). The consensus is that contrastive or marked stress evokes a set of entities that have already been established in the discourse context. These entities are contrasted with the entity referred to by the expression that bears stress—the focused entity. Consider the following example (capital letters indicate marked stress):

(1)   JOHN called Mary.
   Alternative set = {x: x called Mary}

With the indicated intonation, (1) presupposes that there are other people besides John in a position to call Mary. The sentence in (1) can be used felicitously, therefore, as the answer to the question *Who called Mary?* Alternatively, it can be used in a situation, as in (2), where one speaker challenges the assertion made by another speaker about the identity of a specific caller:

(2)   Speaker A: Peter called Mary last night.
   Speaker B: No, JOHN called Mary last night.

In both cases, there are one or more alternatives to the individual in focus—that is, John. These alternatives are referred to as the *contrast set*, and the linguistic expression that receives stress will be referred to as the *focus element*.

The use of phonological stress occurs reliably with focus-sensitive particles, such as *only*, *always*, and *even*, but most reliably with *only*. Depending on which linguistic expression receives stress, different alternative interpretations of the sentence are generated, each with a different contrast set. By identifying the focus element, marked stress signals the relevant contrast set that should have already been established in the domain of discourse. Consider the following examples:

(3)   LAURA even sang at the party.
   Alternative set = {x: x sang at the party}

(4)   Laura even sang at the PARTY.

   Alternative set = {x: Laura sang at x}

In (3), the meaning of *even* carries the presupposition that Laura was one of the least likely of the partygoers to sing at the party. The fact that *Laura* receives stress indicates that a set of alternatives to Laura has previously been introduced. In (4), by contrast, the stress pattern indicates a different contrast set. In this case, *even* carries the (speaker's) presupposition that the party was the least likely place where Laura would sing, among other possible places that were under consideration. In both cases, marked stress designates the set of alternatives with which the focus particle *even* is semantically associated. Thus, the use of stress contributes to the presuppositional content of the sentence. However, the use of stress does not influence the truth conditions of these sentences; (3) and (4) are true just in case Laura sang at the party, independently of the element in focus.

   The focus operator *only* behaves differently from other focus-sensitive elements, including *even*. With *only*, the location of marked stress can affect the truth conditions of a sentence, in addition to its presuppositional content. In sentences with *only*, the speaker not only *presupposes* the existence of a contrast set in the discourse context, as with other focus particles, but the speaker also *asserts* that the entity in focus has some property that other members of the contrast set lack. This uniqueness claim can change depending on the location of phonological stress, yielding a corresponding change in truth conditions. We illustrate this with the following sentences, where capital letters indicate marked stress and italics indicate default stress:

(5)   The mother only brought some milk to *the boy*.

(6)   The mother only brought SOME MILK to the boy.

In English, the final constituent of a sentence typically receives what has been called neutral or default phonological stress (Selkirk 1986; Cinque 1993). The neutral stress pattern makes the noun phrase *the boy* the focus element in (5). Following several linguistic accounts, we assume that whichever happens to be the most prominently accented constituent in the sentence will associate with *only*, becoming the focus element of the sentence. In uttering (5), the speaker asserts that the only person who the mother brought milk to was the boy, as opposed to a man, say. In uttering (6), by contrast, the speaker asserts that the only thing the mother brought to the boy was milk, among the other things under consideration in the discourse context—for instance, coffee. Both sentences presuppose that a set of alternatives (to the boy in (5) and to the milk in (6)) has previously been introduced in the discourse context. However, sentences (5) and (6) make different assertions, so their truth conditions are dif-

Figure 11.1
Example of a test scene corresponding to the sentence *The mother only brought some milk to the boy* and its variants for each of the conditions.

ferent. In the situation depicted in figure 11.1, for example, (6) is true because the mother brought only milk, not coffee, to the boy, but (5) is false, because the man was also given milk. It is clear from (5) and (6) that sentences with the focus operator *only* are potentially ambiguous depending on where focal stress is assigned. Resolution of the ambiguity hinges on the assignment of stress. We exploited these properties of sentences with *only* to investigate the effect of stress in resolving the semantic ambiguity found in constructions with ditransitve verbs. Specifically, we used a head-mounted eye tracker (eye-movement recording system) to investigate the influence of contrastive stress during the online interpretation of spoken sentences, which subjects judged against visually presented scenes. This method allowed us to examine the interaction of the focus operator *only* with changes in phonological prominence. The results of the present study show that phonological stress facilitates the resolution of ambiguity; marked stress results in the rapid calculation of the appropriate contrast set.

Previous Studies

Several studies have shown how the semantic properties of *only* can be used by the parser to override preferences for certain structural analyses that would otherwise be observed. For example, substitution of *only* for the definite determiner *the* has been shown to eliminate garden-path effects typically observed in classic garden-path sentences such as *The horse raced past the barn fell* (Ni, Crain, and Shankweiler 1996). Sentences with *only*, as compared to ones with *the*, as in (7) and (8), do not evoke garden-path effects.

(7) *Only* businessmen loaned money at low interest rates were told to record their expenses.

(8) *The* businessmen loaned money at low interest rates were told to record their expenses.

To explain the absence of garden-path effects in sentences like (7), Ni and colleagues (1996) appealed to semantic properties of the focus operator *only*. Because sentences with *only* were presented in the so-called null context, there was no contrast set to the focus element, *businessmen*, in (7). To minimize the accommodation of the presuppositional failure, the authors suggested that the parser would use the verb *loaned* as a past participle, thereby allowing the parser to partition the set of businessmen previously introduced into a set of businessmen who were loaned money and a set of businessmen who were not loaned money. It was anticipated, therefore, that the reduced-relative-clause reading would be generated in the test sentence with *only*.

Sedivy (2002) replicated Ni, Crain, and Shankweiler's findings, and complemented them by showing that garden-path effects reemerge for sentences with *only* if a contrast set is established in the preceding discourse context. In (9), for example, a contrast set corresponding to *secretaries* (accountants) has already been established in the discourse model when the parser encounters the focus operator *only*. Therefore, the model of Ni and colleagues is led to predict the reemergence of a garden-path effect, which is what Sedivy (2002) found.

(9) All secretaries and accountants were asked to take a tough computing course.
Only the secretaries prepared for the exam got good scores.

In short, the parser's structural analyses in interpreting sentences with *only* depend on the presence or absence of a contrast set in the conversational context.

Other studies have investigated the effect of focus stress on sentence interpretation, using a variety of tasks. For example, Eberhard et al. (1995) monitored the eye movements of subjects attempting to identify objects that were introduced and referred to in spoken commands. These authors found that subjects were faster in visually locating and tracking the appropriate nonlinguistic entities when these entities were identified in commands by marked (contrastive) phonological stress. More specifically, assigning stress to an adjective (e.g., *pick up the LARGE red square*) permitted subjects to (mentally) eliminate certain objects in the display from consideration. In the stress condition, subjects immediately gazed at those objects in the display that contrasted with the target item on the relevant dimension (e.g., size), thus enabling them to subsequently restrict attention to the relevant objects (also see Sedivy et al. 1999). It is pertinent to note that studies by Cutler and Foss (1977) and Cutler and Fodor (1976) report that subjects need less time to identify a targeted phoneme when the phoneme occurs in a word that receives phonological prominence.

These findings imply that marked stress alone often suffices to draw people's attention to certain relevant entities in the discourse context, which then become the semantic focus of the sentence. These studies, however, did not investigate the effect of focal stress in potentially ambiguous sentences with *only*. The literature in child language contains two previous studies that investigated children's use of phonological stress in the resolution of ambiguity (Gualmini, Maciukaite, and Crain 2002; Halbert et al. 1995). These studies found that preschool children ignore contrastive stress in attempting to determine the linguistic expression associated with the focus operator *only*. As a result, these children assign the same reading to (5) and (6), the one corresponding to the default stress pattern. In a review of these studies, Reinhart (1999) suggests that children encounter difficulty when processing ambiguous sentences with *only* because of limited working-memory capacity. Such a limitation prevents children from holding alternative interpretations in mind and leads them to resort to the default interpretation.

The question now arises whether and how adults use phonological stress to resolve ambiguities—that is, whether and how they use phonological stress as an indicator of the relevant focus element in sentences with the focus operator *only*. The present study was designed to address this question, using an eye-tracking paradigm. The aim was to investigate the effect of stress in the resolution of ambiguous sentences, by looking at the association of *only* with phonological stress in online sentence processing.

Diverging Approaches

There are few theoretically motivated proposals about the computation involved in calculating phonological stress. A notable exception is Reinhart 1999. In the model proposed by Reinhart, in interpreting potentially ambiguous sentences with the focus operator *only*, the processing system is compelled to calculate the contrast set associated with the default stress pattern of the sentence, even if stress is assigned to a different constituent (as with marked stress). Therefore, the parser is forced to reanalyze sentences with marked stress patterns, making such sentences more difficult than ones with default stress. For example, speakers are expected to initially compute one reading for (6), taking the focus to be the boy, and the contrast set to be people rather than drinks, because this reading corresponds to the neutral stress pattern of English.

The computation of the relevant contrast set must later be adjusted in response to the observation by the parser that the stress-shift rule (changing the stress to a marked position) has been engaged. Therefore, the prediction is that people will find (6) more difficult than (5) because two possible readings and two stress rules are computed in (6), whereas one interpretation is computed in (5).

(5) The mother only brought some milk to *the boy*.

(6) The mother only brought SOME MILK to the boy.

The overall model Reinhart has in mind is modular in architecture, such that computations made within the grammatical system (including syntax and phonology) are executed independently of computations made within the conceptual system (i.e., semantics and contextual information). The outputs of these different computational systems meet at an interface component of language. Because the two computational systems operate autonomously, the grammatical system is compelled to compute default stress first, with its associated focus assignment. At the interface, if the information that is output from the conceptual system does not match the interpretation of the initial focus assignment, this triggers a recomputation of stress in cases of stress shift, together with its corresponding focus interpretation. This extra operation, according to Reinhart, increases memory load, resulting in greater cost in processing. In the paragraphs that follow, we refer to this as the *interface model*.

Despite empirical support for this model from research on child language, previous findings on adult sentence processing appear at odds with the interface model. As we saw, the previous literature on adult sentence processing suggests that the parser incrementally computes the focus element and its associated contrast set for sentences containing the focus operator *only*. If phonological prominence disambiguates sentences with the focus operator *only* online, it could also turn out that marked stress is used immediately by the parser to decide which noun phrase bears semantic focus and, therefore, which contrast set should be invoked for sentence interpretation. In this scenario, there is no need to fully calculate all alternative contrast sets, including the one associated with default stress. To the contrary, the expectation is that the processing cost of interpreting sentences with marked stress, as in (6), will not be significantly greater than that found in sentences with neutral stress, as in (5). In fact, it is possible, perhaps likely, that multiple contrast sets (one for each postverbal NP) will be built in *only* sentences with default stress, because the element in focus is not decided until the entire sentence has been processed. If the parser processes alternative interpretations of ambiguities in parallel with default stress, the fact that *only* requires the construction of a contrast set could compel the parser to build contrast sets for each relevant noun phrase it encounters, until the focus element is identified. We call this view the *online model*.

Description of the Study

To adjudicate between the expectations of the online model versus the expectations of the interface model, we conducted an eye-tracking experiment with adult English speakers. A head-mounted eye-tracking system was used to identify the patterns of fixations associated with the computation of the contrast set(s) for the target sentences. Subjects were asked to indicate the truth or falsity of sentences presented auditorily relative to visually presented scenes. This task contrasts with the eye-tracking studies mentioned earlier (e.g., Eberhard et al. 1995) in that determining the objects referred to in the visual scene is not the only task performed. Rather, the processor needs to evaluate each piece of information against the visual scene to determine the truth of the statement heard. This is arguably as natural a task as responding to spoken commands, because it is a central part of human communication. This task involves not only identifying the objects referred to by the spoken sentences, but also identifying and judging the appropriateness of the relations established between them.

The study compared three sentence types, as exemplified in (10)–(12).

(10) The mother only brought some milk to *the boy*.
      (Prepositional object)

(11) The mother only brought SOME MILK to the boy.
      (Marked stress)

(12) The mother only brought the boy *some milk*.
      (Double object)

The stressed constituent in each sentence is the focused element that determines the appropriate understood contrast set. Sentences like (10) have default stress on the final constituent in the sentence. This will be referred to as the *prepositional-object construction*. This construction served to establish a baseline for measuring the difficulty associated with marked stress in sentences like (11), which we call the *marked-stress construction*. Note that in figure 11.1, (10) is false while (11) is true, because they have different foci and interpretations. Since there may be an inherent difficulty in judging the falsity of a sentence, we also introduced the condition exemplified in (12), which has the same interpretation and truth conditions as (11) (where *milk* is the focus) but with different word order (we call this the *double-object construction*). Thus, (10) and (11) receive different interpretations but the same word order, while (11) and (12) have the same interpretation but different word order. This design provides separate measures of the processing difficulty associated with marked stress, one associated with the interpretation process, the other associated with the response itself. Comparing the marked-stress sentence to (10) allows us to evaluate the effect of marked stress versus default stress on the interpretation process. Comparing the marked-stress sentence to (12) allows us to determine whether differences between (10) and (11) are due to the interpretation process or to the difficulty of arriving at a false response.

The processor needs to assign an interpretation to be able to determine the truth of a sentence—that is, subjects need to determine the focus object and the appropriate contrast to this object. More specifically, to verify the prepositional-object construction in (10), which asserts that the mother brought some milk only to the boy, subjects need to check whether the boy is the only one with milk in figure 11.1. Thus, fixations on the man's milk are expected because this object falsifies the sentence. By contrast, to verify the marked-stress and double-object constructions, subjects need to check whether the boy only got milk (as compared to something else). Fixations on this object are thus expected. In all cases, fixations on the corresponding contrast sets (the man and the man's coffee) are also expected.

In addition to the fixations required to determine the truth/falsity of the sentences, the predictions of the interface and the online models differ in several respects. The interface model states that processing difficulty in the marked-stress condition results from the initial calculation of the interpretation associated with default stress. Sentences like (11) should prove more difficult for subjects than ones like (10) and (12)—that is, marked-stress sentences should take longer to process and show more incorrect responses than the sentences in the prepositional-object and double-object conditions. In addition, the interface model predicts that two interpretations and two contrast sets will be calculated in the marked-stress condition, one for the contrast set of the boy, another for the milk, because, in this view, two possible interpretations are entertained before responding. Thus, to verify (11) relative to figure 11.1, subjects should fixate on the two alternative contrasts: the man and the man's coffee. In contrast, to verify the default-stress conditions in (12) and (10), only one contrast set should be calculated. In the double-object construction, subjects should fixate on the man's coffee; in the prepositional-object construction, they should fixate on the man (the contrast to the boy). Given that total absence of fixations on scene objects is unlikely (participants often scan all objects), these predictions imply that fixations on the inappropriate contrast for the marked-stress construction (the man) should be longer than in the double-object construction and similar to the prepositional-object construction, where the man is the appropriate contrast.

Alternatively, the online model predicts that the marked-stress construction will be no harder than the prepositional-object construction (provided that this construction is no harder than the double-object one), because marked stress should not tax processing. On the contrary, if marked stress helps to determine the appropriate interpretation, then facilitation in response time, accuracy of response, and identification of the appropriate contrast set for the marked-stress construction (the one corresponding to the stressed material) may be expected. Thus, to verify this construction, subjects need to fixate longer on the boy's milk and its contrast (the man's coffee) relative to the other conditions. In contrast, the online model allows that two contrast sets could be computed in the default-stress conditions, due to the temporary ambiguities in such sentences until the default-stress expression is encountered. Thus, fixations on both alternative contrast sets (the man's coffee and the man) are expected in the default-stress conditions (the double-object and prepositional-object conditions), before the parser settles on the appropriate interpretation. This implies that fixations on the man should be longer than in the marked-stress condition and fixations on both alternative contrasts should not differ significantly for the two default-stress conditions.

Materials

The materials included a total of twenty-four sentences and a set of eight pictures like the one in figure 11.1. The test materials were embedded in a set of forty-two filler trials. The spoken stimuli contained eight sentences per condition recorded from a native speaker: the marked-stress condition, the default-stress/prepositional-object condition, and the default-stress/double-object condition, as exemplified in (10)–(12). The small number of items in each condition was due to the difficulty in obtaining verbs that can both admit the double-object construction and be visually depicted. The test scenes all had the structure exemplified in figure 11.1: there were two possible focus entities (the boy's milk or the boy) and two possible contrast entities (the man's coffee or the man). The scene thus satisfied the contextual presuppositions for two interpretations. Which focus or contrast entity is fixated on depends on which of the final noun phrases is taken to be the focus.

Procedure

Fifty-three native speakers of English participated in the experiment. Each subject was asked to judge whether the spoken sentences were true or false by pressing a key on the keyboard. Fifteen subjects were presented with examples of the prepositional-object construction, as in (10). Twenty subjects were presented with examples of the double-object construction, and eighteen were presented with examples of the marked-stress construction. The visual scenes and filler trials were the same for all three conditions. Because the scenes were fairly complex, subjects first saw each scene for 800 ms. Following this initial presentation, a cross was displayed on the screen for 500 ms, then the scene and the auditory stimuli were presented simultaneously for evaluation. Stimuli were presented using PsyScope, which also recorded response times and accuracy (Cohen et al. 1993). Eye movements were recorded from the beginning of the second presentation, using an ISCAN ETL-500 system.

Results

The behavioral responses by subjects across conditions were consistent with the on-line model, and not with the interface model. The percentage of correct responses was higher for the marked-stress construction than for the other two constructions (see table 11.1). Using the proportion of correct responses as the dependent variable, a one-way ANOVA revealed significant main effects of construction type, both by subjects and by items ($F_1(2, 50) = 2.90$, $p = .06$; $F_2(2, 12) = 7.97$; $p = .006$). Fisher's post hoc comparisons revealed that the marked-stress construction differed significantly from each of the two constructions with default stress. The proportion of correct responses for the marked-stress construction was .84 versus .70 for the prepositional-object construction (subjects: $p = .04$, items: $p = .009$) and .71 for the double-object construction (subjects: $p = 0.5$, items: $p = .002$). Also, there was a significant difference in response

Table 11.1
Mean proportion of correct responses and reaction times for each condition

	Proportion correct		Reaction time (ms)	
	Mean	SD	Mean	SD
Double object	.66	.24	2868	1442
Prepositional object	.70	.19	2465	1170
Marked stress	.84	.18	2178	859

times across construction types (see table 11.1). ANOVA by items revealed that subjects responded significantly faster to sentences in the marked-stress condition than ones in the double-object condition ($F_2(2, 14) = 3.80$, $p = .03$). This difference also appeared in an unpaired comparison across subjects ($p = .07$). However, the marked-stress condition was not significantly different from the prepositional-object condition. Taken together, the findings from these behavioral measures indicate that the marked-stress condition was not harder than the two default-stress conditions. To the contrary, the significant differences in the proportion of correct responses and in response times suggest that subjects are less confident and tend to be slower in assigning an interpretation to sentences with default stress.

We turn now to the analysis of the patterns of fixations and ask whether these differ across the three conditions. In analyzing the data, we concentrated particularly on fixations directed to the possible focus objects and the contrast objects in the scenes. These data were used to infer which interpretations subjects were entertaining during online sentence processing. For clarity, we report the data using figure 11.1. For example, we will refer to fixations on the boy, rather than on boy's milk, but it should be understood that this refers to the averaged proportion of fixations on possible foci across trials, within each condition.

To obtain a measure of the time subjects fixated on various objects, we first calculated the proportion of time spent within a trial on each object across all subjects. Objects in the scene were categorized according to their role in each possible interpretation, as follows: the focus entities (boy, boy's milk), the contrast entities (man, man's coffee), the counterpart of the focus element (the man's milk). Using the mean proportion of fixating time on each object type as dependent variable, ANOVA revealed a main effect of object type ($F_1(6, 357) = 19.017$, $p < .0001$) and construction type ($F_1(2, 357) = 2.74$, $p < .0001$), as well as a significant interaction of object type × construction type ($F_1(12, 357) = 5.92$, $p < .0001$). The item's analysis revealed a significant main effect of object type ($F_2(6, 12) = 11.71$, $p < .0001$) and a significant interaction of object type × construction type ($F_2(12, 147) = 2.76$, $p < .002$), but there was no main effect of construction type.

Post hoc comparisons revealed several significant differences. As figure 11.2 shows, the proportion of fixations on the boy's milk were significantly higher in the marked-stress condition than in the prepositional-object condition ($p = 0.008$), and fixations on the boy's milk were proportionally higher in the double-object condition than in the prepositional-object condition ($p = .05$). This indicates that both marked and, to a lesser extent, default stress on *some milk* drew attention to this focus entity, as

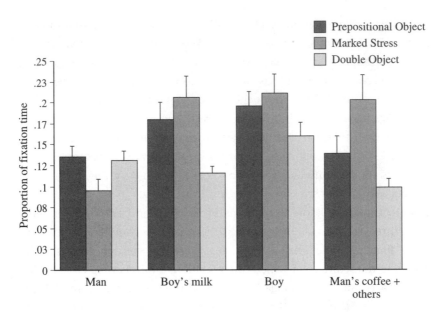

Figure 11.2
Mean proportion of fixation time as a function of construction type and scene object type.

compared to the lack of stress on the same constituent in the prepositional-object condition. Thus, subjects were more likely to fixate on the focus entity corresponding to the stressed constituent, and this was most pronounced in the marked-stress condition.

Next we consider subjects' fixations on the alternative contrasts (man, man's coffee). The interface model predicted that fixations on the inappropriate contrast in the marked-stress condition (the man) should be longer than in the double-object condition and similar to the prepositional-object condition, because two interpretations should be entertained in the marked-stress condition, each corresponding to the interpretations of the default-stress conditions. In contrast, the online model predicted that fixations on the man should be shorter in the marked-stress condition relative to the other two conditions, while fixations on the two alternative contrasts in the default-stress conditions should not differ. The proportion of fixating time on the man's coffee (as well as on the set of contrasting elements such as the teapot taken as a whole) invites the inference that in the marked-stress condition, subjects quickly arrive at the appropriate interpretation. There were fewer fixations on the man in this condition, as compared to the two default-stress conditions (subjects: marked stress versus double object: $p = .02$, marked stress versus prepositional object: $p = .07$). There were also more fixations on the man's coffee in the marked-stress condition than in the default-stress conditions (subjects: marked stress versus double object: $p = .05$, marked stress versus prepositional object: $p = .004$; items: marked stress versus prepositional object: $p = 01$). Within the marked-stress condition, there were proportionally more fixations on the man's coffee than on the man (subjects and items: $p < .01$). This sharply contrasts with the two default-stress conditions, where fixations on possible contrasts did not differ, despite the fact that their responses (and their respective interpretations) differed. These findings argue against the interface model, in several respects. In the marked-stress condition, if considered at all, multiple interpretations do not seem to be entertained for long, whereas there did appear to be temporary semantic ambiguities in the two default-stress conditions, as revealed by the patterns of fixations for all possible contrasts.

Discussion

Overall, the expectations of the online model were met in the present experiment. The sentences in the marked-stress condition revealed more consistent interpretations of the visual scene than did sentences in the double-object condition or ones in the prepositional-object condition. In addition, the proportion of time spent on the focus entity in the marked-stress condition differed from that in the default-stress conditions, indicating that subjects quickly processed the semantic consequences of marked stress. Finally, fixations on the contrast objects in the scenes indicate that subjects quickly arrive at an interpretation in the marked-stress condition: fixations on the alternative contrast (the man) were fewer, and fixations on the actual contrast were greater, than in the default-stress conditions. In the latter two conditions, fixations were evenly distributed between the two possible contrasts, suggesting that subjects were dealing with a temporary ambiguity.

One question that remains open is whether the higher proportion of fixations on the relevant contrast object in the marked-stress condition is simply due to the fact that phonological stress comes earlier in this construction than in the default-stress constructions. Arguing against this scenario is the observation that the mean response time was about 2.5 seconds following the final word of the test sentences in the double-object and prepositional-object constructions. This indicates that even after all the spoken information was obtained, subjects did not immediately settle on a unique interpretation. Instead, they fixated equally on the alternative contrast objects associated with the two possible interpretations. Therefore, both possible interpretations were entertained briefly in the default-stress conditions.

It is worth noting that subjects did not need to fixate on the contrast objects in order to make an accurate decision about the truth or falsity of the target sentence. In the marked-stress condition, for example, subjects need only look at the objects that the boy was given, in order to judge the truth or falsity of the sentence (since the assertion is that the only thing that the mother brought to the boy is milk). Similar remarks hold for the other conditions. Because *only* creates the expectation of a contrast set (via semantic presupposition), however, subjects rapidly search for the alternative contrasts as soon as they hear the stressed constituent in the marked-stress condition. This would be striking evidence that subjects accommodate the relevant presupposition online and incrementally, as suggested by the referential theory (Crain and Steedman 1985).

To conclude, the findings from our study support the view that alternative meanings are computed online during sentence processing, and that marked stress facilitates the resolution of ambiguities involving the computation of contrast sets.

References

Cinque, G. 1993. A null theory of phrase and compound stress. *Linguistic Inquiry*, *24*(2), 239–297.

Cohen, J. D., MacWhinney, B., Flatt, M., and Provost, J. 1993. PsyScope: A new graphic interactive environment for designing psychology experiments. *Behavioral Research Methods, Instruments, and Computers*, *25*, 257–271.

Crain, S., and Steedman, M. 1985. On not being led up the garden path: The use of context by the psychological parser. In D. R. Dowty, L. Karttunen, and A. Zwicky, eds., *Natural Language Parsing: Psychological, Computational, and Theoretical Perspectives*, 320–358. Cambridge, UK: Cambridge University Press.

Cutler, A., and Fodor, J. A. 1976. Semantic focus and sentence comprehension. *Cognition*, *7*, 49–59.

Cutler, A., and Foss, D. 1977. On the role of sentence stress in sentence processing. *Language and Speech*, *20*(1), 1–10.

Eberhard, K., Spivey-Knowlton, S., Sedivy, J., and Tanenhaus, M. 1995. Eye movements as a window into real time spoken language processing in natural contexts. *Journal of Psycholinguistic Research*, *24*, 409–436.

Gualmini, A., Maciukaite, S., and Crain, S. 2003. Children's insensitivity to contrastive stress in sentences with "only." In S. Arunachalam, E. Kaiser, and A. Williams, eds., *Proceedings of the 25th Annual Penn Linguistics Colloquium, University of Pennsylvania Working Papers in Linguistics*, vol. 8.1. Philadelphia, PA: University of Pennsylvania.

Halbert, A., Crain, S., Shankweiler, D., and Woodams, E. 1995. Children's interpretive use of emphatic stress. Poster presented at the Eighth Annual CUNY Conference on Human Sentence Processing.

Jackendoff, R. 1972. *Semantic Interpretation in Generative Grammar*. Cambridge, MA: MIT Press.

Ni, W., Crain, S., and Shankweiler, D. 1996. Sidestepping garden paths: Assessing the contributions of syntax, semantics, and plausibility in resolving ambiguities. *Language and Cognitive Processes*, *11*, 283–334.

Reinhart, T. 1999. *The Processing Cost of Reference-Set Computation: Guess Pattern in Acquisition*. Utrecht Institute of Linguistics Working Papers, Utrecht Institute of Linguistics OTS. Utrecht, The Netherlands: Utrecht University.

Rooth, M. 1992. A theory of focus interpretation. *Natural Language Semantics*, *1*, 75–116.

Rooth, M. 1996. Focus. In S. Lappin, ed., *The Handbook of Contemporary Semantic Theory*. Cambridge, MA: Blackwell.

Sedivy, J. 2002. Invoking discourse-based contrast sets and resolving syntactic ambiguities. *Journal of Memory and Language*, *46*(2), 341–370.

Sedivy, J., Tanenhaus, M., Chambers, C., and Carlson, G. 1999. Achieving incremental interpretation through contextual representation. *Cognition*, *71*, 109–147.

Selkirk, E. 1986. On derived domains in sentence phonology. *Phonology Yearbook*, *3*, 371–405.

12 Children's Use of Gender and Order of Mention during Pronoun Comprehension

Jennifer E. Arnold, Sarah Brown-Schmidt, John C. Trueswell, and Maria Fagnano

A central component of understanding language is identifying who or what the speaker is referring to. This process depends on the situation in which the reference occurs, requiring comprehenders to draw on the linguistic and nonlinguistic context to interpret the speaker's meaning. The contextual dependence of reference comprehension is especially obvious in the case of personal pronouns—the words *he* and *she* are relatively meaningless outside a particular context. Nevertheless, pronouns rarely pose a comprehension problem. Adults are able to draw on a variety of cues to identify the referent of a pronoun, and to do so very rapidly, typically within a few hundred milliseconds (e.g., Arnold et al. 2000a; Boland, Acker, and Wagner 1998; Garnham 2001; McDonald and MacWhinney 1995).

What is the processing architecture that allows adults to do this? We consider this question by focusing not on the adult system, but on the system in progress—that is, the language-comprehension abilities of 3- to 5-year-old-children. Our focus here is not simply on what it is that children know, but also on how they bring that knowledge to bear during the referential processing of pronouns.

On the surface, learning to understand pronouns appears to be a very difficult problem. This is because the same pronoun can refer to vastly different things, even over brief stretches of a conversation. *She* can refer to Mommy, another child, the family cat, and even a talking car in a book. Although some properties of the referents are relevant (e.g., gender, animacy), most are not. This learning situation is quite different from that for common content nouns, which typically refer to entities that share some semantic properties (e.g., mommies, children, cats, and cars). Instead, pronouns typically refer to entities that are currently in the joint focus of attention of discourse participants. This poses a complex modeling problem, both for adults and children. It requires an individual not only to attend to an object over some period of time, but also to infer what one's interlocutor is attending to. The former is difficult enough for small children; the latter is tantamount to mind reading—no small feat for anyone, especially a 4-year-old.

Possible solutions to these learning and processing challenges can be found in the two traditions in psycholinguistics that are highlighted in this book, dubbed the "language-as-action" and "language-as-product" traditions by Clark (1992). Researchers within the action tradition tend to focus on socially situated language use, and emphasize that language is just one component of joint action (Clark 1996). This offers a solution to the seemingly intractable problem of modeling shared accessibility, by focusing on the fact that people, especially children, tend to use language to accomplish concrete, shared goals. This means that shared knowledge can be computed based on heuristics like physical copresence (Clark and Marshall 1981; see also Nadig and Sedivy 2002). Early on, children also use information like speaker eye gaze and plans of action as cues to speaker meaning (Baldwin and Tomasello 1997). In addition, cues from the shape of the discourse, some of which are described below, reflect referent accessibility in ways that can be highly predictive of pronoun use (e.g., Arnold 1998; Ariel 1990; Brennan, Friedman, and Pollard 1987; Givón 1983; Gundel, Hedberg, and Zacharaski 1993).

The language-as-action view also offers an interpretation of situations where the above-mentioned cues fail to result in a perfectly coordinated model of accessibility, as might happen if a child has not mastered them. Referring is collaborative (Clark and Wilkes-Gibbs 1986; Clark and Krych 2004; see also Brown-Schmidt, Campana, and Tanenhaus, chapter 6, this volume), which means that both speakers and listeners take action to ensure effective communication. When there is inequality in the abilities of two conversation partners (as may happen with a child), the more able one may adjust to the perspective of the less able one (Schober 1998).

Thus, the action tradition suggests that numerous sources of information, linguistic and nonlinguistic, are relevant to building a model of joint accessibility. How does the child (and adult) bring this information to bear on the task of pronoun interpretation? One possible solution is offered by processing theories developed within the product tradition. This tradition has tended to take an information-processing approach to language understanding, in which explanations of language use are rooted in understanding the kinds of representations that must be generated and integrated during comprehension. One account in this tradition suggests that much of language comprehension proceeds via constraint-satisfaction mechanisms, in which multiple probabilistic cues, rather than a single heuristic, are used to determine the most likely referential (and syntactic and semantic) representation of the input (e.g., McClelland 1987; MacDonald, Pearlmutter, and Seidenberg 1994; Tanenhaus and Trueswell 1995). Probabilistic constraints can either be linguistic (e.g., *examined* is more likely to be a past-tense than reduced relative verb) or nonlinguistic (e.g., the thing the speaker is looking at is probably but not necessarily the one they are thinking about).

This constraint-based approach offers a potential solution to the processing puzzle posed above, in which highly ambiguous pronouns pose relatively little difficulty for adult listeners. This is because multiple analyses are considered in parallel. Although computationally complex, parallelism allows for simultaneous use of multiple sources of evidence. A constraint-based account also makes clear predictions regarding the development of these processing abilities. For instance, if children approach language learning with a probabilistic system of representing linguistic and nonlinguistic cues, we would expect more reliable cues to be learned earlier, and perhaps weighted more strongly, than less reliable cues (Bates and MacWhinney 1989). In addition, we might expect child performance to improve when multiple cues point toward the same solution.

We investigated these predictions by focusing on two cues that influence adult pronoun comprehension: gender and order of mention (Arnold et al. 2000a). Gender is simply knowing that *he* is for males, *she* for females, and the ability to map these terms onto the appropriate referents. Although this requires children to be able to categorize entities by gender and map *he* and *she* appropriately, it does provide a fairly reliable cue to the pronoun referent—*he* rarely refers to female entities.

Order of mention, as we use the term here, is the tendency for adults to focus on the first of two characters in an utterance as the more accessible one. If a subsequent pronoun is encountered, adults tend to assign it to the first-mentioned character, other things being equal (e.g., Arnold et al. 2000a; Crawley and Stevenson 1990; Gernsbacher 1989; Gordon, Grosz, and Gilliom 1993). First-mentioned characters often occur in the position of grammatical subject, so this has also been described as a subject bias (e.g., Brennan, Friedman, and Pollard 1987; Stevenson, Crawley, and Kleinman 1994; McDonald and MacWhinney 1995; see also Kaiser, forthcoming). This cue represents the more general tendency for adult comprehenders to assign pronouns to entities that are jointly accessible with the speaker.

As a sign of accessibility, order of mention provides a mechanism for the speaker and listener to coordinate a joint model of entity accessibility. When the speaker places one entity in first-mentioned/subject position, this offers a cue to the listener that the speaker is interested in this entity, and is likely to continue talking about it (Arnold 1998; Grosz, Joshi, and Weinstein 1995). Note that this information is available whether the speaker produced it as a signal to the listener or because of the more general tendency to produce accessible information early (Arnold et al. 2000b; Bock 1982, 1986; Bock and Warren 1985; Bock and Irwin 1980).

However, it may take time to learn order of mention as a coordination cue, since it is only partially reliable as either a cue to accessibility or a cue to the referent of a pronoun. One metric of what the speaker considers accessible is what they continue talking about. Although first-mentioned/subject entities are continued more often than other entities, this is not a categorical pattern (Arnold 1998). Even once children know that first-mentioned characters are often central to the speaker's goals, they still may not consider first-mentioned status to be a good cue for interpreting pronouns. Pronouns often refer to the first-mentioned/subject entity, but not always. For example, data collected for Arnold (1998, chap. 2) show that pronouns in children's stories refer to the subject of the previous clause 57 percent of the time (64 percent when the pronoun is also in subject position). In contrast, correct gender assignment is essentially obligatory to the speaker, and so is a highly reliable cue to pronoun assignment under conditions that would otherwise be ambiguous to the listener.

A constraint-based theory would therefore predict that young children depend more on gender than order of mention for pronoun interpretation. This prediction is consistent with results from an online eye-tracking experiment (Arnold et al. 2001). In this study 5-year-old children listened to stories like (1) and viewed a picture of the story. When there was only one character matching the gender of the pronoun, children performed just like adults in a similar task (Arnold et al. 2000a)—they started looking at the referent of the pronoun at 400 ms after the pronoun onset. When the two characters had the same gender, children did not reliably look at the referent until well after the point where the pronoun was disambiguated by the story and scene (e.g., at *umbrella* in (1), because the scene contained only one character that was holding an umbrella). This behavior differed sharply from that of adults, who looked rapidly at the first-mentioned character in this condition.

(1)   Donald is bringing some mail to Mickey/Minnie, while a big rainstorm is
      beginning. He's/She's carrying an umbrella....

Thus, over the course of the temporary ambiguity, 5-year-olds showed sensitivity to gender but not order of mention, whereas adults used both cues simultaneously.

However, it is still possible that young children are sensitive to order of mention, but use it more slowly than gender. The online task would not have revealed offline usage of order of mention, because late eye movements to the correct character can be attributed to the disambiguating information in the subsequent scene and discourse. To resolve this issue, the current study used stimuli that did not include disambiguating material after the pronoun (i.e., pronouns were potentially globally ambiguous). If 5-year-olds are sensitive to this information, it should show up as a first-mention bias in offline responses.

As mentioned above, we suspected that children who are still mastering these cues will perform best when both order of mention and gender point to the same referent.

This prediction is consistent with research showing that children can use accessibility cues in situations where several sources of information together support a single referent as the more accessible one. Song and Fisher (2001) used both online and offline tasks to show that children comprehend sentences better when an ambiguous pronoun is used to refer to the more accessible of two characters—for example, "See the turtle and the tiger. The turtle goes downstairs with the tiger. And he finds a box with the tiger. Now, what does *he* have? Look, he has a kite!" By the time the target (italicized) pronoun is encountered, its referent had been made accessible through three mechanisms: linear order of mention, repeated mention, and previous pronominalization. Wykes (1981) also reported offline evidence that children were better at interpreting pronouns when they referred to the first-mentioned of two characters, in situations where other cues to referent identity were gender and real-world inferences (e.g., John needed Jane's pencil. She gave it to him.). These findings suggest that children can and do use accessibility cues when there is a high degree of redundancy or overlap in the information across several cues. However, each one on its own may not be strong enough to bias the interpretation toward one character.

We tested the above-mentioned predictions by investigating gender and order of mention in children of two age groups, 3;6–4;0 and 4;1–5;0 years. Based on earlier online results with 4;6- to 5;6-year-olds (Arnold et al. 2001), we expected the older group to display offline ability with gender, with perhaps the younger group showing less sensitivity. Of special interest, though, was the use of order of mention. With globally ambiguous stimuli, a situation under which children have ample time to consider referents, would there now be signs of sensitivity to order of mention in offline responses, or even late online measures? Our methods for addressing these issues incorporated elements from both the action and product traditions, an especially important approach for studying language use in children. In particular, we examined online processing in a referentially rich environment—that is, using a partially interactive story describing a visually copresent scene.

Pronoun Interpretation by Children Age 3;6–5;0 Years

Participants

The experiment participants were fifty-two children from the Rochester, New York area, whose parents were recruited from a database of well-baby births. Five children were excluded from the analysis for failing to pass the diagnostic trials ($n = 2$), interference from parent ($n = 2$), or experimenter error ($n = 1$). This left forty-seven children in the analysis. Participants were recruited so as to form two age groups:

(1) twenty-four children age 3;6–4;0 (43–48 months, average 45.3), twelve boys and twelve girls, and (2) twenty-three children age 4;1–5;0 (49–60 months, average 54.3 months), thirteen boys and ten girls.

Methods and Materials

We presented children with short stories appropriate for 3- to 5-year-olds. The characters in these stories were visually illustrated with dolls placed in front of the child during each story. The physical presence of the dolls allowed children to use the visual scene as their memory for the characters, potentially freeing up mental resources to devote to comprehension tasks. It also provided a visual reminder about the gender of the characters, which was established at the start of the experiment. The stories were always about two of the following four puppets: Froggy (f), Bunny (f), Panda Bear (m), Puppy (m). Bunny and Froggy had visual appearances consistent with female stereotypes (e.g., they wore dresses and had long eyelashes). Puppy and Panda Bear had visual appearances consistent with male stereotypes (e.g., clothing like a tie and hockey shirt).

During each experimental session the child sat at a small table facing two experimenters. A play period at the start of the session was used to familiarize the child with the experimenters, an Elmo puppet (the narrator), and the four puppets representing the characters in the stories. The names of the puppets were repeated frequently during the play session, and transparently matched the character (i.e., Froggy was a frog). At the end of the play period we tested the children by asking them to help Elmo learn the names and genders, with the excuse that Elmo has trouble remembering names and knowing who is a boy and who is a girl. Most children were able to immediately name the characters and identify their genders; if they were not, we practiced until we were confident the child had learned them.

Children then listened to one warm-up story and fourteen prerecorded stories like (2), nine experimental and five fillers. Each story mentioned two characters, which had either same or different genders. The second sentence always had the form "{He/She} wants X." The objects were chosen so as to be equally desirable to males and females.

(2) a. SAME-GENDER   Puppy is having lunch with Panda Bear.
                                  He wants some milk.
     b. DIFFERENT/1ST-MENTION   Puppy is having lunch with Froggy.
                                  He wants some milk.
     c. DIFFERENT/2ND-MENTION   Puppy is having lunch with Froggy.
                                  She wants some milk.

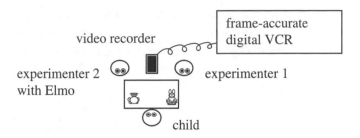

Figure 12.1
Experimental setup.

There were two different-gender conditions, manipulating whether the pronoun referred to the first-mentioned or second-mentioned character. Thus, the three conditions were: (1) different-gender/first-mention; (2) different-gender/second-mention; and (3) same-gender (i.e., ambiguous). One version of each item was recorded by a female speaker, and the other pronoun and name spliced in. This ensured that the prosody was identical across conditions. All pronouns were unstressed, but not extremely so.

The characters for each story were named and placed on the table in front of the child for each trial, as in figure 12.1. During each story, Elmo hid under the table while his "voice" came out of speakers. The two experimenters looked at the table at a point midway between the two characters, so as to not bias the child's response. The stories were digitized and played through PsyScope running on a Power Macintosh. The order in which the two characters were named was counterbalanced across items.

The nine experimental items were rotated through the three experimental conditions and pseudorandomly combined with five filler items to form three lists, presented both forward and backward and with the first-mentioned character on either the left or the right (total number of lists = 12). Two of the filler items were designated as practice items and placed at the beginning of all lists.

After hearing each story, the child was handed a toy (e.g., a play carton of milk) and asked "Can you show me who wants the milk in Elmo's story?" The child then gave the toy to one of the two puppets, thus indicating their interpretation of the pronoun. If the child changed the response, only the first one was counted in the final analysis. The story then continued—for instance, "Panda Bear wants a sandwich"—and the child was presented with a toy sandwich to give to the other puppet. The story continuation always used a name, and was chosen from two alternatives such that it always mentioned the character that the child had *not* given the previous toy to. Only the response to the first part of the story was counted in the analysis.

The five filler trials were identical in format to the experimental stimuli, except that a name was used in the second sentence—for example, "Panda Bear and Puppy are playing in the bathtub. Puppy wants the ducky." These trials were used as diagnostics of the child's ability to pay attention and perform the task; three or more errors resulted in the exclusion of that child from the analysis.

Eye-Movement Data

As a secondary source of data, we also recorded a close-up picture of the child's face, which was used to code the direction of the child's eye gaze during the pronoun and immediately after (see Swingley, Pinto, and Fernald 1998 and Snedeker, Thorpe, and Trueswell 2001 for similar procedures). A videorecorder was placed across the table from the child, and was trained on the child's face only. The characters were placed on either side of the child, but out of view of the camera, thus enabling the coder to be blind to the experimental condition. The sound was also turned off during the coding of eye movements so the coder would not know the condition of that trial. The signal from the videorecorder was sent to a frame-accurate Sony DSR-30 digital VCR, which recorded thirty images per second. Sound was recorded through a microphone connected directly to the digital VCR, yielding frame-accurate sound.

However, the experiment was originally designed as an offline task, so the online data were only included as supplementary data, for three reasons. First, the "correct" referent of the pronoun could only be identified in two of the three conditions. It is possible to compare eye movements in the two different-gender conditions with each other, but in the same-gender condition both interpretations are possible. Second, we expected a possible baseline problem. Unlike in Arnold et al. 2001, where an inanimate object was mentioned immediately before the pronoun, in the current experiment the last thing mentioned before the pronoun was the second-mentioned character. We anticipated that children might have a tendency to be looking at character 2 at the onset of the pronoun, which could make it difficult to observe pronoun-driven fixation preferences. Third, the task in the current experiment did not require the children to manipulate the objects or verify that the story matched a picture (again unlike that in Arnold et al. 2001). This opened the possibility that eye movements to the characters may not be time-locked with the linguistic input.

Results and Discussion

Adult Controls   For comparison to the child results, twelve adults participated in an offline experiment in which the structure and content of stimulus materials followed

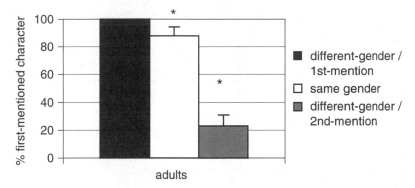

Figure 12.2
Results from experiment 1 (adult participants): percentage of first-mention responses in each condition. * = *p* < .05. All subjects chose the first-mentioned character in the different-gender/first-mention condition.

the same format and in most cases were identical to the stimuli for the child experiment. The stories were recorded by the same speaker, using the same prosody, tempo, and rhythm. Unlike the child experiment, characters were presented as pictures on a computer screen, and adults answered the questions by clicking on one of the two characters. Also, nine additional filler trials were used.

The results from the adults are shown in figure 12.2 in terms of the percentage of items on which the participant chose the first-mentioned character (averaged across participants). As expected, participants tended to choose the correct character in the two different-gender conditions, and showed a first-mention bias in the same-gender condition.

Analyses of variance over arcsine-transformed participant and item means showed a main effect of condition (*F*'s > 38, *p*'s < .001). There was no significant effect of location of first-mentioned character (right/left; *F*'s < 3, *p*'s > 1). Crucially, responses in all three conditions differed from chance (chance = .5; *t*'s > 3, *p*'s < .006), showing that adults interpret pronouns systematically, even when they are technically ambiguous (as in the same-gender condition).

A surprising number of errors occurred in the different-gender/second-mention category, suggesting that the first-mention bias can even lead to errors. This may have been especially likely to occur in cases like this, where participants were less familiar with the characters. Unlike with the child participants, we did not explicitly discuss the gender of the characters, which may have resulted in some confusion about the gender of certain characters.

Table 12.1
Average percentage correct responses on filler items

	First-mention fillers (%)	Second-mention fillers (%)
Younger children (3;6–4;0 years)	80	82
Older children (4;1–5;0 years)	84	84

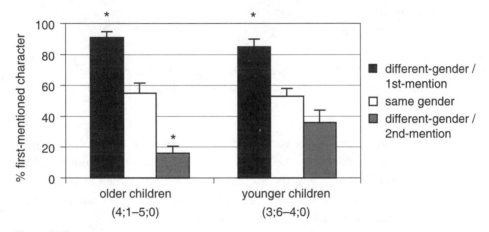

Figure 12.3
Results from both older and younger children in experiment 2: percentage of first-mention responses in each condition. * = $p < .05$.

Children: Diagnostic Data   All children included in the analysis showed evidence of understanding the task by choosing the correct character on at least three of the five filler trials, which did not include any pronouns. Two of the fillers named the first-mentioned character in the critical sentence, and three named the second-mentioned character. Table 12.1 shows that children from both age groups performed equally well on the two types of fillers (t's < 1.5).

Older Children (Age 4;1–5;0 Years)   The pronoun response data from the older children (figure 12.3) are similar to those from the adults for the different-gender conditions: they mostly chose the gender-matched referent. But unlike adults, in the same-gender condition they did not tend to prefer either character. T-tests show that their responses differed from chance in both different-gender conditions (t's > 6, p's < .001), but not in the same-gender condition (t's < 1, p's > .3). The same pattern occurred for both boys and girls.

These data are consistent with the online findings of Arnold et al. (2001), suggesting that 4;6- to 5;0-year-old children are adept at using gender to interpret pronouns, but they have not adopted a first-mention strategy even for globally ambiguous stimuli. That is, even when they are provided ample time, children do not resort to using order of mention. However, there is some indication that the older children were sensitive to the tendency for pronouns to be used for accessible referents, at least egocentrically— that is, they took pronouns to refer to entities in their own focus of attention. In the same-gender condition, the subject's gaze at the time of the pronoun partially predicted their response. The first character was chosen in 78 percent of the items where the subject was fixating on the first character at the onset of the pronoun ($N = 23$), and in only 52 percent of the items where the subject was fixating on the second character ($N = 25$, $\chi^2 = 2.6$, $p = .06$).

Younger Children (Age 3;6–4;0 Years) The response data for the younger children also show better use of gender than order of mention. However, the younger children appear to have a weaker use of the gender cue than the older children. Their responses in the different-gender conditions are in the same direction as those of the older children, but are more variable and tend toward chance. In the same-gender condition, their responses were also at chance (t's < 1, p's $> .5$), but their fixations at the pronoun onset did not predict their interpretation.

Interestingly, the strength of the gender cue appears to differ by both age and condition. The younger children match the abilities of the older children in the different/first-mention condition, choosing the correct referent reliably (t's > 8, p's $< .001$). But in the second-mention condition, where the older children reliably choose the second-mentioned character, the younger children's responses are not statistically different from chance (t's < 2.5, $.05 < p$'s < 1.0). An ANOVA of the subject and item means for all children supports this pattern by revealing an interaction between experimental condition and age ($F_1(2, 90) = 3.5$, $p < .05$; $F_2(1, 8) = 8.1$, $p < .005$).

A closer look shows that this pattern is complicated by a difference between boys and girls (see figure 12.4). The girls performed like the older children, choosing the gender-matched referents in both different-gender conditions (t's > 3), but choosing randomly in the same-gender condition (t's < 1). By contrast, the boys only showed a preference in the different-gender/first-mention condition (t's > 5), and were at chance in the other conditions (t's < 1). The difference between boys and girls is also partially supported by an ANOVA of the subject and items means for the younger children, including only different-gender conditions. This shows an interaction between condition and gender (boys versus girls) but only in the items analysis ($F_1(2, 44) = 0.797$,

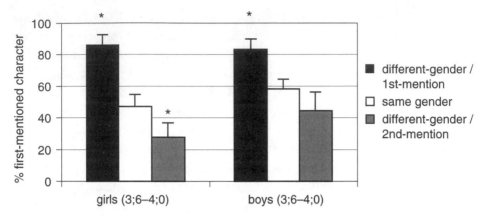

Figure 12.4
Results from experiment 2 for younger children only (age 3;6–4;0), split by gender: percentage of first-mention responses in each condition. * = $p < .05$.

$p = .457$; $F_2(2, 16) = 7.8$, $p < .05$). This difference cannot be attributed to age, since the average ages of these subgroups are 45.8 months for boys and 44.8 months for girls.

Thus, it appears that the children who use gender more weakly also show a dissociation in the degree to which they succeed in the different/first-mention and different/second-mention conditions. This seems to suggest that as children begin to acquire the ability to use gender, they understand gender-marked pronouns better when they refer to first-mentioned characters. Why is this?

To understand why children initially perform better in the different-gender/first-mention condition, we need to understand the processes underlying their responses. There are several requirements for performing correctly on the different-gender trials: (1) know the gender of the characters, (2) know the names of the characters, (3) be able to assign a referring expression to a single character in a context with two characters, (4) know that *she* maps to girls and *he* maps to boys, (5) know that gender information cannot be overridden by accessibility, and (6) have the processing capacity to apply this knowledge while dealing with additional incoming information.

We can be fairly confident that the children knew the names and gender of the characters, since this was established before the experiment began. This is consistent with research on gender knowledge in young children, which suggests that children are able to reliably distinguish females and males by age 2.5 (Martin 1993; Fagot and Leinbach 1993). We also know that they are able to perform the task of assigning a referring expression to one of two characters, given their performance on the diagnostic trials.

Therefore, it is possible that boys age 3;6–4;0 have trouble mapping between pronouns and the real-world gender. This may occur because they have trouble accessing information about the characters' genders during processing. During the preexperiment testing period they named the characters' genders with ease, which suggested that they do have solid representations of the genders. However, using this information on the fly is another matter. Even though our offline task allowed children plenty of time to answer, they still had to interpret the pronoun while simultaneously dealing with the rest of the sentence.

It is important to realize, however, that all the children demonstrated nearly adult-like performance when there was more than one cue pointing toward the same referent, even those who had trouble in the different/second-mention condition. Similarly, most naturally occurring pronouns are used in contexts where multiple cues, both linguistic and nonlinguistic, are present. The contrast between their performance in the different-gender conditions is consistent with the following potential interpretation. It may be that order of mention is present very young, but only as a supporting cue. Children may learn that pronouns refer to entities that are in the focus of attention, where the child's ability to identify the joint focus of attention is limited to the partial use of numerous cues. Order of mention, as a relatively unreliable cue, is not strong enough to produce consistent responses by itself (as evidenced by the chance performance in the same-gender condition). When other cues are absent, children may simply assume that the pronoun refers to the entity that is in their own focus of attention, or that it can refer to any compatible referent. This interpretation is speculative, but it is consistent with findings that very young children interpret globally and temporarily ambiguous referring expressions by choosing a compatible referent, rather than expecting the speaker to identify a unique referent (Flavell, Miller, and Miller 2002, 298; Trueswell et al. 1999). If children initially have an impoverished ability to map pronouns to gender, or if they do not know that the gender cue is inviolable, they may assume that any character they choose is the correct one. It is only when both order of mention and gender point to the same referent that they consider the linguistic input to be strong enough to drive their interpretation of the pronoun. Again, somewhat speculatively, the data suggest that as children develop, they "latch onto" the gender cue, temporarily overrelying on this cue over other partial cues, such as order of mention.

Eye-Movement Data   Our research focus here is on how children develop adultlike mechanisms for interpreting pronouns online, during ecological tasks that both provide a context and require the child to attend to numerous kinds of information. In this regard it is important to probe the time course over which different kinds of information are brought to bear. Do children initially use gender as an offline cue, or is it applied rapidly from a very young age? Data from Arnold et al. 2001 suggested that 5-year-olds used gender just as quickly as adults, starting about 400 ms after the pronoun.

Eye-movement data from the current experiment suggest that 4;1- to 5;0-year-old children are also using gender information online. The videorecord of the child's face was coded in terms of whether the participant was looking at the object to the right or the object to the left, for each 33 ms frame on the digital videotape. We began coding at the onset of the pronoun in the story, and continued for a minimum of 3 seconds, or until the child began to pick up the object presented by the experimenter. Other potential fixation categories were experimenter 1, experimenter 2, center (usually the toy), else, or track loss. Track loss occurred primarily when the child blinked, and accounted for 3 percent of the data overall. Intercoder reliability with this schema showed 87 percent agreement on the location fixated, and $+/-$ 0.4 frames agreement for fixation onset.

The primary result from the eye-movement data was that the older children, who all succeeded in using gender offline, showed use of gender starting at 800 ms after the pronoun. That is, they looked more at the first-mentioned character in the different/first-mention condition, and more at the second-mentioned character in the different/second-mention condition. By contrast, the younger children (both girls and boys) showed no preference for either character during this time period. In the same-gender condition, children in both age groups tended to fixate equally on the two characters at almost every point in time, matching their offline responses where their choices were at chance.

Figure 12.5 shows the eye movements in the different-gender conditions for the two age groups. The x-axis plots the "first-mention advantage" (percentage of looks to the first-mentioned character − percentage of looks to the second-mentioned character). Thus, positive numbers indicate more looks to the first-mentioned character, and negative numbers indicate more looks to the second-mentioned character. Each point represents the average percentage looks over a 400 ms segment.

Analyses of variance were performed over arcsine-transformed subject means for each segment, comparing the two different-gender conditions. For the older children there was no significant effect of condition for the first two segments (F's < 2, p's $> .2$), but segments 3 and 4 both showed a significant difference between the different-gender conditions (F's > 6, p's $< .005$). The younger children showed no difference between the conditions at any segment (F's < 1, p's $> .4$).

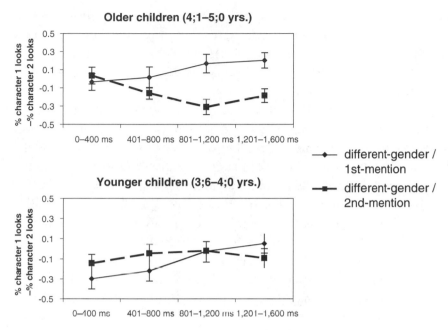

Figure 12.5

Eye-movement data, showing the percentage first-mention advantage (percentage looks to character 1 – percentage looks to character 2), for each 400 ms segment. Top panel: older children (4;1–5;0 years). Bottom panel: younger children (3;6–4;0 years).

It might seem surprising that neither the younger girls nor the younger boys show any reliable tendency to look at the correct character, even in the different/first-mention condition. However, their eye movements are heavily influenced by the fact that they were looking at character 2 more than character 1 at the onset of the pronoun. We had anticipated this baseline problem, since character 2 was the last thing mentioned before the pronoun. This resulted in the same general pattern of eye movements across all three conditions: initially more looks to character 2, followed by roughly equal looks to both characters. This problem was not present in the older children, resulting in a significant effect of age between 0 and 400 ms in an omnibus ANOVA over all three conditions and both age groups (F's > 4, p's < .05).

Conclusions

The main finding from this study is that children learn to use gender before order of mention. All children age 4;1–5;0 and girls age 3;6–4;0 were able to correctly interpret the pronoun when it was gender marked, but showed no preference when the pronoun matched the gender of both characters in the story. This earlier use of gender is consistent with online results (Arnold et al. 2001), and with the notion that cue reliability plays an important role in learning. *She* almost always refers to a female character, and *he* almost always refers to a male character.

Why do young children not follow a first-mention strategy, like adults? It may seem surprising that children are not more attuned to order of mention as a cue to accessibility. Almost all areas of language use require participants to be able to follow the same topic and identify certain referents as jointly accessible. By contrast, gender is a minor morphological cue, and only relevant for pronoun interpretation.

However, learning to use order of mention is a complex task. Children must learn not only that pronouns refer to accessible entities, but that accessibility is jointly constructed—at least that the speaker must have some evidence that an entity is accessible to the listener, as when the listener is looking at an object. Furthermore, they must learn that first-mentioned entities are treated as accessible by others, for example because they tend to continue talking about them (Arnold 1998). Once these patterns are learned, children still need to learn that order of mention can be overridden by other cues to accessibility, and by other cues to pronoun identity, like gender. These properties of order of mention also mean that it is relatively unreliable.

Order of mention is additionally hard to learn because it is rarely the most available cue to referent accessibility. It only occurs in cases where two entities are mentioned in the same utterance, which is likely to be rare in simple, child-directed speech. And even in such utterances, other cues to accessibility frequently co-occur. First-mentioned entities are usually those that have been recently mentioned and are in focus for other reasons. Consider the following exchange between 4;10.0-year-old Adam and his mother (Brown 1973). Evidently Adam is trying to put on a badge.

Adam: Ursuler@c # when I put dis on it keeps falling off me.

Mother: Maybe I can help you fasten it.

The underlined <u>it</u> refers to the entity first mentioned in the preceding sentence ("it keeps falling off me"). However, this is hardly the most important cue—this pronoun can be easily interpreted because the child is physically attending to it, because it is the focus of the entire exchange, and because it is the only salient entity that can be fastened, or referred to as <u>it</u>. The richness of the contexts of normal language use allows children to understand most pronouns without having adopted an order of mention strategy.

This feature, in and of itself, may also help children learn the association between first-mention/subject position and importance to the discourse. Children can use a variety of cues to understand pronouns, and in doing so accumulate a database of the kinds of contexts that pronouns occur in—and more generally, the kinds of entities that are treated as accessible by their interlocutors. Eventually a child will encounter situations in which it is helpful to assume that the first of two entities in an utterance should be considered the more accessible one. These situations may be more likely to occur under conditions with limited contextual support, for example in written stories, which children are more likely to encounter as they get older.

In the meantime, other cues may lead children to focus on the same things as their interlocutor—for example, eye gaze, repeated mention, or physical salience. Most experiences with language also involve an older and wiser conversational partner, who may adjust to the child's focus of attention (see Schober 1998 for similar findings with adults of different abilities). The children in our study may have depended on their conversational partner (Elmo) to adjust to their needs in this way, assuming that the pronoun in the same-gender condition referred to the character they were attending to.

The idea we are proposing is that children learn order of mention through its association with other indicators of accessibility. This idea is consistent with evidence that children can use accessibility cues to interpret pronouns, in situations where several cues point to the same interpretation (Song and Fisher 2001). It is also consistent with our finding that the youngest group in our study, especially the boys, performed best when gender and order of mention pointed to the same referent.

Our finding that children initially performed better when the gender-matched referent was also the first-mentioned one has the surprising implication that very young children are partially sensitive to order of mention. However, this cue remains very weak, and is not observable on its own until some time after age 5. This pattern is different from that observed in other domains, where weak cues are more likely to be observed when other cues are less constraining (e.g., Arnold 2001; Garnsey et al. 1997; MacDonald, Pearlmutter, and Seidenberg 1994; Spivey-Knowlton and Sedivy 1995). The difference here is that order of mention is just one cue to accessibility. Children may consider other accessibility cues more important—including their own capricious view of what is accessible.

Our findings also suggest that children are able to build on their partial understanding of one source of information by integrating another, also partially understood source of information. More reliable cues, like gender, emerge earlier as stable guides to pronoun interpretation. Weaker cues, like order of mention, initially exert pressure only as supporting cues. As children develop the ability to depend on gender, the weak influence of order of mention disappears, even as a supporting cue, as if they over-emphasize gender temporarily during development.

Our findings are more generally consistent with the view that children, like adults, process language by integrating multiple, partially redundant and probabilistic constraints about the pronoun referent and the joint focus of attention of speaker and addressee. The overlap of these cues provides useful information to the language learner, allowing the child to interpret pronouns in real time and thus gather information about additional cues that may facilitate processing in the future.

Note

We gratefully acknowledge Jesseca Aqui for her help in collecting the data, and Jared Novick for discussions of the experimental design and data. We also benefited from discussion with the following people: Richard Aslin, Felicia Hurewitz, Elissa Newport, Jesse Snedecker, and Michael Tanenhaus. Many thanks also to the children who participated in the study and their parents, and to Sandra Loosemore (http://www.frogsonice.com) for use of her frog art for the adult study. This research was partially supported by NIH grant 1-R01-HD37507-01 to John Trueswell, and partially supported by NIH grant 5-R01-HD27206 to Michael Tanenhaus.

References

Ariel, M. 1990. *Accessing Noun-Phrase Antecedents*. London: Routledge.

Arnold, J. E. 1998. Reference Form and Discourse Patterns. Unpublished doctoral dissertation, Stanford University.

Arnold, J. E. 2001. The effect of thematic roles on pronoun use and frequency of reference continuation. *Discourse Processes*, *31*(2), 137–162.

Arnold, J. E., Eisenband, J. G., Brown-Schmidt, S., and Trueswell, J. C. 2000a. The rapid use of gender information: Evidence of the time course of pronoun resolution from eye tracking. *Cognition*, *76*, B13–B26.

Arnold, J. E., Novick, J. M., Brown-Schmidt, S., Eisenband, J. G., and Trueswell, J. C. 2001. Knowing the difference between girls and boys: The use of gender during on-line pronoun comprehension in young children. In A. H. J. Do, L. Domínguez, and A. Johansen, eds., *BUCLD 25: Proceedings from the 25th Boston University Child Language Development Conference*. Somerville, MA: Cascadilla Press.

Arnold, J. E., Wasow, T., Ginstrom, R., and Losongco, A. 2000b. Heaviness vs. Newness: The effects of structural complexity and discourse status on constituent ordering. *Language*, *76*(1), 28–55.

Baldwin, D. A., and Tomasello, M. 1997. Word learning: A window on early pragmatic understanding. In E. V. Clark, ed., *Proceedings from the 29th Child Language Research Forum*. Stanford, CA: CSLI.

Bates, E., and MacWhinney, B. 1989. Functionalism and the competition model. In B. MacWhinney and E. Bates, eds., *The Cross-Linguistic Study of Sentence Processing*, 3–96. Cambridge, UK: Cambridge University Press.

Bock, J. K. 1982. Toward a cognitive psychology of syntax: Information processing contributions to sentence formulation. *Psychological Review*, *89*, 1–47.

Bock, J. K. 1986. Syntactic persistence in language production. *Cognitive Psychology*, *18*, 355–387.

Bock, J. K., and Irwin, D. F. 1980. Syntactic effects of information availability in sentence production. *Journal of Verbal Learning and Verbal Behavior*, *19*, 467–484.

Bock, J. K., and Warren, R. K. 1985. Conceptual accessibility and syntactic structure in sentence formulation. *Cognition*, *21*, 47–67.

Boland, J. E., Acker, M. T., and Wagner, L. 1998. The use of gender features in the resolution of pronominal anaphora. *Cognitive Science Technical Reports* No. 17. Columbus, OH: The Ohio State University, Center for Cognitive Science.

Brennan, S. E., Friedman, M. W., and Pollard, C. J. 1987, July. A centering approach to pronouns. *Proceedings from the 25th Annual Meeting of the Association for Computational Linguistics*. Stanford, CA: ACL, 155–162.

Brown, R. 1973. *A First Language: The Early Stages*. Cambridge, MA: Harvard University Press.

Clark, H. H. 1992. *Arenas of Language Use*. Chicago: University of Chicago Press.

Clark, H. H. 1996. *Using Language*. Cambridge, UK: Cambridge University Press.

Clark, H. H., and Krych, M. A. 1994. Speaking while monitoring addressees for understanding. *Journal of Memory and Language*, *50*(1), 62–81.

Clark, H. H., and Marshall, C. R. 1981. Definite reference and mutual knowledge. In A. K. Joshi, B. L. Webber, and I. A. Sag, eds., *Elements of Discourse Understanding*, 10–63. Cambridge, UK: Cambridge University Press.

Clark, H. H., and Wilkes-Gibbs, D. 1986. Referring as a collaborative process. *Cognition*, *22*, 1–39.

Crawley, R. A., and Stevenson, R. J. 1990. Reference in single sentences and in texts. *Journal of Psycholinguistic Research*, *19*(3), 191–210.

Crawley, R. A., Stevenson, R. J., and Kleinman, D. 1990. The use of heuristic strategies in the interpretation of pronouns. *Journal of Psycholinguistic Research*, *19*(4), 245–265.

Fagot, B. I., and Leinbach, M. D. 1993. Gender-role development in young children: From discrimination to labeling. *Developmental Review*, *13*, 205–224.

Flavell, J. H., Miller, P. H., and Miller, S. A. 2002. *Cognitive Development*. Upper Saddle River, NJ: Prentice Hall.

Garnham, A. 2001. *Mental Models and the Interpretation of Anaphora*. Philadelphia: Psychology Press/Taylor and Francis.

Garnsey, S. M., Pearlmutter, N. J., Myers, E., and Lotocky, M. A. 1997. The contributions of verb bias and plausibility to the comprehension of temporarily ambiguous sentences. *Journal of Memory and Language*, *37*, 58–93.

Gernsbacher, M. A. 1989. Mechanisms that improve referential access. *Cognition*, *32*, 99–156.

Givón, T. 1983. Topic continuity in discourse: An introduction. In T. Givón, ed., *Topic Continuity in Discourse: A Quantitative Cross-Language Study*, 1–42. Amsterdam: John Benjamins.

Gordon, P. C., Grosz, B. J., and Gilliom, L. A. 1993. Pronouns, names, and the centering of attention in discourse. *Cognitive Science*, *17*, 311–347.

Grosz, B. J., Joshi, A. K., and Weinstein, S. 1995. Centering: A framework for modelling the local coherence of discourse. *Computational Linguistics*, *21*(2), 203–225.

Gundel, J. K., Hedberg, N., and Zacharaski, R. 1993. Cognitive status and the form of referring expressions. *Language*, *69*(2), 274–307.

Kaiser, E. Forthcoming. Differences in the referential properties of Finnish pronouns and demonstratives. *The Proceedings from the Main Session of the Chicago Linguistic Society's Thirty-Eighth Meeting*, *38*(1). Chicago: Chicago Linguistic Society.

MacDonald, M. C., Pearlmutter, N. J., and Seidenberg, M. S. 1994. The lexical nature of syntactic ambiguity resolution. *Psychological Review*, *101*(4), 676–703.

Martin, C. L. 1993. New directions for investigating children's gender knowledge. *Developmental Review*, *13*, 184–204.

McClelland, J. L. 1987. The case for interactionism in language processing. In M. Coltheart, ed., *Attention and Performance XII: The Psychology of Reading*, 3–36. Hillsdale, NJ: Erlbaum.

McDonald, J., and MacWhinney, B. 1995. The time course of anaphor resolution: Effects of implicit verb causality and gender. *Journal of Memory and Language*, *34*, 543–566.

Nadig, A. S., and Sedivy, J. C. 2002. Evidence of perspective-taking constraints in children's online reference resolution. *Psychological Science*, *13*(4), 329–336.

Schober, M. F. 1998. How partners with high and low spatial ability choose perspectives in conversation. Paper Presented at the Thirty-Ninth Annual Meeting of the Psychonomic Society, Dallas, TX.

Snedeker, J., Thorpe, K., and Trueswell, J. 2001. On choosing the parse with the scene: The role of visual context and verb bias in ambiguity resolution. *Proceedings of the 23rd Annual Conference of the Cognitive Science Society*, 964–969. Hillsdale, NJ: Erlbaum.

Song, H., and Fisher, C. 2001. Young children's use of discourse cues in language comprehension. In A. H.-J. Do, L. Domínguez, and A. Johansen, eds., *BUCLD 25: Proceedings from the 25th Boston University Child Language Development Conference*, vol. 2, 720–731. Somerville, MA: Cascadilla Press.

Spivey-Knowlton, M. J., and Sedivy, J. C. 1995. Resolving attachment ambiguities with multiple constraints. *Cognition, 55*, 227–267.

Stevenson, R. J., Crawley, R. A., and Kleinman, D. 1994. Thematic roles, focus and the representation of events. *Language and Cognitive Processes, 9*(4), 473–592.

Swingley, D., Pinto, J. P., and Fernald, A. 1998. Assessing the speed and accuracy of word recognition in infants. *Advances in Infancy Research, 12*, 257–277.

Tanenhaus, M. K., and Trueswell, J. C. 1995. Sentence comprehension. In J. Miller and P. Eimas, eds., *The Handbook of Perception and Cognition*, vol. 11, 217–262. New York: Academic Press.

Trueswell, J. C., Sekerina, I., Hill, N. M., and Logrip, M. L. 1999. The kindergarten-path effect: Studying on-line sentence processing in young children, *Cognition, 73*, 89–134.

Wykes, T. 1981. Inference and children's comprehension of pronouns. *Journal of Experimental Child Psychology, 32*, 264–278.

IV Product Approaches to Action Variables

13 A Computational Investigation of Reference: Bridging the Product and Action Traditions

Amit Almor

Linguistic reference can be established in more than one way. One reason is that language allows many forms for referential expressions. For example, depending on the context, a specific robin could be referred to as "it," "the thing," "the bird," "the robin," "the poor little robin," and so on. The multitude of possible referential forms has been the focus of much work in several traditions of language study (e.g., Ariel 1990; Grosz, Joshi, and Weinstein 1995; Gundel, Hedberg, and Zacharski 1993; Sanford and Garrod 1989; Vonk, Hustinx, and Simons 1992). Despite sharing a common goal—explaining the use and distribution of referential forms—researchers working in different traditions have adopted different conceptualizations of the relevant issues. Many cognitive psychologists working in the *language-as-product* tradition (Clark 1996) view reference as problem solving, with speakers needing to decide what would be the best referential form given the attributes of the referent and the discourse, and listeners needing to decide what the referent is given the cues from the referring expression and the discourse. In contrast, researchers working in the *language-as-action* tradition (Clark 1996) have viewed referential form as providing an additional channel of communication between speakers and listeners. In this view, speakers use this channel to convey helpful information about the structure of the discourse, such as common ground and topic shifts, in addition to the identity of the referent (Clark 1996; Clark and Wilkes-Gibbs 1986; Gordon, Grosz, and Gilliom 1993; Vonk, Hustinx, and Simons 1992).

The different conceptualization in the two traditions has led to differences in emphasis and range of questions that are typically addressed. Whereas studies in the product tradition have tended to focus on the processing of referential expressions of different forms (e.g., Cloitre and Bever 1988; Greene, McKoon, and Ratcliff 1992; Sanford and Garrod 1981), studies in the action tradition have instead focused on the effect referential form has on the discourse (e.g., Vonk, Hustinx, and Simons 1992). While research in each tradition has made distinct and valuable contributions to the understanding of reference use and processing, the differences between the two traditions have resulted in some issues not being addressed at all. One such issue is the connection between discourse pragmatics and the cognitive architecture and mechanisms that underlie reference processing. Until recently, there has been surprisingly little research that attempted to explain how various collaborative behaviors in discourse (Clark 1996) are related and possibly caused by the underlying cognitive architecture and processes.

A more specific issue that has received only limited attention in either tradition is the reason for the systematic relation between reference specificity and the salience of referents in memory. Researchers working in both traditions have long noticed that memory salience plays a central role in the use and processing of referential form such that less specific expressions like pronouns are typically used when the referent is very salient in memory, whereas more specific expressions such as definite noun phrases are used when the referent is less salient (Ariel 1990; Garrod 1991; Garrod, Freudenthal, and Boyle 1994). Although this inverse relation has been noted many times, until recently there has been no serious attempt to explain the reason for the inverse relation. Research in the action tradition has attributed this to a pragmatic convention but has not addressed the processing issues responsible for the systematic relation between referent salience and reference form (e.g., Clark and Brennan 1991; Clark and Wilkes-Gibbs 1990; Wilkes-Gibbs and Clark 1992). Research in the product tradition has focused on the differences in processing various kinds of referential forms, mostly ignoring the systematic relation between referent salience and the specificity of reference form (e.g., Cloitre and Bever 1988; Gordon, Grosz, and Gilliom 1993; Greene, McKoon, and Ratcliff 1992).

Some recent work, however, has drawn on both traditions in order to link the study of pragmatics with research on the processing of reference and to offer a principled explanation for the inverse relation between reference specificity and referent salience. This work resulted in a theory of reference—the *informational-load hypothesis* (ILH)—that links pragmatic principles to the architecture of working memory (Almor 1999). Although the ILH draws on certain aspects of both the product and action traditions, it also diverges from each tradition in important ways. In line with the action tradition but unlike much work in the product tradition, the ILH conceptualizes referential form not as a problem that speakers and comprehenders need to solve but rather as the solution to a problem posed by communication needs under the constraints of the architecture of working memory. In line with the product tradition but unlike most work in the action tradition, the ILH incorporates a specific and detailed description of the underlying cognitive mechanisms and processes. By drawing on the strengths of both traditions, the ILH is not only able to provide a fuller explanation of some of the issues surrounding referential form, but also to address some of the questions that could not have been previously addressed in work that fell solely within the domain of either the action or the product tradition.

The original formulation of the ILH was intentionally general and did not include much computational detail, nor was it specific enough about the relation between comprehension and production processes. Whereas this generality was important for the initial presentation of the theory, the further development and elaboration of the theory crucially depend on filling in the computational details of the underlying mechanisms and on distinguishing between comprehension and production processes. The research reported here constitutes the first step in the development of a complete computational formulation of the ILH. The implications of this research for the relation between comprehension and production are discussed in the conclusion. Because the model outlined here is intended only as an illustration of how the notion of the ILH can be quantified, the scope of the behavioral data addressed is restricted to the findings of two previous studies (Almor 1999; Almor et al. 1999).

The Informational-Load Hypothesis

The ILH was originally formulated by applying a pragmatic principle, the Gricean maxim of quantity (Grice 1975), to referential expressions. The maxim of quantity states that "speakers should use the least complex linguistic form that is sufficiently informative for their communicative purpose." The communicative purpose the ILH attributes to referential expressions is identifying the referent and possibly also adding new information to the discourse. The ILH further attributes the complexity of referential expressions to processing cost that is related to the architecture of the semantic working-memory system used for discourse representation. The ILH thus argues that referential processing is governed by balancing discourse function with processing cost.

The processing cost of referential expressions, according to the ILH, is dictated to a large extent by the semantic overlap between the representation of the referential expression and the representation of the referent in memory. This is based on the observation that reference resolution must include a stage at which both the representation of a new reference (or some part of it) and the discourse representation of the referent are simultaneously active before integration has taken place.[1] Consequently, while semantic overlap may eventually help identify the referent, it also accrues some processing cost because, initially, the representation of the referential expression occupies a location in semantic representational space in working memory that is already used for the prior representation of the discourse and referent. This competition for the limited-capacity representational space is affected by the semantic overlap between the representation of the reference and the discourse representation as well as by the amount of activation of both representations. Assuming a model in which capacity is determined not only by the number of stored items but also by their activation (e.g., Just and Carpenter 1992, and the connectionist model outlined here), higher activation can result in more competition and therefore in higher cost. Activation is not only affected by memory salience but also by the amount of semantic detail in the representation. This is because representations rich in semantic detail require bigger chunks of this representational space than representations that have little semantic detail.

In summary, according to the ILH, two main factors determine the processing cost of a referential expression. The first is its semantic overlap with an already-activated representation. The second is the amount of overall activation of both the referent and the referential expression. This implies that when the referent is highly active in memory, a specific referential expression such as a definite noun phrase can become very costly. In this situation a referential expression with less semantic detail would be preferred, because it would be less costly. Thus, according to the ILH, the inverse relation between reference specificity and the memory salience of referents is not a matter of an arbitrary cooperative discourse convention but a direct outcome of the architecture of the underlying working-memory system.

Distributed Representations and the Quantification of Informational Load

In the original formulation of the ILH (Almor 1999), the processing cost of a referential expression was captured by the notion of informational load (IL), but to keep the theory as general as possible, no specific method was provided for calculating IL. The present work explores one possible way to quantify the notion of IL by assuming that referents and referential expressions are represented as distributed semantic feature vectors and that IL is related both to the overlap between the reference and the referent feature vectors and to the amount of activation of both vectors. The activation of the referent vector expresses a somewhat different notion than the activation of the reference vector. Because the currently processed referential expression is not yet represented in memory, it does not have variable memory salience. Therefore, the activation of the reference vector will only vary according to the amount of semantic detail in the reference (its semantic specificity). In contrast, because the salience of referents in memory varies, the activation of the referent vector expresses both the referent's semantic specificity and its salience in memory.

Mathematically, IL could be defined as the product of two scalar values (equation (1)). The first is the inner product of the referent vector, $f^{referent}$, and the reference vector, $f^{reference}$, which provides a good estimate of their semantic overlap as well as their activations. The second is the length of the reference vector, $\|f^{reference}\|$, which represents its degree of overall activation. As can be seen in the second line of equation (1), this formulation assigns a greater role to the activation of the reference, which is related to the amount of semantic detail activated by the reference, than to the preexisting activation of the referent in memory, which is affected by both the referent's semantic detail and its activation. This asymmetry between the two vectors reflects an asymmetry between the reference and the referent in that references that are more specific than the referent are more costly than references that are more general than the referent (e.g., IL(robin|bird) > IL(bird|robin); see Almor 1999 for details).

$$IL(reference|referent) = (f^{reference}, f^{referent})\|f^{reference}\|$$
$$= \|f^{reference}\|^2 \|f^{referent}\| \cos(f^{reference}, f^{referent}) \tag{1}$$

The usefulness of this proposed quantification is illustrated here by using representations based on subject-generated features that were collected by Kenneth McRae and colleagues from thirty subjects who were asked to list the properties of various concepts (see McRae and Cree 2002 for details). These representations are used to demonstrate that the proposed quantification is compatible with the experimental results that originally supported the ILH (Almor 1999). Each feature in the representation of each concept was assigned a strength indicating the number of subjects who listed it as a property of that concept. Only features listed by more than five subjects for the concept were included in these representations. Although McRae and his colleagues collected features for concepts from several categories, the present work only used the concepts from the bird category for illustration. These included forty kinds of birds as well as the concept "bird" itself. One hundred and fifty-four features that were listed for at least one bird concept by five or more subjects are included. Figures 13.1a and 13.1b illustrate this feature representation by showing partial normalized feature vectors for the concepts "robin" and "ostrich." Figure 13.2 shows a two-dimensional plot of the "bird," "robin," and "ostrich" feature vectors. The angles and lengths in figure 13.2 are the real lengths and angles between these three vectors in the 154-dimensional space. The figure shows how semantic overlap is captured by the angle between vectors. The vector for "robin," a typical bird, is closer than the vector for "ostrich," a less typical bird, to the "bird" vector. Figure 13.2 also illustrates how semantic specificity is reflected in the length of the representation vector. Due to differences in the amount of semantic detail, the length of the vector representing the more

ostrich

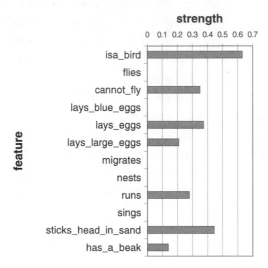

Figure 13.1a
Distributed-feature representation for 'ostrich.'

robin

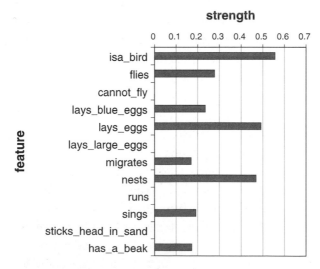

Figure 13.1b
Distributed-feature representation for 'robin.'

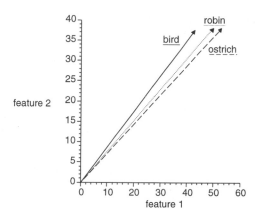

Figure 13.2
Two-dimensional projection of feature vectors.

Table 13.1
Different informational load for different references to the same referent

Fragment	Informational load
The robin ate the big fruit. *It* looked very satisfied.	IL ≈ small
The robin ate the big fruit. *The bird* looked very satisfied.	IL = 130,436
The robin ate the big fruit. *The robin* looked very satisfied.	IL = 246,653

general concept "bird" is smaller than the lengths of the vectors representing the more specific concepts "robin" and "ostrich."

Several basic test cases can be used to see whether this quantification is compatible with the more general theory. According to the ILH, a given referent could be referred to by different referential expressions, which will have different IL depending on semantic overlap. Table 13.1 shows examples of several discourse fragments in which the same referent, "robin," is referred to by different references (underlined). Table 13.1 also shows the IL of these references with respect to the referent, calculated by formula (1) and the subject-generated feature representations. In accordance with the general theory, the IL of the different references varies going from the least loaded pronominal reference to the most loaded repeated reference. Specifically, this quantification of IL can explain the different reading-time patterns found for repetitive and nonrepetitive noun-phrase references. The reading times of repeated and nonrepeated references similar to the ones shown in table 13.1 were measured in experiments 1, 3, and 4 in Almor 1999.[2] In these experiments, repetitive references were read more slowly when the referent was salient in memory than when it was not, but nonrepetitive references were read faster when the referent was salient in memory than when it was not. The original formulation of the ILH attributed this difference to the different IL of repeated and nonrepeated references. The computational formulation described here and illustrated in table 13.1 further supports this claim by showing that, when calculated precisely using realistic representations, the IL of repeated reference is indeed higher than the IL of nonrepeated reference even when the referential expression itself remains identical.

Another significant finding that was reported in Almor 1999 in support of the ILH is the "inverse typicality effect," namely, the finding that category references were read more slowly when coreferring with a focused typical member referent than when coreferring with a focused atypical member referent (experiment 5). This somewhat counterintuitive finding results from the reduced semantic overlap between the atypical referent and the category anaphor in comparison to the semantic overlap between the typical referent and the category anaphor. Intuitively, the typical case is more like repetition than the atypical case. Table 13.2 shows the IL calculated for examples similar to the items used in Almor's (1999) experiment 5. As is evident in the table, a given reference can have different IL when coreferring with different referents (underlined) depending on semantic overlap. In line with the reading-time patterns found in Almor's (1999) experiment 5, the category reference "bird" has a higher IL when coreferring with the typical bird referent "robin" than when coreferring with the atypical bird referent "ostrich."

Together, the examples shown in tables 13.1 and 13.2 illustrate that the quantification proposed here is compatible with the more general theory and the empirical

Table 13.2
Different informational load for the same reference with different referents

Fragment	Informational load
The ostrich ate the big fruit. The bird looked very satisfied.	IL = 55,755
The robin ate the big fruit. The bird looked very satisfied.	IL = 130,436
The bird ate the big fruit. The bird looked very satisfied.	IL = 185,279

findings described in Almor 1999. This in turn supports the general theory in showing that IL could be calculated precisely on the basis of realistic semantic representations.

Processing Dynamics

The discussion so far has focused on the computation of IL on the basis of static distributed feature representations. Because the ultimate goal of the theory is to explain not only the distribution of referential forms but also how reference is processed, the next natural step in developing a computational formulation of the ILH was accounting for the dynamics of reference processing. Specifically, this formulation was designed to account for the variability over time in the activation of referents in working memory, both in normal circumstances, and in abnormal cases when working-memory impairments result in rapid decay of referent representation. This was done using a simple recurrent connectionist model in which feature nodes were connected to concept nodes via weighted links. The weights of the connections between the feature and concept nodes represent the importance of the features for the concepts they are connected to. In the simulations described below, there were 41 concept nodes representing the 40 bird types and the concept "bird" as well as 154 feature nodes representing the subject-generated features described in the previous section. Figure 13.3 shows the architecture of the model. The weights were set to match the strengths

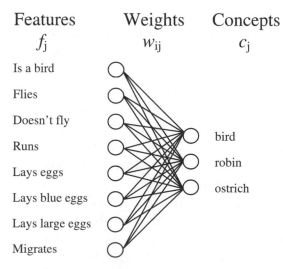

Figure 13.3
The architecture of the recurrent connectionist model.

of the 154 bird features in the representations of the 41 concepts. Activation flows in the model back and forth from the concept to the feature nodes. Equations (2) and (3) describe the activation dynamics of the model. The activation of the concept and feature nodes at time t is a function of the activation of the same node at time $t-1$ and the weighted sum of the activation of its input nodes.[3] The relative importance of a node's own activation in the previous time step in comparison to the activation of the inputs to the node is modulated by the decay parameter $0 \leq \lambda \leq 1$.

$$c_j^t = F\left(\lambda \sum_k w_{kj} f_k^{t-1} + (1-\lambda)c_j^{t-1}\right) \tag{2}$$

$$f_j^t = F\left(\lambda \sum_k w_{kj} c_k^{t-1} + (1-\lambda)f_j^{t-1}\right) \tag{3}$$

When the decay is minimal ($\lambda = 0$), the activation of each node changes independently of its inputs. When the decay is maximal ($\lambda = 1$), the activation of each node changes only according to its inputs. Although in real discourse, the representation of referents can be weakened not only due to memory decay but also for a variety of other reasons including topic change, the processing of new referents, and so on, the discussion here will be restricted to the effect of decay in working memory. Two cases will be considered. The first is normal memory decay, which will be modeled here by a relatively low value of the decay parameter. The second case is abnormally rapid memory decay, which will be modeled here by higher values of the decay parameter. One possible cause for abnormally rapid memory decay is working-memory impairment, as is manifested by people with Alzheimer's disease (AD). The work described below compares the performance of the model with low and high decay rates to referential processing in healthy people and people with AD.

To explore the effect of different values of the decay-rate parameter on referent representation, the model was tested in the following way. Initially, the activation of all the nodes in the model was set to zero except for the node representing the concept "robin." The model was then run for 100 iterations and the activations of both the "robin" and "bird" nodes were recorded.[4] Figures 13.4a–13.4d show the results of four such simulations with different decay rates. With small decay rates ($\lambda = .001$ shown in figure 13.4a, and $\lambda = .01$ shown in figure 13.4b), the activation of the "robin" node weakens but is still higher than the activation of the "bird" node. This could be viewed as the normal decay of representations in working memory over time. In contrast, the higher decay rates ($\lambda = .1$ shown in figure 13.4c, and $\lambda = .2$ shown in figure 13.4d) result in the loss of specific features and subsequently in the winning over of the "bird" node. This illustrates that a high decay rate could result in the rapid transfor-

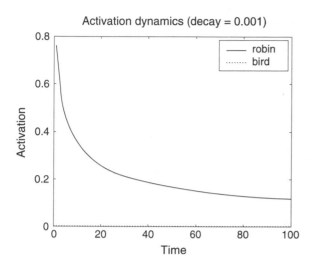

Figure 13.4a
Activation across time $\lambda = .001$.

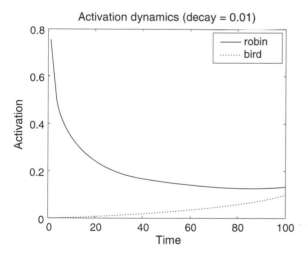

Figure 13.4b
Activation across time $\lambda = .01$.

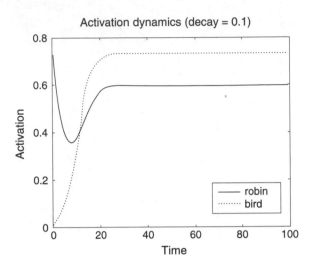

Figure 13.4c
Activation across time $\lambda = .1$.

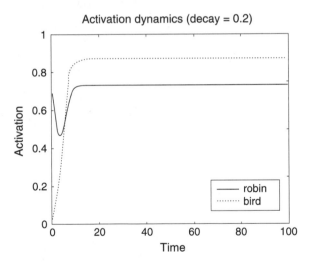

Figure 13.4d
Activation across time $\lambda = .2$.

mation of a representation of a specific concept into a representation of a more general one. The reason this happens is that not all features are equal in their resistance to decay. Features shared by many concepts will strengthen the activation of each other, leading to a general regression toward concepts more strongly associated with these features, which are usually the more general superordinate concepts.

The rapid decay represented by the higher decay rates can be thought of as approximating the poor working-memory performance of AD patients. A possible test of the model is therefore to see whether it can explain the referential behavior observed in these patients. Almor et al. (1999) found that, in language production, AD patients prefer pronouns over other more specific referential forms. In terms of the model presented here, the degraded representation resulting from rapid decay makes the use of pronouns more adequate because what may have started as a detailed semantic representation has within a short time degraded into a more general one. In ILH terms this has the effect of increasing the cost of all referential forms, thus making the use of a more general form more likely. Almor et al.'s (1999) finding that the tendency to use pronouns is related to working-memory performance further strengthens the link made here between the decay rate, which could be viewed as a marker of working-memory performance, and the specificity of referent representation. In broader ILH terms, the coupling of pronoun preference with working-memory performance is the result of the increased cost of using all referential expressions, which increases the pressure to use more general expressions.

Almor et al. (1999) also found that, in language comprehension, AD patients' ability to process and integrate text is hindered by pronouns. In contrast to unimpaired people, AD patients show better comprehension if repeated noun-phrase references are used instead of pronouns. Almor et al. (1999) also found that the comprehension benefit from full noun-phrase references versus pronouns correlates with working-memory performance. In ILH terms, repeated reference could be described as having more function when representation fades as a result of abnormally rapid decay, because the additional information in the repeated reference helps reactivate the faded representation of the referent in working memory. This is important because it shows that referential form is not part of a conventional system but a reflection of an underlying mechanism that is sensitive to the cost and function balance. When cost or function changes, so does the point of balance. In language production, the change of balance caused by AD-related working-memory impairment results in increased cost and consequently in the overuse of pronouns. In comprehension, the change of balance caused by the same working-memory impairment results in repeated reference, attaining extra function that balances its additional processing cost.

Conclusions

The present work shows that a combination of pragmatic principles and an explicit account of memory processes and representations can go a long way toward explaining the distribution and processing of referential expressions in both intact and impaired populations. In particular, the balance between function and the computational cost resulting from competition between representations allows a principled explanation of why referents salient in memory tend to be referred to with less specific references than nonsalient referents. Another important advantage of this approach is that it makes empirical predictions about differences in processing referential expressions from the same grammatical category (e.g., specific versus general definite NPs) that parallel differences in processing referential expressions from different grammatical categories (e.g., NPs and pronouns; see Almor 1999).

The current approach points at a possible problem in previous research under the product tradition, which has viewed referential processing as problem solving and has searched for factors that affect comprehenders' referent identification. If the ILH is correct in that referential processing is directly related to the architecture and performance of the underlying memory system, then asking whether various syntactic, semantic, or discourse factors affect referential processing may be misleading. Instead, one should discern the effect of these factors on the activation and interaction of representations in memory, from which the effect on referential processing would follow. A certain syntactic, semantic, or discourse factor may have different effects on reference processing in different contexts, but according to the current model, all these different effects should be explainable in a consistent way on the basis of the underlying memory representations and pragmatic principles.

The current approach raises similar concerns regarding research under the action tradition, which has viewed reference as an extra channel of communication and focused on speakers' use of referential form as a cue for comprehenders. The fact that the use of certain forms tends to appear in certain discourse situations (e.g., pronouns in topic continuity (Gordon, Grosz, and Gilliom 1993), and NP anaphors in topic shifts (Vonk, Hustinx, and Simons 1992)) does not mean that speakers or comprehenders use referential form as a cue. According to the current approach, it is the underlying memory processes and representations that dictate the choice of referential form in production. Obviously, discourse situations such as topic change will affect the underlying memory processes and representations and thus may appear to be linked with referential form. However, because other factors can also affect the underlying memory processes and representations, it is ultimately the memory processes and representations that are important for reference use and processing.

Originally, the ILH did not specify whether cost and function reflect the underlying architecture of the comprehension system, the production system, or both. Indeed, the model presented here can be applied separately to both systems. Although in principle only one of the production and comprehension systems may operate in accordance with the principles of the ILH, the empirical evidence reviewed here suggests that both systems operate in accordance with ILH principles. The original reading-time data reported in Almor 1999 show that the comprehension system operates in accordance with the principles of the ILH. Similarly, the production data reported in Almor et al. 1999 shows that production is strongly related to the underlying processing cost, and to discourse function. One possibility that merits further investigation is that the comprehension system is merely sensitive to distributional patterns that are driven by production constraints. In other words, although comprehension processes clearly exhibit ILH properties, they may do so not because of the underlying architecture of semantic working memory, but because the principles of the ILH are reflected in the distributional properties of the language to which the comprehension system is sensitive. Thus, although both the comprehension and production systems behave in line with the ILH, it remains to be seen whether the comprehension system's sensitivity to processing cost reflects an adaptation to the distributional patterns of language that are driven by production constraints, or whether it stems directly from the architecture of the underlying semantic working memory.

The work presented here provides an example for research that draws on both the action and product traditions. Whereas the balancing of processing cost and discourse function is a pragmatic principle that is compatible with the action tradition, the characterization of computational cost in terms of the properties of the underlying mechanism lies squarely within the product tradition. Both parts of the theory are important in explaining various aspects of the relevant empirical evidence. Most importantly, this work shows that the balance between processing cost and discourse function reflects the operation of an underlying cognitive mechanism and is not merely a convention.

Notes

This research was supported by grant NIH RO1 AG-11774-04. Thanks to Kenneth McRae for graciously making his database of semantic features available for this research.

1. It is important to note that the processing cost associated with semantic overlap applies at the level of the relevant units for referential processing. These units may be smaller than the entire referential expression. Indeed, there is good evidence suggesting that, in cases where visual context strongly constrains the set of possible referents, complex noun phrases such as "the green square" can be processed incrementally (Sedivy et al. 1999). In such cases, the semantic information conveyed by the initial part of the referring complex noun phrase may sufficient for referent identification (for example, if the only green shape in the visual display is a square). Processing cost would apply at each stage in processing at which referential processing occurs.

2. Experiment 2 in Almor 1999 examined the processing of nonrepeated references that are more specific than the referent such as "the robin" in the following fragment: "The bird ate the big fruit. The robin looked very satisfied." According to the ILH, the high IL of such references is balanced by the addition of the new information, in this case, that the bird was a robin. These cases are beyond the scope of the present chapter because this chapter only addresses the quantification of IL but not the quantification of new information.

3. $f = \tanh$ was used in all the simulations described in this chapter.

4. Each iteration consisted of a sequence of two steps: propagating the activation from the concept to the feature nodes, and propagating the activation back from the feature to the concept nodes. The value of 100 iterations was chosen arbitrarily to demonstrate the working of the model and is not claimed to provide a representation of any cognitive processing time. The current small scale of the model precludes making such claims.

References

Almor, A. 1999. Noun-phrase anaphora and focus: The informational load hypothesis. *Psychological Review*, *106*(4), 748–765.

Almor, A., Kempler, D., MacDonald, M. C., Andersen, E. S., and Tyler, L. K. 1999. Why do Alzheimer patients have difficulty with pronouns? Working memory, semantics, and reference in comprehension and production in Alzheimer's disease. *Brain and Language*, *67*(3), 202–227.

Ariel, M. 1990. *Accessing Noun-Phrase Antecedents*. London: Routledge.

Clark, H. H. 1996. *Using Language*. Cambridge, UK: Cambridge University Press.

Clark, H. H., and Brennan, S. E. 1991. Grounding in communication. In L. B. Resnick, J. M. Levine, and S. D. Bahrend, eds., *Perspectives on Socially Shared Cognition*, 127–149. Washington, DC: American Psychological Association.

Clark, H. H., and Wilkes-Gibbs, D. 1986. Referring as a collaborative process. *Cognition*, *22*(1), 1–39.

Clark, H. H., and Wilkes-Gibbs, D. 1990. Referring as a collaborative process. In P. R. Cohen, J. Morgan, and M. Pollack, eds., *Intentions in Communication*, 463–493. Cambridge, MA: MIT Press.

Cloitre, M., and Bever, T. G. 1988. Linguistic anaphors, levels of representation, and discourse. *Language and Cognitive Processes*, *3*(4), 293–322.

Garrod, S. 1991. Pronouns and cognitive connexity. In J.-P. R. Guy Denhiere, ed., *Text and Text Processing*. Advances in Psychology, *79*, 287–295. Amsterdam: North-Holland.

Garrod, S., Freudenthal, D., and Boyle, E. A. 1994. The role of different types of anaphor in the on-line resolution of sentences in a discourse. *Journal of Memory and Language*, *33*(1), 39–68.

Gordon, P. C., Grosz, B. J., and Gilliom, L. 1993. Pronouns, names, and the centering of attention in discourse. *Cognitive Science*, *17*(3), 311–348.

Greene, S. G., McKoon, G., and Ratcliff, R. 1992. Pronoun resolution and discourse models. *Journal of Experimental Psychology: Learning, Memory and Cognition*, *18*(2), 266–283.

Grice, H. P. 1975. Logic and conversation. In P. Cole and J. L. Morgan, eds., *Syntax and Semantics III: Speech Acts*, 41–58. New York: Academic Press.

Grosz, B. J., Joshi, A. K., and Weinstein, S. 1995. Centering: A framework for modeling the local coherence of discourse. *Computational Linguistics*, *21*(2), 203–226.

Gundel, J. K., Hedberg, N., and Zacharski, R. 1993. Cognitive status and the form of referring expressions in discourse. *Language*, *69*(2), 274–307.

Just, M. A., and Carpenter, P. A. 1992. A capacity theory of comprehension: Individual differences in working memory. *Psychological Review*, *99*(1), 122–149.

McRae, K., and Cree, G. S. 2002. Factors underlying category-specific semantic deficits. In E. M. E. Forde and G. W. Humphreys, eds., *Category-Specificity in Brain and Mind*, 211–250. East Sussex, UK: Psychology Press.

Sanford, A. J., and Garrod, S. C. 1981. *Understanding Written Language*. Chichester: Wiley.

Sanford, A. J., and Garrod, S. C. 1989. What, when, and how?: Questions of immediacy in anaphoric reference resolution. *Language and Cognitive Processes*, *4*(3), 235–262.

Sedivy, J. C., Tanenhaus, M. K., Chambers, C. G., and Carlson, G. N. 1999. Achieving incremental semantic interpretation through contextual representation. *Cognition*, *71*(2), 109–147.

Vonk, W., Hustinx, L. G. M. M., and Simons, W. H. G. 1992. The use of referential expressions in structuring discourse. *Language and Cognitive Processes*, *7*(3), 301–333.

Wilkes-Gibbs, D., and Clark, H. H. 1992. Coordinating beliefs in conversation. *Journal of Memory and Language*, *31*(2), 183–194.

14 The Disfluent Hairy Dog: Can Syntactic Parsing Be Affected by Nonword Disfluencies?

Karl G. D. Bailey and Fernanda Ferreira

The aim of the language-as-product tradition is to develop theories to explain the way linguistic representations are created in real time. The goal of the language-as-action tradition is to develop theories of how conversational participants coordinate their actions and use language to serve their various social and informational goals. Until recently, these two approaches have operated almost entirely independently. Our work bridges these traditions in a unique and important way. We believe the central principles of processing that have been uncovered in the product tradition can be applied to utterances of the type more commonly studied in the action tradition. Of course, as we learn more about the comprehension of a wider range of utterances (such as the ones we will describe below), we will undoubtedly find that these principles need to be reconsidered. But at this stage, our assumption is that the principles discovered in the stark laboratory setting continue to operate after our participants leave the experimental session and go off for coffee with their friends. For an utterance to be understood, the comprehender must group words appropriately, figure out any long-distance dependencies, and deal with any lexical or syntactic ambiguities. The parser, then, is necessary for understanding naturally spoken utterances. The question we are interested in is the following: How does the parser operate when it encounters not the sanitized, pristine, usually visually presented sentences from traditional psycholinguistic experiments, but rather the regular, spoken utterances produced in conversations, utterances that might contain long pauses, *uh*'s and *um*'s, repeats and false starts, and other sorts of disfluencies?

More generally, we are interested in creating theories to explain how linguistic representations are created online during normal conversations. The study of disfluencies seemed an excellent place to begin. Disfluencies are common: approximately 6 percent of all words in naturally spoken discourses contain some type of disfluency (Bortfeld et al. 1999). Clearly, then, this is not an esoteric domain. More importantly, we reason that disfluencies are relevant to syntactic decisions in a couple of fundamental ways.

First, when a person hears an utterance, the parser begins building syntactic structure in real time. If a disfluency is encountered, a parser might in theory take several possible routes. It could filter a disfluency by some mechanism. On the other hand, the parser could use the presence of a disfluency as a cue to pause. In either case, the disfluency will take up time. During this time, the structure already built will have to be maintained. The mechanism by which it is maintained could either cause the structure to build up strength or decay. In the case of structural ambiguities, a disfluency might affect the eventual parse of the sentences, depending on how the parser behaves in response to the disfluency. Second, research from the action tradition has revealed that speakers tend to be disfluent before producing large and complex constituents (Clark and Wasow 1998). The parser might be capable of using this correlation in the input to help it resolve syntactic ambiguities—that is, if at a certain point the parser is trying to choose between a simple and a more complex structure, a disfluency might be a cue to the latter. Finally, it is useful to study disfluencies in an attempt to bridge the processing and conversational traditions because we can avoid having to invent entirely new paradigms, techniques, or stimulus types. Instead, we can build incrementally on work already done, using established psycholinguistic practices from the processing tradition to get at these new and exciting questions.

Basic Principles of Parsing and Their Application to Disfluency

Readers do not need to be reminded that there are many controversies about how sentences are parsed, even if we consider only the type of stimuli normally presented in standard psycholinguistic experiments. Nevertheless, there is agreement on some basic points, and it is on these principles that we have built our current work. First, syntactic structure is assigned to words incrementally and in real time. Second, syntactic ambiguities can cause the parser to pursue an incorrect syntactic path, requiring some sort of reanalysis. For example, the sequence *Sandra bumped into the busboy and the waiter* ... will usually be analyzed so that *the waiter* is part of the object. This preference can be attributed to the minimal-attachment strategy (Frazier 1978, 1987) or to the presence of numerous cues signaling this direct-object analysis (Juliano and Tanenhaus 1994; MacDonald, Pearlmutter, and Seidenberg 1994). If the sentence continues *told her to be careful*, the parser will need to abandon this analysis and create the alternative one where *the waiter* is the subject of a new clause. Again, we assume that all these principles operate when people hear sentences in day-to-day conversations.

In addition, an important principle of parsing that we have exploited in our research on disfluencies is the head-position effect (HPE; Ferreira and Henderson 1991, 1998).

According to this principle, the reanalysis of garden-path sentences is much harder when the ambiguous noun phrase (NP) is lengthened with postnominal modifiers. Prenominal modifiers have no significant effect compared to the baseline determiner + noun condition. Specifically, Ferreira and Henderson found the pattern shown in (1). (The sentences in (1) involve a different syntactic ambiguity than that discussed above, but we will be considering both in our experiments.)

(1) a. Plain NP: While the boy scratched the dog yawned loudly. (62% judged grammatical)

 b. Head-late: While the boy scratched the big and hairy dog yawned loudly. (51%)

 c. Head-early: While the boy scratched the dog that was hairy yawned loudly. (29%)

(The head-early condition included one less adjective than did the head-late condition, to avoid a length confound.) Ferreira and Henderson (1991) explained the effect as follows: The sentence-comprehension system assigns thematic roles at the heads of phrases, and the longer it has been committed to the wrong thematic analysis, the harder it is to reanalyze. In the head-late condition, the wrong thematic role of patient is assigned at the end of the NP, and therefore the disambiguating information *yawned* arrives immediately after (erroneous) thematic-role assignment. In the head-early condition, the wrong thematic role of patient is assigned to the NP early, and so the interpretation has time to build up strength before the disambiguating information is encountered. Reanalysis is therefore more difficult. It is important to note that this study was conducted squarely within the language-as-product tradition, and in particular, subjects read the sentences on a computer monitor and then judged the grammaticality of each.

The question we asked about disfluencies is the following: Is it possible to obtain the HPE with disfluencies rather than with modifiers? Imagine that a person hears *While the boy scratched the dog* and then one or two *uh*'s. The parser has presumably attached *the dog* as object of *scratched*. The disfluencies come after the head noun of the ambiguous phrase, and therefore delay the onset of the disambiguating word. Will the sentence be more difficult to process than it would be if the disfluencies had occurred before the word *dog*, or had not occurred at all?

If we find that the sentence is more difficult when the *uh*'s come after the head noun of the ambiguous phrase, we will have an important result for both the language-as-product and language-as-action traditions. A finding that disfluencies produce the HPE would suggest that the HPE is due to something like the passage of time. Therefore, we will shed light on this highly robust principle of parsing by providing some information about what causes it. And if disfluencies yield the HPE we will have learned something about the way disfluencies influence comprehension. Specifically, if the parser is building an analysis and then encounters disfluencies, the strength of that analysis increases. The structure firms up and becomes more difficult to get rid of when reanalysis requires that it be relinquished in favor of the correct structure. The experiments that we will summarize next provide evidence about these questions, and also raise the issue of whether disfluencies serve as cues to syntactic structure.

Experiments to Examine Parsing of Utterances with Disfluencies

We examined two different types of garden-path structures for the first set of experiments. They are illustrated below:

Subordinate-Main Structures

(2) a. Baseline (plain ambiguous NP): While the man hunted the *deer* <u>ran</u> into the woods.
     b. Head late, words: While the man hunted the brown and furry *deer* <u>ran</u> into the woods.
     c. Head late, disfluencies: While the man hunted the uh uh *deer* <u>ran</u> into the woods.
     d. Head early, words: While the man hunted the *deer* that was furry <u>ran</u> into the woods.
     e. Head early, disfluencies: While the man hunted the *deer* uh uh <u>ran</u> into the woods.

Coordination Structures

(3) a. Baseline (plain ambiguous NP): Sandra bumped into the busboy and the *waiter* <u>told</u> her to be careful.
     b. Head late, words: Sandra bumped into the busboy and the short and pudgy *waiter* <u>told</u> her to be careful.
     c. Head late, disfluencies: Sandra bumped into the busboy and the uh uh *waiter* <u>told</u> her to be careful.
     d. Head early, words: Sandra bumped into the busboy and the *waiter* who was short and pudgy <u>told</u> her to be careful.
     e. Head early, disfluencies: Sandra bumped into the busboy and the *waiter* uh uh <u>told</u> her to be careful.

The subordinate-main structure is the one Ferreira and Henderson (1991) used, and so obviously it was important to include it in any attempt to demonstrate the HPE with disfluencies. The ambiguous phrase in the baseline condition included just the determiner and head nouns (all ambiguous NPs are shown in italics). The head-late, words condition included prenominal modifiers, as in Ferreira and Henderson. This condition should be as easy as the (2a) condition. The head-late, disfluencies condition included two *uh*'s between the head of the ambiguous NP and the disambiguating word (underlined). The same logic applies to the two head-early conditions, which should be more difficult than the head-late and baseline conditions. The coordination structures were included to assess whether we could generalize any effects of disfluencies to a different garden-path structure. Moreover, the coordination ambiguity has been little studied, and so a secondary reason for including it was to see whether the HPE applied to another type of ambiguity. Because this issue is not central to the theme of the chapter and the book, we will not say more about it here (for discussion, see Bailey and Ferreira 2003).

The first author created the stimuli by recording thirty subordinate-main sentences and twenty coordination sentences, each in the five experimental conditions (i.e., he recorded 250 tokens). Care was taken to ensure that there were no biasing intonational cues. In our pilot work, we attempted to naturally elicit the sentences with disfluencies using techniques reported previously (e.g., Van Wijk and Kempen 1987; Brennan and Schober 2001). Unfortunately, it turned out to be difficult to get participants to produce the utterances we needed, and it would have been impossible to collect as many as are required to conduct a proper experiment. We decided, then, that to get started on this topic we had to adopt a different approach, at least in the short run. Our current procedure is to write out the sentence with the disfluency items in the appropriate location. The person recording the stimuli then behaves essentially like an actor, producing the sentence as naturally as possible with the disfluency in the correct spot. The utterance is produced with an adjunct phrase (*According to Mary*), followed by a large prosodic break. This allows the rest of the utterance to be produced as a single prosodic contour, leading to a neutral prosody. An important question, of course, and one especially likely to be raised by anyone working within the language-as-action tradition, is whether these utterances are valid. Up to now, we have found that naive participants cannot distinguish staged utterances from ones produced naturally, but this issue needs to be investigated further and more systematically. We are currently conducting studies to test whether participants behave differently with the artificial sentences than with sentences containing spontaneously produced disfluencies.

As in most psycholinguistic studies of this type, we presented participants with only one version of any one utterance, but across items participants received all conditions of the experiments. Appropriate filler sentences were included as well, half of which contained disfluencies. Participants listened to an utterance and then performed some type of task such as a grammaticality judgment. Their decisions were recorded and then statistically analyzed using analysis-of-variance techniques.

The first set of studies we will describe used the structures shown in (2) and (3). After each utterance, the participant judged whether he or she found the sentence grammatical—that is, was the sentence something that a speaker of English could in fact say? We obtained the following results. First, the pattern of judgments was the same for the subordinate-main and coordination ambiguities. In addition, utterances were judged grammatical equally often in the plain NP and the head-late conditions. Both of these conditions were judged grammatical much more often than the head-early condition (the same pattern as was found by Ferreira and Henderson 1991). Moreover, performance was identical in the words and disfluency conditions, indicating that the disfluencies produced the HPE as effectively as did the modifying words.

We followed up on this basic pattern by asking a different set of participants to listen to the utterances and then judge their prosodic acceptability. The rationale for including this task was that judging grammaticality might draw particular attention to the structure of the sentence and away from its sound, perhaps orienting the listeners' response to the sentence so that it is more consistent with the language-as-product tradition. In the prosodic-acceptability task participants were supposed to pay attention to whether the utterance sounded like something a person would say in normal speech. It was expected that their knowledge both of the sound *and* the structure of the sentence would influence their decision. The data from this experiment were exactly the same as those from the grammaticality-judgment version, which not only suggests that our concern was unfounded but also provides a neat replication of the intriguing HPE pattern. In addition, overall judgments of prosodic acceptability were high (particularly in the plain NP conditions), indicating that the attempt to produce sentences with neutralized intonational cues did not yield unnatural-sounding utterances. Figure 14.1 shows the general pattern found in both the grammaticality-judgment and prosodic-acceptability experiments (and for both coordination and subordinate-main ambiguities).

The results from these first two experiments show that the HPE is produced in exactly the same way when people encounter disfluencies as when they encounter modifying words. These findings are significant, because they are (to the best of our knowledge) the first demonstration that disfluencies systematically influence the oper-

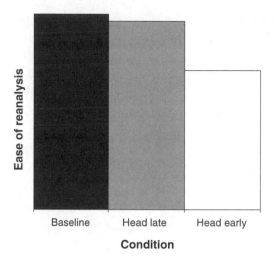

Figure 14.1
The general pattern of the HPE in garden-path sentence reanalysis. Baseline and head-late conditions have the greatest ease of reanalysis, while the head-early condition is significantly more difficult. This pattern of results has been obtained for both modifying words and disfluencies.

ation of the parser. Can we conclude that disfluencies and words have the same effect—that is, that the parser is committed to an incorrect syntactic structure, and then the disfluencies occur in a location that causes the parser to remain committed to that wrong analysis longer, and therefore to have more trouble getting rid of it? It might appear obvious that the answer is yes, but unfortunately, we determined that there are in fact two possible explanations of our effects. One is the explanation we just gave: disfluencies cause the parser to be committed to the wrong analysis longer (just as with the modifying words, thereby suggesting that disfluencies yield the HPE). An implication of this hypothesis, then, is that the passage of time would have the same effect. The alternate explanation is that the parser is making use of possible co-occurrences between disfluencies and structures, and using disfluencies as a cue to upcoming structure. This hypothesis suggests that it is just a coincidence that words and disfluencies produce the same pattern and that the passage of time is not what causes the HPE.

To see why the second explanation is viable, examine the sentences in (2) and (3) again. Disfluencies tend to cluster around the beginning of complex constituents (e.g., clauses; Clark and Wasow 1998; Ford 1982; Hawkins 1971). In the head-late disfluency condition, the disfluency comes right after the determiner that begins a new clause. Therefore, the disfluency predicts a clause, the parser might make use of that information, and the assumption turns out to be correct. Thus the sentence is judged grammatical. In the head-early disfluency condition, the disfluency comes after what seems to be the object of the first clause. The parser might then assume that the disfluency was caused by the speaker's planning of the second clause. That assumption, of course, is incorrect, because the NP that has been attached as object of the first clause is actually the subject of the second. Therefore, the disfluency is misleading, and the sentence as a result is overall more difficult to process and leads to a decreased probability of the sentence being judged grammatical.

To distinguish between these possibilities, we conducted two more studies. In the first, we tested the first explanation by assessing whether the mere passage of time could elicit the HPE. To do so, we could not simply leave silence in the location of the disfluencies, because silence could be interpreted as a pause produced by the speaker for the same reason that he or she might produce an *uh*. We decided to try a creative and somewhat unusual (if not plain wacky) approach: we replaced the disfluencies in (2c) and (2e) and in (3c) and (3e) with environmental sounds such as telephones ringing, cats meowing, and people sneezing. These sounds are not under speakers' control, and therefore they should not be taken as signals to structure. They do not correlate in any way with different structural types. They do, however, cause the parser to be committed to its analysis longer, and so they allow us to see whether the HPE is due to the passage of time, and by inference, whether disfluencies affect parsing because they cause the parser to be committed to the wrong analysis longer.

The experiment had the same design as the ones described previously, and we found the same results: sentences were judged grammatical about equally often in the plain NP and head-late conditions, and much less often in the head-early condition. Performance was identical with modifying words and environmental sounds. Therefore, we have good evidence that disfluencies can influence the parser by causing it to entertain the wrong structure for a longer period of time.

It is perhaps worth mentioning that this experiment might seem strange when evaluated from the perspective of the language-as-product tradition. Nevertheless, the experiment is useful for two reasons. First, it allows us to get at a key architectural question about how time influences the operation of the parser. Second, anyone trying to bridge the product and action traditions would agree that it is worthwhile to try to understand how sentences are comprehended under typical listening conditions—that is, in the presence of noise and extraneous nonlinguistic sounds. In other words, it is not particularly odd to imagine a person in the real world listening to a speaker who ceases speech for a second or so because of a loud horn, buzz, or ringing noise. Indeed, the results from the experiment discussed up to now lead one to expect that those events will influence structure—and interpretation-building operations.

So far we have shown that disfluencies produce the HPE, and the experiment with environmental sounds indicates that the HPE may be due to the passage of time. Do these results imply that the second possible explanation we described above can be dismissed? Recall that this explanation hypothesizes that the HPE occurred because listeners could use information about the co-occurrence of disfluencies and syntactic types to cue upcoming structure. This explanation actually remains viable, because it is possible for both influences to operate simultaneously. Unfortunately, the field of psycholinguistics has not yet produced any evidence that listeners are capable of taking advantage of these disfluency cues.

Thus, the final experiment we will describe was designed to examine this question. The conditions are shown in (4):

(4) a. Baseline (plain ambiguous NP): Sandra bumped into the busboy and *the waiter* told her to be careful.

b. Good-signal disfluencies: Sandra bumped into the busboy and *the uh uh waiter* told her to be careful.

c. Bad-signal disfluencies: Sandra bumped into the uh uh busboy and *the waiter* told her to be careful.

d. Head late, easy with respect to HPE: Sandra bumped into the busboy and *the short and pudgy waiter* told her to be careful.

e. Irrelevant with respect to HPE: Sandra bumped into the short and pudgy busboy and *the waiter* told her to be careful.

(For this experiment we did not include subordinate-main structural ambiguities.) The (4a) condition is simply the "no-disfluency, no-extra-words" baseline. The "good-signal disfluencies" (4b) condition includes *uh*'s before the word *waiter*, thus presumably predicting that the waiter is the subject of a new clause. The "bad-signal disfluencies" (4c) condition places the disfluencies in front of *busboy*, which rather than being the start of a new clause is the final word of the current clause. Note that the use of the term *signal* here refers to the listener's use of the disfluencies and that this use is agnostic with respect to the speaker's intention. The "head late, easy with respect to HPE" (4d) condition is a control for the "good-signal disfluencies" condition—that is, modifiers occur in the same place as disfluencies, but the words should not exaggerate the garden path because they occur prenominally (thus leaving the head noun of the ambiguous NP immediately adjacent to the disambiguating word). The "irrelevant with respect to HPE" condition (4e) is a control for the "bad-signal disfluencies" condition, because it includes words in the same spot as disfluencies. This fifth condition is irrelevant with respect to the head-position effect because the NP that is lengthened is not ambiguous. The prediction from this experiment is that if disfluencies are used by the parser to help it choose among competing structures, the sentences in the (4b) condition ("good-signal disfluencies") should be judged grammatical more often than those in the (4c) condition ("bad-signal disfluencies"). If time is the only variable that matters, then grammaticality judgments in all five conditions should be the same, because in all conditions the head noun of the ambiguous NP ends up adjacent to the disambiguating word.

The data from this experiment provide evidence that people can indeed use disfluencies to help them resolve syntactic ambiguities. First, we found little difference between the two word-modifier conditions and the baseline condition. Sentences were judged grammatical about equally often in conditions (4a), (4d), and (4e). This is what we expect, because in all of these conditions the disambiguating word follows immediately after the ambiguous head noun. The critical comparison is between the two disfluency conditions. Before *waiter*, the disfluency correctly cues the upcoming clause; before *busboy*, it does not. The grammaticality judgments for the good-signal and bad-signal conditions were 97.5 and 90.0 percent respectively—a significant difference, which suggests that the comprehender uses the good-signal disfluency to help it choose the more complex structure and thus avoid being garden-pathed. This is a real coup for the parser.

Further evidence that disfluencies may signal upcoming structure comes from an experiment where we asked subjects to listen to completely ambiguous sentence fragments and then to complete the sentences. The fragments were created by taking the stimuli from the first grammaticality-judgment study reported here ((2) and (3)), and truncating each experimental sentence just before the disambiguating word to create fully ambiguous fragments. Filler sentences were truncated in corresponding places to provide unambiguous fragments as fillers. The subjects' completions of the experimental sentence fragments were then scored as either object or subject completions. An object completion was one that made the ambiguous NP the object of the subordinate clause—that is, the sentence was completed with the preferred structure. A subject completion, on the other hand, made the ambiguous NP the subject of a new main clause, and resulted in the less preferred structure being constructed. The way a sentence was completed should tell us how the sentence fragments have been parsed up to that point. In other words, the structure of the completion depends on whether the ambiguous noun was interpreted as a subject or an object.

Overall, subjects tended not to complete the sentences using the less preferred structure (i.e., a subject completion), even though the sentences that had been truncated originally had that structure. Both modifier conditions and the baseline condition had about the same ratio of object-to-subject completions. A similar ratio was seen for the head-early disfluency condition. However, the presence of a head-late disfluency greatly increased the proportion of fragments that were continued so that the NPs were subjects (36 percent subject completions with a head-late disfluency compared to 13 percent with a head-early disfluency). That is, a disfluency right after the head of the ambiguous NP was interpreted as a sign that that NP initiated a new clause, and this bias caused participants to continue the fragments so that they ended up with the less preferred structure.

Thus, the experiments we have conducted to examine how disfluencies influence the parser point to two significant conclusions. First, disfluencies affect the operation of the parser because when the parser encounters a disfluency, it becomes more committed to the structure it has built up to that point. Second, disfluencies influence the parser because the system is capable of using information about co-occurrences to predict the upcoming structure. If an *uh* or two occurs in a location that could reasonably precede a clause, the parser has a tendency to predict that clause. For many classic garden-path sentences, this cue will allow the parser to avoid being garden-pathed.

Why We Should Bridge the Product and Conversational Traditions

The experiments we have conducted to this point are significant for many reasons. By daring to venture beyond the constraints of the classic product tradition, we have obtained evidence that sheds light on the basic processing architecture of the comprehension system. The study of disfluencies and even dog barks in spoken sentences has revealed that the HPE is probably due to the passage of time. A garden path is more severe when material intervenes between the head noun of the ambiguous NP and the disambiguating word because the passage of time causes the incorrect structure for that NP to "firm up," making it more difficult for the parser to recover the ultimately correct structure. In addition, these experiments have told us a little bit about how people process the types of sentences they encounter in conversations. It is important to realize that we are not claiming that people routinely hear garden-path sentences in their day-to-day lives. What we are saying is that people routinely build syntactic structure, and they frequently have to deal with disfluencies. Our experiments show that when the parser encounters a disfluency, the structure it has built gains strength rather than decaying. Moreover, the last two experiments show that disfluencies are useful to the parser as cues to upcoming structure. It is quite likely that the parser uses disfluencies to help it anticipate structure in naturally spoken utterances.

In addition, these experiments are a first step toward providing the kind of information more typically sought within the conversational tradition. Many researchers
have been interested in how disfluencies influence comprehension, but up to now
most investigations have focused on fairly metacognitive judgments such as the way a
disfluency might signal the confidence the speaker has in what he or she is saying
(Smith and Clark 1993; Brennan and Williams 1995) or whether disfluencies place a
burden on the comprehension system overall (Fox Tree 1995; Brennan and Schober
2001). The experiments described in this chapter go further and demonstrate that disfluencies are not simply filtered out by the comprehension system, just as researchers
from the language-as-action tradition have always suspected. At the same time, we now
know that disfluencies are useful for more than just making high-level decisions about
the speaker's state of mind, and we have described a specific function of disfluencies
within the language-comprehension system. Disfluencies are not filtered, and they
affect comprehension processes because they systematically influence the parser's
operations.

Final Thoughts

A fear that some within the product tradition seem to have about embracing many
aspects of the conversational tradition is that the shift requires that researchers question or even reject the basic principles of comprehension that have emerged from over
thirty years of careful, methodologically rigorous experiments. We believe that this fear
is unjustified. Indeed, our experiments demonstrate that one can build on these basic
principles by shifting orientation just a bit toward an alternative approach to psycholinguistics. More importantly, these experiments only reinforce the obvious fact that
people parse sentences—that is, they build syntactic trees for the utterances they encounter. Just because the sentences are spoken rather than written and contain devia-
tions from ideal delivery does not mean that for some reason the parser chooses to take
a holiday. In some ways, we do not give the parser proper credit. We seem to implicitly
assume that it can only work when it is given a very clear signal, but our results reveal
that the parser can handle and even take advantage of nontraditional material such as
disfluencies. The parser is a powerful device, for it can create syntactic (and semantic
and phonological) representations even for the types of sentences people hear in the
real world. In other words, the parser can even handle something like this:

But I think uh- uh- uh- precisely because technology itself is certainly more and more ... animated
... uh and and is ... moving faster and faster ... uh that's I think that's one reason that the con-

cept of the m- the meme uh has some valence these days uh and and and people are are are f- find it intriguing at least. (From the National Public Radio program *Talk of the Nation*, May 20, 1999)

Clearly, without the parser there would not be joint actions that involve language, because if people were not capable of understanding utterances like the one above they could not extract information and produce their conversational turn appropriately. Basic principles of language comprehension are alive and well in the world of natural speech, and the phenomena found in natural speech can systematically affect these basic principles. The research we have presented here leads us to believe that if we are to understand the entire range of phenomena related to human-language processing, bridging the language-as-product and language-as-action traditions is not only desirable but necessary.

References

Bailey, K. G. D., and Ferreira, F. 2003. Disfluencies affect the parsing of garden-path sentences. *Journal of Memory and Language, 49*, 183–200.

Bortfeld, H., Leon, S. D., Bloom, J. E., Schober, M. F., and Brennan, S. E. 1999, July. Which speakers are most disfluent in coversation and when? Paper presented at the Disfluency in Spontaneous Speech ICPhS Satellite Meeting, Berkeley, CA.

Brennan, S. E., and Schober, M. F. 2001. How listeners compensate for disfluencies in spontaneous speech. *Journal of Memory and Language, 44*, 274–296.

Brennan, S. E., and Williams, M. 1995. The feeling of another's knowing: Prosody and filled pauses as cues to listeners about the metacognitive states of speakers. *Journal of Memory and Language, 34*, 383–398.

Clark, H. H., and Wasow, T. 1998. Repeating words in spontaneous speech. *Cognitive Psychology, 37*, 201–242.

Ferreira, F., and Henderson, J. M. 1991. Recovery from misanalyses of garden-path sentences. *Journal of Memory and Language, 25*, 725–745.

Ferreira, F., and Henderson, J. M. 1998. Syntactic reanalysis, thematic processing, and sentence comprehension. In J. D. Fodor and F. Ferreira, eds., *Reanalysis in Sentence Processing*, 73–100. Dordrecht: Kluwer Academic Publisher.

Ford, M. 1982. Sentence planning units: Implications for the speaker's representation of meaningful relations underlying sentences. In J. Bresnan, ed., *The Mental Representation of Grammatical Relations*, 798–827. Cambridge, MA: MIT Press.

Fox Tree, J. E. 1995. Effects of false starts and repetitions on the processing of subsequent words in spontaneous speech. *Journal of Memory and Language, 34*, 709–738.

Frazier, L. 1978. On Comprehending Sentences: Syntactic Parsing Strategies. Unpublished doctoral dissertation, University of Connecticut.

Frazier, L. 1987. Syntactic processing: Evidence from Dutch. *Natural Language and Linguistic Theory*, *5*, 519–559.

Hawkins, P. R. 1971. The syntactic location of hesitation pauses. *Language and Speech*, *14*, 277–288.

Juliano, C., and Tanenhaus, M. K. 1994. A constraint-based lexicalist account of the subject/object attachment preference. *Journal of Psycholinguistic Research*, *23*(6), 459–471.

MacDonald, M. C., Pearlmutter, N. J., and Siedenberg, M. S. 1994. The lexical nature of syntactic ambiguity resolution. *Psychological Review*, *101*, 676–703.

Smith, V. L., and Clark, H. H. 1993. On the course of answering questions. *Journal of Memory and Language*, *32*, 25–38.

Van Wijk, C., and Kempen, G. 1987. A dual system for producing self-repairs in spontaneous speech: Evidence from experimentally elicited corrections. *Cognitive Psychology*, *19*, 403–440.

15 Context and Language Processing: The Effect of Authorship

Stanka A. Fitneva and Michael J. Spivey

Grounded in the language-as-product tradition, our work seeks to identify plausible cognitive architectures of language processing. We have favored constraint-based models which assume that multiple information sources contribute simultaneously to the interpretation of the linguistic input at the earliest stages of processing. The purpose of this chapter is to introduce authorship—the social identity of the speaker or writer—as a constraint on real-time language comprehension, and offer a first installment of some intriguing experimental results.

Why Study Authorship?

Despite the fact that much research has focused on how context could modulate real-time language processing, the methodologies used have been more geared toward providing the earliest measure of processing, rather than embedding the target stimuli in a rich natural context. The "context" typically consists of a sentence or two—or in some cases only a word—delivered as text on a computer screen or as speech over headphones. Within these confines, the key processes of lexical and syntactic disambiguation have been investigated through manipulating the plausibility of the alternatives, their well-formedness, and the presence of lexical associates (e.g., Boland et al. 1995; McElree and Griffith 1998; Simpson et al. 1989). The work with these and other linguistic variables has been extremely productive. It has not only elucidated real-time language comprehension but also delineated a set of possible cognitive architectures of the language system. Still, despite its productivity and sophistication, this approach may have only led to a limited understanding of contextual influences on language processing. Ultimately, language comprehension integrates many types of information, from lexical and syntactic to visual and social. At a minimum, we need to study these nonlinguistic contextual constraints to know if our models of language processing are robust.

Testing the robustness of language-processing models developed on the basis of verbal context manipulations is indeed what has motivated much of the recent research on nonverbal contextual constraints. New technologies, in particular head-mounted eye tracking, have made it possible to undertake this research and demonstrate how visual context, for example, can aid or hinder the resolution of temporary ambiguities in words and sentences. As one illustration, consider the determination of reference. If one sees two apples, then the italicized fragment of the instruction *"Put the apple* on the towel in the box" is ambiguous. It is not clear which apple *the apple* refers to. People's eye movements prove the reality of this confusion: people look at both apples until they hear the modifying phrase "on the towel" (Spivey et al. 2002; Tanenhaus et al. 1995; Trueswell et al. 1999; see also Sedivy et al. 1999). The visual surroundings appear to immediately constrain the determination of reference.

Word recognition provides another example of a process influenced by visual context. Words overlap up to a certain point with other words—for example, *candy* shares its first syllable with *candidate, candid,* and *candle.* Thus, as a word unfolds, one might construct multiple hypotheses about (or accrue multiple lexical activations for) which word that beginning belongs to (Marslen-Wilson and Welsh 1978). The work of Tanenhaus and his colleagues has demonstrated that visual context can constrain what hypotheses are being considered (Allopenna, Magnuson, and Tanenhaus 1998; Tanenhaus et al. 1995). Someone looking at a display containing a piece of candy and a candle is likely to look at both of these objects when the instruction "Pick up the candy" is spoken. When the same instruction is given but only the candy is in the display, the oculomotor system targets the candy often before the word *candy* is finished being spoken.

Unlike linguistic context, visual and behavioral contexts are not constrained by the temporal order inherent in language. Nonlinguistic contextual information can usually be processed in parallel with language comprehension. This difference suggests that nonverbal contexts might have effects complementary to those of verbal context. Consider, for example, Marslen-Wilson and Tyler's (1980) demonstration that word recognition is faster at the end of sentences than at the beginning. They argued that the effect was due to recognition processes taking advantage of verbal context. As semantic information accumulates over time, listeners narrow down their set of expectations about what will follow.

Now consider the role of authorship in face-to-face communication. As we will show below, the identity of the speaker can also constrain the interpretation of words. But speaker-identity information is available visually and auditorily (via the voice of the speaker) throughout the unfolding of the utterance. Its influence on lexical processing could be as strong when the word appears in the beginning of a sentence as when it appears at the end. This simple mental simulation illustrates how nonverbal context may generate novel results. The implication is that a generic "context" variable may not suffice for models of language processing that aim to capture the pattern of information integration.

Authorship is a particularly interesting variable because it can link comprehension processes with the dynamics of everyday social interactions. Studies of embodiment theory (Lakoff and Johnson 1999) and the theory of situated cognition (Barsalou 1999; Glenberg and Robertson 1999) as well as related theories, including constructivism (Bransford and Johnson 1973), ecological psychology (Gibson 1979), and situational semantics (Barwise and Perry 1983), offer theoretical insights and empirical evidence for the interaction of cognitive processes with spatiotemporal aspects of the situations where they take place. These theories also imply that social aspects of the situations— such as the personalities of the speaker and listener, the stereotypes they hold, their interactional goals, and group membership—affect cognitive processes. Evidence for this position with regards to language comes from research focusing on stereotypes, which often employs language measures. For example, sex words seem to prime violence-related words for men but not women (Mussweiler and Förster 2000). Short (15 ms!) exposure to a picture of a fat woman facilitates access to words associated with negative stereotypes for fat women (e.g., being insecure) (Bessenoff and Sherman 2000). After briefly seeing a picture of an African-American man, a person who firmly believes in and pursues egalitarian goals will read words associated with negative stereotypes of African Americans more slowly than a person who is not as committed to these goals (Moskowitz, Salomon, and Taylor 2000). Findings such as these support the thesis that language processing is critically linked to personal and interpersonal variables.

The language-as-action tradition in psycholinguistics defines more precisely the role of authorship in language processing. This theoretical framework focuses on the illocutionary level of utterance meaning, or what the speaker intends to do by uttering a given sentence: apologize, promise, praise, and so on (Austin 1962; Searle 1969). Community-membership information is an important factor for interpreting the speaker's meaning (Clark and Carlson 1981; Clark and Marshall 1981). The communicative intention of the speaker is sometimes marked in the utterance itself—for example, "I *promise* I will have the car back to you sooner than we have planned." When a verbal marker like the word *promise* is missing, knowing the identity of the speaker is often essential. "I will have the car back to you sooner than we have planned" could be a promise if spoken by a reliable friend, and, if spoken by an unreliable friend, an apology for previous letdowns.

Evolutionary considerations make the involvement of authorship in language processing even more plausible. Dunbar (1996) has argued that language evolved as a
consequence of the need to efficiently maintain social bonds and influence fellow
humans. Primates establish and maintain bonds through grooming, which requires
physical contact. With words, people can show loyalty, persuade, and manipulate with
less effort and even from a distance. Dunbar's theory implies that people and their
identities are at the core of linguistic interaction, defining both its function and its
topic. We intensely care about who is talking, who is talking to whom, and who is
talking about whom. There is no way around *who* because so much in people's lives
(and evolution) depends on social bonds. From this perspective, the identity of the
speaker should be a feature of any model of language processing.

The arguments and evidence reviewed so far compel us to expect that authorship
constrains language processing. However, they are at odds with the implications of
the evidence for egocentrism in language processing and human reasoning. Until
recently, egocentrism was perceived as a stage in children's cognitive development
(Piaget 1929). New evidence suggests that adults are just as egocentric, anchoring
initial interpretations in their own intentions and biases, and only later adjusting for
additional information (Gilbert 1991). The anchoring-and-adjustment framework has
been supported by some results on reference resolution. These results have suggested
that people do not take into account the perspective of the speaker in their interpretations of reference (Keysar et al. 2000; but cf. Nadig and Sedivy 2002). If this position holds, then the identity of the speaker should hardly matter.

Instigating a Rebellion

There is direct evidence for an effect of authorship on language comprehension. However, this evidence may not reflect early stages of processing. As a factor in language
comprehension, authorship acquired prominence first in the 1950s through the work
of Solomon Asch (1952) and related research on persuasion and propaganda. Asch presented people with excerpts from the writings of prominent public figures and asked
for written interpretation of the texts. For example, people read the following sentence:

(1)   I hold that a little rebellion, now and then, is a good thing, and as necessary in
      the political world as storms are in the physical.

The instructions informed half of the participants that the author of the statement was
Thomas Jefferson (the true author) and the rest that it was Lenin. The participants'
interpretations differed dramatically as a result of this manipulation. People who were
led to believe that the author was Lenin "sharpened" the statement by interpreting it

as an instigation of a revolution, which is appropriate to the leader of the 1917 Russian Revolution. Those who were led to believe that the author was Jefferson "leveled" the statement by interpreting it as a call for widespread political engagement, an appeal suitable to the architect of the Declaration of Independence.

Asch (1952) concluded that people take into account the "structural determination" of human actions and utterances in interpreting assertions. He believed that human behavior is determined by the circumstances in which it takes place and argued that "to see facts in their interrelation is a fundamental canon of method and the condition of valid observation and thinking" (p. 442). Note that this is a normative statement. Asch was aware that the interpretations he obtained may have reflected the subjects' intellectual agreement with the canon of method he was describing. Indeed, when explicitly asked whether they took authorship into account when they read the statements, some of Asch's subjects expressed overt opinions about whether authorship should be taken into account.

Although Asch's experiments convincingly demonstrated the effect of authorship on comprehension, they did not address the question of when authorship was integrated into the interpretation of the statement. Did this occur at the moment people responded to the question or at the time they were reading the text? The arguments and evidence for the link between language processing and interpersonal social variables suggests that the effect of authorship could be more immediate than Asch established. We combined his research paradigm with the cross-modal priming methodology to explore this possibility.

Cross-modal priming (Swinney 1979; Tanenhaus, Leiman, and Seidenberg 1979) allowed us to study whether authorship affects lexical processing online and whether its effect is analogous to the effects of verbal context. The cross-modal priming methodology has been used to measure relative activation of the alternative senses of an ambiguous lexical item, and therefore can measure contextual modulation of these activations. As a first step in examining the effect of authorship online, the present studies were not designed to adjudicate between different mechanistic explanations of such an effect; rather they were simply intended to demonstrate its existence.

Investigating *the Case*

The stimuli in our study were spoken sentences rather than typed text, and they contained homonyms (*case, file, slip*, etc.) rather than polysemous words like *rebellion*. Here is an example:

(2)   This case was opened in this very room three years ago.

Our contextual manipulation consisted of showing the participants a picture of the alleged speaker before playing the sentence. For the experimental trials, we selected pictures of people who are likely to use different meanings of the ambiguous words, usually by virtue of their profession. For instance, a judge is likely to talk about a trial "case" and a wine salesclerk about a "case" of wine. We carefully avoided images with background objects that could directly prime either sense of the ambiguous word. For example, there were no boxes or witness stands in the images of the salesclerk and the judge. The participants were given four seconds to form an impression of the people in the pictures while expecting to hear their utterances; no labels were provided.

We dropped Asch's dependent variable, the bias in the interpretations of the texts. Instead, we measured the time necessary to decide whether a probe letter string displayed on the computer screen was a word. Three target words, of approximately equal frequency, were matched with each ambiguous word: two that instantiated its meanings and an unrelated control word. For example, the three targets for *case* were *jury* (related), *box* (related), and *lord* (control). The target probes appeared immediately after the end of the ambiguous word for some subjects and 1,000 ms later for the rest. Our participants were instructed to respond quickly and accurately as to whether the probe was a word or a nonword. The two delays allowed us to track any changes in the activation of the alternative meanings.

To summarize the procedure, in each trial the participants first saw a picture of the speaker. Then the picture disappeared and they heard a sentence. While listening, they had to perform a lexical-decision task. In addition, after each sentence, the participants had to answer a comprehension question meant to ensure that they paid attention to the task. Twenty-four experimental trials were presented randomly along with forty-eight filler trials. The targets for thirty-six of those filler trials were nonwords in English.

We were interested in the differences in lexical-decision time between context-consistent, context-inconsistent, and control probes. The fit between probe and speaker determined these three conditions. While the control probes contributed only to the control condition, each homonym-related probe appeared as context consistent and context inconsistent, depending on the author context in which it was presented. For example, *jury* was context consistent when the judge was speaking and context inconsistent when the salesclerk was speaking.

Previous research has shown that disambiguation is influenced not only by contextual bias but also by the frequencies of the homonyms' meanings (Duffy, Morris, and Rayner 1988; Simpson and Burgess 1985). In the earliest stages of processing, only when context supports a dominant (i.e., more frequent) meaning, does it facilitate access to that meaning (but cf. Tabossi, Colombo, and Job 1987). However, our set of stimuli consisted of both biased and equibiased items. The latter are words whose two meanings are of roughly equal frequency. Usually both meanings of such words are primed early on regardless of context (Swinney 1979; Tanenhaus et al. 1979). Only very strong contextual bias initially facilitates the appropriate meaning (Vu, Kellas, and Paul 1998). Following these previous findings, we expected that the listeners would be faster at making the lexical decision for the context-consistent target than for the context-inconsistent target in the 1,000 ms delay condition, but not necessarily in the 0 ms condition.

Figure 15.1 shows the latencies of the lexical decisions of seventy undergraduate students for the three types of targets in the two delay conditions. A main effect of delay, significant by items only, resulted from some of the participants in the 0 ms delay condition responding faster than some of the participants in the 1,000 ms delay condition $(F_1(1, 68) = 1.81,\ p > .1;\ F_2(1, 23) = 26.211,\ p < .001)$. This difference is probably an artifact of the delay manipulation being a between-subjects variable. Crucially, however, the main effect of target type was significant (though only marginally by items; $F_1(2, 136) = 5.48,\ p < .01;\ F_2(2, 46) = 2.9,\ p = .06$), showing that the

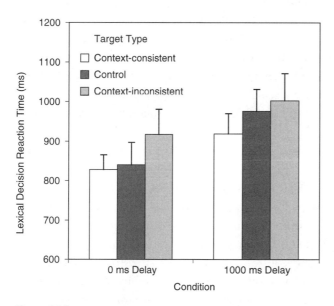

Figure 15.1
Lexical decision times as a function of target type and delay condition. There is inhibition of the inappropriate meaning of the ambiguous word right at its offset (0 ms delay) and facilitation of its appropriate meaning 1,000 ms later (1,000-ms delay).

contextually consistent condition was reliably faster than the contextually inconsistent condition. Mean reaction time for the control condition was in between those two. Although the interaction between delay and target type did not approach significance, previous findings, as well as our between-subjects design, clearly motivate a closer look at each of the two delay conditions.

For participants in the 0 ms delay condition, the effect of context was significant by subjects and marginally significant by items ($F_1(2,86) = 3.194$, $p < 0.05$; $F_2(2,46) = 2.526$, $p < 0.1$). The average reaction time to target words that were inconsistent with the context (917 ms) was much slower than that for the target words that were consistent with the context (828 ms) and the control targets (840 ms). Thus, at the earliest stages of processing that our measure could capture, authorship seems to inhibit access to the contextually inappropriate meaning, not to facilitate access to the appropriate meaning. This early effect is a surprising result given the mixture of biased and equibiased stimuli we used.

As expected, participants in the 1,000 ms delay condition identified the context-consistent targets much faster than the context-inconsistent and control targets (with latencies of 919, 1,003, and 977 ms respectively). Here the effect of context was significant by subjects but not by items ($F_1(2,50) = 3.674$, $p < 0.05$; $F_2(2,46) = 1.682$, $p > .1$). Although some inhibition of the contextually inappropriate meaning is still present, we mainly see facilitation of the contextually appropriate meaning.

These data corroborate Asch's findings. It is possible, however, that the context directly primed the target-probe words, irrespective of the intervening ambiguous word and its senses. This concern is underscored by the lack of significance of the item analyses. To respond to it, we ran the study again, this time without playing the sentences to the participants. The delay between the disappearance of the picture and the appearance of the probe was the same as in the 0 ms delay condition in the previous experiment. The participants were instructed to form an impression of the people in the pictures and then perform the lexical-decision task. We asked them to imagine that they were about to talk to these people. (After the lexical-decision task, they had to come up with sentences that the people might say.) If the images directly affected the probes, we expected to see faster identification of the contextually appropriate targets. The contextually inappropriate and control targets are unrelated to the pictures and should be identified more slowly. The results showed that the pictures did not affect the speed of responding to the targets. This suggests that the effect of target type in the previous study was indeed an effect of the author on the resolution of the lexically ambiguous spoken word, and not just the result of objects in the image priming the visually presented target-probe words.

The control study eliminated the possibility that the effect of authorship was a methodological artifact. However, it did not address the direction of the effect in the 0 ms delay condition. In contrast to the results of previous verbal contextual manipulations, ours led to the inhibition of the contextually inappropriate meaning rather than facilitation of the contextually appropriate one. We wrote in the introduction that nonverbal and verbal contexts differ in their availability to the listener and proposed a mental simulation to show how the two can generate different result patterns in word-recognition studies. The availability of the contextual information might also affect lexical disambiguation. The current data are the first in the field, and much more experimental and computational work is needed to explain their pattern and determine whether it is due to the sustained availability of authorship cues.

It could be that we have documented an effect that is difficult to observe but could have been obtained with any other contextual manipulation. Models of lexical processing that include competitive inhibition are potentially consistent with the selective activation of one meaning of an ambiguous word entailing suppression of another meaning (e.g., Kawamoto 1993; McClelland and Elman 1986).

In sum, these preliminary studies suggest that people can integrate the identity of the author in their interpretation of an utterance online. This conclusion, however tentative, qualifies the proposal that initial interpretations are anchored in the self (Gilbert 1991; Keysar et al. 2000). The present studies were not designed to test this proposal, but the tension brings up questions that require further examination. For example, how did differences in status and perspective between the alleged sentence authors and our participants affect the use of authorship information? College students probably vary in the ease with which they anticipate what judges, salesclerks, firefighters, and boxers will say, and it may be that our effects are more robust with the items where author identities were similar to those of our participants. Although our data do not speak directly to the issue of egocentrism in language processing, they initiate yet another avenue for examining it.

Conclusion

Our goal in this chapter was to introduce authorship—the identity of the speaker or writer—as a constraint on language processing. Much research and theorizing suggest a tight link between language processing and the interpersonal aspects of communicative situations. However, online effects of the social identity of the sentence author have not been previously documented. Our findings contribute to the evidence suggesting that a broad range of linguistic and nonlinguistic factors influence the early stages of online language processing. They also suggest that looking at language as a tool of social interaction may provide new insights about how it is processed and represented.

For a stronger test of the link between language processing and the interpersonal variables in a communicative situation, researchers have to compare different modes of language processing. Could interpersonal variables affect some but not other types of linguistic interchanges? We know of no empirical evidence directly indicating such an interaction between context type (e.g., text, author identity, visual availability of referents, and so on) and language-processing modality (reading or listening). However, the variation in the cognitive and perceptual salience of authors across different language-processing modes—face-to-face communication, book reading, telephone conversation, and e-mail—suggests that this interaction is likely (Baron 1998). A similar proposal has been made regarding the potency of different contextual constraints in online syntactic-ambiguity resolution (e.g., Spivey et al. 2002). Our current work on the role of authorship is aimed specifically at exploring the distinction between text-based language environments and speech-based ones.

References

Allopenna, P. D., Magnuson, J. S., and Tanenhaus, M. K. 1998. Tracking the time course of spoken word recognition using eye movements: Evidence for continuous mapping models. *Journal of Memory and Language*, *38*, 419–439.

Asch, S. 1952. *Social Psychology*. New York: Prentice Hall.

Austin, J. L. 1962. *How to Do Things with Words*. Cambridge, MA: Harvard University Press.

Baron, N. S. 1998. Letters by phone or speech by other means: The linguistics of email. *Language and Communication*, *18*, 133–170.

Barsalou, L. W. 1999. Language comprehension: Archival memory or preparation for situated action? *Discourse Processes*, *28*, 61–80.

Barwise, J., and Perry, J. 1983. *Situations and Attitudes*. Cambridge, MA: MIT Press.

Bessenoff, G. R., and Sherman, J. W. 2000. Automatic and controlled components of prejudice toward fat people: Evaluation versus stereotype activation. *Social cognition*, *18*, 329–353.

Boland, J. E., Tanenhaus, M. K., Garnsey, S. M., and Carlson, G. N. 1995. Verb argument structure in parsing and interpretation: Evidence from wh-questions. *Journal of Memory and Language*, *34*(6), 774–806.

Bransford, J. D., and Johnson, M. K. 1973. Considerations of some problems of comprehension. In W. G. Chase, ed., *Visual Information Processing*, 383–438. New York: Academic Press.

Clark, H. H., and Carlson, T. B. 1981. Context for comprehension. In J. Long and A. Baddeley, eds., *Attention and Performance IX*, 313–330. Hillsdale, NJ: Erlbaum.

Clark, H. H., and Marshall, C. R. 1981. Definite reference and mutual knowledge. In A. K. Joshi, B. L. Webber, and I. A. Sag, eds., *Elements of Discourse Understanding*, 10–63. Cambridge, UK: Cambridge University Press.

Duffy, S. A., Morris, R. K., and Rayner, K. 1988. Lexical ambiguity and fixation times in reading. *Journal of Memory and Language*, *27*, 429–446.

Dunbar, R. 1996. *Grooming, Gossip, and the Evolution of Language*. Cambridge, MA: Harvard University Press.

Gibson, J. J. 1979. *The Ecological Approach to Visual Perception*. Boston: Houghton Mifflin.

Gilbert, D. T. 1991. How mental systems believe. *American Psychologist*, *46*(2), 107–119.

Glenberg, A. M., and Robertson, D. A. 1999. Indexical understanding of instructions. *Discourse Processes*, *28*, 1–26.

Kawamoto, A. 1993. Nonlinear dynamics in the resolution of lexical ambiguity: A parallel distributed processing account. *Journal of Memory and Language*, *32*, 474–516.

Keysar, B., Barr, D. J., Balin, J. A., and Brauner, J. S. 2000. Taking perspective in conversation: The role of mutual knowledge in comprehension. *Psychological Science*, *11*, 32–38.

Lakoff, G., and Johnson, M. 1999. *Philosophy in the Flesh*. New York: Basic Books.

Marslen Wilson, W., and Tyler, L. K. 1980. The temporal structure of spoken language understanding. *Cognition*, *8*(1), 1–71.

Marslen-Wilson, W. D., and Welsh, A. 1978. Processing interactions and lexical access during word recognition incontinuous speech. *Cognitive Psychology*, *10*, 29–63.

McClelland, J. L., and Elman, J. L. 1986. The TRACE model of speech perception. *Cognitive Psychology*, *18*(1), 1–86.

McElree, B., and Griffith, T. 1998. Structural and lexical constraints on filling gaps during sentence comprehension: A time-course analysis. *Journal of Experimental Psychology: Learning, Memory, and Cognition*, *24*, 432–460.

Moskowitz, G. B., Salomon, A. R., and Taylor, C. M. 2000. Preconsciously controlling stereotyping: Implicitly activated egalitarian goals prevent the activation of stereotypes. *Social Cognition*, *18*(2), 151–177.

Mussweiler, T., and Förster, J. 2000. The sex → aggression link: A perception-behavior dissociation. *Journal of Personality and Social Psychology*, *79*(4), 507–520.

Nadig A. S., and Sedivy J. C. 2002. Evidence of perspective-taking constraints in children's on-line reference resolution. *Psychological Science*, *13*, 329–336.

Piaget, J. 1929. *The Child's Conception of the World*. New York: Harcourt, Brace Jovanovich.

Searle, J. R. 1969. *Speech Acts: An Essay in the Philosophy of Language*. London: Cambridge University Press.

Sedivy, J. C., Tanenhaus, M. K., Chambers, C. G., and Carlson, G. N. 1999. Achieving incremental interpretation through contextual representation. *Cognition, 71*, 109–147.

Simpson, G. B., and Burgess, C. 1985. Activation and selection processes in the recognition of ambiguous words. *Journal of Experimental Psychology: Human Perception and Performance, 11*(1), 28–39.

Simpson, G. B., Peterson, R. R., Casteel, M. A., and Burgess, C. 1989. Lexical and sentence context effects in word recognition. *Journal of Experimental Psychology: Learning, Memory, and Cognition, 15*(1), 88–97.

Spivey, M. J., Tanenhaus, M. K., Eberhard, K. M., and Sedivy, J. C. 2002. Eye movements and spoken language comprehension: Effects of visual context on syntactic ambiguity resolution. *Cognitive Psychology, 45*(4), 447–481.

Swinney, D. A. 1979. Lexical access during sentence conprehension: (Re)consideration of context effects. *Journal of Verbal Learning and Verbal Behavior, 18*, 645–659.

Tabossi, P., Colombo, L., and Job, R. 1987. Accessing lexical ambiguity: Effects of context and dominance. *Psychological Research, 49*, 161–167.

Tanenhaus, M. K., Leiman, J. M., and Seidenberg, M. S. 1979. Evidence for multiple stages in the processing of ambiguous words in syntactic contexts. *Journal of Verbal Learning and Verbal Behavior, 18*, 427–440.

Tanenhaus, M. K., Spivey-Knowlton, M. J., Eberhard, K. M., and Sedivy, J. 1995. Integration of visual and linguistic information in spoken language comprehension. *Science, 268*, 1632–1634.

Trueswell, J. C., Sekerina, I., Hill, N. M., and Logrip, M. L. 1999. The kindergarten-path effect: Studying on-line sentence processing in young children. *Cognition, 73*, 89–134.

Vu, H., Kellas, G., and Paul, S. T. 1998. Sources of sentence constraint on lexical ambiguity resolution. *Memory and Cognition, 26*(5), 979–1001.

V Gricean Phenomena

16   The Emergence of Conventions in Language Communities

Dale J. Barr

Communication is made possible through shared knowledge of conventions. Languages are highly intricate, layered systems of conventions—conventions of phonology, morphology, syntax, semantics, and discourse.

The fact that conventions are inherently arbitrary, and that languages are extremely complex collections of conventions, means that there is a vast amount of potential ambiguity in every utterance. The fact that two strangers sharing only a common language can achieve mutual understanding in spite of such ambiguity seems just short of miraculous. Yet one reason that it seems so is because we tend look at problems of language use through a set of lenses whose scope extends no further than the individual dyad. We tend to view each conversation as an independent act of coordination, in which a static system of conventions (a language) is adapted to the needs of individual language users.

Under these circumstances, the only thing close to a guarantee that interlocutors can achieve mutual understanding is that they can exploit their social intelligence to infer a mutually shared body of knowledge, or common ground. It is commonly assumed that this mutuality is the background against which people produce and interpret utterances (Clark and Marshall 1981). By exploiting their common ground, interlocutors use language in ways that will promote shared understanding. However, the process by which individuals track and infer common ground is extraordinarily complex. It involves a database of knowledge indexed according to the individuals and communities with whom it is shared. This database serves as the foundation for an infinite-order, recursive inferencing process that can be short-circuited by certain "copresence heuristics" (Clark and Marshall 1981; but see Lee 2001). Given these assumptions, tracking and using common ground during real-time conversation would seem to place large demands on the cognitive system.

Why are our theories of language use so complex, when using language seems so simple? Because theories focus on the dyad, they tend to place the burden of coordination for the entire community on the shoulders of each individual language user. We do this when we assume that individual language users carry around representations of the generic, conventional linguistic practices in their communities, that they use this knowledge to produce and interpret utterances, and that they expect others to do so as well (Clark 1998; Lewis 1969). The motivation for the idea that language users should coordinate on the basis of common knowledge instead of on what is merely salient or habitual is that it seems likely that different experiences with language will make different things salient to each person.

However, by zooming out our focus from the dyad to the language community, we can obtain a different perspective on this problem. The basic dyad that is the focus of most theories of language use is not isolated, but integrated into a large, complicated information network: the language community. The work of coordinating meaning in the language community is distributed over time and over many interactions. From this perspective, the main question is what is necessary for common symbolic practices to emerge.

In this chapter, I use techniques of multiagent computer simulation to demonstrate how this socially situated view of language use can address fundamental questions about the conventional groundwork of language use. These simulations show that conventional systems of communication can self-organize through the massively parallel interactions of dyads in a language community. These results call into question the accepted theory of conventions, which suggests that they emerge through the accumulation of common knowledge. The simulations imply that by expanding the scope of language research to include processes of coordination in the language community, we can simplify our theories of language use.

Conventions and Common Knowledge

Lewis (1969) proposed that conventions arise out of coordination problems that recur among the members of a community. Coordination problems are problems of interdependent decision making, where the outcome of a decision depends on what other people do. According to classical game theory, people attempt to solve coordination problems by deriving *mutual expectations*; you think about what I will do, I think about what you will do, you think about what I think you will do, and so on. By acting on mutual expectations people can maximize their chances of achieving equilibrium, a state in which no one person would prefer to change his or her action given the actions of the others. People generate mutual expectations on the basis of the salience, precedence, or conventionality of alternatives. Thus, you and I might choose some course of action because we think it is conspicuous to both of us (salience), because we have chosen it in the past (precedence), or because we know that in our joint community this is the regular way of responding to the problem (convention).

Precedents and conventions provide solutions to coordination problems that tend to recur among the members of a community. When a community is small enough that each individual has repeated opportunities to interact with every other individual, there is little need for conventions since any given person can establish specific precedents with every other person. When communities are large, however, there arises a pressing need for communitywide conventions that can provide default standards when mutually shared precedents do not exist, such as when two strangers from the community interact for the first time.

The problem of *generalization*, central to the common-knowledge account, is the problem of how a conventional framework arises and becomes adopted by an entire community. In Lewis's framework generalization is explained through the accumulation of common knowledge. We say that some convention is common knowledge in a community when it is not only known to all members of a community, but it is *known to be shared*. This knowledge can come about through one's own experience with other members of the community: "If one has often encountered cases in which coordination was achieved in a certain problem by conforming to a certain regularity and rarely or never encountered cases in which it was not, he is entitled to expect his neighbors to have had the same experience" (Lewis 1969, 40).

According to theories of language use, it is common knowledge that governs the use of conventions in communication (Clark and Marshall 1981). For example, I use the words *moon, shampoo*, and *red* with you in the way that I do because this is the way that is accepted by the larger community. Furthermore, I believe that you know these standards, that you know that I know them too, and so on. This common knowledge gives me a reason to believe that when you interpret these words you will apply these standards instead of some idiosyncratic scheme. If instead, language users used symbols in the way most salient to them, this would not seem to promote coordination, neither in individual conversations nor in the larger community. This is because "the salience of an equilibrium is not a very strong indication that everyone will choose it" (Lewis 1969, 57).

In Lewis's view, conventions emerge through the joint actions of a community that strategically coordinates its behavior on the basis of common knowledge, and members of the community use this common knowledge to regulate their language use. This assumes that each member of the community has representations of the global behavior of the community. An important question is the following: Are such global representations really necessary for conventions to emerge?

The Self-Organization of Conventional Communication Systems

Another way conventions can emerge in a language community is through self-organization. We say that systems "self-organize" when they exhibit global patterns of organization that are a by-product of low-level, local interactions between the units in the system. For instance, consider the flocking behavior of certain species of birds. Like language users, the individual birds in a flock face the problem of coordinating their behavior with that of other community members. How might birds do this? One way would be for each bird to have a concept of the "flock" that represents the average velocity and direction of the other birds. This global representation could be used to guide its behavior, just as common knowledge might guide the linguistic behavior of the members of a language community. On the other hand, consider the case in which each bird simply locally adjusts its speed and bearing to that of its immediate neighbors. In this case, because each bird is acting on only partial information, one might expect the movements of the birds to lack any cohesiveness. However, Reynolds (1987) has shown that the simultaneous, parallel action of all birds following such a local algorithm yields highly coordinated flocking that is strikingly similar to the patterns observed in nature. The organization that one observes at the global level of the flock emerges out of the many local adjustments that the individual birds make in parallel. Each bird's movements provide the context for the movements of the neighboring birds. Even if it turns out that global representations of the flock's movements could produce the same behavior, we would favor the local explanation because it presumes simpler abilities on the part of the individual birds.

Language communities are like flocks of birds in the sense that language use takes place among many small groups of individuals who seek to coordinate understanding in parallel. Although their interactions seem independent, they reciprocally influence one another, promoting a commonality of representation in the community. In this chapter, I describe the results of a set of multiagent computer simulations that show that the conventions for communication in a language community emerge out of these local but interdependent interactions. The simulations show that common knowledge is not necessary for conventions to emerge. In fact, the development of conventions was sometimes more efficient the *less* each agent knew about what other agents in the system were doing. This casts doubt on the efficacy of common knowledge as a mechanism for community-level coordination.

Previous work on language evolution provides an indirect demonstration that certain conventional behaviors can arise through mechanisms other than common knowledge. For instance, research using multiagent simulation and techniques of artificial life has shown that natural selection can tune languages to become more effective instruments of communication over the course of generations (Batali 1994; Cangelosi and Parisi 1998; Kvasnicka and Pospichal 2000; MacLennan and Burghardt 1994; Parisi 1997). Another line of work uses "iterated learning" to explain the emergence of linguistic conventions (Batali 1998; Hurford 1999; Kirby and Hurford 2001; Oliphant 1999). In the iterated-learning paradigm, language learners are introduced into a population and attempt to induce the language from observed meaning-form pairs. These simulations show that when this induction problem is repeated over many generations, languages tend to stabilize. However, neither the Darwinian approach nor the iterated-learning model provides a solution for the problem of how conventions might generalize to an entire community *within a single generation*, the critical case that the common-knowledge model was developed to explain.

In contrast, the work of Steels (1996, 1998, 2002) as well as that of Hutchins and Hazlehurst (Hazlehurst and Hutchins 1998; Hutchins and Hazlehurst 1995) demonstrates that conventions can self-organize within a single generation. This research is similar in spirit to the work presented here, in that it assumes that conventions can emerge as a by-product of the local actions of agents. As in the current simulations, the agents play a series of language games and update their behavior on the basis of their successes or failures to communicate. However, these simulations do not provide definitive evidence against the necessity of common knowledge, because they leave the locality of agents' knowledge in doubt. First, in simulations by Hutchins and Hazlehurst, small numbers of agents were used such that each agent could potentially interact multiple times with every other agent in the community. The question of generalization to a population is not entirely relevant here, because agents can directly alter one another's behavior. In Steels's work, each agent has an infinite memory that keeps a running score of the success of each mapping. While different from common knowledge, this scorekeeping behavior might be construed as a type of global knowledge because it effectively tracks the most frequent behavior of the community. In contrast to these studies, the current work is more directly targeted at developing an alternative account of generalization by using large populations in which agents have access to only extremely local information.

Finally, in a set of experiments by Garrod and Doherty (1994) that used human subjects, it was found that conventions emerged under circumstances in which common knowledge seemed implausible. However, it remained possible that participants could have inferred common knowledge on the basis of the regularities they observed in their partners' behavior. The current simulations help build a more conclusive case.

The Signaling Game

In the simulations, pairs of agents from a population of 1,000 played a simple communication game. Figure 16.1 provides a schematic overview of the algorithm for a single "epoch" or time step.

The population inhabited the interior of a rectangular two-dimensional space. Each agent played the signaling game with a series of partners who were chosen at random, depending on their spatial proximity in the plane (step 1). Agents interacted most frequently with agents in their "neighborhood," a small portion of space surrounding each agent. Only about 5 percent of the time would an agent interact with a partner outside of its neighborhood. The size of this neighborhood was varied across the simulations. A neighborhood size of 3 means that 95 percent of an average agent's interactions would be with the same three agents; likewise, a neighborhood size of 27 means that 95 percent of an average agent's interactions would be with twenty-seven different agents.

The goal of the game was to communicate a series of four meanings. Each meaning could be conveyed by any of four different forms. Each agent had a "lexicon" that stored mappings between the four meanings and four forms. There were twenty-four different "signaling systems," corresponding to the twenty-four ways in which the forms could be mapped onto meanings in a one-to-one fashion. Initially, every agent's lexicon was randomly initialized to one of these twenty-four settings, so that the population began in a state of disorganization. Because there was no predesignated conventional system, and no possibility of common knowledge, the population could only establish conventions as a by-product of their local interactions with other agents.

One agent in each pair played the role of the speaker, while the other played the role of the listener. The speaker's task was to communicate all four meanings to the listener in a random order (figure 16.1, step 2). For each meaning, the speaker consulted its lexicon and produced the corresponding form (step 3). The listener observed the form and selected the corresponding meaning from its own lexicon (step 4). The two meanings were compared, and the agents were informed of their success or failure (step 5).

Based on this signal, agents updated their lexicons using a simple algorithm called "stay-switch" (step 6). The basic idea behind the algorithm is to retain successful mappings and "switch" unsuccessful ones. To determine how to update their map-

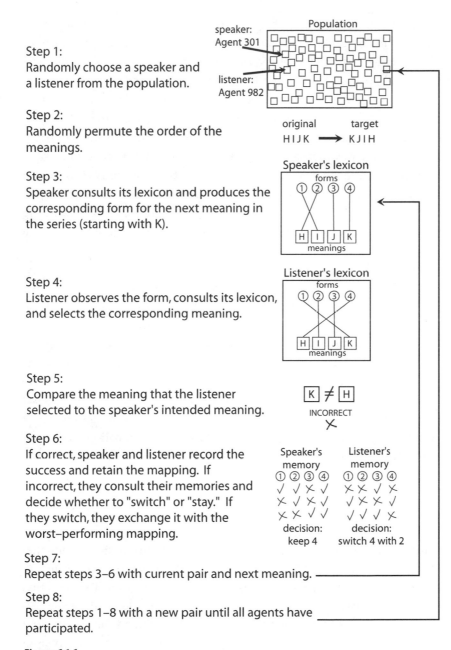

Step 1:
Randomly choose a speaker and a listener from the population.

Step 2:
Randomly permute the order of the meanings.

Step 3:
Speaker consults its lexicon and produces the corresponding form for the next meaning in the series (starting with K).

Step 4:
Listener observes the form, consults its lexicon, and selects the corresponding meaning.

Step 5:
Compare the meaning that the listener selected to the speaker's intended meaning.

Step 6:
If correct, speaker and listener record the success and retain the mapping. If incorrect, they consult their memories and decide whether to "switch" or "stay." If they switch, they exchange it with the worst–performing mapping.

Step 7:
Repeat steps 3–6 with current pair and next meaning.

Step 8:
Repeat steps 1–8 with a new pair until all agents have participated.

Figure 16.1
Algorithm for a single epoch of the simulation.

pings, agents had a primitive memory that tracked the successes or failures of each of the four forms. To force agents to operate on extremely local information, agents' memory size was set to a value of 2. This means that when agents updated their lexicons, they could only consult their memories of the last two rounds.

When a communication attempt was successful, an agent simply recorded that form's success in its memory. When it was unsuccessful, the agent examined the past performance of the form that caused the error and decided whether to switch or retain its mapping. If the form was untested (the memory was empty), they would switch with a probability of .75. If the memory was not empty, the probability of switching was equivalent to the proportion of past failures given memory size. The switch operation consisted of ranking the forms in terms of their past performance, and switching the form that caused the error with the form with the lowest ranking. In the case of a tie, the agent would flip a coin.

After completing all four meanings (step 7), a new pair was drawn and the process repeated (step 8) until all agents had the chance to participate (in each epoch some agents sat out because all agents in their neighborhood were busy with other agents). After the epoch was completed, the counter was incremented and a new epoch began. The simulation was terminated either when 1,000 epochs had been completed or the system had "converged" to a single conventional system—that is, when all of the agents' lexicons had the same mappings.

The simulations reported here examine the performance of the system under six different settings of neighborhood size (3, 5, 9, 14, 20, and 27). The results are robust because they are averaged over 100 runs for each setting. These simulations are part of a larger set that is discussed in Barr, in press, which provides further analysis and exploration of various parameter settings.

Results

Table 16.1 presents, for each neighborhood setting, the percent of simulations that converged before 1,000 epochs and the corresponding efficiency of convergence in epochs (averaging only over populations that converged). The first thing to note is that convergence was more likely than not for all but the smallest (3) and largest (27) neighborhood sizes. Clearly, then, a shared communication system can emerge in a population of agents who lack common knowledge and do not operate on the basis of mutual expectations. The best performance was observed at a population size of 14, where 96 percent of the simulations converged after agents had played the game 352

Table 16.1
Percent of simulations that converged before 1,000 epochs, and efficiency of convergence, at each neighborhood setting

	Neighborhood size					
	3	5	9	14	20	27
Percent converged	19%	62%	85%	96%	69%	44%
Efficiency (epochs)	696	447	280	352	480	526

times. The most efficient setting was 9, where the simulations converged after only 280 times. To get a sense for the quality of this performance, consider that if agents simply flipped their mappings randomly at each epoch, convergence would be observed only once every 24^{999} epochs, a probability so small as to be effectively negligible.

Convergence showed diminishing performance as population size increased beyond 14. This is surprising from the point of view of common-knowledge theory, because the circumstance that best favors the establishment of common knowledge is the one in which agents interact with more partners fewer times, instead of fewer partners more times. In Barr, in press, populations of 1,000 agents operating under stay-switch whose neighborhoods encompassed the entire population, *never* converged to a single system. The fact that repeated interaction with the same agents led to better generalization suggests that situations in which the possibility for common knowledge is greatest may also be the ones least likely to yield convergence.

Even when the populations did not converge by 1,000 epochs, they still exhibited improved coordination over time. In fact, in nearly all populations that failed to eventually converge, the formation of spatially organized dialects could be observed. Figure 16.2 provides an example of this for two different neighborhood sizes, 3 (left panels) and 9 (right panels). In the figure, each agent is represented by a marker that corresponds to whichever of the 24 possible communication systems that agent is currently using. The two panels on each side of the figure display the population at epoch 0 (top) and after 200 epochs. By 200 epochs a larger number of more tightly concentrated dialects appear in the population with the smaller neighborhood size. All populations with neighborhood sizes smaller than 20 exhibited, without exception, a similar development of dialects. Some populations eventually converged on a single system, while others locked into an enduring pattern of two or more competing dialects. In contrast, populations with a neighborhood size of 27 or greater seldom showed the development of dialects.

Neighborhood size = 3   Neighborhood size = 9

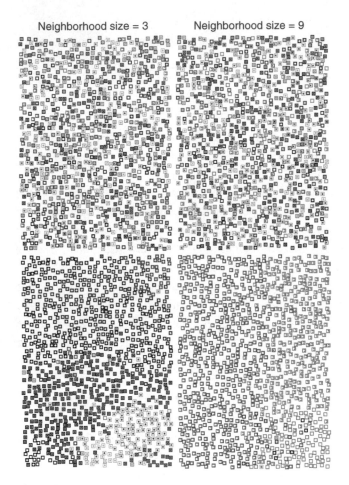

Figure 16.2
The emergence of spatially organized dialects in two populations of 1,000 agents after 0 (top) and 200 epochs (bottom). The neighborhood sizes of these populations are 3 (left) and 9 (right).

Conclusion

The simulations show that conventions can emerge out of the parallel but inter-dependent communicative interactions of individuals in a population. Convergence to a single system was the most likely outcome for populations with moderate neighborhood sizes. The likelihood and efficiency of convergence tapered off at larger neighborhood sizes, a circumstance that, under Lewis's theory, best favors the accumulation of common knowledge. This suggests that there may be circumstances under which coordination through common knowledge could work *against* the evolution of conventions. Even when populations did not completely converge to a single system, they tended to show some degree of self-organization through the formation of spatially organized dialects. Thus, even though a single conventional system sometimes did not prevail, coordination in the community was still quite high.

It should be kept in mind that, when compared to the human activity of language use, the simulations presented here are simply toy models. The linguistic universe of the agents consists of a very simple, highly constrained language game with four forms and four meanings. While the language game is small, it is similar to the signaling games that Lewis (1969) analyzed within the common-knowledge framework. Although this simplification allows for the illumination of the mechanisms of information sharing in language communities and how they pertain to problems of language use, there are ways the simulations should be extended to bring the analogy closer. For one, in human language, forms and meanings are potentially open ended. Perhaps in those circumstances at least some rudimentary form of common knowledge would be needed. For instance, Steels (1996, 1998, 2002) has shown convergence with an open-ended set of meanings and forms, but as noted above, the agents in this case had greater access to global knowledge than the agents in the current simulations.

Could the simulations presented here be construed, perhaps, as an "implementation" of the common-knowledge model? After all, the agents have things in common such as the set of forms, meanings, update rule, and memories. Yet an agent who truly can be said to operate according to common knowledge must also have the following abilities: (1) *membership categorization*, or the ability to identify other agents and to determine whether they are joint members of the agent's community; (2) *metarepresentation*, the ability to represent what others in that community know; and (3) *high-level strategic reasoning*, the preference for conforming to whatever it is that other people in the community do, given the expectation that they will also expect you to conform, and so on. Although the agents in the simulation clearly had none of these abilities, an argument for this "implementational view" could be drawn out along the following lines. Because the agents in the current simulations never encountered an agent outside their community, perhaps they did not need (1). Furthermore, it could be argued that (2) was implemented by agents' memory, and that the update algorithm was a proxy for (3), in the sense that it altered agents' mappings in a way that would make them more likely to succeed within the community.

A close analysis of the simulations shows this view to be implausible. First, agents operated on the basis of extremely local information. Each agent only had a memory for the last two rounds, which hardly could be said to index the most common behavior in a population of 1,000 agents. Moreover, even if the agents were given infinitely large memories, they still would not operate according to the strictures of the common-knowledge model. To see why, consider the following example. Assume that during the first ten rounds some agent, A, interacts with ten distinct individuals who all communicate using signaling system S. For the next ninety rounds, just by chance this same agent interacts over and over with agent B, who communicates using a different signaling system, S'. Note that an agent who operates according to common knowledge would tend to discount its repeated interactions with B and maintain its use of system S. Since nine out of ten agents used that system, it would still be the agent's best guess about what signaling system is most common in the community. In contrast, an agent in the current simulation would stop using S and alter its mappings to look more like S' because it is interested in trying to do what worked most *frequently* in its own experience, but *not* in adopting the system used most frequently in the community.

The fact that common knowledge was not necessary to bring about generalization should not be taken to imply that it could *not* do so. Nonetheless, it would be important to show that it could using analytical techniques or through multiagent simulation instead of accepting it as a forgone conclusion. The results presented here and in Barr, in press, suggest that the circumstances that are most favorable for the establishment of common knowledge—a large memory of one's history of interaction and interactions with more people fewer times—are the same ones that, in the current framework, led to the least efficient convergence.

Finally, these simulations do not entail that people *never* use common knowledge of conventions to regulate their use of language. People have extensive knowledge about the various kinds of registers spoken in different social circumstances and among different community groups, and can adjust their language accordingly. What the simulations do suggest is that people can take much for granted when communicating with members of their home community. Because dyads are organized into an interlocking social network, their parallel acts of coordination are mutually constraining, and will promote similar semantic representations in the community. In a sense, the dynamics of interaction in the community are tantamount to a process of "social concept formation," an idea first advanced by Garrod and Doherty (1994) and further investigated by Markman and Makin (1998). Over time, the variation that individuals encounter in the language use of their partners will promote highly general representations that in turn, support coordination with an ever-wider array of individuals from the community (Garrod and Doherty 1994).

In closing, let us return to the question, Why are our theories of language use so complex when using language seems so simple? One possible answer is that by focusing too much on the isolated dyad, we fail to recognize that language use is situated in the informationally complex environments of language communities. As a consequence, we place too much of the community's burden of coordination on the shoulders of the individual language user, instead of distributing it across the members of the community. As the current simulations suggest, it is important to build models of the macrolevel environments of language use because they can place constraints on our microlevel theories. Specifically, they can inform us as to whether we need to build specialized mechanisms for coordination into the heads of individual language users, or whether the coordination can best be left to social processes. A primary reason why a better understanding of the broader social environment of language use can make our theories simpler is that in solving social-coordination problems, "social feedback mechanisms can substitute for high levels of knowledge and deductive powers on the part of individuals" (Young 1998, 662). Thus, even though problems of coordination might be extremely complicated, theories of language use need not be.

References

Barr, D. J. (in press). Establishing conventional communication systems: Is common knowledge necessary? *Cognitive Science.*

Batali, J. 1994. Innate biases and critical periods: Combining evolution and learning in the acquisition of syntax. In R. A. Brooks and P. Maes, eds., *Proceedings of the Fourth International Workshop on the Synthesis and Simulation of Living Systems (Artificial Life IV)*, 160–171. Cambridge, MA: MIT Press.

Batali, J. 1998. Computational simulations of the emergence of grammar. In J. R. Hurford, M. Studdert-Kennedy, and C. Knight, eds., *Approaches to the Evolution of Language: Social and Cognitive Bases*, 405–426. Cambridge, UK: Cambridge University Press.

Cangelosi, A., and Parisi, D. 1998. The emergence of a "language" in an evolving population of neural networks. *Connection Science, 10*, 83–97.

Clark, H. H. 1998. Communal lexicons. In K. Malmkjær and J. Williams, eds., *Context in Language Learning and Language Understanding*, 63–87. Cambridge, UK: Cambridge University Press.

Clark, H. H., and Marshall, C. R. 1981. Definite reference and mutual knowledge. In A. K. Joshe, B. L. Webber, and I. A. Sag, eds., *Elements of Discourse Understanding*, 10–63. Cambridge, UK: Cambridge University Press.

Garrod, S., and Doherty, G. 1994. Conversation, coordination and convention: An empirical investigation of how groups establish linguistic conventions. *Cognition, 53*, 181–215.

Hazlehurst, B., and Hutchins, E. 1998. The emergence of propositions from the co-ordination of talk and action in a shared world. *Language and Cognitive Processes*, *13*, 373–424.

Hurford, J. R. 1999. Expression/induction models of language evolution: Dimensions and issues. In E. J. Briscoe, ed., *Linguistic Evolution through Language Acquisition*. Cambridge, UK: Cambridge University Press.

Hutchins, E., and Hazlehurst, B. 1995. How to invent a lexicon: The development of shared symbols in interaction. In N. Gilbert and R. Conte, eds., *Artificial Societies: The Computer Simulation of Social Life*, 157–189. London: UCL Press.

Kirby, S., and Hurford, J. R. 2001. The emergence of linguistic structure: An overview of the iterated learning model. In A. Cangelosi and D. Parisi, eds., *Simulating the Evolution of Language*. London: Springer.

Kvasnicka, V., and Pospichal, J. 2000. An emergence of coordinated communication in populations of agents. *Artificial Life*, *5*, 319–342.

Lee, B. P. H. 2001. Mutual knowledge, background knowledge and shared beliefs: Their roles in establishing common ground. *Journal of Pragmatics*, *33*, 21–44.

Lewis, D. 1969. *Convention: A Philosophical Study*. Cambridge, MA: Harvard University Press.

MacLennan, B. J., and Burghardt, G. M. 1994. Synthetic ethology and the evolution of cooperative communication. *Adaptive Behavior*, *2*, 161–188.

Markman, A. B., and Makin, V. S. 1998. Referential communication and category acquisition. *Journal of Experimental Psychology: General*, *127*, 331–354.

Oliphant, M. 1999. The learning barrier: Moving from innate to learned systems of communication. *Adaptive Behavior*, *7*, 371–384.

Parisi, D. 1997. An artificial life approach to language. *Brain and Language*, *59*, 121–146.

Reynolds, C. W. 1987. Flocks, herds, and schools: A distributed behavioral model. *Computer Graphics*, *21*, 25–34.

Steels, L. 1996. Self-organizing vocabularies. In C. G. Langton and T. Shimohara, eds., *Artificial life V: Proceedings of the Fifth International Workshop*. Cambridge, MA: MIT Press.

Steels, L. 1998. Synthesizing the origins of language and meaning using coevolution, self-organization and level formation. In J. R. Hurford, M. Studdert-Kennedy, and C. Knight, eds., *Approaches to the Evolution of Language: Social and Cognitive Bases*, 384–404. Cambridge, UK: Cambridge University Press.

Steels, L. 2002. Grounding symbols through evolutionary language games. In A. Cangelosi and D. Parisi, eds., *Simulating the Evolution of Language*, 211–226. London: Springer.

Young, H. P. 1998. Individual learning and social rationality. *European Economic Review*, *42*, 651–663.

17 Evaluating Explanations for Referential Context Effects: Evidence for Gricean Mechanisms in Online Language Interpretation

Julie C. Sedivy

Modularity claims have served as the focal point for a great deal of empirical work in online language processing over the past two decades. Hypotheses constraining the nature of the information that is consulted during the earliest moments of language processing have held considerable appeal for at least two reasons. First, they provide a way of reconciling the extraordinary speed of language processing with the sheer quantity and diversity of information that must be recruited in order to arrive at an elaborated meaningful representation of a sentence based on its surface input. Second, they are consistent with claims from formal linguistic theory that much of the structure of language can be accounted for by appealing to a highly specialized domain-specific set of representations and principles (or indeed, perhaps even highly autonomous discrete levels of such representations and principles) that interact with domain-external information in extremely limited, unidirectional ways. Thus, the organization of the processing system could be construed as providing confirming evidence for particular hypotheses about the organization of the grammar.

Heated debates have focused heavily on the question of evaluating empirical evidence for the impact of discourse context on the earliest moments of syntactic parsing, challenging some particular implementations of the modularity hypothesis. A great deal of focused research activity has not yielded consensus regarding the exact details of the processing mechanisms and their ordering. However, there is now considerable agreement about the conditions under which discourse context exerts the most powerful effects, as well as acknowledgment that in many cases, the effects of context are evident from the earliest moments discernible through current experimental methods. These findings pose a challenge in that they suggest that the speed of language processing is not purchased as a result of categorical constraints ruling out entire domains of information from initial consideration. It is therefore necessary for the field to explain how the integration of contextual information with linguistic structure can be so rapidly achieved. Part of the explanation no doubt lies in the formulation of more explicit theories of the structuring and organization of extralinguistic information, drawing on work in nonlinguistic domains of human cognition and perception. However, I would like to propose that recent developments in characterizing certain kinds of linguistic phenomena, especially with respect to characterizing the ways linguistic structures and expressions systematically interact with discourse context, may serve as a promising starting point for generating and evaluating hypotheses about the relationship between linguistic form and extralinguistic context in online language processing.

As noted, motivation for modularity hypotheses has come in part from the appealing prospect of using processing data to evaluate questions about grammatical organization. While strong evidence of temporal dissociation of structural from semantic or discourse-context information would have supported arguments for their representational dissociation, the current empirical evidence generally showing a lack of clear temporal dissociation makes it difficult to draw any representational conclusions; even completely simultaneous use of structural and contextual information is consistent with a strict distinction of representational systems. However, it is interesting to note that linguistic research in the fields of formal semantics and pragmatics has itself led to a blurring of boundaries between grammatical and extragrammatical information. Standard theories of semantics have typically assumed that aspects of meaning that are context-general and contributed by lexically specified information together with the combinatorial rules of the language can be sharply distinguished from aspects of meaning that reflect context-specific inferences and expectations; indeed, context-specific inferencing mechanisms have often been assumed to take as input the output of the grammatically determined semantic representations. However, close investigation of some linguistic phenomena has led to proposals for a degree of interleaving of the semantic and contextual information. For instance, recent semantic treatments of focus (e.g., Rooth 1992) require an open variable to be contextually specified before the semantic system can yield its output. Accounts of scalar adjectives incorporate similar formal mechanisms (e.g., Bierwisch 1987; Kennedy 2001; Pollard and Sag 1994), and intrusions of pragmatic inferencing within the semantic system have been proposed by Chierchia et al. (2001). Work along these lines is very interesting because it suggests that knowledge of linguistic representations and structures may also include a specification of points of contact with contextual representations such that the linguistic representation itself may serve as a recipe for pulling out of the context the immediately relevant information. If very rapid context effects are primarily observed under these conditions, then integration of contextual information in language processing may be in some sense inherent to the knowledge of language. The current chapter focuses on some of the linguistic properties of adjectival modifiers as a case study in evaluating in more detail the nature of the context effects now commonly observed in language processing.

A Conservative Hypothesis of Form-Context Interaction in Online Processing

The widely known experimental work of Crain and Steedman (1985) and Altmann and Steedman (1988) first led to discourse-based explanations for well-known parsing biases such as the one responsible for difficulty in processing many kinds of temporarily ambiguous sentences, including Bever's (1970) famous example sentence *The horse raced past the barn fell.* Crain and Steedman (1985) pointed out that the syntactic ambiguity had as one of its consequences the necessity of choosing between a structure involving modification, and a structure involving a simple, unmodified noun. They characterized the discourse requirements of definite modified noun phrases as presuppositional, and argued that the use of a definite modified NP requires the satisfaction of the following presuppositions: (1) that the entire NP refer to a single, uniquely identifiable individual in the discourse model; (2) that the existence of an individual matching the description of the NP be taken as implicitly assumed in the discourse; and (3) that some (nonsingleton) set of individuals identified by the head noun be represented in the discourse model. This view can be seen as a simple extension of presuppositions associated with definite nouns in general (e.g., see Heim 1982), with the presuppositions in (1) and (2) commonly shared by all definite noun phrases, and (3) contributed by modification. Under such a view, there is a fairly direct link between a particular class of linguistic expressions (i.e., definite noun phrases) and relevant contextual information, and this link is simply part of the characterization of the linguistic meaning of these expressions. This proposal makes fairly conservative claims about the relationship between context and form in language processing. Because a particular class of expressions is directly linked to certain inferences about the discourse model, the search for relevant contextual information in interpreting the expression is triggered (and possibly may be constrained by) the linguistically specific presuppositional requirements of that expression.

A study investigating the discourse properties of adjectival modifiers provided experimental evidence in support of referential context effects associated with modification. Sedivy et al. (1999) investigated eye movements in response to spoken sentences involving prenominal adjectival modifiers (e.g., *Pick up the tall glass*). The study used the methodology described by Tanenhaus et al. (1995), which exploits a tight temporal linking between spoken language and eye movements to entities that are referred to in the speech stream. Experiments using this technique have found that subjects attempt to establish reference on the basis of very partial evidence. The Sedivy et al. study aimed to determine the online referential interpretation for vague scalar adjectives such as *tall* in a visual context with two potential tall objects (e.g., a glass and a pitcher). It was reasoned that if modification is inherently associated with a contrastive function, then when the visual context includes a contrasting object of the category denoted by the head noun (e.g., a contrasting shorter glass), there should be a greater tendency to identify the actual target (i.e., the glass) as the referent for *tall* than the competing tall object, because only reference to the target object is consistent with this contrastive function. These displays were compared to ones in which there was no contrasting object of the same category as the target. It was found that the presence of the contrasting object did indeed have a dramatic effect on eye movements to the target and competitor objects; the presence of the contrasting object resulted in convergence on the target object beginning before the offset of the adjective, whereas in the absence of the contrasting object, subjects did not identify the target as the referent of the modified NP until after they had heard the head noun. These results suggest that prenominal modification does indeed trigger inferences pertaining to contrasting entities in the discourse model.

However, Crain and Steedman's specific presuppositional account of modified definite NPs has been called into question by, for example, Clifton and Ferreira (1989), who argue for a much less direct link between modified nouns and their discourse properties. They point out that a hallmark of presuppositions is that they are typically not cancelable, resulting in marked anomaly when the presuppositions associated with an expression are violated. However, modified nouns do not seem to be anomalous even when used noncontrastively (i.e., in violation of clause 3 above). In fact, corpus data suggest that modifiers are used most typically in contexts where the modification is not serving a contrastive purpose (see, for example, Fox and Thompson 1990).

Indeed, more recent experimental work building on the Sedivy et al. (1999) experiments suggests that contrastive inferences are not observed for all noun phrases involving modification. Sedivy (1999) reported data involving eye-movement data in response to instructions containing color adjectives. Unlike the experiments with scalar adjectives reported by Sedivy et al. (1999), no facilitatory effect of contextual contrast was found for identifying the referent of noun phrases such as *the red bowl*. The lack of a contextual-contrast effect for color adjectives is incompatible with the view that adjectives, or modifiers more generally, carry presuppositions of discourse contrast. Under this view, no difference would be predicted in the behavior of color versus scalar adjectives.

The difference in the results for color and scalar adjectives points toward an alternative account of the discourse-context effects on the interpretation of scalar adjectives, initially pointed out as a possible explanation by Sedivy et al. (1999). It may be the case that the referential-context effects observed in that study are due to the relational nature of the scalar adjectives that were investigated, rather than general contrastive properties of modification. Specifically, it is a general property of scalar adjectives that they cannot be interpreted without taking into consideration some relevant comparison class. Formal semantic analyses of adjectives (e.g., Bierwisch 1987; Kennedy 2001) typically capture this requirement by incorporating into the meaning of a scalar adjective a contextually bound variable that stands in for some comparison class, where this class can be determined contextually. Hence, if the lexical representation of a scalar adjective contains a variable whose value must be determined by some salient contrast set, this may be the impetus for the contrastive interpretation of scalar adjectives, rather than some global presupposition associated with modification.

Note that this account is similar to the presuppositional account in that it builds the relevant contextual information into the meaning characterization of a particular class of linguistic expressions, in this case, scalar adjectives. Under the presuppositional account, certain contextual assumptions must be met in order for the modified referential phrase to successfully refer, and hence have a value. Under the alternative account, no potential referents for the scalar adjectives can be identified without fixing the comparison class that would yield the specific values that might count as the entities bearing the scalar property in question. Thus, both explanations represent conservative hypotheses about the intrusion of contextual information into early online processing decisions, in that the contextual information is directly linked to the linguistic semantic characterizations of the words and phrases being processed. The data from both experiments with scalar and color adjectives are compatible only with the lexically based account, given the discrepancy between the adjective types with respect to contextual effects. In the following sections, a more radical interpretation of discourse-context effects is evaluated.

A Radical Hypothesis Regarding Interaction of Linguistic Form/Context in Processing

It has been suggested (e.g., Clifton and Ferreira 1989; Sedivy et al. 1999) that the explanation for the intuition that modified NPs require referential contrast derives from general expectations about cooperative communication. As was first noted by Grice (1975), hearers typically assume that speakers will minimize redundancy in their utterances, and be optimally informative. Hence, if a referent could be identified on the basis of the head noun alone, and there is no other informational value to the modifier, the use of a modified NP would violate communicative expectations, resulting in a bias toward the communicatively motivated form of the noun phrase. Clifton and Ferreira (1989) conclude, however, that such indirect inferences are too computationally burdensome to be useful in rapid online processing.

Indeed, an explanation of the contextual effects with adjectives based on a Gricean account appears at first glance to be empirically inconsistent with the contrast in context effects found for scalar and color adjectives. In both cases, the use of the adjective is redundant for referential purposes if applied to a target object in a display that does not contain a contrasting object of the same category. However, the implicatures account may well be more subtle, because it involves an implicit comparison between possible alternative expressions. A number of factors are likely to determine the choice of actual expressions that are used, in addition to considerations regarding the information necessary to establish reference. For instance, some high-frequency lexical items might be more accessible than others and might be more likely to be encoded in the production process, some physical properties of an object may be highly salient and hence more likely to become encoded, or the visual salience of a property may make it especially useful for speakers to mention as a way of orienting a hearer's attention to the object even though the property does not distinguish it from other objects of the same kind. Thus, a Gricean explanation for the referential-context effects would be consistent with the data if it turned out to be more common for speakers to refer to the color of an object for purposes other than distinguishing from among possible referents than its height or width. Evidence for such an asymmetry in language production was provided by Sedivy (1999). It was found that scalar adjectives were very rarely used (2 percent of trials) in situations where they were not required for purposes of unique identification (i.e., modified phrases such as *the tall glass* were typically used only in situations where there was more than one glass in the display). However, color adjectives were produced with much greater frequency (47 percent of trials) in situations where the color property did not need to be mentioned for unique identification. In other words, roughly half the time, participants produced color adjectives even when redundant for purely referential purposes.

These production data show that a Gricean account cannot be ruled out as an explanation for the referential-context effects with adjectives in the comprehension studies. However, they do not distinguish between this account and the more conservative account in which the effect of a contrasting object on target identification is driven by the lexical requirements of scalar adjectives. Without additional data, the latter explanation appears preferable on grounds of the directness of the link between the linguistic expression under consideration and the contextual information shown to impact its interpretation online. However, the two accounts can be distinguished by investigating a class of adjectives that is neither inherently relational, as are scalar adjectives, nor likely to be produced unless required for referential purposes. A Gricean explanation would predict referential-context effects for such a class of adjectives, while the lexically based account would not. The experiments reported below address precisely this set of predictions.

Experimental Evidence Comparing Color, Scalar, and Material Adjectives

An elicited-production task was used to examine the patterns of production of adjectives in contexts with and without a referential contrast for three types of adjectives. The first two were scalar and color adjectives, as in Sedivy 1999. The third class was a set of adjectives denoting material (e.g., wooden, plastic, metal, and so on). Such adjectives are like color adjectives, in that they lack a lexically specified requirement for a contrast set; they easily receive an interpretation that does not depend on a contextually available contrast set, and like color, material adjectives have a stable core meaning. However, it was speculated that material adjectives would be less likely to be encoded as part of the default description for objects in isolation, perhaps due to lesser salience than the property of color, and hence, like scalar adjectives, their use might be reserved primarily for referential situations where it is necessary to refer to the property to uniquely identify a referent.

Sixteen members of the Brown University community served as participants in an elicited-production study. The experiment was administered with the help of an experimental confederate, who sat facing the experimental participant, with a horizontal display board containing four objects between them. For each trial, participants were given a pair of schematic diagrams of the 5×5 display board, with numbers representing each of the objects in the display. The first diagram indicated the arrangements of objects in the display at the start of the trial, and the second diagram indicated the desired arrangement as a result of moving one of the objects on the board to some new location. Participants were told that their goal was to communicate to the confederate the identity of the target object to be moved and its desired new location. They were told to communicate this information in any way they chose.

The goal of the experiment was to determine whether participants would produce scalar, color, and material adjectives to refer to these properties of the target objects, and to observe whether the production of these adjective types would be limited to visual displays containing a contrasting object of the same category differing with

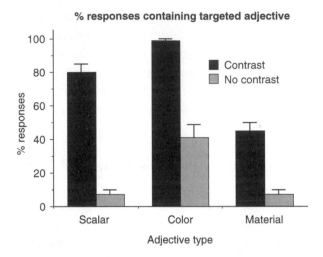

% responses containing targeted adjective

Figure 17.1
Displays the mean percentage of trials in which an adjective was used to describe the targeted property for each adjectival condition. The data exclude adjectives that occurred after the initial formulation of the noun phrase (i.e., excluded repairs and corrections).

respect to the targeted property. To this end, thirty sets of experimental items were constructed, with ten items targeting each of the three property types. Each experimental set occurred across two conditions; it appeared either with a contrasting object of the category denoted by the head noun, or in a display without such a contrasting object. Two lists were constructed so that each participant saw only one version of each item set. The experimental items were embedded in an additional set of thirty distractors, and followed five practice trials.

All of the participants chose to use referential expressions that referred to properties of the objects. Occasionally, these properties involved spatial relations on the grid or to other objects (e.g., *the book on the left*). However, none of the participants adopted a strategy of assigning numbers to squares in the grid as a way to refer to the objects; hence, their descriptions were of the sort that would be useful in a general referential situation.

The participants' responses were scored for the presence of the targeted adjective on the first utterance of the referential expression. Figure 17.1 presents the percentage of trials in each condition for which the targeted adjective was initially produced.

Results for the color and scalar adjectives were similar to the findings reported by Sedivy (1999). Color adjectives were virtually always used when a distinguishing property was required to uniquely identify the referent, and were used almost half of the time when there was no contrasting object in the display. Scalar adjectives were produced frequently, but not always (80 percent) in displays with a referential contrast, and almost never in contexts without a contrast (7 percent). Material adjectives patterned similarly to scalar adjectives, with very few occurrences of material adjectives in displays without a contrast (also 7 percent). Material adjectives were produced more frequently in displays with referential contrast, but not as frequently as either the scalar or color adjectives in similar displays (i.e., 45 percent).

These data were submitted to a 2×3 repeated-measures ANOVA with adjective type (scalar versus color versus material) and display type (contrast versus no contrast) as factors. A significant main effect of adjective type was found ($F_1(2, 30) = 45.82$, $p < .001$; $F_2(2, 27) = 29.29$, $p < .001$), as well as a main effect of display type ($F_1(1, 15) = 106.48$, $p < .001$; $F_2(1, 27) = 146.57$, $p < .001$). The interaction of adjective type and display type was also significant ($F_1(2, 30) = 7.68$, $p < .01$; $F_2(2, 27) = 4.62$, $p < .05$). A Tukey's HSD post hoc test indicated that all cell means were significantly different from one another except the scalar/no-contrast and material/no-contrast conditions, which in fact had identical means.

The results of the production study replicate earlier experiments investigating the production of color and scalar adjectives, but more importantly, they identify a class of adjectives—material adjectives—as a suitable candidate class for distinguishing between competing hypotheses regarding referential-contrast effects in online language processing. To test these competing hypotheses, a comprehension study was undertaken investigating eye movements to the visual displays in response to spoken instructions.

The materials for the comprehension task included the same sets of items as in the production study, with thirty items reflecting three adjective types varying across two display types, with and without referential contrast. Each display had a competitor object (i.e., an object with the property denoted by the head noun that was not the target referent). This was done to create the opportunity for temporary referential indeterminacy at the adjective and to determine the role of context in resolving the indeterminacy. In addition to the experimental trials, there were fifteen counterbalancing trials that had the same structure as the experimental trials with contrast, but in which the target in the first instruction was not one of the contrasting objects, as well as an additional fifteen distractor trials of varying structures.

Participants heard prerecorded spoken instructions to move various objects in the display. The same token of each instruction was used across display types, ensuring that no inadvertent prosodic cues were provided by the experimenter with respect to the contrastive information associated with the adjective across conditions. Each display was accompanied by an instruction to look at a central fixation cross, and then by three instructions to manipulate objects in the display, with the critical instruction always the first of these three. While the participant followed instructions to move objects in the workspace, eye-movement data were recorded using a lightweight ISCAN head-mounted video-based tracking system. A VCR record with a time-code stamp was made for each experimental trial for later coding and analysis.

Eye movements were analyzed by playing the audiovideo record back frame by frame on a digital VCR. For the experimental trials, critical points in the speech stream were identified, corresponding to the onsets of the adjective and head noun, as well as the offset of the head noun. Continuous eye movements occurring from the beginning of the instruction were noted until the participant reached for the target object.

For purposes of statistical analysis, the time-course information was divided into scoring regions of interest. In this case, the scoring regions were established to correspond to pertinent words in the speech stream, offset by 200 ms in order to take into account the approximate time necessary to program and launch an eye movement. Three scoring regions of interest were defined. The first two were designated to reflect eye movements launched in response to the adjective and noun respectively. The third region reflected the fixations initiated in the ten video frames following the offset of the instruction.

Previous experiments on referential contrast in the online interpretation of scalar adjectives (Sedivy et al. 1999) revealed two consequences of the contextual manipulation. First, participants' eye fixations to the target object diverged from fixations to the competitor object earlier in the speech stream when the display included a contrasting object. Second, participants were much more likely to fixate the contrasting object in the display with a contrast than an unrelated object in the corresponding location in displays with no contrast, suggesting that the contrasting object was deemed relevant for the purpose of interpretation. The analyses below evaluate both effects.

To measure the degree of bias in favor of the target object relative to its competitor in the display, a single measure (referred to as the *target advantage score*) was derived that corresponded to the proportion of time in a region spent fixating the target object minus the proportion of time spent fixating the competitor object. Target advantage scores for each region are shown separately in figures 17.2 through 17.4.

The goal of the study was to determine whether material adjectives pattern more like color or more like scalar adjectives. To make this comparison, two separate sets of 2×2 ANOVAs were conducted with adjective type and display type as factors. First, material adjectives were compared with scalar adjectives. An analysis of target advantage scores in region 1 (the region corresponding to fixations launched in response to

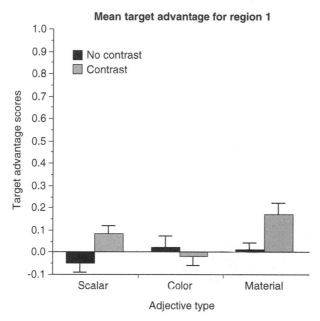

Figure 17.2
Region 1 spanned from 200 ms following the onset of the adjective to 200 ms following the mean offset for each adjective type. Mean advantage scores were computed by subtracting the mean proportion of time spent fixating the competitor from the mean proportion of time spent fixating the target object.

hearing the adjective) revealed a significant main effect of contrast ($F_1(1, 15) = 11.09$, $p < .01$; $F_2(1, 18) = 16.77$, $p < .001$), no main effect of adjective type, and no interaction between adjective type and contrast. At region 2, analysis of target advantage scores revealed a significant effect of contrast ($F_1(1, 15) = 14.36$, $p < .01$; $F_2(1, 18) = 15.21$, $p < .001$). A main effect of adjective type was significant by subjects only ($F_1(1, 15) = 6.72$, $p < .05$; $F_2(1, 18) = 2.04$, $p > .1$), and the interaction did not approach significance.

Analyses of fixations to the contrasting object and its unrelated counterpart were also conducted. These fixations are shown in figures 17.5 through 17.7 for each region. At region 2 (the nominal region), a significant effect of contrast was observed ($F_1(1, 15) = 13.95$, $p < .01$; $F_2(1, 18) = 14.62$, $p < .01$). There was no effect of adjective type, nor was there an interaction. At region 3, there was again a main effect of contrast ($F_1(1, 15) = 71.34$, $p < .001$; $F_2(1, 18) = 25.88$, $p < .001$). There was no significant effect of adjective type, and no significant interaction of contrast and adjective type.

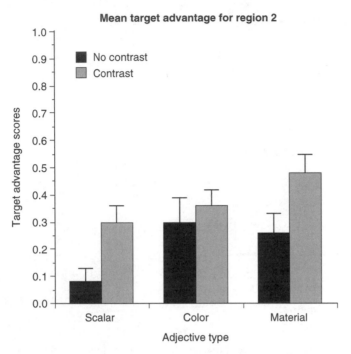

Figure 17.3

Region 2 spanned from 200 ms following the onset of the noun to 200 ms following the mean offset for the noun in each adjectival condition. Mean advantage scores were computed by subtracting the mean proportion of time spent fixating the competitor from the mean proportion of time spent fixating the target object.

While the analyses comparing material and scalar adjectives revealed that these two adjective types showed similar patterns with respect to the early convergence on the target for displays with contrast, comparisons of material and color adjectives showed a different pattern of results in region 1. Target advantage scores at this region showed no significant effect of contrast. There was a main effect of adjective type ($F_1(1, 15) = 5.22$, $p < .05$; $F_2(1, 18) = 4.89$, $p < .05$), reflecting the higher target advantage scores for material adjectives in the contrast condition, and the interaction of contrast and adjective type was significant ($F_1(1, 15) = 4.70$, $p < .05$; $F_2(1, 18) = 6.94$, $p < .05$). This interaction was no longer significant by region 2, because fixations converged on the target object.

Analyses of the contrasting object and its control at region 2 revealed a main effect of adjective type ($F_1(1, 15) = 11.42$, $p < .01$; $F_2(1, 18) = 7.81$, $p < .05$) and a main effect of contrast ($F_1(1, 15) = 8.14$, $p < .05$; $F_2(1, 18) = 11.53$, $p < .01$); both main effects result

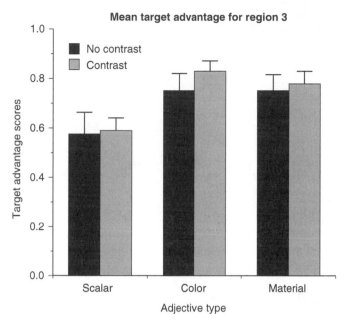

Figure 17.4
Displays mean target advantage scores for the 333 ms following the mean offset of the noun in each adjectival condition.

from the preponderance of looks to the contrasting object in the material/contrast-present condition. The interaction of adjective type and contrast was significant ($F_1(1, 15) = 4.76$, $p < .05$; $F_2(1, 18) = 8.44$, $p < .05$). Similar results obtained at region 3; both a main effect of contrast ($F_1(1, 15) = 17.91$, $p < .01$; $F_2(1, 18) = 7.86$, $p < .05$) and adjective type ($F_1(1, 15) = 8.31$, $p < .05$; $F_2(1, 18) = 9.82$, $p < .01$) emerged, again reflecting a greater number of fixations to the contrasting object in the material/contrast-present condition. The interaction was again significant ($F_1(1, 15) = 7.14$, $p < .05$; $F_2(1, 18) = 6.22$, $p < .05$).

Pairwise comparisons were also conducted for each adjective type to determine whether the contextual manipulation exerted a reliable effect on eye fixations. For scalar adjectives, the presence of a contrasting object resulted in significantly higher target advantage scores for displays with contrast compared to the displays without contrast in regions 1 and 2. The contextual manipulation of contrast also resulted in a significant difference between fixations to the contrasting object and the corresponding unrelated object for regions 2 and 3. Contextual manipulations exerted similar effects with material adjectives: there was a significant difference in target advantage

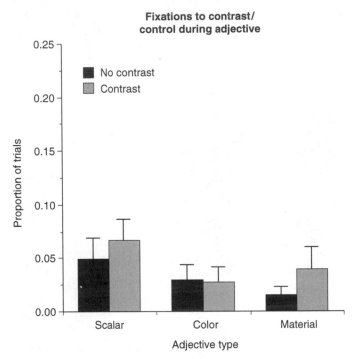

Figure 17.5
Shows the mean proportion of time spent fixating the contrasting object in the contrast condition as compared to the control object in the corresponding location in the display in the no-contrast condition. Region 1 spanned from 200 ms following the onset of the adjective to 200 ms following the mean offset for each adjective type.

scores due to display type in regions 1 and 2, and a significant difference between fixations to the contrasting object versus the corresponding control in regions 2 and 3. Only the interpretation of color adjectives appeared insensitive to the contextual manipulation. For the color adjectives, target advantage scores showed no difference across display conditions in any of the regions. Similarly, no significant differences emerged in any of the regions between fixations to the contrasting object in displays with contrast, and fixations to the corresponding unrelated object in the displays without contrast.

A number of interesting observations can be gleaned from these data. First, the results for the scalar and color adjectives replicate earlier results in an experimental situation where prosody was strictly controlled by using the same token of each instruction across conditions. Furthermore, showing the distinction within a single ex-

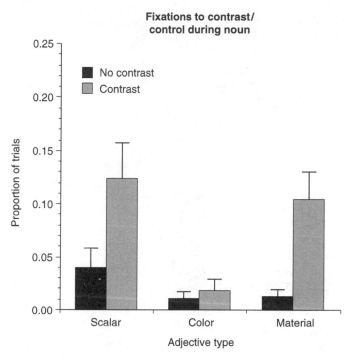

Figure 17.6
Shows the mean proportion of time spent fixating the contrasting object in the contrast condition as compared to the control object in the no-contrast condition. Region 2 spanned from 200 ms following the onset of the noun to 200 ms following its mean offset for each adjective type.

periment also makes it unlikely that when contrast effects did emerge, they were the result of strategic effects due to the salience of contrasting pairs in the display.

The crucial data for evaluating competing hypotheses about the nature of the context effect come from the processing of the material adjectives. It can be seen from the data that material adjectives pattern similarly to the scalar adjectives, and unlike the color adjectives in showing effects of contrast on two important aspects of the eye-movement data (i.e., they show facilitation to the target relative to the competitor, as seen in the target advantage scores, and they also show the tendency for subjects to fixate the contrasting object in the display). The fact that these two measures appear to be tied together is particularly interesting, and supports an interpretation in which looks to the contrasting object reflect a consideration of that object as pertinent for the purposes of identifying the referent. Thus, the results of this comprehension experiment support an account of referential effects that is grounded in hearers' expectations

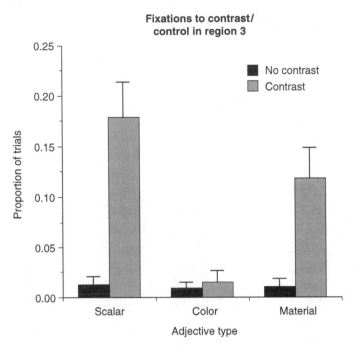

Figure 17.7
Shows the mean proportion of time spent fixating the contrasting object in the contrast condition as compared to the control object in the no-contrast condition. Region 3 spanned the 333 ms following the mean offset of the noun in each adjectival condition.

regarding the encoding of referential expressions and the inferences triggered by the violation of such expectations.

The current study provides suggestive evidence that rapid online contextual effects can derive from expectations regarding the informativity of expressions in a particular context, along the lines of the expectations outlined by Grice in his account of conversational implicatures. The results are not compatible with either a view in which referential-context effects arise due to direct presuppositions carried by modification in general, or a view in which context effects for adjectival interpretation are driven by the need to fill lexically introduced free variables that must be contextually fixed. The claim that communicatively based expectations, rather than information linked directly to specific linguistic forms or expressions, are responsible for referential-context effects, leads to a number of clear predictions. For instance, referential-contrast effects should be observable with expressions that do not involve modification, but that vary in terms of the degree of information they provide, as is the case with basic-level versus subordinate-level expressions such as *loafer* versus *shoe*. Similar context manipulations to the ones in this chapter could be carried out to determine whether the use of a highly specific subordinate-level expression triggers a bias toward a referent that has a contrasting member of the same basic-level category present in the display. Preliminary investigations in our laboratory suggest that this is indeed the case.

The experiments reported here provide evidence for subtle, indirect sources of interaction of linguistic form and context during online language processing that have been characterized as instances of Gricean inferencing. They also lay the groundwork for an experimental paradigm that may lead to the possibility of empirically testing more fine-grained hypotheses about contextually based inferences than has been possible. A number of interesting questions arise from the present study. For instance, it is imperative to consider in greater detail what serves as the basis for expectations regarding quantity of information, such that inferences arising from the deviation from such expectations can be computed. Clearly, a simple notion of information that is required for the purpose of uniquely identifying a referent from among alternative referents is not sufficient. If this were so, there would be no way to account for the different behavior of color adjectives on the one hand, and scalar and material adjectives on the other. Rather, expectations about quantity of information seem to derive from a more fine-grained sense of what the default form for referring to an object would be. These expectations may take into account perceptual factors such as the relative salience of certain properties, or communicative patterns, such as the tendency for conversational partners to persist in using the same label for an entity over time, even when that label does not seem informatively optimal in the immediate local context of use (e.g., Brennan and Clark 1996). A closer examination of these questions is likely to lead to a more explicit understanding of mechanisms triggering inferences due to communicative expectations.

Furthermore, it should be noted that while the current data point to a pragmatic explanation deriving from Gricean principles, they are compatible with a range of claims regarding the automaticity, flexibility, and depth of information representation that such rapid online operations involve. For instance, the inferencing may reflect processes that involve an active evaluation of communicative intentions, taking into consideration a rich array of information about the speaker and his or her beliefs and specifics about the communicative situation. On the other hand, the data could reflect processes that, while having roots in the rational communicative nature of human communication, do not involve actual decoding of communicative intentions at all.

Thus, at the other extreme, the attribution of contrastiveness to material and scalar adjectives but not color adjectives may arise from a general expectation about lexical classes of adjectives and their frequency of usage in referential phrases, coupled with the knowledge that a frequent function of adjectives is to mark referential contrast. While not involving as direct a link between contextual function and linguistic form as a presuppositional account of modification, such a view does not entail that hearers represent anything specifically about the intentions of the speaker or the speaker's goals. This latter view is consistent with some accounts of conversational implicature. Neo-Griceans such as Horn (1984) and Levinson (2000) have argued that inferences that share a common, systematic computational structure (such as implicatures based on the maxim of quantity of information) are qualitatively distinct from inferences that derive from highly idiosyncratic assessments of what information is considered to be relevant in a specific communicative context (such as relevance-based implicatures), and are generated with a higher degree of automaticity and robustness across particulars of context. However, other researchers (e.g., Carston 1998; Sperber and Wilson 1986) have denied the usefulness of such a distinction, arguing that relevance-based considerations are taken into account in the computation of all implicatures.

The notion of a class of inferences that is highly automatic and of limited flexibility in taking into account speaker intentions seems highly plausible in the face of arguments about computational tractability. Further support appears to come from experimental studies such as those conducted by Boaz Keysar and colleagues (e.g., Horton and Keysar 1996; Keysar et al. 1998, 2000). These authors have argued that information pertaining to a conversational partner's knowledge state is not used in the initial stages of language production or comprehension. However, other experimental work reports very rapid use of such information even by young children (Nadig and Sedivy 2002). Even more provocatively, it has been claimed that an understanding of speaker intentions underlying referential acts drives a good deal of early langauge acquisition and may be a prerequisite for the normal process of early word learning (see Bloom 2000; Clark 1990), suggesting that intention decoding is a central and potentially innate aspect of human linguistic behavior, rather than a relatively peripheral one.

In conclusion, while the current experimental data provide evidence for a more complex relationship between contextual function and linguistic form than has previously been argued with respect to referential effects in rapid online language processing, a great deal remains unknown. It is hoped that further investigations along these lines will contribute to the testing of more explicit hypotheses and an elaborated understanding of the mechanisms underlying rapid contextual effects, and more generally, the understanding of language in a communicative context.

Note

The research in this chapter was presented at the Fourteenth Annual CUNY Conference on Sentence Processing in Philadelphia, March 2001, and at the SEMPRO (Cognitively Plausible Models of Semantic Processing) Workshop in Edinburgh, August 2001. I would like to thank the audiences for their valuable comments, as well as the members of the University of Maryland Linguistics Department, where I presented some of these data in a colloquium talk. I am grateful to Alaka Holla and Charlesly Joseph for assistance in data collection and analysis. In addition, I would like to thank Silvia Gennari, Daniel Grodner, and Pauline Jacobson for helpful discussions of the work at various stages in the project. This research was funded in part by NSF grant BCS-0079497 and NIH grant R01 MH62566-01.

References

Altmann, G., and Steedman, M. 1988. Interaction with context during human sentence processing. *Cognition*, *30*, 191–238.

Bever, T. G. 1970. *The Cognitive Basis for Linguistic Structure*. New York: Wiley.

Bierwisch, M. 1987. The semantics of gradation. In M. Bierwisch and E. Lang, eds., *Dimensional Adjectives*. Berlin: Springer-Verlag.

Bloom, P. 2000. *How Children Learn the Meanings of Words*. Cambridge, MA: MIT Press.

Brennan, S., and Clark, H. 1996. Conceptual pacts and lexical choice in conversation. *Journal of Experimental Psychology: Learning, Memory, and Cognition*, *22*, 1482–1493.

Britt, A. 1994. The interaction of referential ambiguity and arguments structure in the parsing of prepositional phrases. *Journal of Memory and Language*, *33*, 251–283.

Carston, R. 1998. Informativeness, relevance and scalar implicature. In R. Carston and S. Uchida, eds., *Relevance Theory: Applications and Implications*, 179–236. Amsterdam: John Benjamins.

Chierchia, G., Crain, S., Guasti, M. T., Gulamini, A., and Meroni, L. 2001. The acquisition of disjunction: Evidence for a grammatical view of scalar implicatures. In *Proceedings of the 25th Boston University Conference on Language Development*, 157–168. Somerville, MA: Cascadilla Press.

Clark, E. 1990. On the pragmatics of contrast. *Journal of Child Language*, *17*, 417–431.

Clifton, C., and Ferreira, F. 1989. Ambiguity in context. *Language and Cognitive Processes*, *4*(SI), 77–103.

Crain, S., and Steedman, M. 1985. On not being led up the garden path: The use of context by the psychological parser. In D. Dowty, L. Karttunnen, and A. Zwicky, eds., *Natural Language Parsing*. Cambridge, UK: Cambridge University Press.

Fox, B., and Thompson, S. 1990. A discourse explanation of the grammar of relative clauses in English conversation. *Language*, *66*, 297–316.

Grice, H. 1975. Logic and conversation. In P. Cole and J. Morgan, eds., *Syntax and Semantics, Vol. 3: Speech Acts*. New York: Academic Press.

Heim, I. 1982. *The Semantics of Definite and Indefinite NPs*. Doctoral dissertation, University of Massachusetts at Amherst. Amherst, MA: GLSA.

Horn, L. 1984. Toward a new taxonomy for pragmatic inference: Q-based and R-based implicature. In D. Schiffrin, ed., *Meaning, Form, and Use in Context: Linguistic Applications* (Georgetown University Round Table on Languages and Linguistics), 11–42. Washington, DC: Georgetown University Press.

Horton, W. S., and Keysar, B. 1996. When do speakers take into account common ground? *Cognition, 59*, 91–117.

Kennedy, C. 2001. Polar opposition and the ontology of degrees. *Linguistics and Philosophy, 24*, 33–70.

Keysar, B., Barr, D. J., Balin, J. A., and Brauner, J. S. 2000. Taking perspective in conversation: The role of mutual knowledge in comprehension. *Psychological Science, 11*(1), 32–38.

Keysar, B., Barr, D. J., Balin, J. A., and Paek, T. S. 1998. Definite reference and mutual knowledge: Process models of common ground in comprehension. *Journal of Memory and Language, 39*, 1–20.

Keysar, B., Barr, D. J., and Horton, W. 1998. The egocentric basis of language use: Insights from a processing approach. *Current Directions in Psychological Science. 7*(2), 46–50.

Levinson, S. C. 2000. *Presumptive Meanings: The Theory of Generalized Conversational Implicature*. Cambridge, MA: MIT Press.

Nadig, A. S., and Sedivy, J. C. 2002. Evidence of perspective-taking constraints in children's on-line reference resolution. *Psychological Science, 13*(4), 329–336.

Pollard, C., and Sag, I. 1994. *Head-Driven Phrase Structure Grammar*. Chicago: University of Chicago Press.

Rooth, M. 1992. A theory of focus interpretation. *Natural Language Semantics, 1*, 75–116.

Sedivy, J. C. 1999. Examining the discourse-based properties of adjectives in on-line semantic processing. Paper Presented at the Twelfth Annual CUNY Conference on Human Sentence Processing, New York.

Sedivy, J. C. 2002. Invoking discourse-based contrast sets and resolving syntactic ambiguities. *Journal of Memory and Language, 46*, 341–370.

Sedivy, J. C., Tanenhaus, M. K., Chambers, C. G., and Carlson, G. N. 1999. Achieving incremental semantic interpretation through contextual representation. *Cognition, 71*, 109–147.

Sperber, D., and Wilson, D. 1986. *Relevance*. Oxford: Blackwell.

Tanenhaus, M., Spivey-Knowlton, M., Eberhard, K., and Sedivy, J. 1995. Integration of visual and linguistic information during spoken language comprehension. *Science, 268*, 1632–1634.

Contributors

Amit Almor
Department of Psychology
University of Southern California

Gerry T. M. Altmann
Department of Psychology
University of York

Jennifer E. Arnold
Dept. of Brain and Cognitive Sciences
University of Rochester

Matthew P. Aylett
School of Philosophy, Psychology, and
Language Sciences,
University of Edinburgh

Karl G. D. Bailey
Department of Psychology
Michigan State University

Ellen Gurman Bard
School of Philosophy, Psychology, and
Language Sciences,
University of Edinburgh

Dale J. Barr
Department of Psychology
University of California, Riverside

Holly P. Branigan
Human Communication Research Centre

Department of Psychology
University of Edinburgh

Susan E. Brennan
Department of Psychology
State University of New York

Sarah Brown-Schmidt
Department of Brain and Cognitive
Sciences
University of Rochester

Ellen Campana
Department of Brain and Cognitive
Sciences
University of Rochester

Stephen Crain
University of Maryland at College Park

Maria Fagnano
Department of Brain and Cognitive
Sciences
University of Rochester

Fernanda Ferreira
Psychology Research Building
Michigan State University

Stanka A. Fitneva
Department of Psychology
Cornell University

Silvia Gennari
Department of Linguistics
University of Maryland at College Park

Joy E. Hanna
Department of Psychology
State University of New York at Stony
Brook

Sarah L. Haywood
Department of Psychology
University of York

Yuki Kamide
Department of Psychology
University of Manchester

Boaz Keysar
Department of Psychology
University of Chicago

Janet F. McLean
Human Communication Research Centre
Department of Psychology
University of Edinburgh

Luisa Meroni
Department of Linguistics
University of Maryland at College Park

Martin J. Pickering
Human Communication Research Centre
Department of Psychology
University of Edinburgh

Amy J. Schafer
Department of Linguistics
University of Hawai'i at Mānoa

Julie C. Sedivy
Department of Cognitive and Linguistic
Sciences
Brown University

Shari R. Speer
Department of Linguistics
Ohio State University

Michael J. Spivey
Department of Psychology
Cornell University

Matthew Stone
Department of Computer Science and
Center for Cognitive Science
Rutgers University

Michael K. Tanenhaus
Department of Brain and Cognitive
Sciences
University of Rochester

John C. Trueswell
Department of Psychology
University of Pennsylvania

Paul Warren
School of Linguistics and Applied
Language Studies
Victoria University of Wellington

Index